Not Flying Alone

FoR ERIKA,

IN FonDEST MEMoRY oF YoUR cousin
AnD MY FRienn AloRWIN SYNnEstvUDt

THAnKS FoR YoUR visit HeRe AT
St LoUIS ER   Ray

Ray Brown

Not Flying Alone

An Autobiography

By Capt. R. A. (Ray) Lemmon
United Airlines, Ret.

authorHOUSE®

AuthorHouse™
1663 Liberty Drive
Bloomington, IN 47403
www.authorhouse.com
Phone: 1 (800) 839-8640

Cover design by Stephen Lenius

Some names in this story have been changed.

Published by AuthorHouse 06/04/2015

ISBN: 978-1-4969-7420-4 (sc)
ISBN: 978-1-4969-7419-8 (hc)
ISBN: 978-1-4969-7418-1 (e)

Library of Congress Control Number: 2015903677

Print information available on the last page.

This book is printed on acid-free paper.

For Margaret

About the front and back covers:

These photos of Margaret, me, and our 1942 Beechcraft D-17S Staggerwing airplane appear courtesy of the Allentown, Pa. *Morning Call* newspaper. The newspaper called me in March 1971, requesting a picture of our vintage biplane for an article they were doing about airline pilots residing in the Lehigh Valley. During the nine-year period Margaret and I owned this airplane, it defined the extracurricular portion of my life as an airline pilot.

Contents

Acknowledgments

My thanks to Steve Smith for many hours of technical computer support; to Ron Littlefield for his tireless editing efforts; to Susan Dreydoppel, Stephen Lenius and R.W. (Bob) Burcaw for their assistance; to Walter Wagner for his contribution; and to the many unnamed who offered their advice after reviewing the basic draft.

Not Flying Alone

Part I

Chapter 1

The Awakening
2011

It's 4 a.m. and I'm wide awake.

"Write to Mark Hanson." Again and again.

Margaret is after me to do *something*, but what? I don't know Mark Hanson; of course, I do know about him. He's the presiding bishop of the Evangelical Lutheran Church in America; I read his commentary each month on the last page of *The Lutheran* Magazine. Margaret knew him from a chance meeting at Chautauqua Institute during an annual gathering of Lutherans that meets every August.

Oh, all right, I'll see to it later — but *"no, you'll do it right now."*

So, I get up, drag out my typewriter and begin a letter (about what, I have no idea).

This was another of many encounters with Margaret's spirit. She died in January 2011, but shortly after, her spirit returned — apparently for the express purpose of getting me on track for salvation and eternal life. The message I received early on was, *"If you want to get to where I am, get your act together."*

What were these encounters like?

Was it a voice, an apparition of some sort, a bright light? It was none of these. It was a definite *presence* — a feeling of having someone very close to me, actually penetrating my mind, guiding, directing, and influencing everything I do.

Knowing that I would be hard to convince, Margaret took elaborate steps to prove to me that it was she, here in the apartment with me.

How would she do this? The first occurrence was immediately after her death when Pastor Mauthe was here to make arrangements for her funeral service. He said, "I know Margaret selected hymns and scripture readings for her service, but I wasn't able to find anything in the church files." A moment or two passed and then I got up and went to her Bible shelf (where there were at least ten choices). Without hesitation I took down the correct one and, needless to say, the hymns and scripture readings were inside.

I didn't dwell on it a great deal until sometime later when another event took place. I made an appointment with Pastor to discuss the disposition of Margaret's memorial fund that friends had so generously contributed to, amounting to about $900. Immediately, Pastor made clear to me that we couldn't do much with a gift of that amount, and suggested we combine it with the small gifts of others to do something meaningful.

"Absolutely not," I replied. "Margaret was a pillar of St. Matthew's and she needs to have her own legacy."

Pastor Mauthe continued, "What the church really needs are new pew torches for the Christmas Eve candlelight service." The ones we had were old, of wrought iron construction, and they clamped to the pews causing damage to the finish.

He took down a book with candelabra offerings. The ones preferred were about 5 feet tall, all-brass finish, and very attractive. They cost about $250 each and 34 were needed. The total cost would be between seven and eight thousand dollars, including the receptacles for their storage. He was about to reject the idea out of hand and put the book away when I spoke up without hesitation, saying that he should make arrangements to purchase them.

Pastor gave me a quizzical look, as if to say, "Are you sure?" Yes, I was quite sure because I was receiving input from Margaret.

There were so many unexplainable events, and I really didn't analyze them too much. I was grieving, confused, and in many ways *disconnected*.

Then, the big moment arrived: a life-changing, transcendent experience of being "filled with the Holy Spirit."

I was downstairs in our storage locker, sorting through Margaret's clothing to be donated, when I noticed a shopping bag up on the shelf. It had been there since we moved, and although I had no interest in it, I took it down and set it aside to take back to the apartment. After completing my project with the clothing, I brought it upstairs and set it by my chair for later consideration.

When I began examining the contents, I came upon a book containing an analysis of the musical compositions for Handel's *Messiah*. I had absolutely no interest in that, as Margaret was the music person. But as I leafed through it, an eight-page folder on grieving popped out.

It was from a seminar she attended long ago at the church. The pamphlet was quite explicit about what to expect during the various stages of grieving, both short-term effects and those longer into the process. Suddenly, it struck me that this was not a coincidence or some other phenomenon. Margaret was truly *with* me, *guiding* me, and *helping* me.

Nearly overcome with emotion, and without warning, an extreme feeling of calm and serenity swept over me. It was like an enormous wave, akin to an empty vessel being filled. It is hard to describe, but it was very real and exceedingly powerful. In an instant I was changed forever.

Previously, I had little interest in the church or any other religious pursuits. In fact, I seldom attended church even though we were members of St. Matthew's for over 40 years; Margaret had given up on me long ago.

One of the principal elements of my "gift" was an intense quest for knowledge — religious study centered on St. Paul. I started with Edgar J. Goodspeed's *Paul* and then continued with Barclay's complete series on Paul's letters, Great Course lectures, etc. I seemed to be able to assimilate vast amounts of text in a very short time.

Another element of my "gift" was clarity; I was suddenly quite sure about things I previously knew nothing about. An example was sitting down with a piece of paper and writing the word SALVATION in large letters. Under it I wrote "Total Faith in God," and next to it I wrote "Belief in Jesus Christ as our Savior," "the Resurrection," and "the power of the Holy Spirit." Finally I wrote "Love," as in the two great commandments — *Love the Lord thy God, etc.*, and *Love thy neighbor as thyself.* That was my theology for the path to eternal life. The strange part was that I had no recollection of writing it. It was as if I were the instrument, not the author.

What a feeling! So completely *well*, as if half of my 85 years had been swept away. I felt energized, tranquil, *born again*. That sounds trite, but it truly is the best description.

What should I do now? Margaret didn't make this wonderful gift possible so that I could sit back and watch the world go by. An excellent place to begin is right here at Moravian Village, where I live. We have hundreds of people here, many nearing the end of their lives. Some, perhaps many, are without hope and unsure about what happens in their next chapter, eternity. (As to my own destiny, I no longer fear death.) We have our own Bible study group; perhaps I should talk to Gordon Sommers, our chaplain, about it.

I would not preach, but perhaps I could teach — Sunday school and Bible Study classes, for example. I have learned so much here at home and in classes I have taken at Moravian Theological Seminary. Perhaps I could share some of what I have learned.

I think of Billy Graham. Yes, I met Billy in the 1970s, when I was Captain R.A. Lemmon, United Airlines, flying Boeing 737s on "Tobacco Road" (airline slang for flights serving North Carolina).

Billy customarily boarded the plane at Asheville and flew with us to New York. Along the way at the various stops, he came up to the cockpit to visit — not about religion, just everyday "stuff." Billy struggled for his "gift of the Spirit." Beginning his ministry in Los Angeles, he knew something was missing and learned about a Welsh evangelist named Stephen Olford. He went to Wales, prayed with Stephen, and that is when Billy received his "gift of the Spirit."

For me, the "gift" just poured down out of heaven, *seemingly through Margaret.*

Perhaps by telling the story of my journey, I can help others. But to do that, I must revisit my career as an airline pilot, going farther back to the 1940s, the 1930s, and yes, even all the way back to the 1920s.

Chapter 2

The Great Depression
1929-1941

I was born June 11, 1929, at home on West 23rd Street in Erie, Pa. Approaching the depth of the Great Depression, my parents, Paul and Pearl Lemmon, were upper-middle-class residents. Dad worked as an accountant at the Erie Foundry, and was sufficiently prosperous to buy a fruit farm west of Erie near the town of North Girard, Pa. In fact, he and his brother Dell owned adjoining farms, with a big sign out by the road that read, "Lemmon Farms, Fruits in Season."

The farms included peach orchards, pears, cherries (sweet and sour), and even grape vineyards. There were huge barns housing horses, cows, chickens, and pigs. Since they were located on the immediate shoreline of Lake Erie, the climate was tempered against fall frosts.

A few years before my arrival, a summer house (actually a cottage) was built on our farm. The Crash of '29 was disastrous for the Lemmon family. Dad lost his job and had to vacate our home on 23rd Street, and our family of six moved into the tiny farmhouse on Lake Road. I had three siblings: Richard, my only brother and the oldest, born in 1919, followed by sisters Mary Elizabeth (Betty) in 1921, and finally Margaret Ann (Peg) in 1927.

The farmhouse was not intended for year-round living; in fact, it was barely habitable for a family of six because of its small size and lack of indoor plumbing. The only source of water was a hand pump on the back porch outside the kitchen, and a wood-burning stove centrally located in the living room provided heat. The only toilet

The farmhouse on Lake Road (Route 5), built in the 1920s. This
was basically a summer cottage that became a permanent home
for the Lemmon family. The only plumbing was a hand pump
(well) on the back porch. The building still stands.

facility was outside in an outhouse. Hot water was obtained from the
wood-burning cookstove in the kitchen. Refrigeration was provided
by an icebox serviced by an iceman. I can still see him approaching
the house with a 25- or 50-pound block of ice on his shoulder,
protected by a rubber pad to keep from getting soaked.

Bathing required a trip down to Grandma's and Grandpa's house
every Saturday night. Uncle Dell was not married and lived in the old
original farmhouse with them. At least it had indoor plumbing and,
of all things, gas for cooking and hot water. Natural gas was plentiful
along the shore of Lake Erie and many farms had their own gas wells.

Typically, the whole family would go down to Grams' house for
dinner and a bath. Times were hard, but food was abundant on the
farm. We had vegetable gardens, and cows and pigs that were housed
in a barn at Uncle Dell's.

A few highlights punctuate my memories of life on the farm in the
early 1930s. An example was my first day at school in the fall of 1935.
A bus traveled Route 5 each morning as far east as Avonia (about 4
miles), picking up farm kids. The elementary school for grades 1–8
was located in North Girard. The school was an ancient structure
with a bell on top, a two-story building divided into eight classrooms.

The wooden stairs were hollowed out after years of endless traffic up and down.

It was such an important day for me that I will never forget it. I recall getting off the bus, not knowing where to go, and being swooped up by a teacher who delivered me to the correct classroom for first grade.

I also remember having a BM accident duly noted by the teacher in a letter sent home with me. Dad was furious, and proclaimed, "I know how to handle that." At Uncle Dell's, there was an elevated spray tank containing at least 1000 gallons of water used for spraying the fruit trees. Dad announced that he was going to put me in the tank for a swim — but I didn't know how to swim yet.

I was terrified, kicking and screaming, as we went down the path to Uncle Dell's. As my father was carrying me up the tank ladder, my mother appeared, screaming, "Stop! Stop!" Dad did finally relent, but I always wondered if he was prepared to drown me in that tank. Needless to say, there were no more "accidents" at school.

Peg was two years ahead of me in school, and she became my teacher. Arriving home from school, she would corner me, eager to teach me everything she had learned that day. We were very close.

All hands worked diligently during the picking season, especially when harvesting sour cherries destined for the cannery. Our bonus was a swim in the cool water of Lake Erie at the end of the day.

In the fall during the Depression, people couldn't afford to buy our peaches. As we lay in bed in the quiet of the night, we could hear them dropping to the ground in the orchard — a total loss.

When winter came, it was very cold everywhere, including inside the farmhouse. I still remember the four piles of pajamas, one on each side of the stove where we dressed for school.

The south side of our property bordered the New York Central Railroad right-of-way. In those days there were no fences, so we were visited by our share of hobos riding the rails. The "bums," as Grams called them, would show up around three or four o'clock in the afternoon looking for food. Most would volunteer to work for their supper by cleaning stalls, weeding the garden, etc. Grams was quite generous with them, but she always made sure they did their share. These unfortunates were not as bad off as those in soup kitchen lines in the city. They migrated with the seasons, south and west, riding in boxcars. They all had interesting stories to tell, victims of the times.

Erie and Cleveland Before the War

By the summer of 1936, our situation had improved dramatically. Dad gave up the job search in Erie and took a position in Harrisburg working for the State of Pennsylvania. He considered moving the family there, but instead he rented a house for us in the city of Erie and relocated to Harrisburg by himself. His visits were rare and sporadic due to the distance involved. I'm sure it was very difficult for him living alone in a faraway place.

Part of the problem was that my two older siblings, Richard and Betty, were nearing graduation from high school. Even during those difficult times, Dad was committed to sending his kids to college.

Life in Erie was markedly improved from what it had been down on the farm, and our rental house was a palace in comparison to the farmhouse. Newly constructed Emerson Elementary School was only two blocks down the street — and for Peg and me, a world away from the schoolhouse in North Girard. Betty attended the brand-new Strong Vincent High on West Eighth, and Richard would soon be off to Kenyon College in Gambier, Ohio.

We weren't used to the heavy traffic of city streets, and Peg and I often sat on the corner of Eighth and Cascade seeing how many different license plates we could identify. Schoolyard activities included marbles, mumbly-peg, and swapping baseball cards.

Our rent was $38 per month, hamburger meat was 25 cents per pound, and a loaf of bread was a dime. The low prices meant that money could be stretched to some degree, but there just wasn't much to go around. Dad earned about $200 per month, out of which he paid his room rent and other meager expenses; the remainder was sent home. I recall instances nearing the end of the month when the evening meal consisted of breakfast cereal; however, we managed fairly well through 1937 and 1938, even with Richard attending college.

For Christmas, Peg and I received a small Boston terrier named Timmy. He was just a pup, and we loved him to death. He disappeared one day and Peg and I were frantic, looking everywhere. We finally found him upstairs; he had grown sufficiently to climb the stairs.

I recall a few other memories of our life on Cascade Street, such as having childhood diseases like measles, chicken pox and whooping cough. Peg suffered with earaches and cried incessantly. We were too poor to seek medical attention for her, and it progressed to mastoiditis, culminating in mastoidectomy surgery in 1937. That could have been avoided with proper medical care.

With all of today's preoccupation with health care, we only have to look back 75 years to see a different world — one with almost an absence of care for the poor. In those days, we wouldn't have classified ourselves as such but, in fact, we were.

Me during the Erie years, 1936-1940, attending elementary school with my sister, Peg.

1939 was a much different sort of year. In March, my mother received word that Dad was in the hospital with peritonitis. Apparently, he had suffered a bout of constipation and taken castor oil for relief. Unfortunately, it wasn't constipation; it was appendicitis, and he ruptured his appendix. In those days that was catastrophic, because it was before the discovery of antibiotics.

Uncle Dell took the train to Harrisburg, arriving shortly before Dad died of massive infection. Dell returned home with our '36 Pontiac sedan, and Dad's body was shipped home by train. It was a terrible shock for Mom, and we were all devastated. Because we couldn't afford a funeral home, arrangements were minimal with the casket placed out on the porch of our house. I still remember people crowding around for the funeral service. I was only ten years old.

Dad's estate was a life-insurance policy for $5000. That may have seemed like a goodly sum of money in those days, but the payout was broken down into five $1000 bonds, each yielding their full amount only after ten years. Their immediate redemption value was $750 each. I always wondered if my father was aware that he only had a paltry $3750 worth of insurance, instead of the more impressive-sounding five thousand dollars. In those days life insurance was cheap, and Dad should have done more to protect his family. I do recall that it was a big deal when it was necessary to cash one of those bonds.

One immediate adjustment after Dad's death was to find less-expensive housing. We rented an upstairs flat two blocks away, saving ten dollars a month. My only other significant memory of '39 was September 1, when Germany overran Poland and Europe was suddenly at war.

In 1940, Richard graduated from college with a liberal arts degree, and we were running out of money. Dad's inheritance was nearly exhausted, and Richard was facing the specter of having to support our family on his own. Sister Betty was just graduating from high school, so her plans for higher education were uncertain. There were four of us to support, and Richard was unable to find a job. Defense plants were gearing up for the war effort, but Richard's education had not prepared him for working in industry. The only job he could find was a bank teller position in Cleveland, 100 miles away.

After school was out for the summer of 1940, we packed everything we owned and a local mover transported us there. We faced major adjustments, but it was exciting to live in such a large city. We rented an ancient duplex on East 93rd Street.

Naturally there was a great deal of mischief for a ten-year-old boy to get into, and I managed to fall off a garage roof and break my right ankle. Today that might not seem like a big deal, but in those days, with little money and no public assistance, it was catastrophic. I went to the neighborhood doctor and had the ankle set without anesthetic. It took both my mom and Peg to hold me down, and the doctor was screaming for me to hold still. Prior to putting a cast on it, I hobbled downtown to a public clinic for an x-ray. I had no crutches and just hopped around. I do recall that it hurt a lot!

On a clear spring day, Richard took us to the top of the Terminal Tower. It was Cleveland's tallest building at the time, and the observation platform provided a spectacular view of the lake and downtown Cleveland. We had so little money that any diversion such as that was a real treat. I also attended one baseball game at Cleveland Stadium where I saw Bob Feller pitch — a special memory.

As the summer of 1941 turned to fall, Richard came to me with the shocking news that I was being sent to an orphanage. Perhaps a more accurate description was a detention home for wayward boys, but before actually being committed, Uncle Dell agreed to take me in. I think my mom wrote to him pleading for help. She didn't want to relegate me to that facility.

Uncle Dell was in difficult straits himself, having recently lost his farm through a Sheriff's sale. He moved to North Girard and secured employment at the Lord Manufacturing Company in Erie, managing their power station.

Dell Roy Lemmon (1882-1952)

I don't know much about Uncle Dell's personal life except that he never married. He achieved a degree in Power Plant Engineering from International Correspondence School; he was the only person I ever knew to graduate from there. He never served in the military.

Dell worked in the power station at General Electric-Erie division in the 1920s, and then branched out into farming with my father, Paul. After losing his farm during the Depression, Uncle Dell worked for Lord Manufacturing Co. managing their power station. Lord's was awarded the Army-Navy "E" for Excellence in World War II and Uncle Dell was on a first-name basis with Tom Lord, the owner of the company.

Dell worked there until 1952, when he died of prostate cancer while still on the job; he was never able to enjoy the fruits of retirement.

Picture taken circa 1949 at our house on Lincoln Ave. Dell is
in his mid-60s and Peg is 22. Her visits were very infrequent.

Rufus Hilt, a coworker, told me on my return from Japan that Dell
had suffered terrible pain at work, yet had refused treatment from the
medical community. By the time he was taken to the hospital it was
too late, and he died before I arrived from the Far East.

Dell was extremely frugal. To my knowledge, he never owned
a new car but was very proud of my dad's '36 Pontiac, which he
inherited in 1939. At that time the mileage was low, and it served us
well throughout WWII. Even after the war, Dell continued to drive
it, and I inherited it upon his death in 1952. During the war, because
he was engaged in war work at Lord's in Erie, he was authorized a
"C" sticker that provided him with almost unlimited gasoline.

On the way home from work one day, Uncle Dell noticed Army
B-25 bombers covering the entire Erie airport — well over 100 of
them. In deference to me, we drove back that evening so I could
see them. What a guy! The planes came to Erie for refuge from a
hurricane threatening their base at Columbia, S.C., and they were
flown out the next day.

The '36 Pontiac 2-door sedan. Purchased in 1937, it was our family car for 15 years, including the war years. Uncle Dell inherited it in 1939 upon the death of my father. Leaning on the car is my older sister, Mary (Betty), at about age 17.

Dell Lemmon was a wonderful, caring man. Adopting an unruly 12-year-old boy was a major undertaking for a single man of 58. My Grandmother Lemmon died at home in 1941. She was bedridden, and needed complete care. Frances G. Case was engaged as her caregiver for over a year, and after Grandma died, Frances stayed on as housekeeper. Uncle Dell made a solemn deathbed promise to his mother that he would never marry Frances. He honored that promise, and Frances stayed on until his death in 1952. He willed the house to her, so I know he loved her devotedly.

Chapter 3

Growing Up During the War 1941-1946

That was my situation in the fall of 1941: returning to North Girard to live with Uncle Dell. Now in seventh grade, I was back at the old block schoolhouse where I had begun my education six years earlier.

After playing outside with my friend Virgil Wright on Sunday, December 7, I came home and found Uncle Dell hunkered down by our old Philco radio. He said the Japanese had attacked Pearl Harbor, our naval base in the Hawaiian Islands, and that it was very "serious." To me, this meant absolutely nothing because I didn't even know the Hawaiian Islands existed.

However, at school the following day I knew something important was taking place when they set up a radio in the classroom. The teacher realized the historical significance of President Roosevelt's declaration of war on Japan. As of that moment, we were at war.

For the next four years, the war dominated our lives. Every able-bodied man of draft age was in the Army, Navy, Marine Corps, or the U.S. Army Air Corps. At that time it wasn't referred to as WWII — it was just "the war."

The dominant characteristic defining that period was scarcity. Almost everything in the nation's economy was rationed, with red tokens for meat and butter and blue tokens for sugar, shoes, and everything else. Rubber was a very serious problem since most of it came from Malaya, now under Japanese control. For a while, the only car tires available were manufactured from sawdust. An entire new industry emerged with the creation of synthetic rubber.

We recycled everything possible, but so much was needed for the war effort that shortages continued to be a problem for the duration. Most of what we didn't need for ourselves went to Great Britain, and during '42 and early '43, a large percentage of what was sent to England ended up on the sea bottom.

The U-boat menace was a scourge, and once war was declared, Germany sent their U-boats to our shores. Oil tankers were frequently seen burning off the Atlantic and Gulf coasts.

Even though the U.S. was blessed with substantial petroleum reserves, we couldn't produce enough. Shiploads of crude oil and gasoline were imported from Venezuela and the Caribbean. The Germans knew this, of course, and made a concerted effort to cut these supply lines. The populace was never told how critical petroleum was.

War information was strictly censored, and pictures of U.S. Marines battling on Tarawa in the Pacific were withheld from public view. Much of our wartime information came to us in movie theaters compliments of Movie-Tone News, shown in conjunction with the feature attraction and a cartoon, such as Bugs Bunny or The Three Stooges.

An enormous amount of money was needed to finance the war effort, and in those days the government didn't just print more currency as they do now. There were war bonds for adults and savings stamps for kids, both of which raised approximately $185 billion.

Returning war heroes and entertainers like Bob Hope went on bond drives to raise money for the cause. Scrap drives were big business. Aluminum (for planes) was recycled and tin was in very short supply. Gasoline rationing was strictly enforced, with an allotment of three gallons per week for those not engaged in war work. As I mentioned before, Uncle Dell was issued a prized "C" sticker that provided him an almost unlimited allotment of gasoline.

There was a black market, but patronizing it was unpatriotic. Car production was suspended for the duration, so a major automobile accident could be catastrophic. Needless to say, people were very careful with their cars. The price of gas was 15.9 cents a gallon, when you could get it.

That's how it was on the home front. Abroad, the scariest time was in '42, when we were losing on all fronts. Cairo was threatened, and a link-up of Germany and Japan in India appeared to be a distinct possibility. The German invasion of Russia threatened Stalingrad. Ships were being sunk at an intolerable rate. The Japanese had undisputed control of the Pacific prior to the Battles of the Coral Sea in May and Midway in June. Twelve thousand soldiers suffered through the Bataan death march in May; it was a frightful time, to be sure.

By 1943, the war was stabilizing. Our troops in North Africa defeated Rommel's Afrika Korps in May, Germany lost at Stalingrad, the Japanese were beaten at Guadalcanal in early '43, and we were winning the U-Boat war. War plants were humming with three shifts of workers.

In North Girard, Frances went from making 2400 coat hangers per day on piecework (sometimes with my help) to contributing to the war effort at Lovell Manufacturing Co. in Erie. Telephone? Yes, we had a non-dial phone. The operator came on the line and asked, "Number please?" There was long-distance service that was used primarily for emergencies because it was quite expensive.

Religiously speaking, Uncle Dell and Frances were Episcopalians and attended Grace Church in North Girard. It was Anglican, ivy-covered, and survives to this day. It was discovered that I had never been baptized; Uncle Dell stated, "That will never do," and Reverend Stetler was duly summoned to administer the sacrament at the first opportunity.

Uncle Dell loved to tell the story about a father taking his son to worship for the first time. After church he asked the boy, "Well, son, how did you like the service?" The boy replied, "Gee, Dad, that was a pretty good show for a nickel."

Uncle Dell was like that. Even after we moved to Erie after the war, he would drive to North Girard to attend church every Sunday morning. I wonder if they still ring the bell for services; I can still see George Hawkes pulling on the rope that rang the bell, and sometimes he would let us kids do it.

Here are some of my own wartime memories:

Being in the backyard and seeing flights of P-38s (distinguishable by their twin booms) on their way to England; B-24 bombers manufactured at Willow Run in Detroit occasionally flying low over town on their way to England to join the Eighth Air Force; trainloads of tanks passing through on flat cars, making their way to embarkation ports destined for England and D-Day. The war was all around us, totally encompassing our lives. D-Day was successful, and I remember being in class on May 8, 1945, for the announcement of V-E Day.

On a personal level, 1945 started out with great sadness for me. In mid-January, I received word that my mother was in the hospital with uremic poisoning and impending kidney failure. She was not expected to live. At that time there were no dialysis machines or kidney transplants, so virtually nothing could be done for her. She perked up a bit when I arrived; however, within 24 hours she was dead at the youthful age of 53.

This picture of Richard and Peg was taken in Cleveland, Ohio, during the war. Although I lived in North Girard, Pa., with Uncle Dell, I visited them and my mother frequently, traveling to and from Cleveland by Greyhound Bus.

Mom's passing put an end to the Lemmons as a family unit. Peg and Richard stayed together for a while, but it wasn't too long before Peg set out on her own. I did have one last visit with them in August, and I was downtown at Cleveland's Public Square for the announcement of V-J Day. An awesome crowd had gathered, and it was absolute bedlam.

During that summer of '45, Uncle Dell bought a row house in Erie at 1703 West 14th Street. It was an end unit, all brick and very well built, but it was a bit run down. It turned out to be an excellent project house. The property included a detached three-car garage, which meant he had an extra space to rent out for $3 per month! Frances and I participated in painting and other fix-up chores.

The move to Erie during the summer of '45 was just in time for me to attend eleventh grade at Strong Vincent High School. Built in the late '30s, it was a large edifice with 1500 students and even by the time I attended, it was still quite new. Sister Betty had been in one of the first classes ten years earlier while we lived on Cascade Street.

Academically, if I wanted to attend college, I was in trouble. I was barely a "C" student at Rice Avenue Union High School, where I had been poorly advised not to take a math course in tenth grade.

My counselors at Strong Vincent were appalled, and said that in order to have any chance for college I would have to make up the missing Plane Geometry course in eleventh grade in addition to taking Algebra I & II. Looking at my GPA, they didn't think that was possible.

I did it, but I would have failed miserably except for a providential alliance with another student. I didn't know any of my classmates there, but somehow a very bright fellow named Jim Smith took a liking to me and it was a renaissance. Suddenly I was studying, doing my homework, and going to the library. Uncle Dell was both astonished and very pleased. Jim saved my bacon that time.

I even did well in Chemistry with Mr. Armagost, even though for most students he was a nightmare. The first day of class, he wrote LABORATORY on the blackboard and said, "In this class the emphasis will be on the first five letters, and not the last seven." It was an ominous introduction, but believe it or not, he turned out to be my favorite teacher.

Jim was concerned about Physics, a twelfth-grade subject currently taught by Mr. Shanor. "Pop" was an affable teacher who let the kids get away with anything. The bottom line was that you weren't going to learn much in Pop's Physics class.

Somehow, Jim learned that Mr. Armagost would be teaching Physics I and II for summer school, 1946 at the old Erie Technical High School in downtown Erie, so we registered. The course was intense because an entire year of study was crammed into three months and no corners were cut: the full curriculum was adhered to. That meant a lot of homework, and we included English 8 in our curriculum as well. Jim said it would be a "snap."

I completed eleventh grade with an overall mark of "A" minus, including the missing math course. That showed I could excel if I applied myself — with help from Jim. He was exceedingly mature for his age and instilled confidence in his parents to the extent they let him take their car to school. That meant we could make use of the library downtown. My allowance from Uncle Dell reflected his frugal nature, so I wasn't able to help out much with the gas. That was okay with Jim, though, and we really appreciated having the use of the car.

Summer school with Mr. Armagost went fine until one Saturday (the class met six days a week to meet the curriculum) when I was called upon to recite Boyle's Law. That was our assignment, and I was unprepared. I was ejected from class with the admonition, "Why don't you leave and prepare for Monday's class."

I was embarrassed, but needless to say, I recited Boyle's Law on Monday. Mr. Armagost did me a favor, though, because after that I never took an assignment lightly. That work ethic stood me in good stead for the many future airline ground schools that lay ahead.

Mr. Armagost didn't hold grudges, and Jim and I approached him with a proposal for more Chemistry Lab study in preparation for college. He was very impressed, and said he would consult the faculty managers regarding an Advanced Chemistry course for the first semester of twelfth grade. Also, as a by-product of summer school, I had room in my senior class schedule for Typing and Drafting classes. These courses proved useful in the many building projects that lay ahead. All in all, my experience at Strong Vincent High was sound preparation for the future.

Chapter 4

<hr/>

Post-War
1946-1950

Greystone Lab

During my senior year at Strong Vincent, the Greystone Laboratory contacted the principal of the school to see if there were any chemistry students who might be interested in a lab technician apprentice position. Greystone was a small organization consisting of Clarence King, his 29-year-old son Vincent (Vinnie), and nurse/secretary Georgia Strucher.

Naturally, the principal contacted Mr. Armagost, who in turn asked his four Advanced Chemistry students if anyone was interested. With the exception of me, all rejected the offer due to college commitments.

I had a few days to decide, so I asked Uncle Dell for his thoughts. "Sounds like a great opportunity to me," he pronounced. We had never discussed college in any serious way because Uncle Dell really couldn't afford it. However, I think he would have managed if I would have been determined to go. Student loans were not an option in the 1940s.

I accepted Greystone's offer and was hired immediately on an after-school basis until graduation. What they urgently needed was a flunky to clean the hundreds of petri plates used for bacteriological studies, and that was the reason they couldn't wait until I graduated.

So, the first of March, I reported to Greystone as an apprentice Lab Tech. My focus shifted from schoolwork to my new job, and in just a few short months I was working full time. Mr. King announced that my starting salary would be $100 per month; that didn't excite me at all, since my classmates working at GE were making almost twice that. I was tempted to quit, but Vinnie convinced me to stay on for a while and promised I would get a raise when I became more productive.

We tested milk for the city and state, checking for purity (bacteria count), butterfat content, solids, etc., and that was how I began my apprenticeship. We also did industrial analysis for Erie metallurgical firms. Samples were prepared for testing by drilling bars of iron to produce filings. We operated a sterilizer in connection with bacteriological procedures, blood tests for marriage, rabbit tests for pregnancy, and much more. There was a lot to learn.

My immediate problem was lack of transportation. It was only a few miles to work, but it was too far to walk, and taking a bus was not a viable alternative. Because Uncle Dell didn't believe in teenage driving, I didn't have a driver's license, so my options were limited to two-wheelers that could be operated on a learner's permit. Vinnie promised to teach me to drive the lab car in due time, but not immediately.

My first "motorized" transportation — not very practical, but it was okay for the summer of 1947.

The best solution was a Whizzer motorbike kit that could be attached to my bicycle, and for $99 I would have motorized transportation. Rain was a problem, but I coped. In 1947, Whizzers were everywhere.

Learning to Drive

As promised, Mr. King assigned Vinnie to teach me how to drive. We used the lab's beat-up '41 Hudson that had seen better days. My driving lessons were in connection with picking up blood samples at doctors' offices and other duties related to laboratory business.

After about a month, Vinnie said I was ready to take the driver's test. The testing facility was 15 miles away in North East, Pa., and I flunked the first time for not putting my arm out the window to signal a right turn — that was before cars had turn signals. Mr. King was furious, but a month later we returned for a successful re-exam.

Joe Martin (the man who sold me the Whizzer) and I became close friends during the summer of '47. Joe sold the business a year later, and he and another vet named Lee Donaldson established a car-repair business named Peach Street Auto Service.

By the spring of 1948, I sold the motorbike and was ready to buy a car.

The Lemmon Family Members — Post-War

Shortly after I learned to drive, I visited my sister Mary in Cleveland, where she was studying for her doctorate in medicine. After her enlistment in the Women's Army Corps (WAC), she preferred using her given name instead of "Betty."

In January 1948, new cars were scarce, with waiting lists at most dealerships. So I borrowed Joe Martin's ancient Hupmobile to make the trip. When I told my boss, Mr. King, about my upcoming trip to Cleveland, his vociferous reply said it all: "Hupmobile! I haven't heard that name in years." His startled reaction was noteworthy, and it depicted the extremes people went to at that time to find reliable transportation.

During my visit, much of our conversation focused on my new job at Greystone Lab. Mary was extremely skeptical regarding my prospects for the future since it was a small family business and I had no professional credentials, such as a diploma from ASCP

(Associated Society of Clinical Pathologists). It would have been wise to listen more closely, because lab work was for the most part women's work, and the money would never be attractive without an advanced degree.

My brother Richard relocated to San Francisco, where he made a career change to become a CPA like his dad. He achieved that goal, and spent the remaining 30 years of his life working the numbers trade. He died of colon cancer in 1972 at the age of 52.

After Peg and Richard went their separate ways in '45, she went to college in Chicago. There she met John Balanoff, and they were married the following year. Peg visited me on two occasions: the first in '49 after my nephew John Jr. was born, and the second in '55 when Margaret and I were married. I visited Peg once briefly while I was based in Chicago. She seemed content in her new role as wife and mother.

After the War

I bought a '37 Ford 2-door 60 that I found in the Erie newspaper for $250, and I was very proud of my purchase — for a while. It was an impetuous decision initiated on my own without adequate investigation or research.

What did the "60" mean? For 1937, Ford offered two V-8 engines for their cars, one with 85 horsepower and the other with 60 horsepower. Most buyers preferred the more powerful model, explaining the low price I paid. Nobody wanted a 60, especially one that was in such dilapidated condition. After I bought it, I was known as "60" at Joe and Lee's Peach Street Auto for as long as I owned it. The small engine wasn't so bad, though, as it burned less gas than the 85.

I was gradually becoming a lab technician, but the work I was doing bore little resemblance to what we learned in chemistry class. The main reason Greystone wanted a chemistry student was to hire someone familiar with lab equipment terminology such as beakers, flasks, Bunsen burners and the like. I got a raise on my anniversary and some bonuses for special occasions. Rather than commit to regular salary increases, Clarence threw me a bone once in a while to keep me from leaving.

Some procedures, like the rabbit test, were unpleasant because in those days the only way to verify pregnancy was to concentrate a urine sample and inject it into the bloodstream of a female rabbit. Then, 48 hours later, it was necessary to euthanize the rabbit for ovarian examination to render a diagnosis. It was my job to keep a supply of white rabbits on hand.

We also kept a female sheep named Maude to provide sheep cells used in Wasserman tests for the diagnosis of syphilis. It was also part of my job description to take care of Maude, including shearing her.

By 1949, I was ready to move up to a better car. A friend of Vinnie King owned a '46 Hudson Super Six with low mileage available for only $800.

1946 Hudson Super 6 4-door sedan, my second car, purchased in 1949. It had engine problems, so I only paid $800 for it (see text). This car was eventually traded for an almost-new 1954 Chevy 2-door in 1954.

Why was it so cheap? It had a knock in the engine, and the Hudson garage tried everything short of engine replacement to fix it. The strange thing was that it ran fine in spite of the noise.

Being affiliated with Peach Street Auto, I was quite certain I could fix the problem, so I bought the car and immediately tore the engine down. I installed new rings, bearings, and valves, but the knock persisted.

Now what should I do? I considered searching for another engine, but the knock didn't seem to be serious. So I just ran it that way, as the previous owner of the car had done.

Joe's partner Lee Donaldson was a very talented machinist who manufactured things on the lathe. To me, machine work was a mystery; after all, I was still just a kid.

One day, Lee came to me with a proposal: "Would you be willing to spend a hundred dollars to get rid of the knock in your engine?" After mulling it over a bit, I replied in the affirmative, but qualified the agreement by saying, "If the noise is still there, will you pay me $100?" Lee agreed to those terms, but insisted that I leave the car with him over the weekend and promise not to interfere while he worked. I agreed, quite sure that I had just earned an easy $100. The expert mechanics at the Hudson garage couldn't fix it, I was unsuccessful, and I was quite sure Lee would fail as well.

He called on Sunday for me to come and pick up the car. "Is the knock gone?" I asked. Lee refused to answer directly and instead replied, "Come and see for yourself."

As Uncle Dell and I drove downtown, I said, "This should be fun. There's no way Lee could have gotten rid of that knock."

At the garage, I started the car and it was quiet as a mouse. In fact, it sounded like a brand-new engine. I accused Lee of putting sawdust in the crankcase — an old used-car trick. He swore up and down he had done no such thing, but also refused to disclose the secret of his success. I reluctantly handed over the money, saying, "Okay, here's your hundred bucks."

Somewhat chagrined, I drove home with the Hudson running perfectly. Lee was like that; he enjoyed teasing the kid. It was worth the $100 to have it fixed, but it really bugged me as to how he did it. One day, Joe Martin finally broke the silence: "Your camshaft was traveling back and forth, and the cam lobes were clipping the lifter guides." Suddenly, I got it. I had noticed the chipped edges on some of those guides when I took the oil pan down, but had failed to associate that with the knock. A ten-cent spring ahead of the timing gear had failed. That spring maintained constant tension on the camshaft, keeping it to the rear at all times. Without the spring tension the camshaft was able to drift forward, permitting the cam lobes to strike the valve-lifter guides, causing the noise. It wasn't sufficient to induce failure — just enough to create that aggravating knock.

To repair it, all Lee had to do was remove the radiator to gain access to the timing gear cover, install a new spring, and it was fixed. It cost him about a dime for the spring and maybe an hour's labor. He figured it out on his own, but kept mum. I learned from that episode.

After my 1949 vacation, while I was hanging around the garage, Joe came to me: "How would you like to go for an airplane ride?" I was aware Joe was taking flying lessons at the Kearsarge Airport under the G.I. Bill, and had just recently gotten his pilot license, permitting him to carry passengers. I had never been up in a plane and was, in fact, apprehensive; at first I declined the offer, but he kept bugging me: "Come on, you'll like it."

Finally, I agreed to go with him, and we headed out to the airport.

Chapter 5

Learning to Fly
1950-1951

You know what? I *did* like it! I liked it a lot, and I didn't get sick after all. The countryside was so beautiful, and everything was in such stark detail. I was hooked, so Joe invited me to go with him again the next Saturday.

1946 Piper J-3 Cub trainer. I took my first flying lessons in this type of aircraft in 1949 at "Mac" McMillen's flying school at Kearsarge Airport in Erie, Pa. My first experience with a light airplane was flying with Joe Martin.

The plane was a J-3 Cub trainer. They built thousands of them after the war in anticipation of a boom in private flying. Unfortunately, that didn't happen, and the light plane market soon became glutted from overproduction.

I met two people who were to have an enormous impact on my life in aviation, Clayton Lafayette "Mac" McMillen and Earl Derion. After Mac left the service in '45, he was intent on spending the rest of his life in aviation.

1953: C.L. (Mac) McMillen congratulates Pauline Herbidian on her first solo in the Aeronca Champion trainer pictured here. Mac was a key person in my aviation journey. We were friends for more than 20 years until his untimely death in 1972.

A new airport opened in South Erie in the suburb of Kearsarge, and Mac and Earl started a flight school there, training students under the G.I. Bill. Earl was the mechanic, but he didn't go to war because he was deemed unfit for military service as a result of a plane crash early in his career. Instead, he made his contribution to the war effort by training mechanics who become flight engineers on B-17 and B-24 heavy bombers. Earl took exceptionally good care of Mac's Cubs, so the flight school prospered. Mac flew 'em, and Earl fixed 'em.

Earl Derion at his maintenance facility in Erie, Pa. in 1980.
Earl was my lifelong friend and mentor.

By December, I was taking flying lessons of my own in the J-3 Cub. My instructor lost patience with me because all I wanted to do was sightsee instead of adhering to the curriculum. Although flying was dirt cheap by today's standards, lessons were expensive for someone of my means. It cost $8 an hour for the Cub rental plus $3 for the instructor. So far I had only taken a few lessons, and was nowhere near soloing.

Based on his flying experience before the war, Vinnie King suggested I buy a plane and hire an instructor instead of renting, so I decided to explore that possibility. At first Uncle Dell was skeptical, but later on he concurred that I should continue my flying. I think he detected just a glimmer of possibility that it might turn into something productive for me. I had virtually no savings, and a plane would cost about $750. I approached Uncle Dell about a loan and he didn't reject the idea out of hand. He simply said, "We'll look into it."

Unlike Kearsarge, Port Erie was a large municipal airport with paved runways, airline service, and two fixed base operations, one of which was Krantz Aeronautical. Julian Krantz was an old-time friend of Vinnie's, so we stopped in to see him during one of our lunch breaks.

He had a deteriorated Aeronca Champion trainer with a freshly overhauled engine for $750 — the plane had the dubious-sounding moniker of "Old 480." Vinnie said we would discuss it and get back to him with our decision, and I was anxious to hear Uncle Dell's response.

Surprisingly, Uncle Dell agreed to lend me the money on the condition that I sign a promissory note. He was all business, and I think he wanted it to be a teaching moment for me. We returned to the airport the next day and I deposited $100 on Old 480.

The following Saturday, I went to Kearsarge Airport to tell Mac and Earl about my purchase, and I thought they were going to laugh me right off the airport. They knew all about Old 480 and the fact that it was a worn-out hulk of a plane, fit for salvage only.

I was crestfallen, and it appeared I had made a horrible mistake. "Go get your money back," was their recommendation. That was easier said than done, as I had signed a purchase agreement with Julian and I suspected he would not be anxious to refund my deposit.

N 9309E 1946 Aeronca Chief. This plane appears twice in the text. It was purchased in early 1950 for $850. This plane was pivotal because it provided the means to acquire my private pilot's license. I flew it approximately 100 hours.

Earl knew the whereabouts of a really nice Aeronca in the Jamestown, N.Y. area available for only $50 more, at $800. It was a 1946 Chief model, with side-by-side seating instead of the front-and-rear arrangement in the Champ. The Chief would be suitable for instruction, and it was a one-owner plane with only 400 hours flying time since brand new.

Somehow I had to undo my purchase agreement with Julian, and the only solution I could come up with was to tell a lie: "Uncle Dell won't let me have the plane, and would you please give me my money back?" That's what I did, and I've always regretted it. I was young, but that didn't excuse it; I knew it was wrong.

"Oh well, what did it matter?" I thought to myself. "I'll be flying at Kearsarge Airport with Earl and Mac, miles away."

Julian did return my deposit, but it wasn't over yet, as we shall see.

Earl and I drove over to the airport at Falconer, N.Y., to examine the Chief. It was top-of-the-line and gorgeous, with a special hand-rubbed "dope" (lacquer) finish. It even came with a radio and a self-starter. The propellers on most small planes of that vintage were hand-actuated, meaning that a helper was needed to stand at the front of the plane and physically "prop it" (rotate the propeller) to start the engine. The Chief had a handle in the cockpit that accomplished the same thing. I couldn't wait to get it home.

"I'll get Joe Martin to fly it back," I mused. Unfortunately, that plan had to be scrubbed because the hangar at Kearsarge was full, and tying the Chief down outside was not an option. There was space in the big hangar at Port Erie, but that was the home of Krantz Aeronautical, and Julian would be right next door. As the saying goes, what goes around comes around. Never lie — it isn't worth it. It was imperative that the Chief be in a hangar.

"Okay, Joe. Fly the Chief to Port Erie. I'll just steer clear of Julian as much as possible and maybe it will be okay." But it wasn't, as we shall see.

Upon arrival at Port Erie, Joe recounted his flight from Falconer, N.Y. "That plane is no trainer! I had my hands full, and you'll crack it up on your first solo." That was not what I wanted to hear. Mac had assured me the Chief would be okay for instruction with its side-by-side seating. I loved the plane, so I said to myself, "We'll work it out somehow," and we did.

Wilbur A. Hahn would be my flight instructor. Bill had trained aviation cadets in WWII, and I think he felt diminished in some respects because he hadn't served overseas in combat. Actually, though, those who trained the pilots here at home were every bit as important as those shooting down enemy planes.

Once the Chief arrived at Port Erie, I joined a new aviation fraternity. Herman Steimer, of German descent and with a distinct accent, was the airport manager. Herman was a great guy, and I can only imagine how he suffered during the war. He was always smiling and cracking corny jokes — the life of the party. In his role as airport manager, he was the key to finding me a spot in the "big hangar."

Massive upgrading of Port Erie Airport was a WPA (Works Progress Administration) project of the 1930s. The big hangar also served as an airline terminal for American and Penn Central Airlines during the war. The street side provided ticket counters as well as office space for airport administration.

The massive hangar doors rolled on tracks in the floor, and since the hangar faced east, the doors were seldom closed except during severe storms and in winter, when no planes were taken in or out. It was fully illuminated and provided space to fully enclose one DC-3 or about ten small aircraft. The rent was $15 per month, and the hangar was usually quite full.

Herman's secretary, Betty, worked in the office, the flight school was operated by Gerald (Gerry) Richardson, and Krantz Aeronautical provided maintenance. Gradually, I became acquainted with the other plane owners who kept planes there. There was no control tower at that time, but there was a small building across the entrance road, known as "the shack," that housed a CAA Flight Service Station.

Prior to 1958, the Civil Aeronautics Authority operated the Federal Airway System, and provided the personnel to staff control towers and weather reporting stations like the one in Erie. It was manned 24/7 and in some ways functioned as a control tower, except the men who worked there were unable to see planes taking off or landing because the big hangar obstructed their view. However, they did provide traffic advisories to planes they maintained radio contact with, as well as disseminating information about weather conditions, altimeter settings, etc. It was also a gathering place for pilots. Weather broadcasts were transmitted on a special radio frequency at 15 minutes and 45 minutes after the hour, 24 hours a day. This facility was a tremendous asset for the pilots at Port Erie.

The Erie airport also had navigational equipment that was monitored and controlled by the CAA personnel in connection with IFR (Instrument Flight Rules) traffic. During bad weather the airlines operated on Instrument Flight plans and followed special rules. Some business aircraft, and a few private aircraft, were also equipped and qualified to fly IFR. The navigational aids previously mentioned were: 1) Instrument Landing System (ILS), and 2) Low-Frequency Radio Range.

Erie was one of the first airports in the nation to have an instrument landing system. The system was developed during the war for the military and was put into service at a few civilian airports, including Erie, on a test basis. It provided very accurate lateral and vertical guidance right down to the end of the runway. This permitted planes to descend to a much lower minimum altitude than could be authorized with the Radio Range. The ILS attracted numerous large training planes to Erie to practice approaches before big cities like Cleveland, Buffalo, and Pittsburgh were so equipped.

The people who worked in the CAA Service Station were first and foremost just ordinary people, like any of us. Some were trained as pilots, but many others were aspiring aviators who wished they could fly, and envied those of us who did. Their official title was Flight Service Station Representative. They briefed pilots on current and forecasted weather conditions and information needed to file a flight plan.

I spent many hours in "the shack." We talked about everything, but much of the discussion focused on aviation. They even taught me how to make the half-hour weather broadcasts. That was quite a compliment because the "briefer," the person whose responsibility it was to convey weather information to pilots, was sticking his neck out by permitting me to do that.

Into the Air

Returning to my flight training: Once I engaged Bill Hahn as my instructor, I was ready to resume flying lessons in my new plane. It was a tight fit with two grown men in the small cockpit. The Chief was equipped with a control wheel, instead of the stick that was the primary control in the Cub. That was not a major adjustment; in fact, it was a real plus not having to maneuver your legs around that protruding obstacle.

Training began with a ground session prior to our first flight. Many of the elements were similar to those used during my J-3 Cub training, and the ground school provided Bill with the opportunity to forewarn me about the idiosyncrasies of flying the Chief. I wasn't required to pay for ground school; the clock for Bill started when the engine did.

The plane handled well, chugging along at 85 mph compared to the Cub's 70. The first landing was a bit dicey, and I began to appreciate Joe Martin's derogatory remarks regarding the Chief.

Discussing that with Bill, his only comment was, "You'll soon get used to it." All in all, I was very pleased with my first lesson. Takeoff was less than stellar with a full tank of gas, but Port Erie's long paved runways more than compensated for the Chief's doggy performance. We did both standard and steep turns, climbs, glides, and even a chandelle (a sudden, steep climbing turn) with an occasional spin thrown in. It was all very exciting, and Bill was an excellent instructor.

After a few more lessons and having logged about 8 hours, I was ready to solo. The instructor never told the student when that defining moment had arrived, lest it stir up anxiety. It began as an ordinary flight lesson, and after a few landings, Bill told me to pull over to the edge of the runway. At that point, he simply climbed out and gave me my instructions: "Take it around for three full-stop landings." That was my first inkling that I would be flying alone, so I really didn't have time to get psyched up. I just taxied back to the end of the runway and took off.

What a feeling! The plane felt light and responsive without Bill alongside. I was thrilled, but so much for the joy of taking off; soon it was time to land. Was it as bad as Joe said? Would I crack-up on my first solo? Of course not — it was "a piece of cake," using old RAF (Royal Air Force) pilot's terminology from the era of flying Spitfires during the Battle of Britain.

Nice and easy now, watch your airspeed, start the flare (get the plane in the proper attitude for landing); the plane is so light it doesn't want to land. Okay, now you've got it; keep the yoke (control wheel) all the way back and let it settle. There was maybe a slight bounce and then I was on the runway for my first landing. Wow, that was great! Let's try it again.

Bill was standing off to the side watching and he gave me a thumbs-up, so I must have done something right. I just had to do two more and I'd be home free, and I did. What a feeling! I had just completed my first solo.

Back at the hangar, I was surprised to see Bill approaching with a pair of scissors. Oh-oh, it's the traditional "tee shirt" ritual: In celebration of becoming a new birdman, I was to be rewarded by having my shirttail snipped.

"You did fine! Just be sure to come out and fly again tomorrow," Bill said. It wasn't a good idea to allow a long interruption after your first solo. When I returned the next day, my expectation was that I would take the Chief up by myself for more takeoffs and landings. No-o-o, that's not the way it worked. Bill got back in for some more stalls and air work. Then, and only then, he exited the Chief and turned me loose. However, this time was different because when he got out he just walked back to the hangar. I said to myself, "That's a good sign." I made three more landings and from that point, I was on my own.

Most of my practice was on weekends, because the days were still too short to fly after work. I was scheduled for a long lunch break at the lab, so I was able to squeeze in a session or two during the week. I was progressing nicely until one lovely Sunday in May.

When I took off, the air was bumpy. So I climbed to 6000 feet, on top of scattered cumulus where the air was smooth. I flew around, just having fun, nipping the edges of the clouds, and soon it was time to return to the airport.

Bill had cautioned me about carburetor icing, especially when gliding down from altitude on a spring day such as this. As instructed, I pulled the carburetor heat knob out, retarded the throttle to descend, and had more fun chasing the clouds on my way down. As I reached "pattern altitude," at about 1000 feet above the airport, I pushed the throttle back in to enter the downwind leg of the traffic pattern.

Bad luck! The engine quit. Oh, it didn't completely die on me then and there; it sputtered and coughed a bit, and then I looked out the windshield and observed the propeller standing motionless, straight up and down. I had been trained for this emergency, so I didn't panic; the procedure was to select a suitable landing site within gliding distance, and make a normal landing while maintaining a safe airspeed and glide angle. I was too far from the airport to reach the runway, but the low-frequency radio range towers were directly beneath me. As I began my approach, that looked like the safest place to land, but the area was planted with winter wheat. I knew a light west wind was blowing, and that was favorable for the approach I was making.

It was only a minute or so from the time the prop stopped, but it was sufficient to adjust my glide angle and with a little forward slip, my glide path was fine. The surprise came just prior to touchdown, when I leveled off three feet too high because the wheat was tall, ready for harvest. The Chief just plopped down for a safe landing with no damage to the plane, and then I got out and looked around, noting the height of the grain.

I was next to a golf course, and saw people on the green at the ninth hole. They weren't paying any attention to me, and I don't think they saw me land. I approached one of the golfers, explaining that I had just made an emergency landing and needed a ride to the airport. He was a bit shocked, but agreed to drive me, and on arrival at the big hangar refused payment; instead, he handed me his business card indicating he was the owner of the Thom McAn shoe store on Peach Street. "When you need shoes, I would appreciate your business." I thanked him very much, and assured him I looked forward to patronizing his store.

Walking through the hangar, I noticed Gerry Richardson sitting outside on the bench right where he was when I left. He was startled, seeing me return without my airplane, and about the same time, Bill Hahn appeared on the scene. I told him what had happened. "Is the plane okay?" Bill asked. "Can we fly it out?" I replied that I thought so, except I didn't understand why the engine quit. Four of us piled into Bill's car and headed for the golf course. When we reached the Chief, Bill told me to get in, and we would attempt to start it. The engine roared to life on the second pull, and ran up perfectly.

Bill agreed to fly it out if we tramped down some of the wheat to create a short runway. He got in and, after a brief run, hauled the Chief into the air. We tried to straighten the wheat as much as possible before we left, because I felt certain the farmer would be thoroughly incensed; fortunately, though, I never heard a word from anyone.

What caused the engine to fail? The answer was really quite simple, and in a way it was my fault. During my descent from altitude, the carburetor iced up because I didn't rev up the engine frequently enough to generate sufficient heat to melt the ice accumulation. Even though I pulled the knob out, very little heat was being generated at idle during the glide down from chasing the clouds. Either Bill failed to clarify the procedure, or I forgot. However, it was a lesson well learned, and I never experienced it again. Except for a few wheat stalks stuck in the landing gear, the Chief was good as new.

Preparing for a Flight

Sometime later, after engine start, I heard a strange noise, and it didn't sound right. "You've got a stuck valve," someone shouted.

Oh boy! I didn't like the sound of that. Now I would be in the clutches of Julian Krantz, the man I had lied to a few months earlier. I dreaded having to go to him, but unexpectedly, he was nice as pie. Julian was no dummy; he valued my business in spite of it all.

"I'll have Brad take a look at it," he promised. Brad was Clarence Bradshaw, Julian's licensed A&P (airframe & power plant) mechanic and shop manager. After Brad had looked at the engine, I asked, "What's the verdict?" and Brad replied, "You need a top overhaul. One exhaust valve is stuck fast, and a couple of the others are sticking as well."

"How much will it cost?" I queried. "About $200, depending on whether the valves can be reused." Then Julian arrived on the scene and said, "I'm sorry, Ray; it's a good idea to use Rislone with your oil changes. Aeroncas are notorious for sticking valves."

Again, the onus was on me because I had been doing my own maintenance to save money and to avoid the shop. Perhaps if I had been truthful with Julian at the outset, he might have counseled me about using the additive.

What was I to do now? I didn't have money for the overhaul, and I dreaded going to Uncle Dell for more money. Vinnie King bailed me out.

Since I didn't have vacation plans that summer, Clarence gave me the option of doing maintenance work at the lab during that period to earn extra money. It was usually contracted out, but if I was willing, I could have the job. As involved as I was with flying, it was the perfect solution.

The overhaul turned out great, and I was soon back in the air again, approaching my goal of becoming a private pilot. Satisfying the cross-country requirements was my last major hurdle. One flight was dual with Bill on board, and the other solo. At least three legs of 50 or 60 miles each were customary. In my case, I flew to Youngstown, Ohio, then to Jamestown, N.Y. and returned home. Bill suggested I check out my radio. There hadn't been any need for it thus far, but Youngstown had a control tower. After installing new batteries, Bill instructed me on its use.

The dual portion was completed in early June without a hitch. Bill taught me how to identify landmarks on the sectional chart such as rivers, lakes, and railroads. The day of my solo cross-country, the weather turned worse with reduced visibility, and I experienced trouble with my radio receiver at Youngstown. Alternatively, I used the "light gun" system, a special procedure for radio failure. It called for a normal entry to the landing pattern while maintaining a watchful eye on the control tower for a green light aimed directly at the plane while making my final turn to land.

My responsibility was to rock my wings to acknowledge the light, signifying I had received clearance to land. If the light was red, I must abandon my approach and go around. I got the green light, so it was okay to land. Fortunately, I was able to get the radio fixed, and departed normally.

On the Jamestown leg, I temporarily lost my way. I circled a town that had a large water tower with the name "Corry" on it, so then I knew where I was, and got back on course. The final leg to Erie was easy; I could scarcely miss Lake Erie and Presque Isle.

Prior to the private pilot flight test, it was necessary to have a recommendation ride with an instructor who was not involved in my training. He would have me perform all the required maneuvers and grade them accordingly, and it usually took about an hour. So, early in July, I went up with Gerry Richardson and got approval for my flight test. The actual exam would be conducted by a CAA inspector or a designee. Luckily for me, Bill had that authority, so I was able to take the flight test with him.

I was anxious, but I needed to concentrate and do my best. It turned out all right, but the jitters interfered with my performance to some degree. The written test of 25 true/false questions was a breeze, however.

At that point, I had about 35 flight hours. After passing the test I was finally a licensed pilot, allowing me to carry passengers.

In the fall of 1950, I accompanied Virgal Swain on an ambulance trip to Philadelphia, acting as copilot. It was fun and provided the first multi-engine hours for my logbook.

Virgal was a WWII vet who operated an air ambulance service out of Port Erie. The plane he used was a Cessna Bobcat, a war-surplus multi-engine trainer that was specially equipped. I guess he observed potential in me and helped me with my flying. Naturally, I was in awe of his extensive experience and went up with him every chance I got.

"Virg" also had a surplus AT-6 Army trainer, an exciting plane with a 600-horsepower radial engine. On occasion, he would invite me to accompany him for aerobatics, doing loops and rolls.

A most memorable flight was in November 1950, when we flew the AT-6 to Kearsarge to refuel. Virgal let me fly the return trip from the "front seat" (command pilot position) for the first time. My only requirement was to buy the gas; however, the AT-6 was very thirsty, and burned 35 gallons of high-octane fuel per hour. It cost about $10, but it was well worth it. That hour of training in an advanced military trainer stood me in good stead later. Virgal also flew with me in the Chief on occasion.

The air ambulance business dried up the following year, and Virgal moved on to bigger and better things in connection with the Korean War. He enrolled at a flight school in Miami for his Airline Transport Rating under the G.I. Bill, and then became a DC-3 captain flying soldiers around the country for Meteor Air Transport based at Teterboro, N.J. He loved that job and it was the fulfillment of his dreams. Two years later, I had an opportunity to make a trip with him to Detroit hauling freight for Ford, acting as his copilot.

Chapter 6

The Korean Conflict
1951-1953

On June 25, 1950, the cold war got hot. From the U.S. point of view it was a "police action," but in reality it was *war!*

North Korea, with substantial Chinese support, invaded South Korea. Within days, Red tanks rolled into Seoul. South Korea promptly appealed to the United Nations for help, but before long the UN defenders were pushed into a pocket on the Yellow Sea called the Pusan Corridor. Their only advantage, under General Douglas MacArthur, was air supremacy. Even though it was a UN operation, the U.S. provided 90% of everything. Our fighter/bomber incursions created a stalemate lasting several months.

On September 15, MacArthur ended the stalemate with an unbelievable coup: UN troops made an amphibious landing at Inchon at an area lightly defended because of its horrendous tidal flows. Within 24 hours, UN forces were back in Seoul and drove north to capture the North Korean capital city of Pyongyang. The fight went all the way to the Yalu River, North Korea's border with China.

All thoughts of the troops being home for Christmas were dashed when 400,000 Chinese troops, with bugles blaring, swamped UN lines. Suddenly, there was a massive retreat to the south in an attempt to escape. Our forces suffered terribly that winter; the Chinese owned the hills, and we controlled the roads in the valleys. There was no hope of getting our people back to the 38th Parallel, which was the dividing line between North and South Korea. Only a massive amphibious withdrawal at Hungnam saved the day. It began to look a lot like World War III.

What did all this have to do with me? Answer: a lot — because by late summer, there was talk of reinstating the draft. Naturally, I watched these developments very closely, but my boss, Clarence, told me not to worry; he could secure a deferment for me because we were engaged in work for the state as well as for the City of Erie. That turned out to be so much wishful thinking.

In early December, I received notice from the draft board to report for a pre-induction physical exam. At that point, China entered the fray in Korea. I saw many familiar faces when I reported for my physical. Clarence submitted more paperwork, but it was all in vain. By early 1951, I had received my "Greetings" from the President of the United States:

"You have been inducted into the Army of the United States and are hereby ordered to report to a certain location in downtown Erie on March 20, 1951, for transportation to an Induction Center to be determined at a later date. Bring only toiletries that will fit in a small handbag." I was 20 years of age.

In the midst of all this gloom and doom, there was one bright spot. On February 11, Virgal Swain and I delivered the AT-6 to Leeward Aeronautical at Fort Wayne, Indiana. After all those years, the AT-6 was still the Air Force basic trainer of choice. Leeward was under contract to train pilots, and by that time, those powerful machines were in short supply.

Since it was midwinter, we dressed warmly for the trip. The flight was uneventful and boring because we didn't have an intercom radio, and it was virtually impossible to talk over the engine. Minimal communication was exchanged by closing the throttle briefly to quiet the engine, but that was quite unsatisfactory. After completing the necessary paperwork, we went to the bus station for the long ride back to Erie.

Having received my induction notice, there was much to do. Uncle Dell suggested putting the Hudson up on blocks and draining the fluids in preparation for long-term storage.

What about the Aeronca? I advertised it for the same $800 I paid for it. With the recent engine overhaul, that price was attractive. It really hurt, though, as I had become quite attached to the Chief while I had owned it. During the past year, I had flown it over 100 hours.

One fact not previously mentioned: I had been careless with my eating habits over the past couple of years and gained a lot of weight. At the time of induction I weighed 250 pounds, and Uncle Dell kidded me about it — "Wait till they get you in the Army," etc. He didn't know how prophetic that statement was.

The morning of March 20, 1951, Uncle Dell drove me downtown to the bus. It was difficult for me to grasp all that was taking place. Arriving at the designated street corner, I saw a crowd of young men all carrying small handbags similar to mine. I recognized a few, but most were strangers. Everyone's destination was the same — the induction center at Fort Meade, Maryland — and we would be traveling by train. The Staff Sergeant assigned to us counted heads with great diligence.

At Union Station, ready to board the train, we were in for a pleasant surprise. Uncle Sam provided Pullman cars — sleeping-car accommodations with stewards to pamper us. Someone piped up, "There's a dining car to the rear."

The train pulled out of the station promptly at 5 p.m., and all 70 of us were invited to the dining car for dinner. The Sergeant in charge kept track of our whereabouts at all times. We were not permitted to visit other areas of the train. The coaches ahead of us were loaded with civilians. The train made numerous stops along the way, but most of the passengers were destined for Harrisburg. In spite of a high level of excitement, we eventually went to bed. At 10 a.m. the next morning we arrived at Fort Meade, and our Pullman cars were shunted right onto the base.

We were definitely in the Army now, with troops marching everywhere. After a final head count, we fell in for the march to the supply room where we were measured for uniforms (dress and fatigues), dress shoes and combat boots, helmets, poncho, and undershirts and shorts. A box was provided to pack civilian clothes to be sent home. From that point on, everything would be G.I. (Government Issue).

Next we marched to our barracks to learn the Army way to make a bed: When tight enough, a quarter dropped on the bed would bounce up so you could grab it. Then we were off to the mess hall for lunch.

After chow, we were marched off to the administration department. Here we encountered endless papers and forms, including an interview for each of us. That was the beginning of my

"201 file," the set of documents the government maintained for every member of the armed forces. The Army wanted to know everything: my occupation, skills, history, criminal record, etc. That file became very important six months later, after I arrived in Japan.

Finally we returned to our barracks. Everyone was discussing our experience this first day in the U.S. Army. I was now Pvt. Raymond A. Lemmon, U.S., 52-077695. We were issued "dog tags" with this information, plus our blood type and religious affiliation: P was for Protestant, C was for Catholic, and H was for Jewish.

Lights-out was 2100 hours (9 p.m.) and "Reveille" bugled at 0500 hours. My assignment at Fort Meade lasted only for ten days. It was rumored that most of us were to be assigned eight weeks of Basic Infantry Training at Fort Jackson, S.C.

Although our status at Fort Meade was "Unassigned," I don't want to create the impression that we were just lying around. We attended classes on military organization, movement of troops (marching), and military courtesy (learning to salute). We were advised to salute anything that moved. And, of course, there was always KP (kitchen police). That meant peeling potatoes and washing trays. The army didn't use dishes; compartmentalized stainless-steel trays were the order of the day. There were also lots of greasy pots and pans. The mess halls' worst enemy was grease because it caused diarrhea in the troops, so they used a lot of soap to avoid the "runs."

Marching: Parade ground drills were defined as the orderly movement of troops. That familiar scene was often shown in movies showing troops in training. While marching, the troops might sing out cadence calls, such as "Your left, your left, your left, right, left," or more commonly "Hut 2, hut 4, 1-2-3-4," and then, "Left, right, left," etc. Another cadence call was, "Jodie was home when you left, Jodie was home you're right, cadence call, 1-2-3-4," etc. We marched by the hour in platoon strength (50) back and forth, column left, column right, to the rear march, etc. It didn't take long to learn; the main element was keeping in step. Corporals led platoons in the drills.

The barracks housed one platoon that was supervised by a Sergeant who lived in the barracks with us, except that he had his own separate room. Bunks for us were stacked upper and lower. The flip of a coin decided who would climb.

An infantry company consisted of four platoons with a Captain in overall command. However, for the most part, you would find a Second Lieutenant out with the troops. Four companies defined a regiment, and four regiments made up a battalion. The whole complement of a camp comprised a division of perhaps 20,000 troops.

The strategy to avoid KP was to not get caught standing around. The Company NCOs (non-commissioned officers) were always on the lookout for stragglers. Typically, when they found some, they would say, "You, you, and you report to Sgt. So-and-so," who was in charge of the kitchen detail.

Soon it was time to move on to my next assignment in South Carolina. The Erie we left was a snow-covered wilderness, compliments of an early spring storm, and we had been pleasantly surprised to find the Baltimore area enjoying spring-like temperatures. Now we would be traveling south to even warmer weather — much warmer. There were no Pullman cars this time. We were guests of the Southern Railway System on a troop train carrying at least 200 of us. With all our duffel bags, it was pretty crowded.

In a couple of days we reached Fort Jackson, home of the Eighth Infantry Division. They identified each company by our "cycle of training" number. (Each company of raw recruits constituted a "cycle.") After eight weeks I would leave as a qualified combat infantryman with the appropriate Military Occupational Specialty number (MOS).

The training was intense. We were issued a Garand rifle, Caliber .30 M-1. We spent a great deal of time on the rifle range, after which we were graded on our shooting ability — "Marksman" was the lowest acceptable rating. With each bull's-eye, the rifleman scored a point. I scored 435 out of a possible 500, for a rating of "Expert." I think there was some mistake, but anyway, it went on my record as such. We also hurled hand grenades and fired a .30-caliber machine gun as well as the bazooka (a tank-busting rocket).

The intense training translated into long days with a very demanding schedule. Performing calisthenics every day melted excess fat away. We ate a 4000-calorie-per-day diet, so I don't remember ever being hungry. There was a lot of marching, and at the end of the course we hiked 15 miles to the bivouac area and back. We were taught the buddy system. Each infantryman carried a shelter half (one of the halves of a two-man tent). The bivouac was tough, but I lucked out when they sent a few of us back to camp for KP. Who says it doesn't pay to volunteer?

At the conclusion of basic training, we underwent inspection by the battalion commander. Because this was a special occasion, we wore our khaki dress uniforms. When the Major came to me, he sized me up and said, "Get this man a proper uniform." I had lost 40 pounds. The training cycle was over, and I was off to my next assignment.

Flying at Fort Jackson

Owens Field, the municipal airport for Columbia, S.C., was located within the city limits and operated by an ex-WASP (Woman Army Service Pilot — the main contribution of the WASPs was freeing up combat-trained pilots for duty overseas by ferrying planes of all types from factories to air bases all around the U.S.). She had a two-place side-by-side Piper Vagabond trainer, and because I had my private pilot's license, she agreed to rent it to me. I invited a friend from camp to join me, and we had an hour ride that included flying over Fort Jackson.

When we returned to the airport, the weather was a bit gusty, and after touching down, the plane swung around in a "ground loop." A wing dipped down and a little gas splashed out, but other than that, no harm was done. The old-time WASP pilot, sitting on a bench, saw it all, and as I sheepishly walked in, she remarked, "Tricky little thing, isn't it?" "It sure is," I replied. That was my first of several experiences of renting planes at my duty stations.

I received shocking news from home! Vinnie King, my mentor from Greystone Lab, had died of a massive heart attack at the tender age of 33. On the surface he was the picture of health, but beneath his radiant exterior there were problems. He smoked heavily, using both a pipe and Old Gold cigarettes, and had been rejected for military service because of high blood pressure.

I tried to get leave, but my request was denied since the emergency was not in my family, so I responded with a telegram instead. It was a tremendous loss for the King family, and for me as well.

I completed my training at Fort Jackson in early June. My new orders read: "Proceed to Fort Sam Houston, Brooke Army Medical Center, San Antonio, Texas, for Emergency Medical training to become a Combat Medic." (Someone had obviously been looking at my 201 file.) The course was called MRTC (Medical Replacement Training Center). Traveling with only a few others, we went by rail; we were escorted by a Sergeant, who made sure we arrived safely. The trip took two days, and since no hotels were authorized, we stayed on the train. At San Antonio we were met by a bus that took us to Fort Sam.

A new class of 30 recruits was being convened, and the first order of business was a comprehensive test. It covered not only our recently completed infantry training at Fort Jackson, but general knowledge about many different topics with a definite slant toward the field of medicine. Assignment to MRTC changed my branch of Army service from Infantry to the Medical Corps. I wore the caduceus for the remainder of my time in the Service. The following day, when class convened, the Sergeant embarrassed me by announcing, "Private Lemmon had the highest score of anyone ever attending MRTC." Of course, with that announcement, great things were expected of Private Lemmon. The course consisted of learning how to administer drugs, including morphine, using hypodermics; bandaging battlefield wounds; and splinting broken bones. It lasted for six weeks — part of June and all of July into early August.

San Antonio was categorized as a Hot Climate Assignment, and it surely lived up to that designation. Even so, PT (physical training) sessions were conducted out in the open, as if it were not. Our fatigues turned white from salt exudation, and ambulances stood by to retrieve those who dropped out of formation from dehydration and transport them to the base hospital. My fat continued to burn off, and by the time I completed training, my weight was down to a trim 180 pounds and I had never felt better in my life.

Training included bivouac in Texas cattle country, a tough assignment because the campsite was infested with cattle ticks. Each night, we stripped naked to pick the critters off each other — the Army was big on the buddy system.

On weekends we were permitted to go in town. San Antonio was a bustling metropolis, and I remember my first visit; getting off the bus, right there in center city, was the Alamo — just as it was back in 1836. That was neat, and I was duly impressed.

Near the completion of our training, some observant clerk discovered those of us from Fort Jackson hadn't completed the infiltration course. So, one morning during troop formation, the Sergeant called our names, and after falling out, we were ordered to report to the front gate for bus transport to Fort Hood, Texas, about 50 miles away.

The infiltration course was a live-fire exercise where you got down on your belly, and with your rifle cradled in your arms, propelled yourself on your elbows 100 yards while they fired a machine gun over your head. To heighten the excitement of the drill, explosive charges were detonated nearby, throwing dirt all over. The machine gun swept side to side, but the height was fixed so they wouldn't kill everybody. Needless to say, standing up was a very bad idea, but there were a few cases of that happening due to a trainee panicking under fire. Even being careful, you got filthy.

At the end of the course, we stood up and fired our rifles, loaded with blanks, at a dummy. If your rifle didn't fire, it meant you had contaminated it with dirt while crawling, and you had to go through it again. Two transits were required to attain qualification for both day and night.

While stationed in Texas I was able to fly at Stinson Field, a small airport on the south side of San Antonio. The base operator had a Piper PA-12 for rent, and after a 30-minute checkout, I was cleared to fly it solo. With a 100 horsepower engine and room for three, it was more advanced than the planes I was used to. The rate was $10 an hour and as usual, I brought a friend. We explored the surrounding area, including Randolph Field, the primary Air Force Academy of the time, and I added 3 hours to my logbook while stationed there.

Leaving for the Far East

I graduated in early August as a full-fledged Combat Medic and was placed in the pipeline bound for Korea. My specific assignment was FECOM (Far East Command) with 30 days' leave delay en route. Subsequently, I was ordered to report to Camp Stoneman in California for transport to Japan via troopship, and after processing would be assigned to a combat unit in Korea.

If I accepted the leave, it was implied that I would report for embarkation by the date specified in my orders. That was the Army's way of not having to provide transportation, because they knew everyone wanted to go home before being shipped overseas.

I bought a half-fare plane ticket on Eastern Airlines to Cleveland, where I boarded a bus to Erie. On arrival, everyone except Uncle Dell was amazed at how five months in the Army had transformed me. (Uncle Dell had predicted the outcome, remember?)

Since my Hudson was still up on blocks out in the garage, Uncle Dell let me use his '36 Pontiac. The Aeronca Chief had been sold in my absence, so I was able to repay Uncle Dell. Vinnie had been right after all — it was a cheap way to learn to fly.

All too soon, it was time to report to California; I decided to travel by train, since it was much cheaper than flying. I took New York Central to Chicago, where I transferred to the Union Pacific. My reporting date was September 15, 1951, and I had been warned not to be late as violation of orders during hostilities could result in a trip to the stockade for 30 days.

The four-day trip west was long and tiresome, and there was no Pullman car this time. I rode sitting upright in what Union Pacific called a "chair car." Sleep was whenever you could get it, and dining was sandwiches and sodas provided by vendors along the way. I recall pulling into Cheyenne, Wyoming and seeing cowboys sitting on horseback wearing Stetson hats. We also stopped at Salt Lake City, Reno, and Sacramento prior to arrival at San Francisco. From there, it was a short bus ride to Camp Stoneman in Pittsburg, California.

I reported with one day to spare, awaiting transport to our troop ship, the USAT *General John Pope*, for the voyage to Yokohama, Japan. The ship was huge, capable of carrying 5000 Army personnel plus dependents.

We marched down to the ferry pier with all our gear, dropping everything on the ground at our assigned location, and then returned to camp for the night. Luckily, it never rained in that part of California during the summer.

The next day, after breakfast, we boarded the ferry that took us to the *Pope*, docked in San Francisco. From Pittsburg, it was about a 30-mile boat ride down the Sacramento River estuary.

USAT *General John Pope* was an Army troop ship that operated between San Francisco, Ca. and Yokohama, Japan. The *Pope* was enormous with over 5000 souls on board. Dependents and other VIPs were quartered topside, while we resided in the hull of the ship. Card games were the preferred pastime during the ten-day transit of the Pacific Ocean to Yokohama.

Red Cross volunteers served coffee and donuts before we transferred to the ship for assignment of bunks in the hull of the *Pope*. It was very crowded on deck, as everyone wanted to be at the rail for departure. With a tremendous blast of the ship's whistle, we sailed out of San Francisco Bay, through the Golden Gate. As we passed under that magnificent bridge, I wondered what the future might hold in store, including the possibility that this could be a one-way trip.

The bunks were stacked four high, so the usual flipping of coins decided who slept where. The bottom bunk was not necessarily the best. Next order of business was to locate the mess hall and latrines. The incessant thumping of the engine required some getting used to. There were the usual questions about how long the crossing would take, etc. It was shaping up to be a boring trip, and then the playing cards came out. Poker and Hearts were the games of choice.

The next day, when we were well out to sea, *mal de mer* began. I nearly succumbed to it, but I found that by going out on deck, and not eating much, I was able to stave it off. A few days later we ran into thick fog, and the ship slowed perceptibly while the foghorns blared incessantly. Because of the fog, we took an extra day to cross the Pacific. By the tenth day, it was evident we were nearing our destination of Yokohama, Japan.

The next stop on the route to Korea was Camp Drake, a processing center south of Tokyo, where I spent about 10 days. Each man was issued a brand-new M-1 Garand rifle. "Medics don't carry a rifle," we protested. Then we discovered the real reason: The new rifles were packed in cosmoline, a very sticky preservative oil that was tedious to remove. Assigning the rifles to non-combatants conferred on the non-combatants the responsibility of removing the cosmoline and getting the rifles ready for combat in Korea.

Sendai

172nd Station Hospital (750 beds), Sendai, Japan, 1951-1952. While serving in the U.S. Army I may owe my life to being assigned here instead of going to Korea. Several of my MRTC classmates were killed in combat on the Korean Peninsula.

A day or so after our arrival at Camp Drake, I was summoned to report to Personnel. It was good news; I wasn't going to Korea after all. They needed a lab tech at the 172nd Station Hospital in Sendai, a large city north of Tokyo. So I turned in my rifle and all my combat gear and awaited transfer to the transportation division. New orders were cut: I was to carry my 201 file with me and I would be traveling alone.

How would I find my way? I didn't speak any Japanese, at least not yet. Not to worry, though; the Army was thorough, and an MP (military policeman) put me on the correct train. Out of the thousands of troops in the Korean pipeline, I was singled out for this assignment.

It was a pleasant ride north to Sendai. Japan was famous for its excellent railway system, and their trains usually ran on time. At the Sendai RTO (rail transportation office) I caught a bus to the hospital.

When it was built shortly after World War II, the 172nd Station Hospital was a magnificent modern structure, located right in the midst of the city's urban squalor. Sendai wasn't bombed extensively, so there was no evidence of the fire damage so prevalent in many Japanese cities. About one million people lived there.

The hospital encompassed several city blocks and contained 750 beds. A product of the occupation, its intended purpose was the care and keeping of U.S. occupation personnel. While it was the focal point for the whole city, it was certainly not for the Japanese people, since only members of the armed forces and their dependents were treated there. At the time I arrived the staff was housed at Camp Sendai a few miles away, but that changed during my stay and by the time I left, everyone was quartered at the hospital.

Master Sergeant Hakes, who was in charge of the enlisted personnel at the lab, introduced me to six other technicians who worked in the various departments, including Hematology, Blood Chemistry, Urology, etc.

I was assigned to replace a certain Cpl. Whitehead, who was due for rotation back to the U.S. I soon discovered that "Whitey" didn't want to be rotated and was prepared to fight — and if he was successful, I would find myself right back in the pipeline to Korea.

One of my principle shortcomings was a lack of expertise in drawing blood for lab tests ordered by the doctors. Some of the staff made a big deal of that in support of Cpl. Whitehead's case. Since it was his job to teach me, he dragged his feet.

What a beginning! I turned out to be a quick study, though, seeming to have a knack for dealing with difficult "sticks." Before long, I was the one called upon when another technician was unsuccessful with a patient.

Sgt. Hakes and the chief of medicine, a Major Serfass, were in Whitehead's corner. They were nearly successful in getting me sent to Korea until Colonel Rigdon, the head of the hospital, intervened to put a stop to it: to wit, Pvt. Lemmon was to stay, and Cpl. Whitehead would be shipping out.

I was totally unaware of any of this undercurrent until sometime later, when I happened to be sitting next to our personnel manager on the bus. When he recognized me, he commented, "You created quite a stir at the hospital for a buck private." There were others working on my behalf that wanted to see Whitehead go; I was soon making the morning rounds by myself, and working in the Hematology section. I also lacked experience with the high-powered microscopes used there, so as I worked through the other sections on a weekly basis, I practiced using the scope on my own time. I did quite well, and soon after I was assigned to Hematology on a permanent basis.

I became rather expert at pinpointing malarial spirochetes on a routine blood smear. It was considered impossible with existing technology, but John Reardon, a fellow Private, pioneered a breakthrough by developing a special Wright's stain. We were receiving a lot of malaria cases from Korea. With utmost assurance, I would call the doctor and say, "Doctor, your patient has malaria." Instead of being offended by the effrontery, the doctors really applauded our expertise. In rare instances the physician would come to the lab, where I would have the slide in place so that he could peer through the scope and see the offender for himself. The presence of these spirochetes was definitive diagnosis.

By Thanksgiving, I was promoted to Private First Class, and my pay increased from $21 to $30 per month. Yippee!

Simultaneously, the 24th Infantry Division transferred from Korea to Sendai. Camp Schimmelpfennig, on the outskirts of the city, was their new base — and also my new home, as it turned out. A lab tech and pharmacist were needed to man their dispensary, so democratically we drew straws and guess who picked the short one? It promised to be a real challenge with my limited experience.

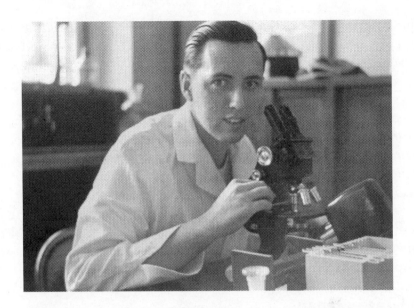

1951: This was my "work station" at the microscope in the hematology section of the hospital laboratory in Sendai, Japan.

"Don't worry," Hakes said. "You'll do fine. If you get something you can't handle, just send it over here."

As it turned out, I did a pretty good job at the dispensary and earned Corporal's stripes long before I could have anticipated another promotion. I was working closely with the doctor running a VD clinic, and when it looked like there was a case of gonorrhea, he sent the man over to me for a microscopic exam. My findings were diagnostic, and if the test was positive it was bad news for the soldier in question. Confirmed VD was "line-of-duty NO," which meant a black mark was entered on his 201 file affecting future promotional consideration.

I also did blood counts and additional malaria studies. After spending Christmas there, by the end of January, I was back at the hospital resuming my assignment as chief of the Hematology department. Because of Korea, the lab was expanding and we were assigned three new men, one of whom was Paul (PG) Fellmeth, about whom we shall hear a great deal more later.

I worked closely with the chief of medicine for the lab, a pathologist and MD: First Lt. John R. McGrath, from St. Louis. Although Mr. Hakes ran the lab administratively, Lt. McGrath was in charge of all professional aspects. He was called up from his research lab, and was very impressed with the work we were doing. One day he remarked, "You guys can work in my research facility anytime."

That was quite a compliment. Lt. McGrath was also instrumental in getting my MOS changed to 1858: "Fully Qualified Medical Lab Technician." Normally, it was necessary to attend a special school to qualify for such a change. Lt. McGrath also helped me become a member of American Medical Technologists, and that would translate to a higher salary expectation if I returned to Greystone Lab upon leaving the Army.

Another function of the lab staff was performing autopsies. We were on 24-hour call to assist Dr. McGrath in the morgue. I hated them and, thank goodness, we didn't have many; once they sent two drowning victims who had been in the water for days — ugh.

Flying in Japan

One day, a Captain Harry Morris reported to the lab for blood work, and during routine conversation I learned that he was assigned to the Army Light Aircraft Detachment at Lanier Field, just a few miles from the hospital. When I told him I had a private pilot's license, Harry was quite surprised.

"What are you doing here?" he asked. I explained that my lack of higher education precluded Air Force pilot training. He left with an invitation for me to come out to the airfield when I had a day off and we would do some flying. That was music to my ears after months of being grounded, so on a nice spring day I took the bus out to Lanier Field.

It was quite an operation. They were part of a medevac unit that trained pilots for Korea. They had helicopters, a De Havilland Beaver, several Cessna L-19s, plus a few other Liaison types. Harry suggested we take an L-19 "Bird Dog" to Matsushima Air Base, about 50 miles north, and I flew from the rear seat. The 230 horsepower engine really enabled the plane to perform. Those Cessnas were capable of operating out of unimproved strips performing observation duty associated with Artillery units. I logged two hours flying time, which was great. He invited me to come again and fly their Beaver, a bush-type plane with a 450 horsepower radial engine able to accommodate stretchers, or up to five people. On another occasion, I was able to fly that as well.

L-19 Cessna "Bird Dog" assigned to the U.S. Army Med-Evac unit in Sendai. I flew this plane (on weekends) several times during my service at the hospital.

Harry asked me a favor. The Detachment Commander needed permission to land a helicopter on the roof of the hospital in connection with a medevac training exercise, and he didn't know whom to contact for this approval, so I offered to look into it for him. About a month later, we had a coordinated drill that involved a helicopter landing on the roof with patients, and many hospital personnel attended. All I did was contact Col. Rigdon's adjutant with a request, and that was it. I was pleased to be able to help.

1952: Trips to Tokyo General Hospital

We were occasionally called upon to escort patients with special needs to Tokyo. Because I was a graduate of MRTC at Brooke Hospital in San Antonio, I was eligible for this duty. Those train trips were very desirable, so we split them up between us and I got to go three times, as I recall. We were assigned a special car with divided staterooms — very cushy indeed. At times, special equipment such as oxygen or IV stands were required, but for the most part, our patients were ambulatory.

This was the medevac exercise referred to in the text. The exercise involved an army helicopter from the aviation detachment at Lanier Field landing on the roof of the hospital simulating delivery of a patient. The scene is reminiscent of many episodes of the *M*A*S*H* television series.

It was a four-hour ride, with a meal provided. An ambulance from Tokyo General Hospital met the train and after admitting my patient, I was on my own. Sometimes two of us would go, which was even better. We visited the Enlisted Men's Club, went shopping on the Ginza (Tokyo's shopping mall), or just engaged in sightseeing at the Imperial Palace and the Dai-Ichi building. Dai-Ichi was UN Headquarters where MacArthur and, later, General Ridgeway had their offices, and the building was frequently shown on the evening news. At the time I made those trips, it was late spring of '52, so the weather was ideal.

The return trip from Tokyo was not so luxurious, just standard military transport like I had used for my arrival the previous September. Things were proceeding routinely that summer — until suddenly, my world turned upside down.

Emergency Orders

In early August, I received an urgent message to report to Personnel. Uncle Dell was hospitalized in Erie, not expected to live, and I hadn't even been aware that he was sick. Frances went to the Red Cross with an emergency request for me to come home. Since I was Uncle Dell's closest living relative, Frances indicated that it was imperative for me to return. Apparently she was successful, as orders had already been cut for my departure. What a shock!

Since I still had seven more months to serve, I assumed I would return to Sendai, so I took only my duffel bag with clothing and other personal effects. My orders read: "Cpl. R.A. Lemmon, U.S. 52-077695 is hereby granted 30 days' emergency leave. Air transport to the U.S. is authorized. Upon completion of said leave, EM (enlisted man) is to report to Indiantown Gap Military Reservation for reassignment in Continental U.S." Signed, Col. Rigdon — it came from the very top.

Wow! It looked like I wouldn't be coming back after all. Fortunately, my closest friend, PG Fellmeth, boxed up my typewriter and other personal effects and sent them to me. That same afternoon, I went to the RTO to board the Tokyo train. I was in a daze. When I arrived in Tokyo, I was immediately taken to Haneda Airport and consigned to MATS (Military Air Transport Service) for the first available flight to Travis AFB in California. I assumed it would be a military transport plane, but it wasn't.

After only an hour or so, I was aboard a California Eastern Airlines DC-4 bound for Hawaii and the West Coast. Only six hours had elapsed since I was first notified; the Army really knew how to get things done. Apparently, they had given me a top priority.

California Eastern was a contract carrier — CAM, for Civilian Air Movement. They were shaky outfits that would never pass muster as regular airlines. They were safe, but only marginally so. We took off with full fuel tanks, 70 G.I.s with their duffel bags bound for Wake Island. We didn't climb above 200 feet for three hours, and an announcement was made not to use the lavatory until further notice. Since the toilet was located in the very rear of the airplane, they didn't want any extra weight back there.

It was a 12-hour flight to Wake. What a relief to get off that plane! We refueled, had something to eat, and then we were back onboard for the next leg to Honolulu. That was another 10-hour flight, mostly in the dark. At daylight, we noticed that the #4 propeller had been feathered (stopped). The captain announced that it was a precautionary shutdown, and everything was okay, but was it? Not exactly, since that engine had to be changed on arrival.

It was beautiful in Honolulu. Since it would take several hours for the engine change, we went over to the main terminal for a good meal. I took pictures of a United Air Lines Boeing Stratocruiser sitting at the gate, with no perception that I was staring at my future.

United Airlines B-377 Stratocruiser at Honolulu, Hawaii, August 1952. I did not get to fly the rest of the way home in it — the plane was parked at the terminal during my stopover on the way home from Japan. The person in the picture was my traveling companion.

Late that afternoon, we reboarded our DC-4 for the final leg to California. It was very hard for me to comprehend all that was happening — it was just too much. After another 12-hour flight we finally landed at Travis Air Force Base, 50 miles northeast of San Francisco.

I was finally home — well, sort of. From Travis, I had two options: Either stand by for a "hop" on a military plane going east, or buy a half-fare airline ticket and fly commercial. I didn't have any money, but that was okay as I could sign a voucher, which was basically an IOU. Since there weren't any free rides going east, I took a bus to

San Francisco Airport. I hadn't been in bed or had a shower for three days. Phew.

On arrival at SFO, I learned my flight to Cleveland didn't leave until 11 p.m., so United customer service took pity on me and allowed me to use their executive lounge to clean up and get some much-needed sleep. When I boarded the flight, they put me up front in the first-class section of a DC-6B for the all-night flight. After a brief stop at Chicago Midway Airport, we were off again for Cleveland. I assumed I would have to take a bus the rest of the way, but a passenger agent announced there was an American Airlines Convair leaving for Erie in just 30 minutes.

I hustled for that one and just made it — 30 minutes later, I landed at Erie. While deplaning, I saw Herman Steimer sitting on the ramp in his Buick, waiting to drive me home. I never figured out how he knew I was on that flight.

I was finally home — only this time, unfortunately, it was to sadness.

Back in the U.S.A.

By the time I arrived, Uncle Dell had died. I was grateful that my sister Peg had come to help Frances. I was exhausted after my 8000-mile trip. I missed the funeral service, but since the funeral director knew I was coming, they delayed interment until I arrived.

The following week I visited Clarence King at Greystone Lab. John Heid was now chief chemist, having replaced Vinnie. Clarence was not satisfied with my replacement and wanted to know my intentions after separation from service in the spring. I said I didn't know yet, but would have an answer for him early in the New Year.

Much had changed during my brief absence, and I felt somewhat out of touch. It was evident the dollar had suffered from Korean War inflation.

There were changes at Port Erie as well. Krantz Aeronautical, Gerry Richardson, and Herman were still there, as well as "Brad" (Clarence Bradshaw), my A&E mechanic friend, who had overhauled the engine on the Chief two summers ago. Bill Hahn was still engaged in flight instruction on a limited basis. The one missing was Virgal Swain, now well established with Meteor Air Transport in Teterboro, N.J., flying Captain on DC-3s and C-46 Curtiss Commandos.

The most startling change was right before my eyes, where there were two large hangars under construction at the northwest corner of the field. Mac's Erie Aviation and Earl's Derion Aviation were on the verge of moving to Port Erie Airport because the Erie City Planning commission had authorized a new mall on the land that was Kearsarge Airport. At first, it appeared Mac and Earl would be forced out of business, but the Erie Airport Authority stepped in to offer them long-term leases provided they built their own facilities (hangars).

The tipping point was the new airplane franchises they would bring with them. Mac was a Piper dealer, and Earl sold Beechcrafts. The missing link was Cessna, and that dealership belonged to Erie County Flying Service in Fairview. They also planned to take up residence at Port Erie in just three short years.

All of that maneuvering would have a direct impact on me, as I planned to enroll in flight training under the G.I. Bill the following spring. In September '52, when I arrived, they were roofing both hangars. Mac's operation was much more elaborate, with a beautiful office on the field side plus restrooms and a special room for the Link Trainer. There was also a basement that provided space for a large classroom and workshop.

After dealing with the immediate crisis of Uncle Dell's death, I needed a few days to unwind, so I drove to New Jersey to visit Virgal Swain. We had kept in touch while I was in Japan, and I was anxious to hear about flying with Meteor Air Transport. He invited me to visit and said that he would only be away one night in case he had to fly.

Luckily, Virgal was home when I arrived, and invited me to accompany him on his trip to Detroit that very evening. What an opportunity! Even though I would end up on the jump seat much of the time, I was anxious to go. I accompanied him during the walk-around inspection, and he showed me what to look for when preflighting the DC-3. I also met the copilot before boarding, and 15 or 20 minutes after takeoff, Virgal gestured that we should change seats.

He turned control of the plane over to me for an hour and a half, until starting our descent for landing in Detroit. What a delightful experience that was!

Once the freight was unloaded and we had something to eat, it was time to start back. The return flight was essentially a ferry flight, as we were empty. Again I flew most of the way to Teterboro, and logged a total of 3 hours and 30 minutes DC-3 copilot time. By the time we landed it was daylight, and we were ready for bed. I drove back to Erie the following day and told Mac about my wonderful experience flying the DC-3.

Flight training under the G.I. Bill for WWII veterans was winding down, but a whole new generation of Korean War vets was coming on board. The emphasis now would be training pilots for the airline industry, which was expanding at a vigorous rate.

Relocating to Port Erie was a gamble for Mac and Earl; I knew that Earl, especially, was cutting it close. For several years he made do without an office and restroom facilities, keeping his desk out in the hangar up against the wall.

The remainder of my emergency leave was spent wrapping up Uncle Dell's estate, and ensuring that Frances would be okay on her own. There wasn't time to get my '46 Hudson running, so it stayed in the garage up on blocks. I drove Uncle Dell's old '36 Pontiac to my new assignment, and it served as my transportation at Indiantown Gap.

Uncle Dell left the house to Frances, and she kindly invited me to stay as long as I liked.

What did my inheritance consist of? Uncle Dell was not a rich man, but as I mentioned earlier, he was frugal. He left everything else to me, including a stash of government bonds amounting to approximately $5000. The money from selling the Aeronca Chief was in a separate envelope marked "Ray." In addition, I had sent money home that had been held for me in a separate account. I wasn't rich, but I wasn't broke, either.

I had taken care of the most urgent business, so early in September I packed my duffel bag and headed for Indiantown Gap Military Reservation (IGMR), northeast of Harrisburg. How strange it was to make the identical trip my dad had made in that very car fifteen years earlier in 1937. I couldn't get over the irony of that.

IGMR

I was not permitted to bring the Pontiac on the base without a sticker, and since that would take some time to arrange, I parked the car in Harrisburg and took the bus out to IGMR. The installation's primary function was a separation center for mustering men out of the Army, and I would be directly involved with that process in just a few short months.

After checking in with Personnel, I reported to Sgt. Ruk, who was in charge of the lab at the base hospital. He seemed quite interested in the work I had been doing in Japan, but pointed out that the emphasis at IGMR was on serology testing. They also served as the laboratory for the on-base hospital, a small facility of 250 beds.

There were huge centrifuges that held one hundred or more test tubes. Blood drawing was on a massive scale, and the staff consisted of three Army lab techs plus two civilian women. It didn't take long to acclimate to my new job.

After about a month, I became deathly sick: malaise accompanied by severe nosebleeds. During lunch break, I retreated to the barracks to lie down. Sgt. Ruk came over to see me and suggested I go on sick call, and added, "Why don't you do a CBC [complete blood count] first and take it with you?"

The white cell count showed 95% lymphocytes, suggesting infectious mononucleosis — more commonly known as "mono." I was in trouble because there was no cure, and it usually took awhile to run its course. I hand-carried the report to the dispensary, where I was seen by the on-duty physician.

Dr. Kopfinger looked at me and said, "I don't need to explain any of this to you, do I? Admit yourself to the hospital and I'll be in to see you tomorrow."

The hospital consisted of frame barracks buildings converted to wards with about 30 beds. Adjacent to my bed, a TV was blaring loudly much of the time. I begged to be moved, but my protests were in vain. It was my first admission to a hospital — ever. I was able to retain bathroom privileges, at least for the present.

The following day, I had extensive examinations including lab work. The admitting nurse noted that my eyes were yellow and ordered an icteric index; those results indicated liver involvement, specifically jaundice. The heterophile antibody test was also definitive, indicating severe mono with the highest titer they had ever seen. My failure to address the disease early on had led to complications. The final diagnosis was an extreme case of infectious mononucleosis with liver damage (infectious hepatitis secondary to the mono). Prescribed treatment was an indefinite period of complete bed rest.

I did retain bathroom privileges but was unable to eat much, and remained in a fog much of the time. I don't really recall much of my hospitalization except having to put up with that stupid TV. After about two weeks, I began a slow recovery. My weight was down to 150 pounds, taking me back to the days when I was a skinny kid.

By Thanksgiving I had rebounded with a voracious appetite, and Dr. Kopfinger decided I had recovered sufficiently to be released on medical leave. His prescription was, "Corporal Lemmon, what you need now is good home cooking. Come back and see me after the holidays." I was weak as a kitten; it was ill advised for me to drive home, but there really wasn't any alternative.

Recovery Time

Shortly before going to the hospital, I had finally received a sticker for on-base parking, and the old Pontiac had just been sitting outside in the parking lot. It should have been driven periodically, but it wasn't touched during the entire period of my hospitalization.

The last thing on my mind was the car, so I really had doubts about getting it started. I didn't say anything, though, and obtained my release to go on leave. I went to the car saying a prayer.

The Pontiac groaned a lot, but hallelujah, it did start and I made it to Erie okay. I decided then and there that it was time to get my Hudson back in service. When I arrived, Frances was shocked at my appearance — my uniform was just hanging on me.

"I'll fatten you up," she said. And you know, that's exactly what she did — there was no place like home for recuperation.

Since I was home on leave to recover, I was careful to maintain a low profile. I did go down to see Clarence at Greystone Lab. My clothes were still "ill fitting," even though my weight was slowly returning to normal.

I also stopped in to see Joe Martin and Lee Donaldson at Peach Street Auto to ask them for help with the Hudson. They lowered it off the blocks, pumped up the tires and towed it back to their garage.

It had survived storage fairly well, except for a coat of rust forming on the top. They suggested having it painted; Joe knew a guy at the Chevy body shop who did excellent work. He thought he could get a special price, as they were slow during winter. Two weeks later it was finished and looked very sharp, with shiny gun-metal gray enamel and red wheels.

I stayed with Frances through the holidays. Then suddenly it was January 1953, and time to drive the Hudson back to IGMR. I had recovered nicely, but now my problem was how to put a stop to the weight gain.

Back at IGMR, during a few days off, I decided to pay a visit to Virgal Swain to explore the possibility of a copilot job with Meteor. He indicated prospects were excellent if I had the required ratings, specifically Commercial Pilot, Instrument and Multi-Engine. He encouraged me to return to my old job at Greystone Lab and work towards those ratings under the G.I. Bill with Mac, right there in Erie.

"It shouldn't take you more than a year," Virgal said. That made the New Jersey trip well worthwhile, providing food for thought. Although Virgal's plan for me sounded fairly ambitious, it was quite clear there would be no chance for a job at my present level of experience.

End of My Service Time

Clarence King wrote in February that he would be attending a meeting in Harrisburg on state business, and asked if I could show him our facilities at IGMR. I decided that a tour might prove advantageous if I planned to return to Greystone Lab.

I found Clarence at his Harrisburg hotel, and we drove out. He was very impressed with our facilities and we discussed the new state-of-the-art test for syphilis, the cardiolipin antibodies test. Clarence had already been notified by the Pennsylvania Department of Health that Greystone Lab would soon be required to adopt this new procedure; the old Wasserman test was out. Since the lab at IGMR performed hundreds of cardiolipin antibodies tests every day, I was supremely qualified, providing yet another incentive to rehire me. The principal purpose of our meeting was to finalize my intentions after leaving the Army on March 19.

Clarence was prepared to deal with my salary requirements. I pointed out that my broad-based research experience in Japan, plus being a Registered Medical Technologist with AMT, and especially my extensive recent experience with the new syphilis test, qualified me for a substantial raise. Clarence agreed that my credentials were impressive and offered $250 per month, with more increases to come "pending circumstances." That seemed rather vague, but the $250 figure sounded pretty good.

It was imperative that Clarence not learn that I was using the lab job for a bridge; if I could get a flying job, I was going to accept it. Clarence needed my decision immediately, so I accepted the offer and dropped him off at his hotel. The die was cast; I would start again at Greystone Lab on April 1, 1953.

However, I wasn't quite finished with Uncle Sam yet, still having a few weeks to go. At that point, though, I was marking time. During my final barracks inspection, the Captain approached me and remarked, "We need more men like you to stay. What would it take to get you to re-enlist?" I replied, "Well, sir, Captain's bars might."

The Captain continued down the line; he knew I had already been offered Sergeant's stripes. No, I wasn't interested in continuing service in the Army, and couldn't wait to get out. Two weeks later, on March 19, I was separated from service. Notice I didn't say discharged — that wouldn't happen until 1958. All inductees were required to serve five years in the Ready Reserve.

What I did receive, though, was the all-important form DD 214. That sheet of paper provided all of my service information: where I served, my MOS (Military Occupational Specialty — we talked about that earlier) and, most important, my eligibility for education under the G.I. Bill. It also included insurance documentation, allowing me to continue my government-sponsored $10,000 life insurance policy. The initial premium was only $6.60 per month, and I kept it in force for the next 40 years.

Chapter 7

Building a Flying Career
1953-1956

What a feeling to be a private citizen again! However, I suddenly realized I no longer had any civilian clothes that would fit. Fortunately, I was allowed to wear my Khakis for thirty days, after which my uniforms would be consigned to the cedar chest. The Pennsylvania Turnpike never looked so beautiful with my whole life stretching out before me. Arriving in Erie, the first thing I got was a welcome-home hug from Frances.

Since my starting date at Greystone Lab was still ten days away, I had a little time to relax, so naturally I went out to the airport to visit Earl and Mac. Kearsarge Airport was no more, and everything had been moved to their new hangars at Port Erie. Mac's office was especially nice, with an unrestricted view of the airport.

Mac and I discussed the flight-training syllabus for my Commercial and Instrument ratings under the G.I. Bill, and since he didn't own a twin-engine plane at that time, I would have to take the Multi-Engine course at Erie County Flying Service six miles west of town. All I needed was the previously mentioned DD 214 form to begin the enrollment process.

However, I still wanted a plane of my own. While stationed at IGMR I rented a Cub at a nearby airport and a low-wing, two-place plane called the Swift was also based there. I admired its clean lines and retractable landing gear, a feature that translated into higher cruising speed.

When I got home, I asked around to see where I might locate one. One of the local pilots, Red Rhudman, had purchased a brand-new

Swift five years earlier that was now based at nearby Titusville, Pa., and was rumored to be for sale. "It only had a couple of hundred hours on it when I sold it," Red said.

That sounded like a great place to start, so I began there. The Swift was indeed based at the Titusville Airport, and the owner confirmed that it was for sale. The following Saturday, Otto (Ott) Luthringer and I borrowed Mac's Stinson to fly down to evaluate it. The tachometer indicated 276 hours, and except for sorely needing to be polished, the plane was in excellent condition. Instead of being painted, the Swift was almost entirely bare aluminum, so it would take a lot of tender loving care to keep that plane looking sharp. There wasn't time for a test flight, and I needed to think it over. It wasn't long, however, before I called Bob Cronn, the plane's owner, and said, "Okay, Bob, I'll take it for $2400; fly up on Saturday and we'll close the deal."

1948 Temco Swift purchased in 1953. This plane was also pivotal to my aviation career. See text for transcontinental trip with PG Fellmeth in 1954. The plane was sold in 1955 after my marriage to Margaret. I flew this plane over 500 hours during the two years I owned it. It cruised at 140 mph. (At right in the photo, note Mac's office, which had a commanding view of the entire airport.)

Saturday was a fine spring day, and around lunchtime I observed the Swift in the landing pattern. It looked sleek with its wheels retracted, zipping along. We completed the transaction, and they boarded their plane for the return flight to Titusville.

I needed a checkout in this new and more complicated plane, so I asked Mac to go along. He had never flown a Swift either, so it was the blind leading the blind; however, it turned out fine, and after a short test flight we put the plane in the hangar. Mac signed my logbook certifying my qualification to fly it solo.

A review of my logbook for this period shows my total accumulated flying time was only about 200 hours. Eligibility for professional pilot status would require at least 1000 hours, in addition to the pilot ratings previously mentioned, so I had my work cut out for me. At the time, however, it was mostly just about having fun. Building up flight time with the Swift was my objective, and during the next two years I flew it over 500 hours. Of course I flew other planes as well, seizing every opportunity to fly, but after April 1 it wasn't just about flying; I now had a job to devote my attention to as well.

Back at the Lab

Acclimating to being back at Greystone Lab wasn't as simple as I had thought it would be. During my absence, there were new regulations and ways of doing things — for instance, Clarence informed me that I would have to attend a Dairy Bacteriology course at Penn State for three weeks in August. Someone at Greystone needed to be State Board-certified to test milk. That meant no vacation for me in '53, but I couldn't really complain since, being in the Army, I hadn't earned one.

Once the rules for state certification to perform serology changed, requiring the new cardiolipin procedure, I had ample opportunity to demonstrate my prowess. We received test samples periodically from the Pennsylvania Department of Health, and Clarence promptly laid them on my desk. He was pleased when the results came back with the correct resolution. At least I didn't have to shear the sheep any more, Maude having disappeared at some point during my absence.

Working with John Heid, the new chief chemist, was a distinct pleasure. He was an accomplished technician, but not being schooled in laboratory medicine, it was up to me to cover that part of the business.

No more rabbit tests. Now, we used the African clawed frog with the scientific name of *Xenopus laevis.* We injected a female frog with urine, and if it was positive, she would lay scads of eggs. We also kept a few guinea pigs for special tests.

Margaret Taylor loved the guinea pigs. Oh, yes, there was someone new at the lab — but, in fact, Margaret was new only to me, as she had been at my old job of washing the petri dishes (and other sink goodies) for almost a year.

Margaret Taylor washing lab dishes at Greystone Lab in 1953;
shortly after I returned there from my Army service. She was
22 years of age at that time.

Her full name was Margaret Minnie Taylor (she hated the "Minnie," a gift from her paternal grandmother). Born May 26, 1931, in Erie, she attended Thiel College in Greenville, Pa., until health issues forced her to drop out. Georgia, the nurse/secretary at the lab, knew Margaret from church and offered her a part-time job at the lab. Her home was at 720 West Seventh St., only a bike ride away. Frankly, I didn't pay much attention to her at that time, as my focus was directed toward flying and my work at the lab. Our relationship my first year back was one of friendly cordiality, just coworkers.

August '53 arrived, and it was time for me to head for State College. It was my first experience in higher education, so I didn't know what to expect. I rented a room from a widow in town who catered to students. Rent included breakfast, and she was also generous with fridge privileges.

The class began with an introduction by the professor, to wit: "My name is Dr. Cohn, pronounced like ice cream *cone*," etc. There were about 20 of us from all over the state, including a man named Woody who was an Inspector for the Pennsylvania Department of Health. Since Woody would be checking my work at Greystone Lab, he was a person I wanted to be on good terms with. We got along famously.

Most of the students were fairly young women. Pennsylvania is an agricultural state, so the university's animal husbandry department was fairly extensive. The duties of graduates of Dr. Cohn's course included farm inspections, and lab-testing milk for cleanliness, butterfat content, etc. Our work for the course centered on microscopic studies of bacteria and other contamination aspects. After successful completion of the course, we were awarded a certificate to hang in the workplace.

I was more interested in the proximity of the Piper Aircraft factory in nearby Lock Haven. The only Cub still in production was the Super Cub, and as the name implies, it was a far cry from the old J-3. Of greater significance on the line was the Tri-Pacer, certified to carry four people. It was sensitive to overloading, especially since it held 36 gallons of fuel. It was really built as a family plane, with room for a couple of small children in the back. At that time, I was permitted to just roam around the factory talking to the workers; that would be unthinkable today.

I did a little flying at the State College Airport. My logbook shows three flights during late August in three different types of planes. Most memorable was the Cessna 170, a four-place plane with a 145 horsepower Continental engine. It was fairly new, and I was impressed with its performance. The only other flying during this period was a local flight in the Swift when I came home one weekend.

With the diversion at Penn State, I had drifted off course from my goal of becoming an airline pilot. It happened partly because Clarence was not forthcoming in February about his plans for me, and also because of my own conviction that I could have it both ways. In retrospect, my expectations were unrealistic. If, however, Clarence had been honest with me about the Penn State hiatus, I might have considered alternate possibilities to attain my goal. My decision to return to Greystone, admittedly a lazy one, almost cost me my career as an airline pilot.

At the time of my separation from the Army, if I had attended a professional airline pilot training academy under the G.I. Bill, I would have been hirable much sooner, at age 24 or 25. By 1955, I was nearing the maximum age for joining a major airline. On the other hand, if I had gone that route, I would never have met my bride-to-be and true soul mate, Margaret Taylor.

Over Fourth of July weekend, I flew to New Jersey to visit Virgal Swain. I got lost temporarily over the wilds of Pennsylvania and I attempted to use my radio range receiver to navigate, without much success. It was no big deal, though, as I had plenty of fuel. In due time I identified the Allentown airport, and landed at Teterboro shortly thereafter. As a result of that difficulty, I was spurred to buy a new navigational radio for the Swift.

The system was called Omni, or more correctly, Visual Omni Range (VOR). By 1953, Omni was in service nationwide and had already replaced the Radio Range as the mainstay of aerial navigation. It was to aviation at the time what GPS (Global Positioning System) is today. This wonderful new device, the Narco Superhomer VOR receiver, cost about $500, and I had to have it for the Swift. Oh-oh, there goes another one of Uncle Dell's bonds. It was around that time I entered the realm of deficit spending, dipping into my reserves day by day just to get by.

After Penn State, I resumed the Instrument Rating course with Link Trainer sessions taught by Otto Luthringer. "Ott" served in WWII as an instrument flying instructor for the U.S. Army Air

Corps. I was indeed fortunate to find such an experienced instructor right there in Erie.

The Link Trainer

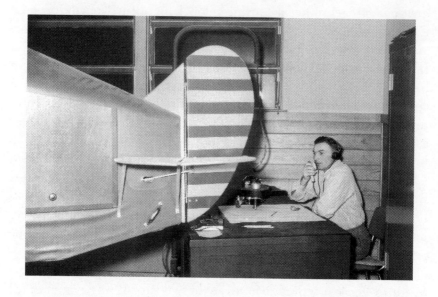

"Link" instrument trainer. Ott Luthringer is talking to me during a training session. Note the chart on the table with the "crab," displaying my flight with an ink stylus.

The Link Trainer was developed by Edwin Link of Binghamton, N.Y. for the military, and it was used by both Army and Navy aviators in WWII. This device was equipped with a complete array of blind-flying instruments with a cockpit setup identical to the AT-6 airplane, an advanced military trainer. In addition to being fully instrumented, it had full radio capability, so the pilot could navigate radio range legs and communicate with the instructor. Its ability to move on all three axes gave the pilot a realistic impression of actually flying a plane.

Once the trainee climbed aboard and the top was lowered, he was in a total "on instruments" environment. It was as close as you could get in those days to actually flying blind. It earned the nickname of "the box." The primary importance of the Link Trainer was the ability to work all sorts of navigational problems associated with the Radio Range using only the sounds coming through my headset.

A heavy cable of wires connected the trainer to a large table, where a "crab" device crawled over the chart, depicting exactly what the trainee was doing and where he was flying. Today, the Link is archaic, but during the war it was indispensable. The crab indicator was an ink stylus moving over the chart, so at the end of the lesson the instructor could show the trainee everywhere he had traveled during that session. Mac had the foresight to allocate a separate room just for this special training. For the early fifties, it was state-of-the-art.

My first Link session with Ott was actually prior to leaving for Penn State. I also practiced Radio Range flying in the Swift as well. Under the G.I. Bill, my dual instrument training sessions were in Mac's well-equipped Stinson, including required IFR cross-country flights.

Margaret Taylor taking her first ride in the Swift, 1954.

I also initiated a night-flying program around this time, and took Margaret Taylor for her first ride in the Swift to Niagara Falls. By the fall of '53, I was using the Link Trainer extensively and practicing instrument flying in both the Swift and the Stinson. Much of that training was with Ott as dual, but other times I practiced with a safety pilot acting as lookout.

Accrual of at least 40 hours of actual instrument flight time was required for eligibility to take the flight test. The Swift was not an ideal instrument platform because it lacked some of the advanced gyro instruments found in the Stinson and Link Trainer. For the foreseeable future, virtually all my flying would be directed toward acquiring the Instrument rating.

Nearing the end of the year, the days were short, and the weather turned cold and snowy. Often the weather was unsuitable for flying, so we would practice using the Link Trainer instead.

Even though the new Omni Range system was fully operational, I was not permitted to use it for my instrument flight test. The ancient Radio Range system was still commissioned, and since it was considered more difficult to use, the examiner reserved the right to have the applicant demonstrate proficiency with it. The Instrument Landing System (ILS) was considered to be a luxury, and I wouldn't be tested on that, either. Later that criterion changed dramatically with my introduction to airline flying. All periodic and rating flight checks focused on ILS approaches and were graded. The Radio Range was considered antiquated, was seldom if ever used, and was decommissioned circa 1958.

Touring With PG in 1954

In early March of '54 I flew the Swift to Erie County Airport in Fairview for the installation of the Narco Superhomer. The new radio included VHF (very high frequency) channels for communication with control towers and flight service stations. It was very compact and fit the instrument panel space previously occupied by the GE low-frequency radio, and I couldn't wait to take a trip using it.

At first glance, it looked like my vacation plans for a trip out west were overly ambitious considering the time available. As I probed deeper into the planning phase, it was apparent I was underestimating the capabilities of my little airplane.

A brief outline of the proposed trip was as follows: Flying to California via the southern route, then swinging north to Seattle, and returning home via Salt Lake City and the high plains. Naturally, this would have to be completed by the end of my two-week vacation break at the lab. Ostensibly, a high point of the trip was to visit people PG and I had worked with in Japan, and the new Narco Superhomer radio was an integral part of the plan.

Mac's Stinson provided the platform for several lengthy cross-country IFR flights that spring, one of which was to visit Virgal Swain again at Teterboro — he was urging me to move quickly with my program. "Meteor is expanding and will be hiring new copilots in the near future," he tantalized.

"I should have both my Commercial license and Instrument rating soon," I replied. In fact, on May 19, after a successful flight test with Mac, I had my commercial pilot license. I had aspirations of completing the Instrument course before my cross-country vacation trip, but I failed to achieve that goal.

Paul G. (PG) Fellmeth

PG Fellmeth on our arrival in Dallas, Texas for our overnight stop there in August 1954. This was our second night out after visiting St. Louis the previous night. Temperature was in the high 90s.

PG Fellmeth was my closest friend while working at the hospital in Japan. He lived in Akron, Ohio, and returned to his pre-induction craft of making dental plates and performing other work characteristic of a dental lab. We continued our friendship in civilian life, and I frequently flew to Akron to visit. Recently, we had hatched a plan to fly around the country during our 1954 summer vacation to see some of our ex-Sendai comrades.

In order for that to work, I pointed out the need for PG's vacation to coincide precisely with mine. He assured me that would not be a problem, since he was director of the facility. PG had never flown in a light plane before, so a brief test hop was in order. That went fine, so we proceeded with our plans. Since baggage space was limited, I bought two matching suitcases that would fit the plane's luggage compartment. I delivered PG's during a July visit, cautioning him to pack judiciously.

I left Erie on August 7 to pick him up in Akron, and from there, we flew to Terre Haute, Ind. for our first fuel stop. The days were still quite long, so we continued to Lambert Field in St. Louis for our first overnight stop, where we took in a show.

The next morning dawned rainy with poor visibility, but we decided to press on using a special VFR departure. Thank goodness for the new radio; navigation was a cinch. We flew south to Little Rock, Ark., where the weather was clear but very hot.

Stifling heat would be a major impediment for the first half of the trip. The temperature at LIT was 104 degrees. After refueling and a bite of lunch, we enjoyed a pleasant ride to Dallas, Texas, where it was well over 100 degrees as well. The adiabatic lapse rate (the amount the temperature decreases as altitude increases) is three degrees per thousand feet, so by flying at 10,000 feet we enjoyed ambient temperature inside the plane in the low 70s. We stayed in a downtown Dallas hotel with luxuries we only could have dreamed about in Japan.

Early the next morning, we took off to revisit our old barracks at Fort Sam Houston in San Antonio. Both of us attended MRTC there, so it was a bit of nostalgia to return. After a morning of sightseeing, we returned to the airport for lunch, taking off again heading northwest to Midland. We were in west Texas oil country, and our overnight stop there was very pleasant. It was amazing to see tall buildings rising out of the desert in such barren wasteland; petroleum was obviously king in this west Texas city. It was only our third night out, and we were already halfway across the country.

The next stop, El Paso, was still in Texas, sharing the border with New Mexico and Old Mexico at the Rio Grande. Our route took us straight west, and there was no sign of habitation until we were within 100 miles of our destination. That was our crossing point of the Continental divide, and El Capitan towered on our right. We filed flight plans for each flight segment in case of an emergency.

Nearing civilization once more, we lined up with a single-lane highway, straight as an arrow, leading directly to El Paso. The Swift ran perfectly, and we landed at 9:30 a.m. We decided to cross the Rio Grande for shopping in Juarez on the Mexican side.

A Teaching Moment

Re-entering the United States after our visit south of the border, we were faced with a crucial decision. Although we had completed our business, I was hesitant to take off on our next leg to Arizona.

I noticed that the Air Force planes that had been training locally when we arrived were not flying anymore. I didn't attach much importance to that, but I should have. We fueled up and decided to continue on to Tucson.

The El Paso Airport was 4400 feet above sea level, in the heart of the Rocky Mountain chain. Although there were no 14,000-foot peaks in our vicinity, we still faced mountain flying conditions.

Had I consulted the Koch chart for a density altitude computation, I would have realized that we had no business flying, period, as the reduced air density effectively elevated the airport by at least 2000 feet. We taxied out and did our usual run-up of the engine at the end of the runway. Everything seemed normal, so I advised the tower we were ready for takeoff and then pulled out onto the active runway. Our acceleration was much slower than usual, but I continued the takeoff roll. After an exceptionally long ground run, we finally lifted off.

When I retracted the landing gear to reduce drag and reached about 200 feet, the plane simply refused to climb any higher. It would fly level, but it would not climb due to a phenomenon in the atmosphere called "ground effect." A cushion of compressed air lies very close to the surface of the earth, and because it is denser it provides a bit of additional lift. Unfortunately, that cushion is only 200 feet thick. That's where we were: stuck at the top of that ground effect layer.

The engine was doing all it could, in view of the thin desert air, when I decided to call the tower and declare an emergency. The controller had obviously seen this before and replied somewhat laconically, "Swift 35 Bravo, start a shallow left turn to a south heading, and you should be able to gradually resume your climb."

He was right; we were heading toward higher terrain, and the breeze coming off those hills created just enough downdraft to disrupt our climb. By that time I was really sweating and wondered if we would clear wires and other obstructions to our immediate front. Finally, about the time we were to cross the Rio Grande again into Mexico, we had staggered to 500 feet and turned west on course for Tucson. I humbly thanked El Paso Tower for their assistance.

As we turned west on course to Tucson, I breathed a sigh of relief. It took a very long time to reach our cruising altitude of 8500 feet. I turned to PG and stated with conviction, "No more afternoon flying in mountainous terrain."

As we flew west, more and more thunderstorms were developing and as we threaded our way through a pass, we were in very close proximity to another plane going the opposite direction. Finally, the welcome sight of Tucson's 12,000-foot runway came into view, and we landed without further incident. I was totally exhausted by that experience; mountain flying could be very dangerous in a light plane. Although I had just learned a valuable lesson, it would not be our last encounter with high-elevation airports.

The next morning we resumed our trek, and this time our destination was California. My log shows that we landed in Phoenix to file a special flight plan for entering California's air space. Next stop was Bakersfield, in the San Joaquin valley, where we gassed up again for the short hop to Fresno, where we rented a car. After five grueling days of flying, we finally reached a recreational destination: Sequoia, Kings Canyon, and Yosemite National Parks.

Driving ever higher into the Sierras, it cooled off to the point a jacket was appreciated. It was truly delightful, and we enjoyed three days visiting California's national parks. We were disappointed to discover the waterfalls in Yosemite had run dry. We saw the redwoods and all the sights, but soon it was time to head back to Fresno for the next leg of our trip.

For our visit to San Francisco, it was wise to avoid SFO and land at Oakland instead. I wrote my brother Richard that we were coming for a visit. Not receiving any response from his phone, we took a cab to his house, where neighbors informed us he had gone on vacation and didn't know when he would return. That was a significant disappointment, and almost 20 more years elapsed before finally seeing him; by that time, he was terminally ill with cancer.

PG's Flying Lessons

As we flew along, it was only natural that PG's curiosity about flying the plane would be piqued. He had no flying experience whatsoever, so I felt that it would be prudent to teach him at least the fundamentals of flying the plane, in case of emergency.

I knew of instances where a plane crashed for no reason other than the passenger sitting next to a disabled pilot had no knowledge of how to control the plane. Since we were spending so many hours together, I decided to conduct a little basic flight instruction. PG was agreeable, provided I kept it simple. Conversation above the engine noise was difficult, so there was a lot of gesturing and innuendo.

I began with the airspeed and altimeter. I stressed the utmost importance of being able to interpret those two instruments, and occasionally, in different stages of flight, I would ask, "PG, what's our altitude right now?" Regarding the airspeed, I probed, "What should our speed be now?" as we turned on our final approach to land.

In the interest of simplicity, I pointed out that the throttle controlled the airspeed, and moving the control wheel in and out controlled the altitude. I let him fly the plane frequently so he could see for himself how the controls worked. Then he inquired, "What about the landing gear and flaps? How do I handle them?" I answered quite emphatically, "Don't even think about it. Just maneuver the plane, maintaining control, all the way down to the ground for a 'wheels-up' landing. Staying alive is more important than damaging the plane."

I said that probably nothing serious would result, except for breaking the wooden propeller, and bending some aluminum on the belly. An attempt by an inexperienced pilot to land a complex plane like the Swift on its wheels could easily result in flipping upside down, spilling fuel on the hot engine resulting in fire, and being trapped inside.

PG seemed to grasp my explanation, which was reassuring. I also instructed him on the use of the radio. One of the transmitter crystals was 121.5 megahertz, the emergency frequency. I made sure he knew how to tune that in and use the headset. I explained that airliners, all CAA weather stations, the Coast Guard and all military bases were required to monitor that frequency.

"Just call out 'May Day, May Day,' numerous times until someone answers. Help will come in the form of instructions." PG wore his own headset much of the time anyway, so he was used to listening to aviation conversation. He did okay, and I showed him how to use the elevator trim tab to assist gliding down. There could come a time when all this might be important.

We enjoyed our visit to San Francisco; when I had passed through there two years earlier, there was no opportunity to explore the city. The day we were ready to leave, visibility was restricted and I wondered about our chances for taking off. Sure enough, it was still foggy at the Oakland airport, and visibility was down to one mile.

As part of the Instrument Rating course, I learned about a special procedure to leave a fogbound airport. Special VFR wasn't recommended for the average pilot, because it called for familiarity with instrument flying. Under that rule you could take off with only one-mile visibility instead of the customary three. By staying in contact with the control tower and avoiding other traffic, you could leave controlled airspace and continue your flight.

On our short flight to Sacramento to visit our comrade, Fred Yee, we broke out of the fog crossing the ridge. We were back in the Central Valley, where we would remain until leaving the Golden State.

It was nice to see Fred and to observe Chinese culture. We had lunch (no chopsticks, please) and met his mother and father. They spoke almost no English, so there was a lot of gesturing and head-nodding. We explained to Fred that our visit would be brief, as we wanted to reach Red Bluff, at the northern end of the valley, before nightfall.

We had a pleasant layover at Red Bluff, but I had some concern about the challenge we would be facing the following day. Our route crossed the Cascade Range — a high, forbidding obstacle blocking our passage to the Pacific Northwest. We would need to fly above

10,000 feet much of the time in the shadow of towering, 14,000-foot Mt. Shasta. I had a very good briefing at the Red Bluff CAA shack, and filed a three-hour VFR flight plan to Portland, Oregon. We would pass over Crater Lake on our way.

As we climbed out of the valley, it got colder and colder. Even with the cabin heat on, we were freezing. Suddenly, the tachometer started screeching and the needle fluctuated. It was not threatening, just distracting, and I would need to have it checked when we arrived at Portland. The scenery was spectacular but also forbidding. Fortunately, the weather cooperated as forecast, and we arrived at Portland on schedule. The tachometer problem turned out to be minor; after lubricating the cable, all was well again.

The next stop was Seattle, the last outbound leg of our trip; from there we would be heading for home. At that time, Boeing Field was Seattle's municipal airport and the home of Boeing aircraft, where over 5000 B-17 bombers were built. After leaving Portland the weather worsened, and by the time we landed at Seattle a light rain was falling.

We were in Seattle to visit Chuck Beaudreau, another Army buddy from our tour of duty in Sendai. Chuck was brilliant. His IQ was very high, and he worked as a graduate student at the University of Washington. Chuck always intimidated me because he was so smart. He seemed happy to see us, and gave us a tour of the University. We were also treated to a nice dinner. It was a great reunion.

The following morning, on our first homeward-bound leg, we faced another significant challenge. We intended to cross the Cascades to Spokane and fly southeast to Salt Lake City. A check of the weather at Snoqualmie Pass made it quite clear that wasn't going to happen.

What should we do? We didn't want to be stuck in Seattle, so the only alternative was to fly south to Portland and then turn east through the Columbia River gorge. It wasn't that much out of our way, and at least we would be able to continue the trip. We were rapidly depleting our allotted time, so it was time to be heading home. It was a rainy, gloomy flight south to Portland where we landed, gassed up, and had lunch.

Taking off and heading east, we were in for an unexpected treat. The flight through the Columbia River gorge was filled with stunning scenery: waterfalls, snow-capped mountains and the thread of the Columbia River winding through the cleft. We flew low following the river, and when we reached Cascade Locks the weather became "severe clear"—blue sky forever.

We spent the night at Pendleton, Oregon, a wartime Army air base that became the new municipal airport. Pendleton was the home of Pendleton Mills, the makers of quality woolen blankets and clothing, and they conducted guided tours.

The leg to Salt Lake City was over hostile, forbidding territory, and we carefully adhered to our flight plan for safety's sake. Landing was uneventful, and since we arrived early, I sought out the maintenance hangar to give the Swift a much-needed oil change. I preferred to do that every 30 hours, and we had already exceeded that.

The maintenance would take awhile, so it provided an opportunity to explore Salt Lake City. Our sightseeing included a brief tour of the Mormon Tabernacle — what a church! We bought souvenirs, including a trinket for Margaret.

When we returned to the airport, the work on the plane was completed. Even though they discovered a few minor glitches, there was nothing major, so we were good to go.

Not so fast, though — since it was too late to tackle the Wasatch Mountains to the east, we decided to stay overnight for an early start the following day. I was aware our elevation was over 4000 feet, and even though it was much cooler than El Paso, I didn't want to repeat our experience there.

The Wasatch Mountain Range was a formidable barrier to the east, and to get to the other side, we would fly north to Ogden, where Uintah Pass provided a pathway to the high tableland to the east. I wanted to fill the plane's auxiliary fuel tank (nine gallons), but because of the 4000-foot field elevation, I declined. Later on, I would regret that decision.

The takeoff from Salt Lake in the coolness of early morning was a piece of cake. We climbed to 9500 feet and made the turn to the east at Ogden. Everything was going splendidly until I checked weather east of us, discovering that low ceilings were going to be a problem for us.

Our flight plan was in jeopardy partly because an anticipated tailwind didn't materialize, causing our fuel range to be diminished.

Filling the auxiliary fuel tank would have made a tremendous difference. We needed an alternate airport, but where? Rawlins, just ahead of us, had a long runway, but the field elevation was almost 7000 feet. Since it was really the only suitable airport west of Cheyenne, we landed there at 9:30 a.m.

Because of the extreme elevation, I considered putting PG on a Union Pacific train, but that would never do. What a quandary.

Well, it was early and still relatively cool, so I decided to try it. If we couldn't get airborne, I would taxi back and put PG on the train. Rawlins had been an old WWII AAF training field for heavy bombers, and that was the reason for the generous 7000-foot runway.

By the time we were refueled, it was 10 o'clock. The weather in Nebraska was favorable, so we filed a flight plan for Scottsbluff.

We did lift off, but then just as at El Paso, we were stuck in ground effect again and couldn't climb — only this time there was no way to turn to get a break. Even though I feared we might stall out, I had to turn because we were headed right for town. With the greatest gentleness, I eased the rudder in; any increase in bank would have been suicidal. I considered landing off-airport, but by the time that was possible, we were through the worst of it. I carefully circled the airport three times before turning east on course.

A feeling of nausea and lightheadedness swept over me. The stress and failure to eat breakfast had caught up with me. We were over Wheatland Reservoir, Wyoming. I told PG I felt faint and feared that I might pass out; I saw the blood drain from his face, but I pointed to the control wheel and said, "Take over for a bit, PG, you can do it. Just fly like we practiced." He hesitantly took the controls. I even considered a wheels-up landing right where we were, but that seemed like a bad idea. Besides, I didn't think I had that much time. I stuck my head down and took a sip of water. We flew along like that for a while, with PG at the controls, until I revived.

Whew! That was close. PG did fine. He only lost a hundred feet or so. I mused, "What if I hadn't taught him those basic flying skills?"

He handled it well, and I was proud of him. The rest of that leg to Scottsbluff was uneventful, and we landed without further incident. After the usual fueling and lunch, we continued, descending to 2000 feet at Grand Island on the Platte River, and that felt very good indeed.

Remarkably, we made it all the way to Des Moines, Iowa that day. Salt Lake to Des Moines was a very good day, any way you slice it. An unanticipated tailwind made all the difference in the world.

We were anxious to get home now, and I finally had a chance to use the auxiliary fuel tank. With 35 gallons at reduced power, we had a range of five hours. That was also just about maximum flying time for bladder endurance, so I cautioned PG to go easy on the coffee; it was going to be a long ride.

In fact, sitting on top of broken clouds at 9500 feet, it took us four hours and fifteen minutes to reach Toledo, Ohio. We were throttled back and scooting along at 160 mph. We had a nice view of Chicago off to our left.

It was showery approaching Toledo, so I made an instrument approach off the Waterville VOR to locate the airport. My instrument training came in handy that day. We had a quick lunch, and then took off again for Akron to drop off PG. Arriving there, I asked PG for his impressions of the trip, and he replied, "It was great, but I wouldn't want to do it again." At least he was candid. We kept in touch for many years with an occasional visit while I was on Canton/ Akron layovers, flying the Boeing 737 for United Airlines.

What about my own reflections? It was an excellent first step toward my goal of becoming a professional pilot — the first page of a book of experience culminating in over 33 years of flying over this magnificent country of ours, the United States of America. I've seen it in all its beauty, ferociousness and cunning, every season of the year, in so many different types of planes.

With vacation over, I needed to fully concentrate on attaining my Instrument rating. To get back up to speed I did extensive review with Ott Luthringer, both in the Stinson and the Link Trainer. Finally, on September 26, I successfully passed the flight test; two down, and only one more to go. The Multi-Engine course with Andy Kudlak would be in a Cessna Bobcat like Virgal Swain's air ambulance.

Clarence King was very curious about my intense flying activity. Did he suspect my true intentions? I couldn't shut him out completely, because occasionally I needed time off to take the written exams administered once a month by CAA examiners from Pittsburgh. I refused to lie or call in sick, so I told him everything, except my ultimate goal of becoming an airline pilot.

On one occasion, Clarence asked me flat out, "Why are you doing all of this?" I answered that since I had earned the benefits under the G.I. Bill, I intended to take advantage of them.

Wedding Bells

Something else was going on, which I suspect the reader might guess: romance. Yes, I was smitten with Margaret Taylor. Unfortunately, it was complicated, since Margaret already had a boyfriend and they had been dating for well over a year. Al Kochik was Polish, and predictably Catholic; the relationship between his parents was troublesome, because they didn't speak to one another. In spite of these issues, Margaret continued to date him.

I decided to intervene with an attempt to win her away from him, but how should I go about it? (Dealing with the opposite sex was obviously not my strong suit, as evidenced by my total lack of interaction with girls up to that point.) I agonized for an entire weekend over the best way to accomplish it, and then I recalled Margaret's recent habit of teasing me at work. The next time she tried that, I would take it to a new level.

Margaret frequently came to the back room of the lab, where I did my serology microscopic work. So, on the following Monday, I got up from my stool and planted a big kiss on her.

She was shocked, to say the least, but she didn't pull away; in fact, she kissed me back.

I was in love. When things cooled down a bit, I said we should talk. She admitted thinking about me a lot, but didn't expect anything to ever come of it. I told her she was on my mind, too, especially during the Swift trip, and that I had missed her. I had been taking her home after work, so that evening in the car we picked up where we left off with the necking. I really liked that, and I guess she did, too; I know she was late getting home for supper.

Margaret attempted to break it off with Al, but he refused to give up without a fight. Since I hadn't met her parents yet, we parked on Seventh Street returning home from a date. Al recognized my Hudson, and would drive by and harass us. That tactic just made it easier all the way around. Before long, Al was out of the picture, and I did get invited into the house. It was an invitation for Sunday dinner, and I was very nervous at first because I had seen her father, and he appeared to be all business. Margaret said, "Relax; he's really a cream puff." And he was.

The Taylor residence on West Seventh Street in Erie, Pa. — the house where Margaret Taylor grew up in the 1940s.

Sometimes Margaret and I drove to the public dock and just talked for hours. We liked the same things; we had graduated from the same school with similar backgrounds. Because she had been two grades behind me, I hadn't known her at Strong Vincent.

Margaret had an adventurous spirit, always ready to try new things. We discussed future plans and I admitted I couldn't offer her any measure of stability. My life was a deck of cards, and I wasn't holding any aces. I told her about Virgal and my aspirations of getting a copilot job with Meteor Air Transport. During our next vacation, I intended to drive to New Jersey and apply for a job. Starting out at the bottom of the ladder, new copilots didn't make much more than

I did at the lab. None of that seemed to matter, and Margaret shared my enthusiasm for flying.

I presented Margaret with an engagement ring for Christmas, and we made plans for a June '55 wedding. Louis Vogt, my old jeweler friend, helped me out by coming up with a really nice-looking diamond ring for $200. I didn't ask questions, but I wondered if it was "hot," and I even asked Lou about it. "No, it's not stolen," he assured me. Margaret was thrilled.

Later, after we were married and I was still working at the lab, I examined her ring under the microscope and discovered a huge flaw not visible to the naked eye. I was ashamed, but Margaret just laughed. It didn't matter to her, and she wore that imperfect ring all of her married life. As the holidays gave way to 1955, the focus shifted to preparations for our June wedding.

I wondered why my Multi-Engine course was being delayed until Andy Kudlak explained that their sod field was too soft in the winter and early spring for the heavy Twin Cessna. He said we would be able to start by early May, and that was fine with me as I was deeply involved with "other things."

At the end of March, I saw an ad in *Aviation Week* for pilot openings posted by United Air Lines. With my Commercial and Instrument ratings I met their basic requirements, and they didn't insist on a Multi-Engine rating. Could it be that easy? I wrote a letter, and United responded with an application and an invitation to report to LaGuardia Airport (N.Y.) for tests and an interview.

Coincidentally, I was to attend a dinner for graduates of Dr. Cohn's Dairy Bacteriology course in State College. Clarence wanted me to go because Woody, a State Inspector classmate of mine, was assigned to our lab and checked my work.

The time frame for the dinner coincided nicely with the United Air Lines interview; however, it required me to leave work early the previous day and drive all night. It was a stretch, all right, and I would be dead tired by the time I got to New York. But Margaret was insistent: "You must go; it's just too important an opportunity to pass up."

What a drive! All night, over Route 6, arriving at LaGuardia Airport at daybreak with just enough time to grab a few winks before my appointment at 9 a.m.; the effort I was making was really a push. I took a battery of written tests, culminating in an appointment with Personnel after lunch. The interviewer was not a pilot, and quickly pointed out my bare-minimum experience and lack of college credits. It lasted for about 30 minutes, and then I was dismissed: "We'll be in touch with you by mail. Goodbye."

I still had to drive to State College for the banquet the following day. It was tough over secondary roads, but I arrived without incident and checked into a room. Boy, was I tired! I attended the banquet, talked with my friend Woody, and drove home the next day.

I couldn't wait for the reply from United, but when their letter arrived it was quite explicit: "Although we find you to be well qualified in some respects, we have applicants that more nearly meet our requirements. Thank you for your interest in United Air Lines." Margaret was with me when I opened it, and I almost cried. I learned later that United Air Lines did not hire pilots without university accreditation. I have that letter to this day, but now it is only a conversation piece. Ironically, I joined the ranks of the United pilots by coming in the back door as a consequence of the United/Capital merger in June 1961.

On May 1, I began the Multi-Engine course with Andy. It was a rather intense program consisting of 10 to 12 flying hours. The Bobcat burned 30 gallons of fuel per hour, so I was glad Uncle Sam was footing the bill. I finished the course a couple of weeks later, and I now had my Multi-Engine rating. I wrote Virgal in New Jersey informing him that school was out, I now had all my ratings and would arrive in August to apply for a job at Meteor.

Wedding bells were set to ring on June 4. The invitations had gone out and Margaret and her mother were almost finished with the bridal gowns — Margaret sewed her own wedding dress from a pattern she liked. The ceremony was at St. Matthew's Lutheran, her home church. A small luncheon reception for family and close friends was hosted at Palokos, a nearby Greek restaurant.

Family members gathered after our wedding ceremony, June 4, 1955 in the backyard of the Taylor residence. Left to right are Dad Taylor, John Balanoff, Peg Balanoff and son John, Jr., Margaret, me, Jane Taylor and Rich McGee, Mom Taylor and Ray Phillips, Margaret's sister Nancy's husband.

Frances G. Case and me on June 4, 1955, Margaret's and my wedding day. This photo was taken at our home on Lincoln Avenue in Erie before leaving for the church. Frances is in her mid-50s.

June 4, 1955, dawned bright and clear, which was a good omen. Sister Peg came from Chicago with her husband and John Jr. — John Sr. was Best Man. Everything went as planned, and as we stood in the receiving line Margaret's mother came by and said to me, "Take care of her." That admonition didn't register at the time, but after the chain of events four years later it was crystal clear, as we shall see. By 2 p.m. we were on our honeymoon trip in my recently purchased '54 Chevy. Margaret was now Mrs. Raymond A. Lemmon.

Goodbye to an Old Friend

The Swift had to go. It just didn't fit in anymore, and I couldn't afford it. Besides, the engine was reaching the point where Earl warned me that a major overhaul would soon be required. Selling it now would bring in money sorely needed for us to set up housekeeping.

I ran an ad in *Trade-A-Plane* offering the Swift for $2400, coincidentally the exact amount I had paid for it two years earlier. I got a call from a potential buyer in upstate New York who wanted me to fly over so he could look at it, but I emphatically refused: "No, I won't be able to do that; you'll have to come to Erie to see it." I had been on those wild-goose chases before. A compromise was finally reached, with him agreeing to pay my expenses to fly to Buffalo Airport the following Saturday.

After ironing out a few glitches, the transaction was completed and with check in hand, we returned to Erie by bus. I was sad for a while, but my logbook shows I resumed flying, now as a renter.

The summer of 1955 was lovely, with numerous outings to Presque Isle State Park. We rented a canoe one day and, quite unexpectedly, it tipped over. Fortunately, it was shallow water, and we walked the canoe to shore to upright it. We were soaking wet (including the licenses in my wallet). That was typical of how we spent our first summer together. Soon it was August, and time to begin my job search in New Jersey.

I informed Virgal we were coming so he could arrange an appointment with the chief pilot at Meteor. When we arrived, he told me about a new development: Pan Am was hiring pilots, and I might want to check that out before committing to Meteor.

Pan American World Airways! That was the big leagues, and a tremendous opportunity. Virgal had a phone contact for the Chief Pilot, Atlantic Division at Idlewild Airport (now Kennedy International). The next day I met with Captain Clark, who was all decked out in his Pan Am uniform. He was extremely candid: "The seniority list is long and it will probably take you 10 to 15 years to reach the Captain's seat. However, it is a career opportunity, if you have the patience to stick it out."

He made note of my bare-minimum qualifications, but respected the tenacity I demonstrated by earning an Instrument rating on my own. He indicated Pan Am was willing to give me a chance.

That "chance" meant a full day of intense testing called "stanine." It was not only written and oral exams, but also dexterity tests to determine levels of coordination. It would be a busy day, to be sure. It sounded challenging, but I said that I would like to try. "Okay, report to our office at LaGuardia Airport at 9 a.m. tomorrow."

When I arrived back at our motel and told Margaret about the interview, she was very excited and acknowledged it as a great opportunity.

"Not so fast," I said. "Remember what happened with United?"

Reporting as instructed, I was with a group of six other candidates. Discussing our chances, as all applicants do, it was apparent I was low man on the totem pole. Most of the others had flown in the military and had much more impressive qualifications.

It was a difficult day, and very intense. When it was over, they sent us to the medical department for an eye test using a modern device with little checkerboards, and I failed it. In order to give me every chance, they took me to the old 20-foot wall chart with the big "E". Unfortunately, I failed that as well, and I was crushed. Failing the eye test meant that I couldn't get the job. The medics indicated they would send the report to the chief pilot, and that I should check back with the flight office.

The next day I returned to Idlewild, where Captain Clark said he was sorry, that in fact I had passed the grueling tests and it was their intention to hire me. I saw a folder on his desk with my name on it, and underneath my name was a stamp that said "Atlantic Division." That really hurt.

I am relating this in such detail to illustrate that the path to an airline cockpit was a rocky road indeed. I was so very close to being a pilot for Pan Am. Bad news loves company; somehow Ken Johnson, chief pilot for Meteor, learned about my application at Pan Am and declined to interview me. I was shot down on all counts and my program was a shambles. However, stay with me; the quest is not over yet.

Since we were still on vacation, we drove north to the Adirondacks and other New England haunts before returning to Erie and our jobs. Margaret continued to work at the lab, so everything appeared normal on the surface.

What about my eye problem? I made an appointment with an ophthalmologist for a thorough exam, but the earliest appointment was mid-October, so I would have to wait. I toyed with the concept of another career path, just in case. At the time, the airlines required 20/20 uncorrected vision, period. I was aware of a slight astigmatism in my left eye, and had worn glasses briefly in high school.

The CAA was hiring controllers, and veterans had preference, so I thought I should look into that in case I couldn't fly. Although that's not what I really wanted, sometimes compromise was unavoidable. I filled out an application with Cecil Chartley at the "shack" and sent it in to the CAA in Oklahoma City. During my dilemma, my logbook showed only a few hours of flying time for the fall of '55. Then I finally went in for my eye exam and was told, "There's nothing wrong with your eyes. You have a mild astigmatism in the left eye, but it's certainly not disqualifying. You do have 20/20 uncorrected vision, and I am willing to provide you with documentation saying so."

"Why was I turned down by Pan Am last summer?" I asked the doctor.

"Based on the information you provided, it was probably due to eyestrain from the intense test program you were engaged in that day." What a relief! Now it was back to the search for a flying job, but where?

Someone said Eastern Airlines was hiring. Yes, I had seen an ad in *Aviation Week* that said to contact Captain F. B. Kern at Miami Operations. But how would I get there, and even more problematical, how would I get time off from work? It looked like the time had finally come to be straight with Clarence. I waited for one of our Monday lunch conversations at the public dock, and simply blurted out that I needed a couple of days off to apply for a pilot job with Eastern. It turned out that he knew all along that I had been trying for the airlines. What he said was, "Ray, I know you want to fly, so I will go along with you this one time. Go ahead and pursue your dream, but if it doesn't work out, I want you to snap out of this foolishness and apply yourself here at the lab. You're a married man now and you have responsibilities." Clarence sounded more like a father than my employer.

I had to admit he was being fair with me, and his response took me by surprise. By that time the holidays had come and gone, and it was 1956, so my clock was ticking. Eastern sent the usual application. Upon receiving it, they offered to provide space-available passes from Pittsburgh to Miami and return, but I would have to get to Pittsburgh on my own.

The die was cast, and it was make-or-break for me now. After Groundhog Day, I bought a round-trip ticket on Capital Airlines to Pittsburgh. It was definitely winter in Erie, with lots of snow on the ground, but I got to Pittsburgh okay. The Super Connie for which I was on standby was packed to the gills, and I got one of the last seats. We landed briefly in Jacksonville, and then we were off for Miami.

What a plane! I couldn't imagine flying something so enormous. The Lockheed Super Constellation was powered by four 3000 horsepower engines, and hydraulic pumps produced all kinds of strange noises during the operation of the landing gear and flaps. I was definitely impressed.

I located a hotel room near the airport and briefly enjoyed warm and sunny Miami. How could it be this nice in February? That was my first trip to Miami.

The next morning, I checked in with the Eastern Airlines personnel office and completed the usual pre-employment tests. By now, I was getting accustomed to them. A bit later, it was time for my interview with Captain Kern.

"You don't have any multi-engine time," he bellowed — as if to say, what are you doing here? My heart sank and it looked like another dagger in the chest. "We'll let you know," he said. End of interview.

While going through the process, I befriended one of the other applicants. His name was Paul Ferguson, and his experience was similar to mine except that he had over 2000 hours. Paul suggested we rent a car and see the sights, so I said, "Sure, why not?" Paul received the same treatment I did, as his flight time was in a Beechcraft Bonanza, which was a deluxe four-place high-performance single-engine plane with retractable landing gear. Paul hadn't logged much multi-engine time, either.

He was convinced that our Eastern Airlines application was going nowhere, and said that after leaving Miami he was flying to Washington to apply with Capital Airlines. Paul had heard they were expanding and buying prop-jet Viscounts from England.

The following morning, I checked out of the hotel and boarded a Connie flight to Pittsburgh. Space was not a problem going north, because during February most of the heavy loads were on southbound flights. At cruising altitude, the stewardess asked if I would like to visit the cockpit and talk to the crew. She could tell from my ticket that I was a pilot on company business.

I said, "Sure," and went up front. What a cockpit! The first crew member I encountered was the flight engineer, who gestured for me to take one of the jump seats. I was amazed at all the gauges and switches. I also talked to the captain and copilot, and after 15 minutes or so, returned to my seat.

Back at the lab, Clarence asked me how it went. I said that I didn't know yet, but a week later the bad news came: "Sorry, check back with us later." When I showed Clarence the rejection letter his only comment was, "I guess you'll just have to stay here with me and run a lab." End of discussion.

Spring was fast approaching, and my job search was coming to a head. The CAA offered me a position as apprentice briefer at the Erie Flight Service Station. I would start at Grade GS 5, earning approximately the same money I was making at the lab.

Another job offer came from Pure Carbon Co. in St. Marys, Pa., flying company officials around in their Cessna 180. Margaret definitely did not want to move there, so that was out.

Shortly after returning from the Eastern fiasco, I received a penny postcard from Paul Ferguson: "Ray, call Doc Reid at Capital, they are hiring." He also mentioned that he had a class date for early April, indicating that he now had a firm commitment.

I never considered trying at Capital because they required a minimum of 2000 hours, and since that was far more than my meager 800, I didn't apply. It was becoming a blur.

Then I received the real shocker. Earl said Forrest Beckett from Youngstown Airways was hiring pilots for their business fleet. I knew Forrest from the Erie Airport, so I thought I had a good chance. Forrest instructed me to report for an interview Saturday morning. Oh well, what did I have to lose? A lot, as it turned out: my job.

I asked Clarence for Saturday morning off to take care of some personal business. "Yeah, and I just bet I know what that is: another job interview. I've had it. I'm giving you two weeks' notice, as of right now. You're fired." And he stomped away. John Heid was there, looking for someplace to hide. I was stunned; this time I had pushed Clarence too far. I should have just called in sick, but no, I insisted on being honest with him. So that was that, and now I was out of work. Wait until I tell Margaret.

I thought I might as well go to Youngstown, since the damage was already done. It was a bust.

I did put that call in to Doc Reid at Capital, who immediately transferred me to Ralph Sewell, Chief Pilot. Ralph asked a few pertinent questions, including one that was very specific: "Do you have your Instrument rating? We have two airplanes a week arriving from England, and we need qualified pilots immediately." Wow! That did sound promising. "I'll put the paperwork in the mail today, then come down and see me." I sent the application in, and Capital responded immediately with a round-trip ticket to Washington. It was April 1 again, and I was hoping this wasn't another April Fool's joke.

When my two weeks were up, I went to Clarence's office to say goodbye and turn in my keys. I said I was sorry, that I had tried to be honest with him: "People do make career changes. I was just trying to do the right thing."

"You did, and you didn't," he said. "I warned you last winter, and you ignored me. I'm fed up with it all, here's your check, goodbye." I never saw Clarence again, but Margaret did; she ran into him downtown one day, and they exchanged pleasantries like, "How's Ray," etc. It was fortunate that I didn't have to deal with him on the Capital situation — that would have been even more stressful. I was with Clarence for nine years, including the two-year service break. I knew I wasn't family, but because I was so close to Vinnie, I felt we shared something other than a cut-and-dried working relationship.

Well, reader, that's the end of the Greystone Lab saga — let's move on.

I had to fly to Washington immediately, but in spite of the chief pilot's invitation to "come and see me," I still ended up in the personnel office first. "You'll need a first-class medical exam; go over to see Dr. Jarmin," the secretary suggested. Capital's pre-employment tests weren't anything like those I experienced at United, Eastern and Pan Am. There was no stanine requirement there.

Immediately, I sensed a different atmosphere at Capital. It was much homier and laid-back. Many of the senior captains had their roots as airmail pilots back in the '20s and '30s. (Wait until I recount my experiences flying with those guys.) I met Ralph Sewell, the chief pilot; he was one of the old-timers who graduated to management. No uniform was evident in his office, not even a suit coat.

He was quite candid: "It might be a little while before I can give you a class date, but I definitely will have a spot for you. Go over and see Doc Jarmin and get your first-class physical, and we'll get all this paperwork out of the way." I left on a decidedly positive note. (I flew with Ralph years later after the United/Capital merger. He didn't survive as "management" on United's team.)

That same afternoon, I went to see Dr. Jarmin in downtown Washington. What a character! He was a Flight Surgeon in the Army Air Corps and loved to tell stories. Naturally I was nervous, as I had never taken a Class I physical before.

"Relax," he said. "Go pee in the bottle and I'll be with you in a jiffy." No nurse, nobody, just "Doc" Jarmin. There were a couple of other Capital pilots there for physicals. I passed with flying colors: "No Limitations," indicating corrective lenses were not required.

"There, that wasn't so bad, was it? Give me 15 bucks and don't be so nervous next time; it raises your blood pressure." I did return, several times, while I was based in Washington.

I'm sure by now you have deduced that all this had a favorable outcome. But please bear with me — there's more excitement ahead.

The next day I boarded a Capital DC-3 bound for Erie. I should point out that the Capital personnel in Erie were rooting for me, especially John Hennigan, the station manager. We had been friends since I first learned to fly at Port Erie in 1950. Mac was also very supportive. He wanted his students to succeed. I was one of the lucky four who made it.

Early Married Life

Margaret Taylor Lemmon at our new apartment on Japan Street, Erie, Pa. Obviously, it is Christmas, 1955. Note vintage TV set and dial telephone on stand.

After our wedding in June, Margaret and I moved into a furnished upstairs flat at 804 Potomac Ave., near the airport. Lacking air conditioning, we were uncomfortable during the heat of summer. That, plus other considerations, motivated us to look for another place.

We frequently went into town to Mom and Dad's house for dinner. Since I was an orphan, I was soon adopted by the Taylors. Margaret often said she wanted to avoid in-law troubles like she had experienced at Al's house. Her father John managed a liquor store in downtown Erie. Jane, Margaret's younger sister, still lived at home, so there were often five of us at the table. Mother Taylor was an excellent cook.

Mom and Dad Taylor with me at their home on West Seventh Street, Erie, Pa. This picture was taken shortly after I started working for Capital Airlines in 1956.

My long lunch break at the lab provided sufficient time to come home, but there were no more trips to the airport to fly. It was a tranquil summer, but by fall we were ready for the move to a one-bedroom apartment at 628 Japan Street, near Strong Vincent High School. It was a complex of small houses built during WWII, and ours even had a basement. The rent was $55.

Margaret was very excited and couldn't wait to start fixing it up. Since we owned virtually nothing, shopping was the order of the day. Bedroom and living room furniture, kitchen appliances and a washing machine were all on the list. I recall spending many evenings downtown at Erie's main shopping outlet, The Boston Store. We settled for a used TV set.

Dad did much of the painting inside the apartment — what a guy. We splurged on a silverware set for $55, but we didn't need much else for the kitchen; Margaret's mom had extra "stuff." We bought a used Crosley "Shelvador" refrigerator and a used apartment-size gas range for $40. The stove was like new, but a bachelor had turned it into a mess. I still remember working out on the driveway at 720 restoring it to pristine condition.

Wringer washers were commonplace in the '50s, but Margaret bought a used Easy Spindrier washing machine instead. It was a precursor of today's automatic washer, and as the name implies, it eliminated the need for a wringer. She was very proud of that, and we moved it four times. Prepare yourself, reader; we moved a lot. Because I had no job, we bought some of the furniture "on time."

I got a break — a small one, to be sure, but important nonetheless. A church member at St. Matthew's heard that I was out of work and offered to help. Walt Konji owned and operated Erie Pepsi-Cola Bottling Co. He approached me after church one Sunday and said, "I can put you on for 10 bucks a day working the trucks." That offer implied delivering cases of pop to stores, large and small, all over the city. It wasn't much, but there were no unemployment checks at that time.

"I'll take it," I said. After a week or so, I transferred to the advertising department. It sounds like a promotion to an inside job, but it wasn't. Walt assigned me an old beat-up truck equipped for erecting signs at beer distributors. Those signs were much like the ones the "Pickers" buy on TV. Walt was a great guy, and I treasure the memories of my brief employment at Pepsi-Cola.

———

Finally, that all-important letter from Capital Airlines arrived. It was a solid commitment of employment: "Your class date is May 25, 1956; you are directed to report to Captain Don Stiff at the training department, Hangar 3, Washington National Airport at 0830. Your assigned payroll number is 5036. Welcome aboard."

A penny postcard from Paul Ferguson just turned into a multimillion-dollar career with what would become, as a result of a merger, the finest airline in the world: United Airlines.

Chapter 8

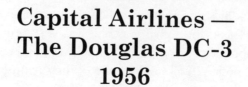

Capital Airlines —
The Douglas DC-3
1956

Overjoyed as Margaret and I were at landing my new job with Capital Airlines, it was apparent we were facing a major transition: We were about to leave our home on Japan Street that we had painted and furnished with such devotion. It was impossible to anticipate our needs in Virginia, where we planned to live; for example, most apartments came with kitchen appliances, so we took steps to rid ourselves of those. "Not my Easy washer, I'm keeping that!" Margaret stated emphatically.

Margaret needed the car, so when I arrived in Washington, it was shank's mare. She took care of the Erie end of our relocation while I concentrated on the Capital DC-3.

I left Erie with a suitcase full of clothes and a thankful heart. Since I had no idea where I would be living, I returned to the hotel where I had stayed previously.

The Airline Industry and Capital Airlines

A brief history of the airline industry up to the mid-1950s may be in order. Just a few years earlier the field had been dominated by a few embryonic domestic companies, notably American, United, and TWA. All had their roots in the allocation of airmail routes by the U.S. government in the '20s and '30s.

The industry grew by leaps and bounds after the 1925 passage of the Air Mail Act, which allocated contracts to deliver airmail and gave the plane owners an incentive to also carry passengers. At that point the Air Commerce Act of 1926 gave the Secretary of Commerce power to establish airways, certify aircraft, license pilots, and issue and enforce air traffic regulations. Prior to 1938 it was a cutthroat industry; the establishment of the CAB (Civil Aeronautics Board) provided much-needed stability. The CAB's two most significant functions were to assign airlines' routes of travel and regulate fares.

Early on, routes were flown by single-engine planes that were surplus from the Great War. The first serious multi-engine contenders were the Boeing 247 and Ford Tri-Motor, both of which were available in the early '30s. A giant of the aircraft industry was Donald Douglas, father of the famous DC-3 (manufactured by the Douglas Commercial Airplane Company).

A Capital Airlines DC-3 at Buffalo, N.Y. at the close of its service in 1960. Inset is Captain OV Pezzi, who took the photo.

Even though aviation had grown enormously during WWII, the airlines were still in their infancy when I arrived on the scene in 1956. Just a few years earlier, before and during the war, the DC-3 was king. It was through design of the DC-4 as a long-range troop transport that the airlines leapt into the future. One other significant development during the war years was the production of the C-69 by Lockheed, which would become the Lockheed Constellation. Both of those planes would have a distinct impact on my future.

A few giants emerged: Howard Hughes (TWA), C.R. Smith at American (AA), W.A. Patterson at United (UAL), and Eddie Rickenbacker at Eastern (EAL). The next largest airline was Capital, headed up by an ex-airmail pilot named "Slim" Carmichael.

Capital Airlines originated in Pittsburgh as Clifford Ball Airlines, and that split up to become Pennsylvania and Central Airlines. They later combined to become Penn-Central, which shortly after was renamed PCA, The Capital Airline. After the war, they dropped PCA to become present-day Capital Airlines.

Airlines were primarily composed of route structure, planes, and fares. Until the passage of airline deregulation in 1978, two of those entities were controlled by the Civil Aeronautics Board. Under its supervision, the nation's airline route structure was divided geographically along the lines of their route origins. American and United enjoyed somewhat of a monopoly on coast-to-coast service. Because of his financial clout, Howard Hughes inherited a vast domestic network as well as international routes — hence the name Trans World Airlines. Pan Am and TWA dominated the nation's international airline service.

The Capital route structure evolved from its origination in Pittsburgh to become the nation's fifth-largest airline. With its home offices in the nation's capital, it was aptly named at first: PCA, the "Capital Airline." Its initial triangular route structure was Pittsburgh-New York-Washington, later expanded to include Chicago. A southern branch was added that became known as "Tobacco Road," principally including Virginia, North Carolina and Tennessee. Shortly after, an extension farther south to New Orleans, Huntsville, and Memphis was approved. All of Capital's operations were east of the Mississippi River, including the fairly recent Midwestern additions of Milwaukee and Minneapolis/St. Paul.

Although not massive like American and United, Capital served a definite market niche, and that was sufficient to encourage the company to embark on a massive expansion by pioneering the first jet service in the U.S. In 1955, "Slim" Carmichael entered Capital into an agreement with Vickers Aircraft in Great Britain to purchase 60 Viscount aircraft at exceedingly favorable terms. The Viscount was not a true jet because it still used propellers, thus earning it the designation "prop-jet." Even so, it was a huge leap forward for the airline industry, and there was nothing comparable to it here in the U.S. The British were well ahead of us in jet aircraft development, and that continued until Boeing launched the 707 program near the end of the decade.

There were economic downsides. The Viscount was equipped with four engines, yet it only accommodated 44 passengers. Still, Capital's agreement with Vickers was a bold move, and Carmichael's bravery paid off briefly in spades. In fact, the majors were stunned by this development, as they could only offer large piston aircraft such as the DC-6 and Constellation in competition. The mid-1950s was an exciting time for me to begin my airline career.

What defined a major airline? Was it just planes, or was there more? I will attempt to reconstruct the fabric of Capital as it was in May 1956.

First, of course, were the planes. We owned 20 DC-3s, 5 Super DC-3s (a modern variant of the original with streamlining and more-powerful engines), about a dozen war-surplus DC-4s, and 12 Lockheed Constellations. At that time approximately half of our order of 60 Viscounts from Britain had been delivered.

Next, pilots: Broadly estimating approximately six crews per airplane, our complement was about 600. In fact, my original seniority number was 628. There was nothing more important to an airline pilot than his seniority number.

I don't recall the total workforce at Capital. The number of flight attendants ("hostesses") was between 700 and 800. As to the number of mechanics, ticket agents, baggage handlers, ramp agents, catering people, and a host of others, it is beyond my recollection.

The Career Begins

The morning of May 25, I reported to Hangar 3 in search of Captain Stiff. There were eight in our new-hire class, all reporting for the first day of training and orientation. I was surprised to find that I was younger than most of my classmates. I struck up a conversation with Pete McIntosh from Connecticut, who was the youngest.

Hangar 3 was typical for the industry: an enclosed space large enough for several planes, with an office complex on the street side. At each airport we served, we owned or leased space for a ticket counter and equipment used to service the planes.

Before long, Captain Stiff arrived and invited us into the classroom that would serve as our home for the next two weeks. It was Don's job to teach us about airline operations, as well as the information we needed to fly the Douglas DC-3. Ours was one of the last classes to train on this venerable plane; starting in July, new hires would train initially on the Viscount.

Don recommended rooming houses in Alexandria with accommodations available at very reasonable rates. Starting salary was $375 per month for the first year, increasing to $450 the second. After that, a formula known as increment pay was used. Gross pay was calculated based on the type of plane, hours flown both day and night, and even mileage pay. In addition, we received an expense account for hotels and meals while away from home. That was a major perk for Margaret and me, as it provided the luxury of eating out when I returned from a trip. Since I seldom spent much on trips, it was essentially additional pay.

After the basic introduction, Don asked if there were any questions. Foremost in everyone's minds, of course, was where we would be based. Most assumed it would be Washington, but that turned out to be incorrect.

An outline of the Capital pilot domicile structure was as follows: There were nine crew bases, beginning with Washington (Capital's corporate headquarters) and then Norfolk and New York on the East Coast. Moving inland, additional domiciles were located at Buffalo, Pittsburgh, Detroit, Chicago, and Minneapolis/St. Paul. Detroit was established to serve the Michigan cities and Ohio, but was soon to be eliminated. The only southern domicile was New Orleans, La.

Several crew bases no longer provided DC-3 service. Minneapolis was strictly Constellations, and New Orleans and Norfolk were Viscount-only. Don emphasized that the whole system was in flux, but for the time being DC-3 crews were most needed in the Midwest, notably Chicago. This instability interfered with our plans to move to Virginia.

The first week at Hangar 3, we focused on an intense study of the DC-3 itself, followed by operational procedures relating to our assignment as copilots (second in command). Special radio procedures were used, such as calling in arrival and departure times and fuel on board. All Capital stations had VHF radio sets to communicate with our planes on an assigned company frequency.

It was the crew's responsibility to perform a walk-around inspection, checking to make sure everything with respect to the plane's operating condition was airworthy. An example of dereliction of this duty would be failure to remove control locks from the tail surfaces that ground service personnel may have installed to prevent wind damage. That happened at least once with disastrous results: The plane crashed.

We were not responsible for fueling the plane, only to verify that the specified fuel load was on board. Sometimes, it meant climbing up on the wing with a dipstick, a hazardous enterprise in winter. Most items we checked were obvious, such as proper tire inflation and evidence of collision damage of any kind — that sort of thing. The next step was to enter the cockpit and determine that everything was shipshape there, including examination of the ship's log for maintenance discrepancies.

Ground School

Ground School sessions addressed aircraft systems like engines, propellers, hydraulics, fuel, oil, etc. There were differences in some of the planes. Ours were "original" DC-3s, meaning they were powered by Wright Cyclone radial engines, as opposed to the Pratt and Whitney power plants used on war-surplus military C-47s brought into service by many startup carriers postwar.

In fact, our Wright Cyclone engines were identical to those used on B-17 bombers of WWII. After the war, Capital purchased an entire warehouse filled with brand-new Cyclone engines, still in cans. No DC-3 engines were overhauled by Capital until well after I joined the company — when a replacement was needed, maintenance simply went to the warehouse and picked up a new one.

The bomber engines were 1200 horsepower, versus ours rated at 1100. No alterations were necessary to "de-rate" them; we simply limited manifold pressure to 43 inches of mercury.

Airline ground schools followed a predictable pattern, but since this was my first, I was diligent in class. There were a lot of "what if" questions at first, but Don Stiff was exceedingly competent and many of these questions were answered by just exercising patience. About all I remember about the DC-3 after 50-plus years is that its maximum gross weight allowance was 25,346 pounds; it held 28 passengers and cruised at 145 knots.

Flight training began with flying old #210, a cargo version that was used primarily for transporting engines and other outsized material to stations on the Capital system. Even though #210 didn't fly the line, it sported the regular Capital "bird" livery. Six seats were arranged in the forward cargo area for trainees to occupy when not flying. Even though only one trainee at a time could be at the controls, idle time in the rear was used for preparation. There was also one jump seat in the cockpit for the next man up to observe and prepare for his turn. We started the session with full fuel tanks (600 gallons), and flew for four hours to Baltimore, Harrisburg, and other nearby airports. Each man was allotted one hour of flying time beginning with familiarization (most had never flown the DC-3 before), how to feather (stop) a propeller and restart the engine, takeoff and landing practice and ILS approaches.

The Instrument Landing System had not been part of the Instrument Rating course in Erie. At Capital, the ILS approach was the primary criterion used to measure pilot proficiency.

Don was delighted to learn that I had logged over 3 hours previous experience flying the DC-3. That was my round-trip flight from Teterboro, N.J., to Detroit with Virgal Swain four years earlier. As a result, my training was abbreviated to some extent for the benefit of those who needed more time. Tragically, old #210 crashed on a training flight near Baltimore three years later, killing all on board.

Nearing the end of our training and prior to becoming working copilots, we needed 10 hours observer time (sitting on the jump seat) on flights of our choice throughout the system. I chose what we called the "around the horn" sequence. Starting in Washington, the route traveled through Baltimore, Harrisburg, Williamsport, Elmira, Rochester, Buffalo, Erie, Pittsburgh, Morgantown, and then returned to our starting point at DCA.

Oh boy! That would provide an opportunity to fly into Erie and see Margaret; wasn't that great? We hadn't been issued uniforms yet and we wouldn't be permitted to fly the line until they arrived, so I wore civilian clothes. Margaret and her parents came to the airport to visit while I was passing through.

Nearing the end of the course, I received two training sessions in the Link Trainer. The second period included practice flying ILS approaches, a new innovation for me and a viable substitute for valuable aircraft time. An ILS approach would be the highlight of my final flight check.

My DC-3 training ended with a two-hour copilot qualification flight on June 6, 1956. We convened as a class one last time to celebrate our graduation.

What about seniority numbers? Did we draw straws? No, a more equitable method was to award the oldest member of the class the lowest number. That logic was based on the premise that an older pilot would have less opportunity to climb the seniority ladder through attrition. The oldest class member was 28, so he was awarded the lowest number. Pete McIntosh got the highest, and I was second-youngest so I was senior to him. That system had adverse consequences for me in the future.

We used Pete's car one weekend to check out apartments, and I found a nice two-bedroom unit in Arlington for $97.50. It was in a very desirable location near Shirley Highway and was attractive, with parquet floors throughout but no air conditioning. I told the superintendent I was interested and asked if he could hold it until July 1. He refused to do that without a deposit, so I said I would check back in two weeks. When I learned my domicile assignment was Chicago (Midway Airport), I erased it from my mind.

My uniform arrived during my observer flights. It looked sharp: double-breasted with brass buttons, wings and three stripes on the sleeves. By then, it was time to leave Alexandria and ride jump seat on a DC-4 bound for Chicago.

Air Line Pilots Association

As a new hire, I was limited to associate membership in the Air Line Pilots Association (ALPA) for my first year, and in that capacity, I didn't pay dues. Capital was a closed shop, so all pilots were required to join the union.

June 1956: The author decked out in his new Capital Airlines uniform. This was at our apartment in Arlington, Virginia near Washington National Airport.

For one year I was on probation and could be fired for the smallest infraction. As an example, if I were flying with a captain who didn't like the way I combed my hair, he could simply call the chief pilot and I would be history. It was scary at first, but I learned the secret of diplomacy. Yes sir, no sir — just like the Army. Virtually all the captains I would be flying with had been in the service and were familiar with military protocol.

I recall one disturbing encounter, well beyond my probationary period, while I was flying Viscounts. I was assigned to fly with a captain unfamiliar to me, and upon arrival in the cockpit, my instructions were, "Push your seat back, keep your feet on the floor, and shut up." That was a difficult beginning, to be sure. Fortunately, such instances were rare, and most of the captains were great to fly with.

Flying Out Of Chicago

I checked in with Chicago crew scheduling and was informed there were bunks and showers on the second floor of the hangar. It was intended to be a crew lounge, but when I arrived, it looked more like a hotel. There were already pilots living there temporarily, so at least I didn't have to pay for a room.

My first scheduled trip was June 10: Chicago (MDW), Muskegon (MKG), Grand Rapids (GRR), and Milwaukee (MKE). Bill Barnhart would be my captain. I arrived at flight dispatch early to prepare the flight plan, and was quite nervous with typical first-flight jitters. When Bill arrived, I introduced myself and explained that it was my first trip. I was hoping my first hop would be in daylight, but very little of it was. We took off at 7 p.m., crossed Lake Michigan and arrived back in Milwaukee around 10 p.m.

Many of our Michigan flights were scheduled so businessmen could put in a full business day in Chicago and arrive back home across the lake the same day. Those DC-3 flights were very popular because the alternative was to drive around Lake Michigan by car, which was hundreds of miles. Car ferry service was available, but that was not suitable for commuting.

Bill was very patient with me. He indicated he would do most of the flying so I could familiarize myself with the charts and radio stations that defined the airways we were flying. My experience flying Omni to California proved invaluable, but the geography and terminology were unfamiliar. After dark, reading the chart was even more challenging.

I had used U.S. government charts for my instrument training, and they differed markedly from the Jeppesen navigation charts used at Capital. Jeppesen had been an airmail pilot for Varney Airlines, and by 1934 he developed an aeronautical chart book for pilots which became an international standard.

Leaving Chicago eastbound, it was still light for a while. It was a warm evening, so we opened the windows and shortly flew over the stockyards. What an odor! We filed a VFR (visual flight rules) flight plan implying good weather, which meant we didn't need to talk to anyone. By the time we arrived at Muskegon on the lee side of Lake Michigan, it was completely dark.

There was a quirk of flying known as "night vision," which was basically eye adaptation to dim lighting. Captain Stiff warned us to be very careful using a flashlight in the cockpit at night. A surefire way to get off on the wrong foot with your captain was to shine a bright light in the cockpit. The instrument panel lighting was red, subduing ambient light. Don taught us to use red nail polish to paint the lens, so if we needed to read the chart it would be a dim red light and not a white one.

It was a clear night, but we still used radio navigation to fly airways. A trace of light was needed to determine VOR frequency and course from the chart, and Bill was aware of my difficulty. He suggested for my next trip that I preplan the flight on paper and tabulate all the courses and frequencies so I wouldn't need to refer to the map so much in the cockpit. Of course Bill, being an experienced captain, had committed everything to memory. He said I reminded him of his early days with the airline, living out of a suitcase and having that "lost" look.

The next day we flew several shuttle flights across Lake Michigan between MKE and MKG — back and forth all day, with the usual stops in between. We called it the Michigan Special. The final leg ended up in Chicago after a total of almost eight hours in the air. What a day! Welcome to the airline world; I was bushed. Bill offered me some more tips, and then we said goodbye.

That was the only trip I flew out of Chicago. When I checked back in with the crew scheduler, he handed me a note from the Chicago flight office. It was good news; I was to return to DCA immediately for reassignment. Washington would now be my permanent domicile, and suddenly I realized the Shirley Park apartment was still a possibility. I couldn't wait to call Margaret.

I had hoped to see my sister Peg briefly before I left. It was a tight timetable, but I was able to squeeze in a short visit. She and her husband John lived in South Chicago, on the second floor of a poultry shop owned by his father. I didn't stay long, as I really needed to get back to DC.

Arlington, Va.

Two days later I was assigned another trip, and this time it was a Washington pairing. I barely had time to pay my room rent in Alexandria and call Margaret, in that order. If I had time, I wanted to check on the possibility of renting the apartment in Shirley Park.

Yes, the upstairs two-bedroom unit was still available, so I bummed a ride to sign the lease. I looked at it again and decided it would be fine, but it was a stretch on my meager salary. I felt having a nice apartment was important for Margaret. I mailed her a copy of the floor plan for approval.

It was ours as of July 1, so I suggested she start packing right away. Margaret was excellent preparing for movers, a skill she honed throughout my career. Unfortunately, this time I would not be able to help and she was on her own; a trip to Erie was just not possible for me at that time. It was a huge load to dump on her, and I felt sorry. I refused to push her, though: "We'll just let the apartment stand empty until you can come," I told her.

My second trip sequence on the DC-3 was very interesting. It was the "Tobacco Road" run, Flight 575/14 (June 14, 1956): DCA-TYS (Knoxville), with stops at Newport News, Norfolk, Raleigh-Durham, Greensboro, Winston-Salem, and Charlotte. The TYS designator for Knoxville came from the name of the airport, Tyson Field.

My captain was Paul Miller, a gentle man if ever there was one. He flew B-29s out of Saipan and Tinian in the Pacific theater during the war. That mission was 1500 miles round-trip to Japan and back. He found it both exciting and boring. Sounds like airline flying.

When I walked into Washington operations, Paul was already there and I'm sure the crew desk alerted him that he had a new copilot. Exchanging the usual pleasantries, I informed him this was only my second trip and that I had just arrived from Chicago. I sensed right away it was going to be a pleasure flying with Paul and felt he would be patient with me. I would need all the tolerance he could spare. The DC-3 was a small airplane and not that much more complicated than the Piper Cub I learned to fly in. The captain could easily fly it all by himself without much help from anyone.

His greatest requirement was to have someone raise and lower the landing gear.

Applying Bill Barnhart's suggestion from my Chicago trip, I carried a notebook that fit in my shirt pocket. In it, I wrote all the frequencies and the courses to and from each station. Preparation of the flight plan was always the copilot's job, except in the most unusual circumstances.

Because of the six intermediate stops, I would be very busy indeed. I had to radio in the takeoff and landing times, estimated time of arrival (ETA) for the next stop, fuel requirements, changes in weather, etc.

Once again, it was an evening flight, starting at dusk. Fortunately, it was still summer, and we enjoyed predominantly good flying weather. Even though it was dark, we flew VFR (Visual Flight Rules) on airways defined by lighted beacons and low-frequency radio stations. Since we met the necessary illumination and safety requirements, it was perfectly legal.

This was at the conclusion of the period when airline flights could be conducted under visual flight rules. Before long, all flights were operated IFR, and monitored by radar. There was no approach control in the '50s; we just called the control tower five miles out with a landing light on and they would clear us to land.

Summer was the happy time for flying the DC-3. VFR conditions usually prevailed under temperate climatic conditions with long days. The worst adversity I faced was getting my pants wet during occasional summer downpours. The DC-3 was unpressurized, so you could fly with the side windows open if you could stand the noise. The windshield leaked, and Douglas thoughtfully provided a rubber apron to address that problem, but it met with only limited success. Somewhere along the line, the plane earned the not-so-flattering nickname of "bug smasher."

Contrast that with flying the DC-3 during winter: freezing temperatures, ice forming on the wings and propellers, opening the side window and reaching around with a putty knife to scrape ice off the windshield so you could see to land. In winter, field conditions were a major concern; was the runway plowed? How about snow banks? Was the wind favorable, or was it a vicious crosswind that could put us off the side of the runway?

I'll offer just a few more comments relating to climate control during winter operations with the DC-3. Heat was ducted to the passenger cabin from the engines by way of a manifold. Unfortunately, almost no heat reached the cockpit, so a separate Janitrol heater was provided. It was the most cantankerous device known to man, and we copilots were supposed to make it work. A sure way for a new copilot to get off on the wrong foot was to freeze his captain.

The reality was that the cockpit heater seldom worked. If you saw pilots in operations all bundled up in huge overcoats, you could assume it was a DC-3 crew.

Fortunately, my assignment wasn't long enough to face those nightmares; however, I dealt with them all later, in more advanced planes.

Returning to our flight that day, some of the legs (segments) of the trip were very brief, like the one I flew from Newport News to Norfolk, and between Greensboro and Winston-Salem. The cities were so close it was scarcely necessary to retract the landing gear. The average flight time during good weather was less than 15 minutes. However, if instrument approaches were required during bad weather with low ceilings, then the en-route time was much greater. Some of this was built into the schedule, so on a clear night like June 14 we were early everywhere, and we arrived at TYS ahead of schedule. My principle memory of Knoxville was the station manager, a real go-getter named Ned Lee. He was famous throughout the Capital system for the way he ran the Knoxville station.

The return flight, 574/15, was unremarkable except that we needed an IFR clearance for the Charlotte leg. Occasionally, in summer, ground fog would delay our departure, and then it was my job to call the control tower and file an IFR flight plan. It seldom caused us much delay.

The combination of Flights 575 and 574 was the most sought-after DC-3 trip pairing. I only got it because the regular copilot was out sick. Paul was a joy to fly with, and I told him how much I enjoyed his company.

My next trip, two days later on June 17, was Flight 561, the "around the horn" sequence I had taken on my observer flight. My captain, Roger Taylor, was also a great guy, and we would fly together again in 1966 on the B-727.

Since I was landing at Erie again, Margaret and her parents came out to visit during the brief stopover. That was the first time she had seen me in uniform, and she was quite impressed. Sometimes, at whistle-stops like Erie, we would only shut down the left engine, depending on how many passengers and bags there were. In deference to me since we were early, Roger shut down both engines, and I conducted a tour of the plane. The stopover was short but sweet.

June 1956: The author, smiling and looking out of the cockpit window of a Capital Airlines DC-3. This photo was taken by Margaret during a stopover on my first DC-3 line trip through Erie, Pa.

I logged another seven-hour day. I was really building up my flying time; in fact, I needed to watch my legality. We were only permitted to fly 30 hours in any seven-day period. And so it went, all through July and part of August. I racked up nearly 200 hours during that period. When I think back how I struggled early on for flight time, and how quickly the hours were accumulating now, the difference was astonishing.

Ship #215

On June 26 I was summoned for a DC-3 test hop. My captain was B.K. (Kirk) Watkins — we hadn't met up to that time. When I arrived at operations and discovered it was ship #215, my memory suddenly kicked into high gear. During my DC-3 training, our classroom had windows that looked down into Hangar 3. I had noticed one of our DC-3s sitting along the side without wings, and there was quite a bit of activity around it. "What's with ship 215?" I asked.

"Oh, she's down for an 8000-hour overhaul."

"How long will it take to put her back together?" I asked. Not receiving any credible answer, I dismissed it from my mind. It was that same ship #215, now parked outside the hangar, that we were scheduled to do our test hop in. It would be her first time back in the air after being totally dismantled.

"What do you think about flying this 'bucket of bolts'?" I asked Kirk.

"Somebody's got to do it." Hmmm. Then I learned that the chief mechanic assigned to the job would be going along to supervise the flight test and take notes.

"Well, that's encouraging — the mechanic will be with us as part of the crew," I said to Kirk. He's the only reason we're going; no mechanic, no test," Kirk replied.

We went out to the plane, chocked on the hangar line. "Do a thorough walk-around, Ray. Check everything." And I did!

Soon we were taxiing out to the runway with a clearance for a test hop in the immediate airport area. The flight went really well, and the mechanic took notes on necessary adjustments, etc.

"I'm finished. Let's go back and land," said the mechanic. Captain Kirk called for "gear down," so I lowered the handle as he instructed. The expected response to that command would then have been, "Handle down, latched, green light, pressure's up and I have a wheel." Unfortunately, there was no green light, so it was not safe to land.

I could see the extended landing gear out my side window. At that point there was some confusion, and we were nearing our touchdown point for Runway 18, so Kirk ordered me to "Call the tower and tell them we have an unsafe gear indication and are going around." By that time, both the mechanic and I recognized the problem. I had not latched the landing gear lever, and that was why there was no green light. Kirk saw it too, and I was keenly embarrassed. My seniority date showed I was still quite new, and Kirk knew *that* also.

"Call them back and tell them we're re-entering the pattern; everything is okay now." With the green light illuminated, we were cleared to land. I think my anxiety over having to fly the hangar queen caused me to slip up. Back in operations, Kirk tried to console me: "Don't sweat it, we all make mistakes." Years later, while flying Connies together, Kirk would say, "Remember that test flight on old 215? We've both come a long way since then."

Then we would laugh.

Chapter 9

The Capital Constellation
1956-1957

On August 20, the flight office called with the shocking news that I was scheduled for "049" training the following Monday. That was the very first model designation for the Lockheed Constellation, an airplane also affectionately known as the "Connie."

Connie School? I was stunned. While still grappling with the DC-3, they suddenly wanted to add two more engines. Recalling my recent Eastern Air Lines trip to Miami, the Lockheed Constellation was a gigantic airplane.

"Yeah," he said, "everybody is moving up to Viscounts, and now we need Connie people."

With all this airline discussion, whatever happened to Margaret? Did she survive the move to Arlington? Yes, and she did it mostly by herself, with a little help from Mom and Dad. They inherited our refrigerator, and Margaret was able to sell the gas range. The Easy Spindrier washer went to the Taylor basement for safekeeping. The small stuff was packed into boxes and shipped via Allied Van Lines to Virginia.

I managed a couple of days off to fly to Erie and wrap up a few loose ends. After the furniture was loaded, we drove our '54 Chevy to Arlington. Margaret was delighted with the apartment, and we were soon contented in our new home.

She gradually adjusted to my comings and goings at all hours of the day and night. As a diversion and to save money, Margaret made many of her own clothes with the White sewing machine I gave her as a wedding present.

Our life together revolved around my flights, and since it was only ten minutes to Washington National Airport, Margaret usually took me to work and picked me up. (Two-car families were a rarity in the mid-1950s.)

I recall one amusing instance when our system backfired. In 1956, Margaret was able to drive right up to flight operations, and only a three-foot chain link fence separated the public from the planes. The gates were never locked, and a mobile stairway was used to deplane passengers.

It was a Connie flight and the crew was always last to deplane, so Margaret patiently waited until everyone got off. Guess what? No Ray. Most wives might be concerned, but not Margaret — she simply walked into operations and asked the senior agent to determine my whereabouts. "Oh, he was reassigned to another flight; didn't they call you?" Normally the crew desk did call, but not always. Usually, in case of abnormality, I would do the calling, but for some reason, I wasn't able to get through. I only mentioned this to give you some perspective of the relaxed nature of airline operations in the '50s, even at a major terminal like Washington.

Being so close to the airport made it possible for Margaret to keep the car, and her favorite pastime was window-shopping at the Shirlington Mall. She didn't have much money to spend, but she would patronize the sewing store for patterns and fabric to make blouses. Frugality was the order of the day. She loved eating at the Hot Shoppes drive-in, so when I got in off a trip, we would splurge. The days and weeks slipped by and now it was August. Let's move on to Connie School.

Lockheed Constellation Model L-049

I won't go into technical detail here. Suffice it to say that the Connie was a large four-engine transport, built to fly lots of people over great distances. Unlike most airliners, the Connie had three vertical stabilizers, earning it the rather uninspiring nickname of "the three-tailed monster." That simply meant that instead of a single vertical fin and rudder, the Connie had three. They were smaller in size, to be sure, but it presented a rather unique appearance. The other distinguishing feature was the fuselage; instead of being a long straight tube, like the DC-4, it projected a curvaceous profile. It might have looked ungainly sitting at the gate, but once it was airborne there was nothing like it, appearance-wise.

Capital Airlines Connie (Lockheed Constellation) at Hangar 3, Washington National Airport, 1956. Having just been released from maintenance, it is ready to be towed to the terminal for a flight. The man approaching the plane is Captain Mike Kardos, manager of flight operations in Pittsburgh. Our managers were not "deskbound."

The Constellation fleet operated by Capital was not made up of the latest model; in fact, they were the earliest. More advanced versions, specifically the 749 and 1049 Super series, were equipped with reversible propellers, more powerful engines, and a stretched fuselage. Half of our fleet originated from BOAC (British Overseas Air Corporation) in connection with our agreement with the Vickers Company to buy Viscounts. We traded our coveted Model 749s for their cast-off 049s. They were refurbished and painted in Capital livery, creating the illusion of being "born again."

Our class convened in Hangar 3 for the introduction. The Connie was gorgeous, a truly magnificent airplane. Because of its size, standing next to it was an intimidating experience. Our tour guide, Jim Kelley, was head of the engineering section and supervisor of flight engineer training.

Yes, the Connie was my introduction to a three-man flight crew. I reflected on my recent visit to the cockpit of the Eastern Airlines Connie barely six months ago, when I was returning from Miami. Now I was being trained to fly a version of that very aircraft. I would not have believed it possible for me to advance this far so soon. We spent an hour touring the exterior, and then it was time to separate into smaller groups to check out the cockpit.

The class consisted of eight captains and copilots; flight engineers were trained separately in classes of their own. The cockpit was quite roomy, with three crew member positions plus two observer seats. Next to the flight engineer there was a small service door that, when opened, provided an excellent view of #3 engine. The engines were identified by number — #1 being the left outboard, and then advancing left to right facing forward: #2, #3, and #4. Thus #4 was the outboard engine on the starboard wing.

Flight Engineers

We spent an hour or so on cockpit orientation, focusing on the complexity of the flight engineer station. Capital had a rather unique method for staffing that crew position; unlike most of the other major airlines, we used pilots from our seniority list. If an insufficient number of bids were submitted, assignment was in inverse order of seniority to fill the vacancies. Since pilots love to fly, it usually resulted in the most junior pilots being assigned to a two-year stint as a flight engineer before resuming flight duty as copilot. There were some interesting provisions of the ALPA Union contract, one of which had a direct bearing on me: Pilots on probation were not eligible for the flight engineer draft, so I was safe for the time being, at least.

Because of Capital's rapid expansion, some pilots already assigned as flight engineers were moving up the seniority ladder with such expediency that they were able to hold a DC-3 Captain position before completing their flight engineer assignment. Our union contract did not cover that remote possibility, so those flight engineers were free to bid Captain at any time.

Since most of these flight engineers had no recent experience at the controls, they were very rusty. The impact of their "rustiness" on me was frequently finding myself displaced from the copilot seat to man the flight engineer station. Protestations regarding not being qualified were ignored.

"You can do it, Ray; I'll show you; the throttles are the black knobs, the props are green, and the mixtures are red. Be careful with the mixtures, though, a wrong move there might shut down all four engines." My past experience working at Joe Martin's garage stood me in good stead. I guess I was a quick study, because before long, I was a relatively accomplished flight engineer.

One specific instance of being displaced comes to mind: Pete Gallant was a young Connie captain who never left flight operations to board the aircraft until they were in the process of closing the door and rolling the stairs away. The flight engineer had already taken my copilot seat, and I was sitting at the engineer's panel. Pete looked around, surveying the situation, and then he focused on me with one question: "Which way do those mixtures go for 'full rich'?" As a response, I made a gesture with my left hand, away from where I was sitting.

"Okay," Pete said, "You're the engineer." Then he climbed into the captain's seat and I started the engines.

Back to School

I mustn't jump ahead. After the cockpit orientation, there was a brief Q&A session, and the next morning I started ground school. We were given five days of concentrated study to master the intricacies of the Lockheed Constellation.

It was far more complicated than the DC-3. The cabin was pressurized, the hydraulic system was a plumber's nightmare, and the engines were over 2000 horsepower each, equipped with two-stage superchargers. A complete fully instrumented flight panel was provided for each pilot, contrasting the DC-3's single centrally mounted unit. There was a rudimentary vacuum-operated autopilot, plus loads of other goodies.

Because of the plane's size and weight, the flight controls were hydraulically boosted; however, on flight checks, we were required to demonstrate the ability to fly the airplane with the hydraulic boost turned off using "manual reversion." That made you acutely aware of the enormity of the Connie.

An engine analyzer was included, which was a 5-inch oscilloscope that graphically depicted how all 144 spark plugs were firing. I took manuals home to study, as there was no way one could learn it all in class — at least not with my experience level. I was the junior pilot with less than three months on the line.

Flight training began as an observer on Flight 911 to Milwaukee (MKE) with Captain Frank Wunderlich. We stopped in Detroit (YIP), where Frank offered me the copilot's seat for the leg to Milwaukee. We returned the following day, with stops at Cleveland and New York (LGA).

After additional classroom work, we resumed flight training with Captain Lee Hetterman as our instructor. I and two other copilot trainees flew a Connie to Baltimore for takeoff and landing practice, including ILS approaches. There was no designated training plane; we simply "borrowed" a Connie at the hangar that had been released from maintenance. We all got a chance to fly, and returned about three hours later. After a few more sessions, I was up for my certification ride.

The flight check replicated maneuvers we had practiced in training, culminating in an ILS approach under the hood (no outside reference) to "minimums" (the lowest altitude permitted to establish visual contact with the runway), followed by a missed approach and a visual approach and landing using only three engines. The examiner always "failed" (shut down) an outboard engine to make the exercise more demanding. Even with full rudder trim, when pulling power from the remaining engines you practically had to stand on the rudder to maintain your heading.

As of September 7, I was a qualified Connie copilot released to the line, immediately placed on reserve. There was much more to learn, and the captains I'd be flying with now were very senior and not as tolerant of inexperience as my DC-3 captains were. They were accustomed to having an experienced copilot in the right seat, and did not relish the role of instructor. Norm Hunter, alias "Daddy Warbucks," was a case in point. By this time, many experienced Connie copilots had joined the ranks as captains themselves.

MSP! (Minneapolis-St. Paul)

30 days TDY! (Assignment away from one's permanent domicile was TDY, "temporary duty.") I had never been to the Twin Cities before; what a panorama! It was so expansive, and it was awesome to fly up the Mississippi River, paralleling it all the way from La Crosse, Wisconsin during our letdown for landing at Minneapolis.

Ten complete crews — captains, copilots and flight engineers — were transferred from Washington to fill in during MSP's transition to Viscounts. Then it would become another all-Viscount base like New Orleans and Norfolk. Now we understood what the emphasis on Connie training was all about.

We didn't have much time to prepare, since I was scheduled to fly my first Minneapolis trip on September 15. What about Margaret? And what should I take with me?

I worked it all out because I had to. It was my dream to fly for the airlines, right? Well, yes, but it would be nice to be able to catch one's breath. My new home was the Nicollet Hotel in downtown Minneapolis, and Margaret returned to Mom and Dad's for the duration. The really good news was the extra money I would make being on full expenses when not flying. There was an air of excitement about it, something decidedly new.

The airline history at Minneapolis as it pertained to Capital — and, of course, its ultimate effect on me — is noteworthy. In terms of air service for the Twin Cities, Northwest Airlines was king. It had always been so, back to the airline's inception before the war. Subsequently the Civil Aeronautics Board decided that Northwest Airlines needed a little competition, since their equipment was marginal at best. Capital was providing reliable service in the Chicago, Detroit, and Milwaukee markets, so they awarded us a route extension to Minneapolis.

In the early '50s we inaugurated Constellation service, while Northwest was still operating DC-4s. They didn't appreciate our Connies outclassing their ancient deluxe bug smashers, so they acquired a small fleet of Boeing Stratocruisers.

The realm of the double-deck Stratocruiser, Model 377, was transoceanic travel, and Pan Am was its principal operator. United also operated a small fleet between the West Coast and Hawaii, and I had taken a picture of one during my brief stopover in Honolulu four years earlier.

Northwest's inauguration was probably the first application of these Boeings on domestic routes. They were very powerful, with 14,000 horsepower, and our Connies couldn't begin to keep up with them.

Who cares? Why did it matter to us what they flew? It mattered because Northwest scheduled their Detroit and Milwaukee departures later than ours and, utilizing their planes' superior performance, they arrived in Minneapolis before we did. The impact on Capital flights was Air Traffic Control's practice of vectoring our flights off the airway so Northwest could pass.

That rankled some of our captains like Ham (Hambone) Wilson. If we increased to climb power during the final stages of the flight, we would be just fast enough to prevent Northwest from passing. How fast was that? Almost 300 mph. We burned extra fuel in the process, so it was a stalemate. Now in late '56, we were introducing the Viscount. With its increased performance, it would be a game changer, and I was a very small part of that.

Horsepower and the Different Engines

Let me break away from the narrative briefly to describe the engines used on airliners of the mid-1950s. They were exclusively radials; by that I mean that the cylinders were arranged in a circular fashion, as opposed to being "in line" like those used in many fighter planes of WWII. Why radial? The simple answer was that they cooled more efficiently without the complexity of a closed system using a radiator. Also, streamlining was less important than compactness.

What about horsepower? That was where the radial design really shone. Want more power? Just add more rows of cylinders. They began with a single row, like those used on our DC-3s, and progressed to the giant 4-row Pratt & Whitney 3500 horsepower/4360 used on the Boeing Stratocruiser that Northwest Airlines now operated.

Another path to increased horsepower was supercharging. Instead of letting the engine "breathe" on its own, air was fed to the cylinders under pressure, thus compressing the air used for combustion. That feature was highly developed during WWII on bombers like the B-17 and B-29, since they required the capability of flying at very high altitudes. The superchargers used on the early bombers were the most primitive. They simply installed a turbine wheel in the exhaust pipe that compressed the air ducted to the engine.

When the B-29 was introduced, engines suddenly became much more complex. Those engines had two rows of nine cylinders and produced 2200 horsepower. Wright Aeronautical designed an internal supercharger to supply air under pressure, with one other wrinkle. It was two-stage, operating in one mode at low altitudes and another in the high-altitude strata of the atmosphere.

Capital Connies were equipped with B-29 engines. Those 3350-cubic-inch engines caused Uncle Sam such immense grief early on that the entire program was delayed for a year, attempting to resolve the overheating issues and resultant engine fires.

Even though extensive corrective measures were instituted, Capital had to live with the basic design flaws associated with the Wright 3350 engine. Boeing would have preferred to design the B-29 for Pratt & Whitney engines, but there just weren't enough to go around. It was the age-old battle between the Army and the Navy. All top-line Navy fighter planes used the P&W engine. Also, the Republic P-47 fighter and others were similarly equipped. The enormity of the B-29 program was another significant factor. Thus, the B-29 contract for engines went to Curtiss Wright by default.

We preferred to operate the Connies at high altitude (especially later on for the Miami run), but there was a catch. In order to shift the superchargers (also known as "blowers") to the high-altitude setting, it was necessary to reduce propeller RPM from the normal revolutions of 1850 down to 1600 to avoid failure of the "quill" shaft during the shift.

That procedure struck fear into some of our passengers, who were convinced the plane was going down. Those sitting behind the wing could actually see the propellers slowing down. In the interest of public relations, we often flew below 15,000 feet to keep the engines in low blower. Climbing any higher would necessitate a shift to high.

Later, as more and more Viscounts became available, the Connie was relegated to intercity (short-range) service, a far different role than that for which the plane had been designed. In connection with that, all of the inherent weaknesses of the B-29 engine were exacerbated in spades.

On-the-Job Training, Pure and Simple

There was no other way to describe what I was attempting to accomplish. Placing an inexperienced pilot like myself at the controls of a plane the size and complexity of the Lockheed Constellation was ludicrous. Yes, I demonstrated the basic skills, and knew how to get the beast on the ground in one piece. I could even do it under adverse weather conditions, but to fly the Connie in airline service with precision was quite another matter.

For example, when we were flying along and encountered a line of thunderstorms blocking our path, did we reverse course? Oh no; we would descend to 6000 or 7000 feet, reduce airspeed to 160 knots, and drive right through it. I've flown in rain so intense it seemed impossible for the engines to run, and a severe thunderclap at close range is an unforgettable experience.

I remember one captain in particular. Approaching an imposing line of thunderstorms, he would call for METO (maximum except take-off engine power). After reaching the far side of the storm, still intact, I asked, "Captain, why do you call for METO power when encountering such forbidding conditions?" His reply was, "Son, we aren't in it so long that way." Oh? That was an interesting perspective.

Developing the ability to assess adverse weather conditions, and then plan a course of avoidance, takes years to perfect. The fact that I spent so many years of my life in airplanes attests to the fact that I did achieve that ability — especially at the end, flying close to 40,000 feet in a DC-10 and deviating hundreds of miles based on observations and evaluating reports coming through my headset. In 1956, I didn't have that ability to deliver the smooth ride that everyone wants, so I was engaged in "on-the-job training."

There were two primary ways to learn: through experience and being taught. Experience was the best teacher, but it took too long. I would have appreciated more help from the captains sitting to my left. Some would lavish their expertise, while others refused to part with their trade secrets and hoarded them. I was dealing with very complex individuals; the best path to gaining useful information was through humility and diplomacy, and I worked at both of these devices. If one admits inadequacy at the initial encounter, human nature usually kicks in and assistance will be rendered.

An exception to that was working with Norm Hunter, a.k.a. "Daddy Warbucks." I tried everything I could think of to get along with him. He had already gotten one copilot fired, and I didn't want to be next. Daddy was king of the heap and egotistical beyond description.

He would buddy up to the flight engineer to gain an ally in his war against the occupant of the right seat. He needed the engineer, but not a copilot. At that time I had no control over whom I was assigned to fly with.

As it turned out, Daddy didn't either, and therein lay the core of the problem. For years he flew with seasoned copilots whom he enjoyed working with. And now, all of a sudden, his world was turned upside down with inexperienced copilots assigned to his flights. Some got along with him, and if he happened to like you, everything was fine.

Every day or so, I would be called out to fly. It wasn't like the DC-3 days, with multiple stops culminating in an eight-hour day. Many flights were quick turnarounds to Detroit and back, with a stop in Milwaukee. Some even scheduled a layover, returning the next day. Average flight time was only about three hours per day — one trip was all the way to New York and back, but that was an exception.

I finally finished TDY the end of October. I met some great guys in MSP, like Hambone Wilson, Russ Kirbert, Cal Jazzman, Jack Rigan and others. I learned a lot at MSP, but it would take time. I craved returning to Arlington, and Margaret.

Where was Margaret? In September Mom and Dad Taylor came to Arlington for a visit, and she returned to Erie with them. It was best for her to stay there during my temporary duty assignment. Our '54 Chevy remained parked at Washington National, just in case I needed it.

When the time came for Margaret to return to Arlington, Mom and Dad drove her to Buffalo to board a flight to Washington. Surprisingly, it was a National Airlines DC-6 at the termination of their seasonal operations in connection with the Washington-Buffalo-Miami interchange agreement.

The Capital/National Interchange

When I discussed route allocations by the Civil Aeronautics Board, I left out one small piece of the pie. That was under the heading of interchange agreements. The Board authorized Capital to enter into an agreement with National Airlines that benefitted both parties, due to the seasonal nature of the Miami-Buffalo air corridor. Under said agreement, Capital was permitted to fly Washington-Tampa-Miami during the winter months, and National flew Washington-Rochester-Buffalo during summer.

There was no swapping of planes or crews; we flew our Connies, and they flew their DC-6's; the schedules remained the same year-round. Their planes were newer and faster than ours, so they were always early flying our schedules. Conversely, since our planes were old and slow, we were always late using their schedules to Florida.

That scheduling practice should never have been permitted, because it legalized a violation of CAA flight-time regulations which stated that a pilot must not be scheduled to fly more than eight hours in any 24-hour period. The Miami run was a juicy plum for Washington-based Connie pilots, because we flew the trip nonstop to Miami as a one-day turnaround. Occasionally, flight time exceeded nine hours, which meant that on average our Connie crews only worked nine days per month with 21 days off. Schedules don't get any better than that.

Naturally, the Miami trips were awarded to the most senior pilots, but I was assigned on the basis of my reserve status. Because the airline was in flux, copilots who normally bid those trips were frequently unavailable, possibly sick but more likely in training, moving up to Captain.

That was great for me. I was able to fly to Miami, Jacksonville, and Tampa frequently on trips I could never dream of holding schedule on. The downside was that our top-seniority captains flew those schedules, and they didn't come to work to teach green copilots how to fly.

I never could understand why National agreed to trade Washington-Buffalo for DC to Florida. It was a very lopsided agreement. The schedule started on December 1, and my first Miami trip was one-way, deadheading there to fly a scheduled return.

When I arrived at Miami, I found myself reminiscing about my previous trip in February. If I hadn't applied at Eastern, I would never have met Paul Ferguson so that he could mail me that penny postcard making it possible for me to be back in Miami now.

The return trip took four hours and six minutes at 15,000 feet; my captain preferred not to shift blowers to climb higher. It was nice to see the airplane performing the type of mission it was designed for. I averaged one Florida trip per week — two more in the month of December and, of course, I flew other trips in between. I was home for Christmas, a rare event in my flying career, and then I was called out for a Miami layover returning New Year's Day — my introduction to 1957.

Worship in Arlington

After she was confirmed at St. Matthew's in Erie, Margaret was always a churchgoer. I drifted away from regular worship after being in the service, but once we were married, I joined St. Matthew's. When we were settled in Arlington, we began our search for a new church home. We located a Lutheran congregation nearby that held services at an elementary school. We met our lifelong friends the Hestons there: Bob, Ruth, and their two children, Linda and Bobby. They lived in Shirley Park as well, and we became close friends as well as fellow parishioners.

———

Spring returned and I continued honing my skills with the Connie. I hesitate to use the word routine, but that best describes most of my flights. I was gradually becoming more proficient, at least from the perspective of the copilot seat, and I met many interesting people along the way.

Even though the pressures that led to me relinquishing my copilot position to senior flight engineers no longer existed, I frequently exchanged places with the unfortunates sitting behind me. Most were delighted to learn that I was able to "work the panel" with competency so they could fly — of course, always with the captain's permission. It was usually okay with them as long as things ran smoothly. The word spread that "Lemmon is pretty good on the panel." I liked that. Mastering the pressurization and cabin heaters was the real challenge. If I erred with the heaters, the hostess bell would ring — "It's cold back here." Mishandling the pressurization was obvious to all on board.

This photo was taken during the winter of '57/'58 while flying the Connie on the Capital/National interchange between Washington and Miami.

Initially, the engineer would occasionally have to leave his copilot seat to stabilize things, but before long I was able to manage on my own. I did well starting and leaning the engines. Interpretation of the engine analyzer was tricky at first. A "shorted secondary" was the critical thing to watch for, because that meant both spark plugs on the affected cylinder had their electrodes hammered shut by a disintegrating piston or valve. Immediate shutdown of the engine was imperative to prevent fire.

Engine start, especially in hot weather, called for a delicate touch. Managing 2200 horsepower required precise technique, and miscalculations were readily apparent. Too much throttle resulted in a bang. Overpriming might cause a fire. It was really a good feeling to handle the engines proficiently. Working the panel was fine on a limited basis.

By spring, National once again took over the Florida route, and I was back flying New York-Chicago, with occasional flights to Detroit, Milwaukee and Minneapolis.

I had a little time off in March, so we flew to Erie for a visit. Employee passes for Margaret were restricted at first, but as we approached my one-year anniversary, she still had a few left.

During our stay, I visited with Mac and Earl at the airport. Earl's nephew, Lew Kane, was leaving Derion Aviation to take a job as an aircraft mechanic in Connecticut, and his replacement was Tom Apple, returning to Erie after a stint in Dallas, Texas.

Thomas Paul Apple

Tom made a distinct impression on the recreational side of my life as an airline pilot. I was always fascinated with people who had the ability to make and fix things. Up to that point my own efforts had been amateurish, going back to working on cars at Peach Street Auto.

Tom Apple and Gene Olson servicing Gene's new Beechcraft Bonanza, circa 1981. Picture taken at Derion Aviation in Erie, where Tom was employed.

He wouldn't answer to the name Thomas; in fact, I never heard anyone address him that way. He was always just Tom. He was born and raised in Saegertown, Pa. After graduating from high school, he was promptly drafted into the U.S. Army.

After being discharged, Tom attended The Pittsburgh Institute of Aeronautics (PIA) under the G.I. Bill to become an aircraft mechanic. After graduation, he worked a number of different places before finally ending up at Derion Aviation working for Earl, where he was employed for over 30 years.

I met Tom during our March '57 visit. Margaret enjoyed visiting her mom and dad, and that was fine with me, but I liked going out to the airport. Tom and I hit it off right away, and he invited me out to his house. On arrival, we went downstairs, where I was in for a shock.

Tom was rebuilding a Piper Cub in his basement! I was flabbergasted; how could you possibly build an airplane in the cellar? How would you get it out? Since his house was built on a hillside, I discovered later that he had an on-grade exit door to the back yard.

The Cub was drop-dead gorgeous. Tom had scrounged wings, a fuselage and tail group from wrecked or discarded hulks to come up with a finished plane. Tom was also a pilot, having owned a surplus Waco trainer in partnership with two other guys. Making less than $3.00 an hour, he needed to be resourceful to have "toys."

Instantly, I knew Tom was my kind of guy, and we became lifelong friends.

———

When summer arrived, I was finally off probation at Capital and got a $75 raise. That may not sound like much, but it was most welcome.

However, being off probation also meant that my temporary reprieve to avoid flight engineer duty lapsed. I was now eligible for a two-year draft, and as much as I enjoyed working the panel, I didn't want two long years of it. I sweated it out all summer, and dodged the bullet by only five seniority numbers; it was that close. Seniority really was a roll of the dice.

Believe it or not, I had Christmas off again, so we drove to Erie to enjoy the holiday. I recall putting an American Flyer train set under the tree for my nephew Scott.

1958

The itinerary of our Constellation flights was changing. Many of my trips in early '58 were Washington-Cleveland-Detroit-Milwaukee. These averaged only about three or four hours per day, flying out one day and back the next. For the schedule holder, it meant working more than 20 days per month — not a premier schedule. The downward spiral continued until the following year, when we were flying five days on with only two off. That translated to four nights in hotel beds for every three in my own.

DC-3 service was all but terminated. Short segments such as the "around the horn" trip through Buffalo and Erie and back to DCA were still in place, but that was all. All of our Viscounts had now been delivered, and that would have a direct impact on my immediate future.

Chapter 10

The Capital Viscount — Introduction to the Turbine World 1958-1961

It was my third airplane transition assignment in two years, but it did not come as a surprise. The company wanted as many pilots as possible to be "dual qualified." Proficiency checks would alternate between planes to assure currency. We will soon see an instance where I was briefly "triple qualified," but that was an unusual circumstance and not an entirely safe practice, even for second in command.

Viscount School

A new Capital Viscount that had just arrived from England, 1957. Note the black nose, indicating it was "radar equipped."

By early May, I was in Viscount Ground School, which was even more difficult than my most recent one for the Connie. The Rolls Royce jet engines were totally different from those on the other planes I had been flying. The engines were extremely smooth, although their high-pitched whine was troublesome (ear protection was a must for those working outside). The engines were very sensitive to high temperatures, especially on start. The propellers were also very different because after landing, the blades automatically went to zero pitch, acting as a brake to slow the plane. That feature was labeled "ground fine pitch."

Classroom work once again lasted approximately one week prior to advancing to the simulator. Unlike the Link Trainer, the Viscount simulator was a complete cockpit, just like the airplane. It could replicate everything except actually providing an airport environment for taking off and landing. That trainer was a precursor of even more exotic machines to be developed later.

Soon it was time to fly to Baltimore for training in the airplane. The instrumentation was state-of-the-art, incorporating a computerized steering needle into the approach system that refined the ILS approach to much tighter limits. (Future flight director systems would prove to be even more sophisticated.) The autopilot was excellent, and the first I had experienced that really worked. Next on the agenda was observer time to gain experience in line operation. I chose the Tobacco Road run that I had flown in the DC-3 with Paul Miller.

On May 26, coincidentally Margaret's birthday, I flew my first scheduled trip with Bill Lively. Not only was I taking on a new plane, I was entering an entirely new operational realm — middle- to high-altitude flying. Jet engines relished thin air.

When Capital initiated jet service, operational problems were a certainty. Because jet engines burned excessive fuel at lower altitudes, the Viscount normally operated between 15,000 and 20,000 feet. Everything was fine prior to the spring and summer of '57, but then Viscounts began sustaining hail damage at an alarming rate. In one or two instances, the leading edges of the wings were battered flat. The previous practice of descending to 6000 or 8000 feet for penetration of storms was no longer an option.

As a solution, Capital purchased Bendix weather radar for the portion of the fleet yet to be delivered, and also conducted classes for pilots on convective avoidance at high altitude. An additional resource not previously available was Air Traffic Control (ATC) radar. Even though their scopes were set up to blank out all but the most intense storm echoes, controllers were still able to detect the most severe areas and issue appropriate radar vectors for avoidance.

The last 30 Viscounts arrived from England with black noses, the visible sign of being radar equipped. The Bendix unit was a tremendous help, but with only half the fleet equipped, we had not solved the problem. Dispatchers did their best to route the planes with radar south and west, where the threat was greatest. Arguably, it was just a Band-Aid, but it was the best we could do.

Stress Aloft

I began flying the Viscount at the worst possible time of year, the start of thunderstorm season. On a typical flight during the period of maximum convection, the captain would be busy with the radar — which meant it was my job to take care of everything else. I had to fly, communicate and navigate. Fortunately, the autopilot was available and was, in many cases, indispensable. Even so, close coordination between the pilots and ATC was essential.

The radarscope was not ideally located on the forward panel, where it should have been for both pilots to be able to use it. Not having space there, they installed it at the far left of the cockpit where only the captain had access to it. He faced left when looking at the scope, instead of forward as he normally would. That odd placement resulted in the captain constantly turning his head to correlate the radar information with what was going on outside. Attempted use of the radar under bright daylight conditions exacerbated the problem even more.

So, along comes Ray, brand new on the airplane, struggling to cope with everything. We filed our flight plans above 15,000 feet whenever possible but, unfortunately, that was the portion of the atmosphere rife with convection and, worst of all, hail.

Adding to the stress was the fact that now I was flying with the most senior pilots on the airline, and some had little regard for compliance with our ATC clearance.

During a typical confrontation, my captain might say, "Get a clearance on Victor Airway so-and-so at such-and-such altitude and in the meantime we're on a heading of 240 degrees." I knew that such a clearance was impossible to obtain because of conflict with planes going the opposite direction or other reasons. Some captains refused to acknowledge the existence of one-way airways.

I didn't argue, and called the appropriate Air Traffic Control center as ordered. Naturally, the request was denied, but in the meantime my captain was flying off course in a direction we didn't have clearance for. In the most diplomatic terms possible, I would encourage him to return to our cleared route.

"We can't go that way; the weather is too bad. Declare an emergency and tell them we are on a heading of 240 degrees."

Then the fight with ATC would begin, and I was right in the middle of it. Talk about stress. The captain would prevail, of course, because he had just declared an emergency. The word "emergency" translates to priority, which might require vectoring other planes out of the way. Then there would be a pronouncement by the controller that he intended to file a report.

What should my captain have done instead? In the interest of safety, a pilot could always exercise his option to reverse course, and stand by for further clearance.

I flew Viscounts almost exclusively all summer, with an occasional Connie flight just to keep my hand in. By then, I had sufficient seniority to hold a Viscount schedule, which meant for the most part that I would fly with the same captain for the entire month.

Then came August '58, and who did I get? Norm Hunter, a.k.a. Daddy Warbucks. He had been the scourge of new Connie copilots just two years earlier. When I discovered I was scheduled to fly with him for the entire month I first considered calling in sick, but then I said to Margaret, "What the heck — the worst he can do is fire me."

What a difference! Norm was a changed man, nice as apple pie. He no longer had an engineer to buddy up to, so now he needed his copilot. I still treated him with kid gloves, and at some point during the month he asked me, "Do I scare you?" I didn't quite know how to answer that one, but before long I started to feel quite at home working with "Daddy," and we got along fine.

California Visit

In the fall of '58, the International Association of Machinists (IAM) struck Capital, and I was furloughed for the duration of the work stoppage. Since I was unemployed anyway, Margaret and I decided to take a trip to California. She had never been there, and I told her how much PG Fellmeth and I had enjoyed our visit there four years earlier.

TWA offered space-available passes, at ten dollars each, for transcontinental service out of Washington National with the latest and greatest Connie, the 1649 Starliner, nonstop to Los Angeles. What a plane! It had a new wing and the latest Wright turbo-compound engines with PRTs (power recovery turbines). Earlier, we had gone over to the airport just to see it; now we were anticipating an opportunity to fly in it.

On October 10 we went for the flight, and fortunately first class was wide open. It was a smooth ride, but because of headwinds the flight took almost nine hours. We stayed at a Hyatt House Motel, and the next day we rented a VW Bug. We went to Disneyland, Knott's Berry Farm and other attractions in the L.A. Basin.

Then, to replicate my national park tour of '54, we boarded an older TWA Connie for Fresno. We had a great time hiking and climbing a trail from Yosemite Valley to Glacier Point. Hiking down was much easier, but even so, the hike left us lame. The next day we were both hobbling around the airport for the flight to San Francisco.

Once again I was unable to meet with my brother and sister, as neither was in town during our visit. After touring the Bay Area, we flew back home with just enough time to squeeze in an Erie trip before the strike ended. Except for an occasional Connie flight, all my flying for the remainder of the year was in the Viscount.

I bid a Connie schedule for December to get Christmas off, and it turned into a month of misery because it was the old five-on-and-two-off pairing. I was almost never home.

As my experience with the airline grew, I almost always bid to work on Christmas, and then I was able to fly the best schedule in the base.

Happy 1959? No, a Year to Forget

My March schedule was on the Viscount with a layover in Mobile, Ala. It was delightful, and the entire crew visited Bellingrath Gardens while the park was abloom. Welcome, spring '59.

Back home in Arlington, Margaret was sick, and at first I thought she would get well on her own. She wasn't sick-in-bed sick, and we were still able to go to the Jefferson Memorial and enjoy the Japanese cherry blossoms. Eventually, though, she went to the doctor, who promptly referred her to an internal medicine specialist.

It was her old nemesis, ulcerative colitis. Margaret had suffered with it many years earlier as a child of fourteen. It is an autoimmune disease, impossible to cure. In 1945 Mom and Dad feared for her life, but she slowly regained a measure of health. I qualified that because she continued to have recurring attacks from time to time. I mentioned earlier that she had given up college at Thiel for reasons of health.

Occasionally, while working at the lab, I would see her doubled over with pain. In essence, it was a disease that caused the body to be at war with itself by rejecting its own viscera; thankfully, the disease was confined to the large intestine.

Her internist continued to be optimistic. He believed he could successfully treat her with diet and medications utilizing new treatments. It turned out that he was wrong and she got worse and worse, ultimately ending up in Doctors' Hospital in downtown Washington, D.C.

Then I received a horrible shock. Capital's hospitalization benefits were grossly inadequate, designed primarily to assist with childbirth. Suddenly, I was personally responsible for all Margaret's medical expenses for both the physicians and the hospital. Needless to say, I was devastated.

She was hospitalized for nearly a month, constantly losing ground, getting thinner and thinner. Her weight was down to 87 pounds from her normal of 120. The outlook was grim indeed, and I feared for her life. Mom and Dad Taylor came from Erie to be by her side.

Eventually her internist announced he was referring her case to a surgical group. By that time, the only way to save Margaret's life was to perform an ileostomy.

According to Wikipedia, an ileostomy is "a surgical opening constructed by bringing a loop of small intestine (the ileum) out onto the surface of the skin, allowing gastrointestinal waste to leave the body through this outlet. A bag, called an ileostomy pouch, is then attached to the skin to collect the waste."

Even with my fairly comprehensive medical background, I had no knowledge of this procedure. The operation isolated the small intestine from the colon, which meant Margaret would have to wear an appliance (bag) for the rest of her life. That's why they allowed her to descend to such depths of physical despair. We all needed to realize that this life-altering procedure was Margaret's only option to survive. The decision was made by the three of us, as Margaret was unable to comprehend the implications.

A blood transfusion was administered prior to Dr. Carlos Dominguiz performing the surgery. The operation was brief, of necessity, since she couldn't endure much more. Afterward, Dr. Dominguiz said everything went well and she would be out of recovery soon. Margaret was going to live.

Financially, we were a basket case, and I even considered selling our car to raise money. The Taylors stepped up to the plate by mortgaging their house to raise $5000. We were now deeply in debt. Frances Case sent us $500.

After a period of rehabilitation, Margaret would be facing even more extensive surgery to remove her diseased colon. Was there any good news in the midst of all the bad? In fact, there was.

As a result of our catastrophic health insurance experience, and some others as well, Capital adopted massive improvements to its hospitalization plan. I think the Air Line Pilots Association (ALPA) had a hand in it as well. By the time Margaret returned to the hospital in September, she was fully covered.

I reflected back to 1955, when Margaret and I were in the receiving line at St. Matthew's church on our wedding day and Mother Taylor asked me to "Take care of her." Those four little words were so general in nature that I failed to detect the undertone. Somewhere, deep in her heart of hearts, Mom knew this day would come. In the excitement of our marriage, Margaret enjoyed a brief remission, but the eventual outcome was not to be denied.

Before getting too mired down in grief and despair, we must realize that Margaret went on to live a full and productive life for almost 80 years before succumbing to health issues totally unrelated to her bowel disorder.

What Margaret needed most was TLC. She did stage a remarkable recovery in spite of the diseased colon still inside her which, in its dormant non-functioning state, actually attempted to heal itself. In some cases, it was possible to reconnect it and return to normal function, but that was a rarity. Post-op examination revealed that it was far too damaged to ever function again.

Margaret returned to our apartment by ambulance. Although walking was impossible for her at that point, she had an appointment to see Dr. Dominguiz in just two weeks, and he wasn't making a house call. He felt certain that she would be ambulatory by then, and fully capable of handling an office visit.

In 1959, ostomy support groups were in their infancy, and those companies making appliances and other products for maintenance were in an embryonic state. While Margaret was still in the hospital recovering, a nice young woman stopped by to visit her.

Appearing normal in all respects, and leading a full, dynamic life, she told Margaret that she too had an ileostomy. That visit probably did more to bolster Margaret's well-being than any medicine she could have received. The realization that a return to normal life was possible was most inspiring.

Mother Taylor stayed with us for an indefinite period. Margaret utilized the services of a private-duty nurse three days a week to supervise her recovery. The cost was $300. I paid Doctor's Hospital $1100 at the time of her discharge. The cost for the ambulance to bring her home to Virginia was 15 bucks.

The purpose of this itemization is mainly to point out the different medical world we lived in at that time. Dad returned to Erie by himself to resume his managerial position. Everyone was making sacrifices, and I wondered if we would ever get out of debt.

Doctors Claude & Dominguiz charged $315 for both operations, and the total colectomy was a six-hour operation. I continued to fly through this entire period because it was imperative that I do so. Sick-leave benefits were miniscule at that time.

Back at the apartment, Margaret staged an amazing recovery. After just a few days she was up and about, and a few days later she was exploring the stairwell outside our apartment. She knew that she needed to be able to navigate those stairs in just over a week. Before long, she was making it down to the landing and back. As predicted, she was able to keep her office appointment with Dr. Dominguiz.

Freed from the debilitating effects of her diseased colon, her body couldn't wait to recover. It took time, but with her mother's care (and cooking), Margaret's resiliency prevailed. Norma Fowler, her nurse, made a significant contribution by being well versed in ileostomy care.

One day, I stepped into Mom's room for something, and I could see she had been crying — she was obviously homesick. By mid-July it was evident Helen needed to return to Erie to be with Dad, and he came down the following weekend to take her home. Once released from Dr. Dominguiz's care, Margaret might be able to fly to Erie; however, she wasn't sufficiently recovered to withstand the car trip with Mom and Dad.

So, at the end of July, I put Margaret on a DC-3 bound for Erie. It was certainly going to be lonely by myself in the apartment, but Margaret needed her mom in order to gain strength for major surgery in September. I would fly to Erie to visit as often as possible.

Re-qualification — Back to the DC-3

During Margaret's ordeal, there was some good news for Capital Airlines. The CAB awarded us the long-sought-after Great Lakes-to-Florida route, and it was to have a tremendous impact on my career. Implicit in the award was the authority to fly unrestricted from Buffalo, Cleveland, and Pittsburgh to all major Florida cities including Jacksonville, Tampa-St. Petersburg, West Palm Beach, and Miami. That was a critical development, positively saving my airline piloting career. It would take awhile for implementation, but we should see something toward the end of the year.

Even with that sensational news, the airline was in turmoil. The red ink was so deep, everything looked pink. Part of the demise was attributed to the recession of the past two years, but Capital's financial woes ran much deeper. We weren't able to pay Vickers Aircraft for the planes, and they began repossession proceedings.

The Viscount was no longer competitive against the new pure-jet transports. Slim Carmichael entered into an agreement with De

Havilland to buy Comets, but that deal fell through for a number of reasons, one being an increasing tendency for them to crash. I'm sure that cost us money, as all such ventures do.

Other Band-Aid measures were explored, such as leasing a fleet of late-model DC-6s from Pan Am. Six brand-new Lockheed Electras, painted in the new Capital livery, were sitting on the ramp at Lockheed's Burbank facility awaiting delivery. Ultimately, we lost our deposit on those as well.

It was a whole pattern of deficit spending that resulted in drastic schedule cutbacks system-wide, and the Washington domicile was on the cusp of these reductions. For me, the decision was to either fly reserve on the Viscount, or re-qualify on my old friend, the DC-3. I chose the latter.

We still flew the "around the horn" trip pairing that was good for a seven-hour day. It was one of the last schedules remaining for the ancient bird. A schedule like that would provide sufficient consecutive days off to visit Margaret.

In order to bid a DC-3 schedule, I needed to re-qualify. A group of us took a plane with an instructor to Baltimore, where we made three takeoffs and landings. That was it, and I was re-qualified on the DC-3.

What a step backward! The noise was awful; it was an antique that should have been relegated to a museum. The DC-3 had a tail wheel, and that made landings "interesting." Altogether, I flew it about 50 hours and my last flight was September 28, with a Buffalo layover. I called Margaret's sister Nancy to come to the airport to see our old airplane. They brought the kids and we had a great time. During the month of September '59, I flew all three planes I was qualified on: the DC-3, Connie, and Viscount. It was the only time during my entire career that I was "triple qualified."

Hostess Hazing

One of the DC-3 trips was with Capt. Ray Newsom. Ray was a member of our TDY Connie group that had gone to Minneapolis three years earlier. At that time he was a flight engineer, and now he was my captain for the sequence around the horn. We enjoyed flying together again, and Ray was part of a great story about the DC-3.

We were peacefully flying along on the way to Williamsport, Pa., when there was a knock at the door.

The Wobble Pump

It was the hostess asking permission to flush the "john." Simultaneously, she actuated the wobble pump handle situated between our seats, and then without saying another word, closed the door and left. I looked at the other Ray, and he looked at me, and we both burst out laughing. It was a trick the pilots used to play on new stewardesses, fresh out of hostess training.

The scenario went something like this:

The captain calls the hostess to the cockpit for a briefing and tells her that when anyone uses the toilet in the back, she must immediately come to the cockpit and flush it. In reality, it's a chemical unit with absolutely no plumbing whatsoever. The captain shows her the wobble pump handle, and demonstrates the "flushing" procedure. The wobble pump is a hand-operated fuel pump used for starting the engines; except for temporarily raising the fuel pressure, operating it in flight does absolutely nothing.

Where's the Pilot?

Capt. Ray said, "This gal is new; let's have some fun with her." Sure enough, she came up to the cockpit twice more before landing in Rochester to "flush" the toilet, and we went along with the gag. After arriving at ROC, Ray went down the aisle to the rear door and told the hostess he was going to the terminal for something and would be right back.

Once outside the plane, he observed the ground crew loading baggage in the forward compartment using a belt loader. Instead of going inside the terminal, Ray climbed up the belt and got back in the captain's seat. None of that baggage area was visible from the passenger cabin.

After everything was buttoned up, the passenger agent gave us the hand signal to start engines. About the time we cranked the right one, there was a furious pounding on the cockpit door, with the hostess screaming that we mustn't leave yet because the captain was not on board.

Ray ignored her protestations, and she eventually went back to checking passenger seat belts. Fifteen minutes later we arrived in Buffalo.

Captain Ray alerted ground personnel to bring a belt loader to the forward baggage door immediately. They had seen this before, so they gleefully complied.

Ray scampered down the belt, and pounded on the rear door for the hostess to open up. When she opened the door, there was her missing captain.

"I ran all the way and didn't know if I could catch up," Ray exclaimed. I thought we were going to have to call an ambulance. I don't know if she ever figured it out, but the Buffalo gang was splitting their sides.

Buffalo

It was time for Margaret to return to Arlington. She had regained 15 pounds and appeared to be the picture of health. Driving to Arlington, she remarked on the impending surgery and how she dreaded returning to the hospital. But the surgery was not an option for her, because she still had that diseased colon inside and it had to come out. Her pre-op visit with Dr. Claude was very positive, and he was delighted with her progress over the summer.

"Margaret will come through just fine," he said. She did do fine, but we underestimated the impact the operation would have on her. It took over three months of recuperation for her to return to the level of wellness she had achieved in Erie. She really needed her mom again, but we managed. Then I received a surprise phone call from the flight office.

"Would you still like to transfer to Buffalo? We're moving most of the Connie flying up there in connection with the Great Lakes-to-Florida route award." It only took me about ten seconds to reply, "Sure, I'll go." It wasn't necessary to consult Margaret, because I knew she would be thrilled.

"Okay, pack your bags; you'll start up there December 15."

Initially, when I hired on with Capital, I filled out a form denoting my preference for domicile assignment. I had put Buffalo at the top of the list, never expecting to go there because it was a small base and very senior. The plan called for 12 lines of flying with all Florida destinations, and since I was a fairly senior copilot on the Connie by now, it should work out fine.

Margaret *was* delighted at the prospect of living near her sister, Nancy, whom she adored — and it wasn't far from Erie, either, which meant it would be easier for me to visit Tom Apple.

Still in the recuperative phase of her recovery, Margaret was not able to help much with the packing. This time the ball was in my court. In early December we loaded the car with fragile, hard-to-pack items and drove to Erie. Fortunately, our lease was up at the end of the year, so we weren't penalized. But where were we going to live in Buffalo?

"For now, we'll just move in with Mom and Dad," Margaret suggested.

Within a month, though, we rented a brand-new apartment at 1015 Wehrle Drive in Williamsville, a suburb of Buffalo near the airport. Having only one car, being close to work was always a top priority. By Christmas we were settled, and it was nice to be living near family again.

———

Although I came to fly Connies, my first BUF trip was on the Viscount to Newark, with Les Gallagher. My first Connie flight was not until after Christmas, and that was a Tampa layover. Dual qualification really did enhance utilization.

Flying out of Buffalo in winter was no piece of cake, and I had my share of canceled trips. January was all Viscount flying, but not to Florida as I had expected; it was to New York and Chicago. February was much the same, except at the end of the month I was back on the Connie again with Florida destinations. Between trips, we frequently drove to Erie to visit Mom and Dad. Now it was only 90 miles instead of 400. Even though I expected to fly Connies in Buffalo, the first half of 1960 was predominantly Viscount.

Life in Buffalo was relaxed and the summer was great, with many trips to Erie to visit Mom and Dad, and frequent excursions for me to the airport and Tom's house.

Tom Apple was finishing the Cub in his basement, and he expected it to be ready to assemble at the airport by spring. There were a few glitches for him to work through, but overall the project was nearing completion.

I wished I could rebuild a plane myself, but we simply couldn't afford it at the time. Until the mortgage on Mom and Dad's house was paid off, I would have to remain a spectator. We were still deeply in debt, and it would take several years for us to achieve solvency.

The Airline Industry, 1960

Please permit me to digress for a moment on Capital's financial woes dating back to the previous year. At that time I spoke about the increasing difficulty for Capital Airlines in meeting its financial obligations. My retrograde movement to fly the DC-3 was evidence of the downward spiral, and the company's desperate moves to stop the bleeding were to no avail. Slim Carmichael was out, and a General Baker was the new president.

A year later, the situation had worsened to the point that our very existence was threatened. Vickers began repossessing the Viscounts one by one and flying them back to England. Capital was awash in red ink.

Even our recent Florida award, received with such hope and expectation, failed to produce a meaningful turnaround. The handwriting was on the wall, and by the summer of 1960 the specter of Chapter 7 bankruptcy was a distinct possibility. Chapter 11 was for reorganization; Chapter 7 was closing the doors. Capital's financial situation was desperate indeed.

A last-ditch effort to launch Capital into the jet age was a temporary lease agreement with United Air Lines to operate Boeing 720 jets (an intercity version of the much heavier 707) between New York, Atlanta, and New Orleans. Jet service on our Cleveland, Pittsburgh, and Miami route was also included in the deal. The 720s remained painted with United's corporate logo, but Capital pilots were checked out to fly them.

By the summer of 1960, a feeling of despair was creeping in. Some of the Buffalo captains (like OV Pezzi) were exploring job possibilities in the corporate aviation world. It certainly didn't look promising.

The current management team introduced a new paint livery. The red bird was gone forever, a casualty of the times. Eleven DC 6Bs leased from Pan Am were painted with our new corporate logo.

Other big news that summer was in Chicago: The shift from Midway to O'Hare had begun in earnest. Midway Airport was inadequate for the volume of jet traffic now in place, and a coordinated move by all the majors was imperative to prevent chaos. By then, Capital was a minor player, but we still established a presence at the new airport.

Chicago's O'Hare Airport began its life as Orchard Airport back in the 1930s. When the decision was reached to convert it into Chicago's primary municipal airport, it was renamed in honor of Butch O'Hare, the heroic Grumman Wildcat Navy pilot of WWII.

Some airlines continued to serve both airports, but with the inauguration of pure jet service, O'Hare became the hub.

Since Capital obviously couldn't survive independently, the search had already begun for a merger partner. Under CAB jurisdiction, airline mergers were tricky and fraught with peril. Most attempts simply failed miserably. It was around this time that rumors of a Capital-United merger began to surface.

Although most of the industry's major players rejected the idea out of hand, there were two important reasons for United's interest in partnering with us. Primarily, it was to reduce competition on the New York-Chicago route, and secondly: Florida. Without our recent award for service to the Sunshine State, there would have been no merger and Capital would have gone under like so many others of recent times.

Chances of finding another flying job in that environment would have been miniscule at best, especially since I didn't have an ATR. (ATR was the abbreviation for Airline Transport Rating, needed for a flying job anywhere outside of the ranks of scheduled airlines and especially in the world of corporate flying.)

Capital's contract with ALPA specified that all copilots, upon reaching their fifth anniversary, would be offered the opportunity to upgrade to Captain. Facilities necessary to achieve that important goal would be provided; however, said applicants were required to complete the written requirements on their own prior to training. On the first of June, 1961, I would be celebrating that magic fifth anniversary, and I was well aware of my obligation to complete the "writtens" at the earliest opportunity.

During the summer of 1960, I started taking the exams at the nearest FAA district office located in Rochester, 60 miles away. I passed everything except Meteorology, and I had a terrible time with that. I think I took it three times, with a 30-day waiting period in between. Somehow I had the notion that warm air was unstable, when the reverse is true. I had been warned that failure to pass it after three attempts could invalidate my Commercial Pilot's License, at which time I would be grounded. I hit the books with renewed vigor, and finally passed.

By the end of the year, serious discussion centered on the merger with United. Evidently it was really going to happen. What a break for me; what a break for us all.

Apparently, I had flown my last trip on the Connie. From that point on, all my trips were on the Viscount, and none were to Florida. The company had recently established a domicile in Miami, and thus much of the Connie flying formerly out of Buffalo was now flown from Florida on Viscounts. Our faithful old Connies were relegated to the boneyard at Easton, Maryland.

For a time, an attempt was made to fly Viscounts nonstop from Cleveland to Miami. To make it, they had to fly at 24,000 feet, and that was just too high for the turboprop. Due to the prevailing southerly winds, it turned into a fiasco; the flights frequently had to stop in Jacksonville to refuel. Northbound was not a problem, but the fuel stop flying south killed it. By 1961, the Viscount was obsolete for long-haul flights.

Merger Day

Spring '61 was a glorious time, and I'm sure the rosy job outlook contributed to our euphoria. It had been so turbulent and uncertain for such a long time; it was nice just to relax and contemplate our future at United Air Lines.

On a side note, Tom Apple finally succeeded in getting the Cub out of his basement, and flew it at every opportunity. It was a beautiful restoration job, attracting attention everywhere he went. We spent much of my free time in Erie, so whenever I had a few consecutive days off, we went to visit. When we stayed in our Williamsville apartment, we saw a lot of sister Nancy's family in Tonawanda. They had just broken ground for their new home on Lorelee Drive.

As M-Day, June 1, approached, anticipation increased. United sent coordination teams to all Capital domiciles to brief pilots and station personnel on plans for the transition. However, the outlook was chaotic at best. It *was* nice to know the bills were getting paid, and so far as I know, no one's paycheck bounced — but there was anxiety, and occasional rumors to the contrary.

I was on a trip to Chicago that magical day, and O'Hare was a nightmare. Since our flight dispatch office no longer existed, we were unable to get a release for our flight to New York. Because all of the United fuel trucks were loaded with high-octane gasoline, we couldn't locate fuel either.

Taking matters into our own hands, we found Capital personnel out on the ramp and drove to our hangar, where we found a kerosene truck. We fueled the Viscount ourselves the old-fashioned way, over the wing, and my uniform reeked of fuel for the rest of the trip. Once that was accomplished, we convinced United ramp service personnel to round up our Buffalo/Rochester passengers and then we simply loaded up and took off, bypassing the entire UAL dispatch system at O'Hare.

We had no flight release, but all we really needed was weight and balance data, and we were able to get that from the Capital station personnel still on duty. Fortunately, it was summer and the weather was good. All our flights that day used a special call sign — UNICAP, for United/Capital, followed by the flight number. ATC was not a problem; I think they were enjoying our chaotic operation.

Subsequently, I had a week off while United attempted to sort out the mess. UAL issued all-new wings and hat insignia for our Capital uniforms. It would be some time before everyone had complete UAL issue.

Whatever happened to Capital Airlines? The merger that had been announced July 28, 1960, saved our company from bankruptcy, and Capital ceased to exist after June 1, 1961.

Chapter 11

The United-Capital Merger
1961-1964

Let's take a look at the new United Air Lines. It was a bold move to merge the second- and fifth-largest airlines into the nation's first mega-carrier in aviation history. Until then, American Airlines had always been the biggest, and arguably the best in the business. Looking at United's combined statistics, we find: 30,275 employees, almost 3000 pilots, 18,000 route miles, 264 planes, serving 118 cities.

The airplane inventory consisted of 36 Douglas DC-8s, 18 Boeing 720s, 41 Vickers Viscounts, 39 Douglas DC-7s, 87 Douglas DC-6s, 27 Convairs, and three DC-3s. Also included was an assortment of 13 DC-6 and DC-7 cargo-liners. How's that for a serious fleet of airplanes?

These numbers disregarded Capital's 10 Constellations and a like number of DC-4s that would never display the United logo. They were flown to the airline graveyard at Easton, Md.

Merging Crew Bases and Domiciles

The impact on crew bases was consolidation and elimination. Buffalo, Detroit, Minneapolis, Norfolk, New Orleans, and Boston were all slated for closure. Chicago and New York would be combined. Pittsburgh was retained as a Viscount domicile for the present, and Newark was slated for expansion utilizing relocated personnel from Boston.

As for the District of Columbia, the recently dedicated Dulles International Airport (IAD) would replace Baltimore Friendship as

Washington's jetport. Pure-jet operations at Washington National (DCA) were not anticipated at first, but new smaller jets like the Boeing 737 and DC-9 would eventually be accepted there.

The Washington, D.C. domicile was permanent, and the western domiciles at Denver, Los Angeles, San Francisco, and Seattle were not affected by the merger.

Prior to the merger, Capital established a Miami crew base in connection with the Florida route award, and they had been flying the 11 DC-6Bs leased from Pan Am. Miami was projected to remain as a domicile indefinitely. After the Pan Am aircraft were returned, Miami continued to be a Viscount domicile until 1965, when Capital pilots were permitted to fly jets.

A major provision of merging the pilot seniority lists was that Capital pilots were ineligible to bid any pure-jet openings for four years. To understand why that stipulation was incorporated, it was necessary to examine the Capital pilot seniority structure. A large percentage of Capital's pilots were old-timers, so if they took their position on the combined list based solely on date of hire, United's pilot group would suffer grievously. That provision also provided a way for United to maintain the status quo and avoid horrendous training costs. The end result was that even though we kept our jobs, most Capital pilots faced stagnation, in both assignment to more desirable airplanes and the pay increases implied therein.

My seniority number was 2150 on a roster of 3000. I was hoping for a lower one, but it was for the most part based on date of hire. Some unfairness did emerge when Pete McIntosh, my new-hire classmate, ended up ahead of me on the combined list. That had future ramifications when we were both flying the DC-10, based in New York. In retrospect, an appeal on my part might have been in order.

My new employee number (file number) was 89628. All Capital pilots were "89ers." The last three digits were our Capital seniority number. Today, not many 89ers are left, but OV Pezzi, now 90 years of age, lives just down the street from me.

Moving to New York
With the closure of the Buffalo domicile, Margaret and I were faced with another move; so what else was new? We tried not to let

it ruin our summer but, inevitably, it affected everything we did. The first order of business was to buy another car — nothing fancy, mind you, just a beater for me to use at LaGuardia Airport, since Margaret would need our car in Williamsville until we moved. Finding something affordable seemed impossible, since we were so deeply in debt.

While poking around a local used car lot, I found a '54 Chevy four-door — a snow-belt rust bucket that was amazingly clean inside. It was blue with a white top, and the paint was good except for the rusty sheet metal. The asking price was $200; I offered $150 and it was accepted, State Inspection and a brake job included.

The company granted time off from work to house-hunt in the New York area. The consensus was that living in New Jersey was preferable, largely because of the horrendous tax structure in the Empire State.

Limiting our search to Bergen County, we saw an ad in the *Bergen Record* newspaper for new Cape Cod homes in the town of Wood-Ridge, near Teterboro Airport. The houses had two bedrooms and a basement that incorporated a one-car garage. The upstairs was unfinished, suitable for storage only. After living in apartments for five years, it seemed like a palace. The rent was $145, with the option to buy for $19,900. We signed up on the spot, and since occupancy was flexible, we planned to move in on October 1.

After Labor Day I left Williamsville in the old Chevy, and stayed at the LaGuardia crew lounge until I found a room to rent in Jackson Heights. Two weeks later, I returned to Williamsville to close up and drive to our new home in New Jersey. United footed the bill for all expenses connected with the move.

As a matter of necessity, I became familiar with the George Washington Bridge, Grand Central Parkway, and Harlem River Drive. After bitter experience during rush hour, I also set a deadline for crossing the GW Bridge no later than 7:30 a.m., no matter what time my flight left.

Rumors were circulating that the LaGuardia domicile would soon close, and all New York propeller operations would be moving to Newark — I could hardly wait.

The weather in New York was a huge improvement over Buffalo; crippling snowstorms in the metropolitan area were infrequent. All

157

my flights were across the northern tier: Cleveland, Detroit, Chicago, Philadelphia and Washington, D.C. I didn't have a single trip to Florida all winter long.

I finally had a Memphis layover. So many stories circulated about the ducks at the Peabody Hotel: The hosteller accommodated wealthy guests who kept pet ducks in their suite. Periodically, the house servant would bring them down the elevator and through the lobby on their way outside. We arrived at just the right time to experience this spectacle. There were about six ducks, and they paraded single-file to the front doors, quacking as they marched. For years I had heard stories about the Peabody ducks, and now I finally had a chance to see them in action.

Captain Training at DENTK

Early in 1962, I received a directive from the Newark flight office confirming my assignment to the United Flight Training Center in Denver (DENTK), March 1, for upgrade to Captain and transition to the Douglas DC-6. It was my long-anticipated promotion, but the last thing I would have expected was to be checked out in the DC-6.

Since all the affected Capital copilots had extensive experience on the Viscount, I logically assumed that would be the airplane of choice for my "upgrading." I guess United wasn't logically inclined, because it was going to be their way in Denver, on the DC-6.

Class TU-4 ran for six to eight weeks, and wives were strongly advised to stay home. The demands of the course were such that any distraction could be exceedingly detrimental. Few Capital First Officers had ever flown the DC-6. Yes, there was new terminology at United Air Lines: there were no copilots and engineers anymore. Now we were First and Second Officers.

What was the interpretation of the Class TU-4 designation? It was Transition to the DC-6 airplane including Upgrade to Captain. Mine was the fourth of those contractual classes thus far. United insisted that all future captains receive their training at DENTK, on a plane with which they were very familiar.

A United Air Lines DC-6, circa 1966. This is the plane I trained
on in 1962 to attain my ATR. It was a reliable transport and
served with United for almost 20 years. The DC-6B variant
was very deluxe and identical to the one I rode on in 1952 for
my flight from San Francisco to Cleveland, returning home
from Japan.

Rumors circulated that DENTK held Capital pilots in low
esteem, dating back to B-720 transition before the merger. Rowdy,
undisciplined, discourteous, disrespectful, and inarticulate were some
of the adjectives used to describe our group. Is it any wonder they had
reservations about upgrading such people to the rank of "Captain"?

It was no secret that the TU course was DENTK's toughest, and
not all made it through. The understanding was that if you didn't
pass, you would be terminated. How's that for a stress builder?

Why was it so difficult? Because it was a combined course
including both Transition to the DC-6 airplane and Upgrading
from First Officer to Captain. In other words, it was a double dose
of training, and a brief outline of the course follows:

The ground school portion (airplane systems and operation) lasted
for three weeks; it was very intensive and detailed. United demanded
a much higher level of aircraft systems knowledge than Capital's
one-week blitz. The classroom work was followed by six simulator
periods of two hours each. Graduation from the ground portion
progressed to flight training, and up to 10 hours in the airplane were

programmed. What was the cost of the course? I can't even imagine. The DC-6 airplane consumed 400 gallons of 100-octane fuel each hour. Doing the math, it comes out to at least 4000 gallons for each student. Staggering!

Returning to real time for attending Class TU-4, Margaret planned to stay in Erie with Mom and Dad during my Denver stint. In late February we drove to Buffalo together, where I boarded a DC-6B bound for Chicago. My most memorable trip in this airplane had been ten years earlier, when I returned from Japan. This time, I was advised to ride in the cockpit for familiarization purposes. Unfortunately, the DC-6 was approaching obsolescence. In just five short years, the Boeing 737 would sound its death knell, and I would play a key role in its demise.

At O'Hare, I was booked, first class, on a Boeing 720 flight bound for Denver, and guess who I ran into? It was Paul Ferguson (the penny postcard guy), and comparing paperwork, we were surprised to learn that we were assigned to the same class. Since Paul was senior to me, such a coincidence would have been unlikely, and it happened only because the company delayed his release from line flying due to schedule commitments. That was a stroke of good luck for me, because Paul had been flying DC-6 Second Officer for over a year. He knew the airplane inside out, so ground school would be a breeze for him, and a significant boost for me in the form of extracurricular tutoring.

That flight from Chicago to Denver was my first ride on the B-720. What a plane! What a meal! It was all very impressive, and I had never experienced such luxury before. United truly was a first-class airline.

Normally, our crews stayed at the Gotham Hotel in downtown Denver. But because of the heavy training schedule, United leased an apartment house across the street and named it Gotham West. Jesse Poole, Paul and I occupied one of the suites; they were quite spartan, but did include a kitchen. At times, we did our own cooking, mostly frozen dinners and take-out.

The class consisted of nine former Capital copilots, and it began the very next morning. During the ground school portion we all studied together, but upon completion of that, we split up into groups of three for the simulator phase.

The instructor began with orientation and an overview of the six-week course. We would study each aircraft system in detail, after which there would be an examination. Unlike the old DC-4, the "6" was pressurized and modernized in many other ways. All of this was a snap for Paul, so he just coasted. Evenings and weekends, he coached Jesse and me at the apartment. Much had to be committed to memory, especially emergency procedures. The Cabin Heater Fire Checklist consisted of 28 steps. And so it went, day after day, being inundated with more and more material we were responsible for.

Eventually ground school was over, and we moved on to the simulator. We were reduced to groups of three students and a flight instructor for each group. Those simulators were archaic, built by Curtiss Wright after WWII, so their usefulness was limited. They were most helpful doing cockpit set-ups, as the instrument panels were exact duplicates of the DC-6. By the time we flew the airplane, the panel was familiar to us.

The cockpit arrangement was nothing like the Connie, since there was no separate flight engineer station. The Second Officer sat facing forward behind and between the pilots. Since the DC-6's heritage dated back to the DC-4, there was no provision for flight engineers. After the war, the plane was upgraded with much more powerful engines (2000 horsepower vs. 1200), pressurization and a substantial gross weight increase. The CAA, in all their wisdom, mandated that all aircraft grossing more than 80,000 pounds must have a flight engineer as a member of the crew.

Ross Frederick, our instructor, briefed us at the beginning of flight training that the trainee not flying would take over the flight engineer position. Even though by that time we were well trained to manage the engines, some of the finer points were lacking. During our training flights at Stapleton Airport, we often saw our other DC-6 trainer (painted white) stationary on the runway with four dead engines.

Because of Denver's high altitude, careful leaning of the mixtures after landing was essential or the engines flooded and died. That's where I was so fortunate having Paul as my flying partner; I never needed to worry about engine management. Unfortunately, I didn't manage quite as well when it was my turn, but my experience with the Capital Connie engineer panel stood me in good stead and I soon got the knack of it. Ross, our instructor, complimented us on our expertise with the engines because it made his job so much easier. It wasn't often he had a line Second Officer for an ATR (Airline Transport Rating) student.

The flight training portion of the syllabus consisted of the usual familiarization program: doing stalls, turns to headings, steep turns, climbs and letdowns, visual and instrument approaches, and landings. At the conclusion of each session, Ross's customary evaluation remark was either "no problem" or "I don't see any problem." Now that we were in flight training, word filtered back about other pilots in the program. Bill Benton failed his rating ride, and at first we thought he was terminated but later heard he would repeat the entire program after spending two weeks at home.

During one of our training sessions at Colorado Springs, I failed to retract the landing gear on a missed approach. I didn't think Ross was aware of it, but it was blatantly evident a few minutes later when I called for, "Gear down, landing checklist," and Paul responded by saying, "It's already down; you didn't retract it on the missed approach." Ross wasn't overly concerned, and all he said was, "Don't do that on your rating ride or it will be an automatic down."

It was more and more of the same until April 12, the day of my recommendation ride. That was a three-hour session during which I was tested for every conceivable maneuver the examiner might call for. At the conclusion, the instructor said, "Ray, I think you are ready. Fly like that tomorrow and you will pass with flying colors." You can't get a better endorsement than that.

Show Time: My ATR Flight Test

The next day was Friday the 13th of April (was I superstitious?), and it dawned sunny and bright. You couldn't ask for a nicer day, but I was a basket case, battling the check-itis that always plagued me. Bill Lively, from United Flight Standards, was my acting First Officer. The flight engineer was a line Second Officer. Sitting on the jump seat was an FAA examiner, Bill Hitztaylor. I was tense, and Bill Lively noticed, pleading with me to relax.

"You can do it, Ray. I talked to your instructor and he said you did fine yesterday. Just treat it as another training session, and fly the airplane." "What about the FAA guy?" I asked.

"Just ignore him. Pretend he isn't even there. Our standards are so much higher than his that he might as well not have come."

I guess that helped a bit; we climbed aboard, ran through our checklists, started the engines and taxied out for takeoff. Since it was early in the day, Bill decided to conduct the flight test right there at Stapleton Airport in Denver. I would have preferred Pueblo or Colorado Springs, but it wasn't my call.

We took off and flew to the practice area first, doing turns to headings, steep turns, stalls, etc. My mouth was so dry that I could scarcely speak. I knew my whole future was riding on my performance that day, and that created tension I couldn't escape. When Bill Lively realized the extent of my anguish, he called for a break in the action.

"Go back to the galley, get something to drink and come back in five minutes or so." That was a thoughtful gift, and it worked wonders. After the short break, I got back in the seat and was much better. Later, Bill gave me some advice for future rating checks: "Whenever it hits you like that, just call for a break in the action; say you need to use the bathroom." That was sage advice, and I wish I had recalled it during one particular rating ride 23 years later on the DC-10.

Before long, we returned to Stapleton to shoot approaches. It was all very straightforward with no surprises: A normal ILS to 200 feet with a missed approach, then an engine-fire warning climbing out, declare an emergency, go through the fire drill, then set up for a three-engine ILS approach. Lose a second engine on the downwind leg; execute the procedure for that, then the weather suddenly improves for a visual landing on the remaining two engines. Come to a full stop after landing and while taxiing back, the plane miraculously returns to normal.

Make another takeoff and experience an engine-fire warning immediately after takeoff; declare an emergency again, requesting immediate landing on Runway 15 (a supplementary runway at Stapleton that was seldom used). I knew we wouldn't land out of that, because it would shut down the entire Denver airport if we did. That three-engine visual approach was flown down to 100 feet, at which time Bill Lively called out, "There's a truck on the runway."

We executed this missed approach on three engines, climbed out once more and requested clearance for a three-engine landing on the main runway. Once we landed out of that, it was over.

Did I pass? I saw Bill shoot a glance back at the FAA examiner. I couldn't see, but he must have nodded okay, because Bill turned to me and said, "Congratulations, Captain Lemmon." I couldn't wait to call Margaret, as I knew she, too, was anxious about the flight test.

I was pleased to learn that Paul passed as well. However, there were five failures or incompletes around that time.

DC-7 Qualification

Because the Type rating printed on my pilot's license signified certification to act as captain on either the DC-6 or DC-7 airplane, I needed that endorsement before leaving Denver. Paul Ferguson, I, and two other recently graduated captains met with instructor Bob Clipson for checkout on the DC-7.

The main difference between the planes was the engines — 3300 horsepower for the DC-7 versus 2000 for the DC-6. The Wright 3350 engines used on the DC-7 were powerhouses that bore little resemblance to our old Connie engines. The version used on the DC-7 was turbo-compound, implying that it was equipped with power-recovery turbines linked directly to the crankshaft of the engine. The engine analyzer used to monitor operation was much more sophisticated. Four-blade propellers provided additional performance and efficiency. It was also equipped with a speed brake; pulling that handle extended the main landing gear to effectively reduce speed.

We commandeered a DC-7 freighter passing through Denver. It was fully loaded with huge electric motors that were cabled to the floor. Paul was pressed into service as the flight engineer. We cranked it up and took off for some air work; steep turns, stalls, etc. We were only supposed to approach a stall and then recover. However, before Bob could stop him, one of the new captains yanked the control column all the way back into a full stall. The DC-7 fell off sharply on the right wing, and started down in a steep spiral.

Remember those electric motors I alluded to? If one broke loose, it would head for the cockpit and just keep going, right through the instrument panel and out the nose. Those of us sitting in back were petrified. Bob took over and made a very gentle recovery, keeping everything intact.

Needless to say, that gentleman did not get his DC-7 endorsement that day. My logbook shows my individual time was only 45 minutes to complete the requirement. For the remainder of its service life with United I only flew one line trip in the DC-7, from Newark to Pittsburgh.

Having survived "TK," I gained respect from my peers, the captains I worked with on a daily basis. Most of the ex-Capital pilots hadn't been to Denver yet, but from what they heard, they knew it was no pushover. George Anderson offered to let me fly a leg from the captain's seat of the Viscount. Changing seats was a no-no with United, and I thanked George and never mentioned it to anyone.

DC-3 service was terminated one year after the merger. The "around the horn" sequence was now flown by the Viscount. Service to Erie ended on the day of the merger.

Changes at Port Erie

The Erie Airport underwent significant change after I left to fly for Capital. During the summer of '57, a new terminal with a control tower on top was built on the north side of the field. Now, as a controlled airport, transmitters and receivers were required for all flight and ground operations.

Much of the air service to small cities like Erie was relegated to local-service airlines such as Allegheny, Mohawk, and Lake Central. At first it was strictly DC-3s, but gradually larger, faster planes like the Martin 202 and Convairs were introduced.

The big news of General Aviation interest was that Erie County Flying Service had moved their Cessna dealership from Fairview. Two formidable hangars with an office were built at the northwest corner of the airport, and then the company was renamed Erie Airways, competing directly with Mac and Earl. Private flying grew by leaps and bounds in the '60s, but even so, there was intense competition. The theory was that the Piper and Beech people would continue to patronize Mac and Earl, while the Cessna business would go to the Kudlaks at Erie Airways as it always had.

Tom Apple and I remained close. I no longer got to Erie as frequently as in the past, but we kept in touch by phone. Shortly after moving to New Jersey, Tom sent me a note saying Joe Kudlak, the mechanic at Erie Airways, had a 65 horsepower Continental engine for $75; was I interested? Tom knew that I wanted some small project to occupy me at home.

"Yes," I said, "I'll take it." It was a steal, even though it needed overhauling. That was my first small step into an avocation that would occupy me on a recreational level for 40 years.

Ringwood, N.J. (1962-1967)

The Ringwood, N.J. house, spring, 1963. We lived there four years.

In early '62, Margaret and I saw an ad for houses at Cupsaw Lake, near the New York border. By the time we went to see them, I was about to leave for Captain training at DENTK. Any commitment to buy a house was obviously contingent on a successful outcome at Denver — but it didn't hurt to look, and dream.

These California Contemporary homes were unlike any we had seen before. It was the pictures of them that captured our imagination: they were ranch-style, with a gently sloped roof and large windows. Opposite the entrance door, the living room featured floor-to-ceiling glass with a spectacular view of Bearfort Mountain off in the distance. Our choice was the "Palo Alto," priced at $19,900; it had three bedrooms, a large open area downstairs, and a one-car garage. Built on a sloping lot, the lower level also featured large windows facing the mountain.

Once I had earned my Airline Transport Rating, we were ready to buy. The down payment was only $1000, with favorable mortgage terms. It was in a brand-new subdivision carved out of the wooded hillside — very exciting.

As predicted, the LaGuardia domicile closed and the propeller-flying there moved to Newark. It was wonderful news for me, as the driving time from Wood-Ridge to the Newark airport was only 30 minutes.

The northern edge of the New Jersey metro area terminated at Oakland, a small community at the base of Ramapo Mountain. There was only one road across, called Skyline Drive; it was a pretty drive, but at the crest it was 1000 feet above sea level. Ringwood was at the far side of the mountain with its cluster of lake communities, the largest of which was Cupsaw at 65 acres.

Until the mid-'50s, Ringwood was strictly a resort community with very few year-round residents. Route 208 to Oakland opened the area to development, making year-round living much more feasible. Whenever possible we drove over Skyline Drive, but occasionally during winter the road would close. An alternate route via Pompton Lakes was available, but it took twice as long.

I bid reserve during the summer of '62 to take advantage of the additional time off that reserve status usually provided. The downside of being on reserve was the necessity for me to keep the crew desk informed of my whereabouts at all times. That was long before cell phones, but beepers were available. I had eight guaranteed days each month when I was not subject to call, so it worked out well for one of us to visit the building site on a daily basis.

By July, the framework was constructed, and it was exciting seeing the house take shape. Also that summer, I overhauled the Continental engine Tom located for me; at that time, its destiny was unknown. Coincidentally, I joined EAA (Experimental Aircraft Association), the focal organization for recreational flying. And it wasn't just for "home-built" airplanes; there were separate divisions for antiques, vintage, and racing planes. My involvement was slight at first, and escalated from that point on.

An early snow in October was a harbinger of things to come. The weather in Ringwood during winter was entirely different than that of the metro area just 35 miles away. We had many treasured memories of the five years we lived there.

The township altered Robin Lane, our new address, by raising the street five feet in front of our house. That "improvement" rendered our driveway virtually unusable and forced us to park on the road all winter. There was lots of snow in Ringwood, and the only food market was at the base of the hill in Cupsaw Lake. Margaret and Sandy Weber, our next-door neighbor, borrowed the kids' sled to haul groceries. That was how we spent our first winter: with me flying Viscount First Officer, and settled into our new home.

———

Just because I now had an Airline Transport Rating, it didn't mean that anything had changed at work. I would still be a First Officer for five more years. The most direct consequence of my promotion was being able to fly DC-6 First Officer. Since very few of the ex-Capital First Officers were qualified, it was an opportunity for me to fly some really good schedules, mostly south to Atlanta and Birmingham.

Under the provisions of our new contract, my paycheck was nearly $1000 a month, and I received a sizable retroactive paycheck that we used to buy furniture for the new house. Hallelujah! We were finally getting out of debt.

———

Because of the elevated roadway, our driveway was so steep that a bulldozer was needed to pull the paving truck up the hill. We ended up with an unsightly earthen bank in front of the house that I corrected with a stone wall spanning the entire width of our property. It was a substantial project that incorporated a set of stairs leading up to the road.

I hadn't flown with any United captains since the merger. None were qualified on the Viscount, so in that respect, Capital Airlines was still somewhat intact at Newark within the UAL framework. We were all frozen in place until 1965, at which time United was set to explode. Fleets of jets, both B-727s and 737s, were on order, so even though we still faced two more years of stagnation, there was the promise of a great future ahead.

During the summer of '63, the Pittsburgh domicile needed Viscount First Officers, providing another opportunity for a TDY assignment. I volunteered for the month of August — Margaret and I stayed at a Holiday Inn, swam in their pool and lived like tourists. Even though I was on reserve, we were able to drive to Erie on several occasions; that was especially nice, since we hadn't seen Mom and Dad all summer. With very few call-outs to fly, the assignment turned into a vacation.

Tom Apple sold his Cub and decided to build an experimental plane, the "Trail Air," from scratch — in his basement, of course. I flew the Cub a number of times and wondered about the selling price.

La Belle Caravelle

United was undergoing a gradual shift to turbine aircraft even though we, the Capital pilots, were not part of it. Shortly before the merger, a new intercity jet arrived on the scene. It was named Caravelle, a two-engine, 64-passenger commuter manufactured by Sud Aviation, Toulouse, France. It required a three-man crew and filled in as an interim jet replacement for United propeller planes until the new Boeings came on line three years later.

About 20 Caravelles were ordered, providing over 100 bids for each crew position. Very sleek-looking with great passenger appeal, these planes flew primarily on the New York-Chicago route, and a significant percentage of Caravelle schedules were flown out of the Newark base. Newark United DC-6 pilots filled those vacancies to a man, creating openings in the prop fleet that we Capital pilots were eligible to fill. Even though I was still too junior for a Captain slot, my position improved concerning the trips I could fly as First Officer. I flew DC-6 schedules in the fall and winter of '63 and '64. Since I no longer had to fly reserve, my home life improved considerably.

1964

After looking at the two-door Super Sport in the '64 Chevy lineup, Margaret and I put our order in right after Christmas. We liked the burgundy exterior, with black bucket seats and center console. We splurged on all the power options, including air conditioning, for a price of just under $3000. We sold my old '54 Chevy airport car to the salesman without loss of investment — $150. Since we only had a one-car garage, I installed roofing on the deck outside the living room to create a carport below, and that worked out really well.

1964 was shaping up to be a great year, as we anticipated the New York World's Fair running for two years: April 22 to October 18, 1964, and April 21 to October 17, 1965. We were expecting lots of company.

Chapter 12

Revisiting the Aeronca Chief
1965

N 9309E

During our spring vacation in 1964, I was anxious to drive to Erie to show Tom our new Super Sport and check on his progress with "Trail Air." From recent conversations, it sounded like it was nearly ready to fly.

Shortly after we arrived, Tom sprung a surprise on me: "I know you've been looking for a project, and I've found one you might be interested in. The Paynes still have your old Aeronca Chief, and I hear they are trying to sell it." (They bought it not long after I was drafted.)

"It hasn't flown since the wing fabric failed to test years ago, and has just been sitting in their barn. They've been telling potential buyers the fuselage fabric is still good, but after 13 years, I'll bet it's rotten too. Why don't we go out and look it over, and I'll bring the Maule tester. I'll bet the punch will 'go right through'; when they see how bad it is, I'm sure they'll come down from their $1000 asking price."

Tom was alluding to the way the Maule fabric tester worked. It was a punch-type tool that, in good fabric, made a small dimple that usually disappeared after the test. On deteriorated fabric, however, sometimes the probe penetrated all the way through, requiring a doped patch for repair.

Although I was surprised, it sounded exciting, so we called Rex Payne. "Sure; come on out, it's a great plane." I had never met the

Paynes, and I wasn't anxious to disclose the fact that the original owner was coming for the inspection. While shaking hands when we arrived, Rex's brother Vance picked up on my name immediately and said, "Aren't you the guy that owned it before, and had to go into the Army?" The cat was out of the bag.

Well, hopefully, no real harm was done. Once they saw the test results, I was quite sure they would be forced to acknowledge that the plane was due for complete restoration. Tom explained that he was representing me, and we needed to test the rest of the fabric.

"Sure, do whatever is necessary as long as you patch it afterward." Tom had brought a kit along for that purpose, so we got out the Maule tester and created some "dimples" in the fuselage fabric. Unbelievably, it passed the test.

"See," Rex chortled, "I told you the fabric was good."

Oh, boy! Tom couldn't believe it. When we began discussing the price, Rex was steadfastly resisting any lower figure — and to drive the dagger a little deeper, he said, "I know you'd like to have it back again, wouldn't you?"

Tom was crushed. He was so convinced the fabric would fail, and now the project was doomed. Well, maybe not quite yet — patience, please.

———

Back in Ringwood, the summer became a blur. I had a fairly heavy work schedule flying the Viscount, and Margaret and I had lots of company. The Hestons, from Virginia; Margaret's parents; her sister, Nancy, and all their family; plus the Kanes, from Connecticut, came to visit. We brought in extra beds for downstairs — Margaret had her work cut out for her. Everyone wanted to attend the New York World's Fair.

———

In mid-August, Earl Derion called to see if I was still interested in the Aeronca Chief. I told him the deal was dead, reminding him of our frustrating attempts to deal with the Paynes months earlier.

"Don't give up just yet. They've written you off as a potential buyer, and have approached me; I think they are anxious to sell. I told Rex I might have a buyer but not at the price they were asking, so they came down to $800. If you want it for that, you can have it." I said I would call him back after discussing it with Margaret. After all, it was her laundry area that I would be confiscating to create a restoration shop.

"I'll need a new dryer," Margaret announced. What could I say? The clotheslines would have to go. She also made me promise not to stink up the house with smelly dope. Other than that, she had no objections.

"I'll dope in the garage," I promised, "or even outside, if it's warm enough." With that settled, I called Earl back to say that I would take it. He ended the conversation with, "They'll have to fly it here, and you'll need a ferry permit if you intend to fly it home."

The Chief hadn't been out of the Paynes' barn for over 10 years, and we weren't quite sure how they would manage to make it airworthy. However, after Labor Day, Earl called again to say, "Vance called. He intends to fly the Chief over on the next suitable day."

Sure enough, at the appointed time, the Chief appeared in the airport traffic pattern. It was Vance, and he was circling the field, searching for the magic green light indicating permission to land. Finally he landed but lost control and veered off the runway, dragging the left wing. The plane righted itself, and then Vance got out.

The retrieval committee, consisting of Tom and Bob Berchtold, sprang into action to drag it back to the hangar. The fabric at the left wingtip was torn, but that appeared to be the extent of the damage.

"Are you willing to pay to patch the wing?" Earl asked. Vance replied that he had little choice, since he couldn't fly it back home the way it was; the proceeds for the Paynes were now reduced to $750. The Chief was tied down outside at Earl's hangar. Tom called that evening and agreed to go over the Chief on his own time and patch the wing tip to save me some money. In addition, Earl agreed to issue the ferry permit to fly it home.

What is a "ferry permit"? The FAA, in all its wisdom, recognized that under certain conditions, aircraft not meeting all airworthiness requirements could be safely flown to a maintenance station for repair. Approval for a ferry flight was contingent on certain limitations:

1. It must be one continuous flight between two specified locations.
2. The route flown should be clear of populated areas.
3. No passengers. Personnel on board are limited to necessary flight crew.
4. Immediately prior to the flight, the aircraft must undergo a comprehensive mechanical inspection by a certified A&E mechanic, endorsed in the aircraft logbook, to satisfy basic airworthiness requirements.
5. VFR weather conditions must prevail over the entire route.

Regarding the poor condition of the Aeronca Chief — even though the wing fabric was not airworthy, Tom felt quite certain it wouldn't tear off in flight.

I had a break in my schedule after Labor Day, so I told Tom I would come to Erie then. Since United didn't fly into Erie anymore, I rode jump seat on Allegheny from Pittsburgh. Everything worked out, and I arrived in Erie to fly the Chief home.

While waiting for Margaret's mom and dad to pick me up (I would be staying with them until I flew the Chief home), Tom and I discussed the Chief's condition. The wingtip had been repaired but not finish-painted, as I would be removing all the fabric anyway. Tom realized I would need the eight-gallon reserve tank to make the trip nonstop. After filling the tank, there was leakage around the fuel gauge, so I asked Tom about using it. He said, "It's not too bad from an airworthiness standpoint, but it is going to reek of 80-octane gas."

"Okay," I said, "I'll select the auxiliary tank right away and use it down to where the fuel level is below the gauge. How does it run?" "Amazingly well, considering it was in that barn all those years. You should be okay — just pick a good day."

On September 10, I flew home — it was an uneventful four-hour ride, and I was relieved to see Greenwood Lake Airport appear on the horizon. The trip was boring, and I arrived with an hour's fuel remaining. The Chief was tricky to land, since I hadn't flown it for many years. At least I did better than Vance and didn't drag a wing.

I rented a T-hangar (an airplane shelter shaped like the letter "T") for a month, and now I faced a humongous job. Tom was a long way away in case I got stuck, but there was always the telephone.

Margaret's Grand Piano

I'll leave the airplane for a moment to discuss something that was very important to Margaret in 1964. She wanted a piano — a baby grand, to be specific. After getting out of debt, we could consider buying a few things like cars, airplanes and, yes, even a grand piano. We went to a shop that rebuilt them and picked out a Hardman, 1926, that was due for restoration. It cost $800 — coincidentally, the same price I had just paid for the Chief.

When we first saw the piano, it was in sad shape; it needed everything, including a new soundboard, strikers and ivory keys for the keyboard. Shortly after flying the Chief home, we got a call that the baby grand was ready, and Margaret was very anxious to see it. The piano was beautiful, and she loved it. The following week it was delivered to Robin Lane and from that point, there was music in the house. We moved that piano 10 times.

Margaret playing her newly restored grand piano in 1965.

Some Minor Dis-Assembly Required

The Chief looked forlorn sitting there in the hangar at Greenwood Lake Airport (GLA). Now it was important to determine what was usable and what needed to be replaced. The interior was shot, although it hadn't been that great when I had learned to fly in it 14 years earlier.

Naturally, the people at GLA were curious; that included the shop manager, Sam Teece, and his wife Lee. When I announced my intention to dismantle it and put it in my basement, Sam gave me a puzzled look as if he were talking to a mad man. Then he shrugged his shoulders and went about his business. I only had three weeks remaining for the disassembly and transport to Robin Lane, so when I wasn't flying for United I spent all my free time at the airport. I was a fair mechanic, even in those days, and the task of removing the wings and tail pieces was straightforward.

When it was time to remove the wings, I called my old Buffalo captain, Jack Spiegleberg, to come and assist. I used roof racks for the car, and tied each wing down for the seven-mile trip. In one afternoon, "Spieg" and I had both wings delivered to the Ringwood house and standing up against the lower-story wall.

Next came the smaller pieces: the ailerons, stabilizers, elevators, and rudder. Finally, all that was left at the airport was the fuselage. On a quiet Sunday morning when the traffic was light, we towed the fuselage to Robin Lane. I sat in the trunk, holding the tail wheel in my lap, and Margaret drove. Finally, everything was home, and the basement was full of airplane parts. Perusing the scene, I thought, "What have I gotten myself into?"

During the winter of '64 and '65, I spent almost every available hour downstairs working on the plane. That was the advantage of having a project at home: total availability. Even after supper, I would often go down for an hour or so.

Working on the Chief

I started by removing the engine and propeller, and then I carefully uncovered the fuselage, marking all the old fabric for future reference. During that process, I made an interesting discovery. I found clumps of what appeared to be old grass wedged between the cowling sheet metal where it overlapped. I didn't attach any significance until I recalled my emergency landing at the Erie Range towers back when I was learning to fly: "I'll bet it was wheat from my forced landing." I put it in a jar and saved it.

Why? It was because that was such a pivotal moment. If I had not been so lucky in landing without any damage, my entire future would have been altered. A dead furrow in the field, a rut of any kind, could have flipped the plane upside down with catastrophic consequences. Since the Chief wasn't insured, the damage to the plane would have been significant enough to end all my flying aspirations right then and there. That embryonic phase was critical, and at the time, I had no perception that I was living so close to the edge.

Once the fabric covering was removed from the fuselage, I examined the steel framework and wooden formers. Some of those formers were rotted, so it was evident that considerable woodwork was going to be required. A more serious discovery was a bent steel tube ahead of the left door, caused by a hard landing — maybe even as recent as Vance's landing at Erie.

Fortunately Bill Brown, from Buffalo, was building a home-built airplane similar to Tom's, and he offered to bring his welding outfit over. Bill told me to "Inspect it carefully — I want to fix everything while I'm there."

"Loophole" Legality

"Wait a minute, Ray," I hear you saying. "How are you able to restore a plane? Aren't you supposed to have a license?" Tom had to attend PIA (Pittsburgh Institute of Aeronautics) for over a year to become "certified" as an A&E mechanic.

Yes, indeed. That's a very good point, but there was a loophole called "direct supervision" — a vague term, to be sure. In other words, an unlicensed mechanic (like me) could make repairs to a certified airplane if:

1. The licensed mechanic concerned (in this case, Tom) felt that the person he was supervising was capable of doing the work to the standards required, and

2. That he (Tom, the licensee) observed such person actually doing the work. It's the second part that was a problem for me, because Tom lived so far away.

The FAA does grant leeway to the extent that another licensed mechanic can step in to approve specific work. Although these regulations were poorly defined in many ways (for example, because they did not put restrictions on how close the supervising mechanic needed to be), only an idiot would work on an airplane if he didn't know what he was doing. I had worked on various projects at Earl's over the past seven years, and in the course of that, Tom taught me many things. That's why he was willing to sanction my work even though he was not able to inspect the work firsthand. "Take pictures of everything," Tom advised.

How Do You Restore a Plane?

To restore a plane, you take it apart. But before you do, you take notes and pictures of everything possible, for reference later.

As part of FAA Part 23 (aircraft certification), every aircraft manufacturer makes available an approved parts and service manual. The parts manual illustrates a detailed breakdown of the plane's components and how they relate to each other. The maintenance/service manual also exhibits diagrams and pictures, and in addition furnishes many specifications and limitations regarding pressures, temperatures, and torque values for the different systems. Much of the restoration work is straightforward, in the sense that what needs to be done is obvious. Other steps are less so, and require a certain level of experience and/or knowledge.

After a few weeks all the fabric had been removed from the plane, and what remained was a skeletal frame. Replacing all the formers and stringers that gave the plane its shape was a separate task. For a while, the basement looked like a carpentry shop. As part of the woodworking, I made new floorboards for the cabin. The interior disassembly work included other items, such as the headliner, seats, door panels, fuel system, instrument panel, and carpeting.

Once the Chief was reduced to its most basic components, the predominant piece remaining was the steel-tube fuselage; this was the largest single element to be dealt with. The framework was thoroughly cleaned of dirt, oil, or other contaminants and then sanded down to bare metal. That was followed by a careful inspection for cracks or other damage, such as the bent tube that my friend Bill Brown replaced by welding in a new one.

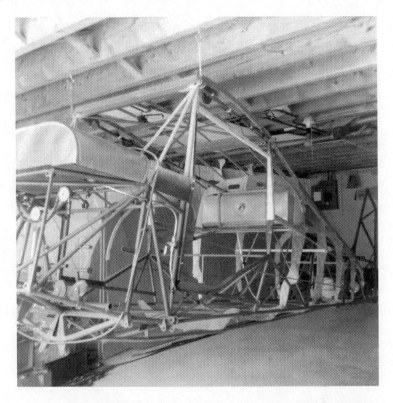

Early stage of rebuild on Aeronca Chief, Ringwood, 1965.

After these preparatory steps, I coated the steel with epoxy primer. Regular paint was not used, because the special cement used to apply the fabric was so volatile that it dissolved ordinary paint, which allowed the frame to rust.

Each tiny part removed was examined and refurbished. Some aluminum parts, such as the cowling, doors, prop spinner, wheel pants, and the like, had to be straightened (if possible), primed and painted. Hammering on sheet aluminum causes the metal to stretch, creating unsightly bulges that can only be removed by shrinking.

Much of the aluminum needed replacement. Aircraft aluminum components were often held together by rivets that were also made of aluminum. Some were round-headed and others were flush, "flat" rivets. Steel bolts and screws were also used, and those were usually cadmium-plated for longevity.

Margaret in the Chief, late 1965. The plane was flying six months later.

You get the idea. Aircraft repair and restoration work was somewhat technical and demanding. That's why my apprentice work with Tom encompassed such a long period of time before I felt competent enough to take on a project like the Chief.

Even so, in many cases I was not skilled enough. On several occasions, I loaded the car with parts that required expert handling and took them to Erie for Tom. He had a special talent for restoring used parts to good-as-new.

By the end of the year, the steel fuselage frame was finished and all the wood stringers and formers were reinstalled. Much of the aluminum cowling had been stripped of the old yellow paint, and the Continental engine that I overhauled in Wood-Ridge was ready to lift into place.

The aluminum fuel tanks were in excellent condition, so I just reinstalled them. No fuel was carried in the wings; the main 15-gallon tank was located in front of the instrument panel, and the 8-gallon reserve was mounted up high behind the baggage compartment. I resealed the leaking gauge that had plagued me on the way home (the part number was identical to that of a 1931 Model A Ford). Finally, the fuselage was ready to be covered with new fabric.

Now it was time to tackle the wings, where many restorers underestimate the amount of work involved. The wings are a large part of any airplane, and surprises often lurk inside. The main structural elements are the spars, which extend the full width from the fuselage attachment to the tip. They are made of spruce or Douglas fir and last many years, provided they are kept in a dry place and protected by varnish. The leading edge is covered with sheet aluminum to shape the airfoil, and the metal often becomes dented over the years. Frequently, a navigation light is installed at the tip.

All that the Chief's spars needed was a thorough sanding and a couple of coats of varnish. The airfoil (curve) was shaped by aluminum ribs that were delicate and easily subjected to damage in a flip-over accident, as I alluded to earlier. The curved bow at the left wing's tip had been damaged in Vance's "ground loop" at Port Erie. After extensive cleaning and inspection, the wings were also ready for new fabric.

With everything prepared, it was necessary for a licensed mechanic to inspect my work and certify that all components were airworthy. What I have described in just a very few minutes took months to accomplish, so it was spring '65 before I was prepared for the inspection.

Around the Christmas holidays, Gene and Jane Olsen stopped by. Margaret met Jane at church while we lived in Wood-Ridge two years earlier. Gene was employed by American President Lines (APL) as Chief Mate on the *President Jackson*, a Mariner-class cargo ship that sailed around the world. His voyages lasted the better part of a year, earning him six months' vacation.

Gene had swapped his Taylorcraft plane for a Cessna 180 since we last saw them, and they invited us to Kobelt Airport for a ride in the spring. Then, around March or April, they called again: "How about flying over to Hershey for a tour of the chocolate factory?"

"Gee, that sounds like fun," I said; "Count us in." Hershey Air Park had a paved runway located immediately north of the factory, within walking distance. The Cessna 180 was a good performer, even with a full load. Because Gene wanted to do some practice instrument flying on the way home, we requested a clearance from New York Center. Gene suggested a longer trip to Florida around Memorial Day.

Margaret's New Convertible

Margaret with her '65 Pontiac convertible at the Erie Deck House in 1978.

Margaret wanted a new car of her own! What could I say? She ordered a 1965 Pontiac Catalina convertible, loaded with goodies, at a modest cost of $4200. Since it was manufactured at the GM assembly plant nearby at Trenton, N.J., we hoped for a price break on the shipping, but did we get it? No, it was still $92, the same as for a much more distant destination.

Al Weidenthal, from Blue & White Pontiac in Hackensack, called April 10 to say that the convertible had just arrived and asked, "Would you like to come down and see it just as it came off the truck?"

"Yes, of course, we'll be right down." The black fabric top was protected with aluminum foil, and the car was gorgeous. I still own that convertible to this day, nearly fifty years later.

Dressing the Chief

Sam Teece from Greenwood Lake Airport agreed to come to our house for the Chief's pre-cover inspection. He examined everything, including the welding repair by Bill Brown and the wood formers and stringers that I had replaced. It was not unusual to end up with a short "to-do list" prior to obtaining the inspector's signoff in the Aircraft Log Book. Occasionally, a return visit might even be necessary to verify compliance — all at the owner's expense, of course.

I was lucky. There were a few things to address, but a return visit wouldn't be necessary. Sam signed off on everything, declaring the fuselage, wings, ailerons, elevators, stabilizers, and rudder "ready to cover."

Methods and materials had changed significantly from the time Tom restored his Cub five years earlier. Those were the "grade-A cotton and Irish linen" days. In 1965, it was all about synthetics, specifically Dacron, sold under the name of "Ceconite." It was far more durable than natural fibers, with an expected service life of 10-15 years provided sufficient silver coats were applied to prevent ultraviolet deterioration. For that reason, I chose the Cooper process that was, essentially, two specially formulated butyrate dope products: "DacProofer" and "Sprayfil."

I ordered all the materials I would need for the job at one time. Because of the volatile nature of the shipment, special rules applied, and the cost of the kit was $625. Arrival at a Jersey City truck terminal was in early June, and I drove there to pick it up, saving a delivery charge.

Since I didn't know how to begin, I took the rudder to the airport where Sam's wife, Lee, showed me the ropes. After gluing the fabric on, she used a household iron to shrink it. Lee was an old hand at this, and she soon had me gluing, trimming and shrinking. By learning on the small pieces, I was ready to tackle the larger wings and fuselage at the appropriate time. I worked tirelessly, whenever I wasn't flying. Margaret was so patient with me, and as I reminisce now, I realize how unfair it was.

What about applying the stinky dope? It was summer, so I worked outside much of the time. The wings were the biggest challenge, and I constantly needed help turning them over on the sawhorses. I'm sure, by now, you can guess who my helper was: Margaret. The fabric was fastened to each rib with small screws and washers spaced two inches apart.

Covering and shrinking everything took most of July, and then it was time to apply "dope." The initial coats were brushed on, and then it was time to break out the spray gun for the Sprayfil. Margaret's flat iron tightened the fabric. It worked beautifully and if I had a wrinkle, I just turned the heat up a bit higher, and the wrinkle would disappear. Inevitably, I ended up spraying in the garage and Margaret's new convertible was relegated to the carport. The bulk of the paint work was completed by the end of October, preparing the way for reassembly during the winter months.

Yes, 1965 was the year of the Chief. Was it worth it? No, not really, especially based on future developments. At the time, however, I was truly driven.

B-727 School — 1965

In the fall, it was back to school again for jet training on the B-727. Finally, four years after the merger, the Capital pilots regained unrestricted bidding rights to any and all openings — systemwide. OV Pezzi and I ended up in the same class and were instructed to report to the Denver training center (DENTK) in late September.

There were dynamic changes from my previous experience in Denver three years earlier, reflecting the school's transition into the jet age. 727 ground school was intensive, using complicated mock-ups with lights indicating valves opening and closing and, for the electrical system, lots of switches identical to those in the cockpit. We spent hours with each of these, creating various scenarios for failures within the systems. There were a lot of "what-if" situations. Interspersed with classroom discussion were numerous trips to the hangar to examine the real airplane.

It was tough, all right, and it was clear why some of our most senior pilots were struggling. Actually, we all were, because the B-727 was so complex.

Finally, after three weeks we moved on to the simulators. They were state-of-the-art for that time: full-size, with all three crew stations equipped the same as the airplane. There were also CPTs (Cockpit Procedures Trainers) that were fully instrumented, but extremely limited in function.

Everyone was anxious to start flying, and eventually we did. That was before the advent of full-motion simulators, so we trained extensively in the airplane itself. We filled our 727 trainer plane with Jet "A" fuel and loaded up with several crews to fly south to Pueblo, Colo., where we trained in four-hour shifts.

When I finally got my chance at the First Officer seat, it was quite a thrill. The B-727 was totally different than anything I had flown before. It was really two airplanes — one with the flaps up and cruising along at 500 mph, and yet another in the traffic pattern with landing gear and flaps extended. In the last configuration, at 150 knots, it was docile and handled much like the propeller planes I was used to. The 727 airplane was really all about its dual-purpose wing.

We did our airport traffic pattern work and landing practice as previously described. It was really fun, and I was having a ball. Unfortunately, the 727 had some unusual landing characteristics that could surprise the overconfident and unwary. In the final stages of the approach, just about the time you thought you were ready to land, you might be rewarded with a landing so hard it resembled a crash.

Because the main landing gear was located so far to the rear, a special landing technique was required. After a gentle flare in the landing zone to arrest the rate of descent, it was prudent to push the control column forward to lower the nose of the airplane. Once the main wheels contacted the runway, continued forward pressure on the control column would lower the nose wheel until it also touched down.

Since the activation date of my 727 bid was still six months hence, I went back to flying the Viscount and DC-6. Later that policy of returning to one's previous airplane for the pre-activation period was discontinued, but in 1965 the practice was still in place. Except for an occasional interruption, the months following my qualification on the 727 were spent flying the DC-6. That was because many of the United DC-6 First Officers at Newark (EWR) had moved up to the Caravelle, and in some cases to Prop Captain. At EWR, many of the copilots senior to me were not checked out on the DC-6 and were therefore limited to flying Viscount schedules. That created a rare opportunity for me to fly some really good "6" (DC-6) trips during the final months of '65 and early '66.

Finishing the Chief

That in-limbo period was utilized to finish the Chief. The engine was now mounted on the fuselage, and the instrument panel was refinished in black wrinkle finish, with all the instruments overhauled. It now sported a 12-volt electrical system for the radio and navigation lights. Since there was no onboard generator, I used a motorcycle battery that was light and easy to maintain; a charge would last several hours.

Airtex Products supplied all the new interior components, including seats, carpeting and headliner. I bought new tires and brakes, and I found a set of used wheel pants in Brooklyn. They were in sad shape and needed extensive repair. Tom really came through for me on those. He was an artisan when it came to reworking aluminum. All-new Plexiglas, including the windshield and side glass, was installed. A refurbished baggage compartment went behind the seat, and even the onboard starter mechanism worked.

By spring of 1966, the Chief was ready to roll out for engine start. I tied the tail wheel to a post in the carport, and the engine started on the first pull. It was a great moment to stand there and see it running outside the garage.

I was not alone for long, however; how often do you see an airplane engine running outside someone's garage? I was able to log a couple of hours' break-in time so that when I got to the airport, the Chief would be ready to fly. It had yet to sprout its wings and tail; I had gone as far as I could before hauling everything back to Greenwood Lake Airport for final assembly.

I re-rented the T-hangar and then fastened the wings and ailerons on top of the car, one by one. Shortly after, we towed the fuselage over, with me in the trunk and the tail wheel in my lap as we had done a year and a half earlier.

Spring, 1966 at Ringwood: The Chief project is complete and ready for transport to Greenwood Lake Airport. (Note fender of Margaret's new '65 Pontiac convertible.)

The Restored Chief Takes to the Air

Now I finally did require some professional assistance, and Sam and Lee came to my rescue. As soon as I had the wings reinstalled, I put the plane in their shop, followed by installation of the tail group. It was beginning to look like an airplane again.

The test flight in late April was anti-climactic, which is my way of saying everything worked — at least for the most part. There were always a few glitches (adjustments). After a few hours of flying around the airport, I was anxious for a trip.

You ask, "Where might that be?" Erie, Pa., of course, as I'm sure you already guessed. Early one Sunday morning in May, Margaret and I loaded up the Chief, and we were off. "Loaded up" might be an overstatement; in fact, with the baggage compartment's small space and meager weight allowance, we could only take a few essentials.

With a full tank of fuel, and the two of us, it was suddenly a much different airplane.

The Aeronca Chief leaving for EAA Fly-in, Rockford, Illinois, July 1966. This photo was taken by Tom Apple at Erie, Pa. The paint scheme was designed by Tom, but the judges were not impressed and rejected it from competition for an award.

All during the project, my friend OV Pezzi kept harping, "It's a dog." He repeated it again and again. You know what? OV was right: it was a dog. Oh, boy! Now what have I done? Well, it's no use crying over spilt milk; we would just have to make the best of it, and we did.

The first leg to Elmira, N.Y. was pleasant enough, and since they had a control tower, it provided an opportunity to try out my new radio. At the gas pump, a crowd gathered around the Chief and there was a lot of ooh-ing and aah-ing, with people asking questions about how did I do such-and-such? It was time to come to grips with flying a restored classic. Margaret was totally unprepared, and couldn't believe we were attracting so much attention.

Soon we were off again — only this time the flying was quite different, as the air had become turbulent. Since our destination was the Buffalo area, I flew the length of Seneca Lake, the biggest and longest of the Finger Lakes, to enjoy the smoother air that was over the water for a while. Eventually, we were paralleling the N.Y. Thruway on our way to Buffalo but, unfortunately, the prevailing west wind had increased to the point we were moving at a snail's pace, and traffic on I-90 was passing us.

We landed at a small airport near Tonawanda, so Margaret's sister wouldn't have a long drive to pick us up. The original plan was to have lunch, then return to the plane and fly to Erie together. But by the time we arrived at 3 p.m. Margaret was exhausted, and she left me to fly the rest of the way to Erie by myself, stating her desire to spend the night with Nancy and join me in Erie a day or so later.

I was hesitant to take off again, but I really wanted to get the Chief to Erie. By the time I left it was late afternoon, and the wind had died down. It was a very pleasant flight to Erie out over the water, following the lakeshore. That trip forced me to come to terms with the fact that what I had with the Chief was really a decent "single-place" airplane. With a passenger on board, it truly was a "bow-wow."

By the time I got to Erie it was nearly sundown, and none of my friends were at the airport except Mac. He commented, "Nice job, Ray," but didn't seem to be overly impressed. We put the Chief in his hangar, and Margaret's mom and dad picked me up. I was disappointed that the plane hadn't performed better. Never allow nostalgia to get in the way of making sound decisions.

The next morning, by the time I returned to the airport, Tom had gone over my job with a fine-toothed comb. "You did fine, Ray. I don't see a lot wrong, but . . . ." Then came a flurry of minor criticisms, mostly fine points where Tom would have done things differently.

My worst mistake was failure to obtain a waiver to revert to the original lettering system of 24-inch wing numbers and 3-inch numbers for the tail, as it was originally. Current regulations called for 12-inch numbers placed on both sides of the fuselage, but the waiver permitted antiques and classics more than 25 years old to display their original markings. Even though my Chief was postwar, it qualified for antique and classic status under the original Aeronca Chief model specifications of the late 1930s. Tom's point was well taken, and I wouldn't make that mistake again. I wondered how I missed it, since we were in close touch throughout the entire process.

Margaret arrived from Buffalo, and before long we were headed back to Greenwood Lake. It was a smooth flight home, with another fuel stop in Elmira. The return flight took four and a half hours, and we had no trouble with the plane; it ran just fine.

Chapter 13

The Turbojet World — Denver
1966-1967

Going back to 1960, large jets like the DC-8 and Boeing 707 were primarily flown internationally or domestically on long-haul schedules, coast to coast. At the time of the merger in 1961, United had a substantial fleet of DC-8s and B-720s (a lighter version of the 707) for its long-haul routes. With that part covered, United's extensive intercity route structure had yet to be addressed.

B-727 at Denver, 1967. Mom and Dad Taylor were returning to Erie after their Denver visit.

Enter the B-727, Boeing's only tri-jet aircraft at the time. It was as close to airborne perfection as you could get: a plane that really did it all. The first models delivered in late '64 were the 100 series, a shorter, lighter version of those that came later. The 727-100 carried between 150 and 180 passengers on short- to medium-range flights of 1500 miles or less and was able to use the relatively short runways at smaller airports. It was a great performer, because it was powered by the same Pratt & Whitney JT8 engines as the stretched 200 series. We affectionately referred to the 100 series as the "sport model," because it would climb right up to maximum cruising altitude of 41,000 feet.

A Short Primer on Commercial Jet Engines

Initially the engines for large jet transports were versions of the military Pratt & Whitney J57. Slightly modified, that engine became the JT3 (JT for "Jet Transport"). It was a great engine except for compromised takeoff performance; optimum airflow was not achieved until the plane was traveling hundreds of miles per hour. At high-altitude airports like Denver, jets equipped with those engines used almost the entire runway to become airborne. A water-injection system was used on the DC-8 in an attempt to address that deficiency — we called them "water wagons."

For shorter-range flights and smaller airports, we needed something more suitable. Enter the P&W JT8 turbofan engine. What is a fan engine, you ask? Take a conventional turbojet engine and install a multiple-fan-disc section in front, and you now have a "turbofan" engine with vastly improved air supply (actually, compressed air) feeding the hot section behind it.

What's the tradeoff for that fan out front? Slightly reduced power output for cruise, because driving the fan consumes thrust; however, that concession was well worth it — in spades. Notice the large air inlets on today's planes; their engines are all massively fan-driven. The fans aren't that obvious on the Boeing 727's JT8s, but they are there and they work. Later, when I get to my stint on the B-720, we will discuss the comparison between turbofan and conventional turbojet engines in greater detail. For now, I must stick with our newest plane, the B-727-100. That was where we were in 1965.

Air Traffic Control

The Air Traffic Control system had undergone massive changes due to the increased volume of traffic and the complexity introduced into the system by jet aircraft. One word described the overall change: RADAR (Radio Detection and Ranging). Radar used radio waves to determine the range, altitude, direction, or speed of objects.

The use of radar began in Air Traffic Control centers. The country was divided up into sectors and awarded city names — such as New York Center, Boston Center, Cleveland Center, Miami Center, Chicago Center, etc. For instance, Cleveland Center was located at Oberlin, Ohio. All IFR (Instrument Flight Rules) traffic en route was controlled by the appropriate geographical facility. Before radar, estimates for arrival at checkpoints along the route had been provided by the flight crew.

When use of radar by Air Traffic Control began, we still had to make station passage reports to facilitate "hand-off" to the next sector. If the controller had numerous "blips" on his radar screen, the flight might have to make an identifying turn.

In the early '60s, DME (Distance Measuring Equipment) arrived on the scene and virtually eliminated that requirement. Your plane sent out a signal to the nearest Omni station and the signal bounced back to your receiver, which then displayed how many nautical miles you were from the station. "Identifying turns" were no longer required.

The next logical radar application was in the area of Terminal Radar Control (TRACON). Remember me telling you long ago how we could just call the tower five miles from the airport with a landing light on? Not anymore. They instituted Radar Approach Control to sequence arriving traffic at the airport. At first, it was sufficient for the pilot to call in his geographical location, such as a town, river, mountain, etc. With radar and DME, that also was no longer required.

Just one more goodie, and then we will return to the story. The Air Traffic Control transponder was your own little radar set in the cockpit that sent out a signal to the FAA controller, so that when you pressed the "ident" button, your blip lit up his screen and identification was instantaneous. The refinement of that came in the form of "discrete code" capability. The controller assigned the flight a four-digit code that the pilot dialed in on his cockpit unit. Those four digits were the flight's own discrete identifier, because no one else held that combination. That was very important, since the controller attached his own marker with matching code on his radar screen and you were constantly monitored. "Squawk ident" requests were seldom issued anymore.

So now you are somewhat up to date on the workings of the Air Traffic Control system as it exists today. It is vastly different from the way it operated in 1956, when I began my airline career. In so many ways, the application of radar made it a much safer aviation world.

For airline transports, VFR (Visual Flight Rules) was a thing of the past. It went out with the DC-3. All airline flights today are dispatched under Instrument Flight Rules, and they have been since the 1960s, where we presently are in my story.

Flying at JFK

The activation date for my B-727 bid was June 1 out of JFK, which resulted in a domicile change for me; I would now actually be flying my trips to and from there. I underestimated the gravity of that decision, and it turned out to have far-reaching consequences. Under the best of conditions it took over two hours to drive, and during rush hour it was beyond consideration. The route was similar to when I was based at LaGuardia, except that from Ringwood it was much farther to Kennedy.

Flying the B-727 in schedule was a major adjustment for me. The pace was ratcheted up, and my captains were not always gracious having to put up with my shortcomings. It wasn't so much flying the airplane as acclimating to the new environment we operated in.

JFK International was a big airport and it was very easy to become disoriented, especially while taxiing in unfamiliar territory. Since the captain was busy steering the airplane, it was my job to provide directions to the runway and back if he so desired. I sat there with the airport diagram on my lap for constant reference, and sometimes it took ten minutes just to reach the runway. Often the active runway was 31, at the far eastern end of the airport, and departing northwest called for strict noise-abatement procedures as well as avoidance of LaGuardia's airspace.

Departures were one problem, but arrivals were quite another. That was before the current regulation of reducing airspeed to 250 knots within a 30-nautical-mile radius of the airport, and we came barging in at 340 knots, contacting approach control much closer in. As the pace accelerated, quick thinking and response were imperative. The 727 cockpit was so quiet that it was impossible to tell how much power the engines were producing without consulting the instruments.

I gradually adjusted to the new operational aspects, and my captains were patient, for the most part, with my newness on the airplane. Paper flight plans were a dinosaur of the past; now we were under radar control during all phases of flight. Flight plans were "center stored," eliminating the redundant readback of en-route clearances. Center stored simply meant that our flight dispatch facility pre-filed our flight plans with ATC.

Part of the departure procedure was to contact "clearance delivery" prior to engine start. After giving our flight number and destination, the controller would usually respond: "Cleared as filed," with whatever altitude restrictions and other special instructions might apply. By necessity, the communication was brief and concise. In an airport like Chicago O'Hare, it would have been impossible using the old system.

Strict departure (SID) and arrival (STAR) procedures were issued by Jeppesen and periodically revised. Even while I was still flying DC-6s I was putting those revisions in my flight manual, so I was somewhat aware of what was in store.

Now I understood why some of our senior Capital captains were having difficulty at DENTK. The training and new operating environment was very complex for some of the old-timers. They either took early retirement or remained with the piston fleet until it was replaced in 1969 by intercity jets like the Caravelle and the new 737.

Flight Levels — A Brief Primer on the Kollsman Sensitive Altimeter

Since I will be making many statements and references throughout the narrative regarding the altimeter, a brief explanation of how it works may be in order. It is truly a marvelous instrument and has changed very little from its inception early in the twentieth century. It has been constantly refined over the years, but the principle of operation has remained unchanged. There are three hands varying in size, depending on their sensitivity: The longest and most sensitive is the 20-foot hand and registers 1000 feet for one revolution. The next longest is the 1000-foot hand, and it registers 10,000 feet for one revolution. The tiniest, and barely visible, is the 10,000-foot hand, and it registers 100,000 feet for one revolution.

The face of the instrument displays large numbers one through zero, with four small gradations between the numerals. The outer scale is also labeled at the top with "100 feet," indicating that each large number represents that increment of altitude. Below the zero at the tip of the smallest hand, we find "1000 feet" and "10000 feet" respectively, in very small numerals, denoting the value for the two smaller hands.

Also on the face of the instrument, at the three o'clock position, there is a rectangular box with small numbers ranging from 28.1 to 31.0 inches of mercury, with an indicator arrow in the center. At the lower left corner of the instrument (at the seven o'clock position), we find a knob that, when turned, will move the numerals described above through the entire range. The dial coverage is arbitrary in the sense that ambient barometric pressure will fall much lower than 28 inches during a hurricane or typhoon, but it serves us well 99% of the time.

Air Terminal Information Service (ATIS) broadcasts continuously at major terminals, and a key element provided is the current "altimeter setting." The first officer will normally tune to that frequency when he reaches the cockpit and "set" the plane's altimeters accordingly by turning the knob described above. A rough crosscheck is comparing the indication of the 100-foot hand with the field elevation of the airport. It should agree within 100 feet.

Since we almost always flew well above 20,000 feet, I was introduced to another procedure and chart system. Climbing above or descending below 18,000 feet called for resetting our altimeters. During climb-out, leaving 18,000 feet, our altimeters were reset to 29.92 inches of mercury (mean standard atmospheric pressure as recognized by the aviation community), and below FL 180 (altitudes above 17,000 feet were identified in that fashion) on descent, we reset them to the nearest geographical location; that barometric setting was provided by the appropriate FAA Control Center. Standard Operating Procedure required verbal announcement of that transition. Those procedures became second nature in a relatively short period of time.

Special (HI) charts were issued by Jeppesen for flying at "flight levels." The jet airways system portrayed far fewer checkpoints, and intersections and airways were realigned and defined by VOR stations every 100 NM (nautical miles) or so.

Descending below FL 180, we reverted to low-altitude charts. It was vital to stay mentally ahead of the airplane, and it wasn't always easy to do so. Most of our flight segments exceeded 500 miles (for example, New York to Cleveland or Cleveland to Chicago).

The Flight Director

The Collins FD-109 mounted in the plane's instrument panel was a fabulous flight director system. All inputs to the flight instruments were computerized, resulting in very precise approaches. Instead of the "miniature airplane" presentation on the attitude gyro, it now displayed a small delta wing flying into yellow "command bars." All that was required of the pilot was to fly the little plane tightly into these yellow bars, and he would arrive at the destination with extreme precision.

The Swept Wings

The 727 was an engineering marvel with its flight controls, swept wing with Krueger flaps, T tail, and three rear-mounted Pratt and Whitney JT8 engines.

The wing was mounted well aft to compensate for the rear-mounted engines. In cruise mode (clean configuration, with no flaps extended), it would yield speeds in excess of 550 mph. Normal cruise was Mach .82 at all altitudes up to 41,000 feet.

There was a penalty for the swept wing; it was angled to delay Mach-buffet as the plane approached speeds above Mach .80 at the upper limit of its operating range. In so doing, that delay introduced "adverse yaw" into the longitudinal axis. In simple terms, it caused the 727 to oscillate back and forth, which was an unpleasant experience. For prevention, the autopilot and rudder system were equipped with a yaw-damping system consisting of computerized hydraulic actuators that anticipated the oscillation before it occurred.

Part of the training syllabus was to turn off the yaw damper to simulate failure, and maintain control of the plane as it oscillated first one way and then the other. It was quite a challenge and an unpleasant drill.

Converting that clean wing into an airfoil suitable for approaches and landings was a marvel in itself. The entire wing virtually "disintegrated" as flaps were selected. The flaps' one-degree position barely extended the trailing-edge Fowler flaps, but what happened at the leading edge was far more significant.

The first set of Krueger flaps extended (they looked like boards), and upon selection of the flaps' five-degree position, the remainder deployed. Those leading-edge devices radically changed the airfoil of the wing, transforming it from a high-performance regime to a slow-speed, lift-generating camber. To assist in lateral control (banking), the ailerons (wing flippers) suddenly more than doubled in size as the inboard and outer sections locked together, providing excellent maneuverability in the landing pattern.

To augment lateral control of the airplane in cruise flight, there was a spoiler system built into the wing. Hydraulically controlled panels raised and lowered in response to banking commands from the control column in the cockpit. Another function of these "spoilers" took place after landing. Either by automatic or manual command, they extended fully, effectively destroying all lift of the wing and, in so doing, immediately transferred the weight of the airplane to the landing gear. This was exceedingly important, especially under snowy conditions when tire traction was compromised.

"Greasing It On" With a Flare

Oh yes, about the landings. I thought I was an ace, touching down like a pro every time. My first month on the 727, I was flying with Roger Taylor, who was judiciously assessing my technique. After "greasing it on" (making an exceptionally smooth landing) a number of times, he asked me, "Do you know what you are doing? Do you really know?"

Apparently Roger detected something in my flamboyant handling of the 727 that was not in keeping with his understanding of the best way to fly the airplane. He suspected that my superb display of airmanship was about to come to an abrupt end, and it did. In response to his question, I simply said, "It seems to be working okay so far," or something to that effect.

In any case, his point was well taken. On my very next landing at Cleveland, a stiff northerly breeze was blowing, so the active runway was 36 — seldom used because it had no Instrument Approach Procedure. I brought the airplane down to the runway environment and flared with my usual aplomb and we hit so hard, I thought I broke something. Of course, the landing gear was built to withstand that (and much more, really) but incurring damage to the plane was not the issue; customer relations was. When we reached the gate to deplane the passengers, Roger said, "You did it; you go back and take the heat."

On arrival at the terminal, in the interest of public relations, it was customary for the captain to greet the deplaning passengers. You should have heard the abusive comments I received.

When I returned to the cockpit, Roger asked, "Did you learn anything?" I admitted that I had no idea what caused our jarring arrival.

"You're flaring it too much; when it works, it's great, but when it doesn't, you're in for trouble. You need to push forward immediately after checking the descent and just let it 'roll on'."

I was in for a rough siege with my 727 landings. After my experience at CLE, I had a persistent tendency to flare too high, and that resulted in a poor landing every time. My captains tried to help, but I was really in a funk. It was a new experience for me, and I wasn't quite sure how to resolve it. I disliked the push-to-land method, but it was the only sure way to land a B-727 smoothly unless, of course, you really did know what you were doing. Flying as First Officer never provided the measure of exploration and reliance on basic flying skills to feel truly at home with the airplane. After moving to the left seat as captain, I was in a position to investigate those areas more deeply.

There were some uncomfortable moments, to be sure, but eventually I was able to make acceptable landings with consistency. The funk was over.

IAM Strike

On July 8, 1966, the IAM (International Association of Machinists) struck United, and the work stoppage lasted 43 days.

When the walkout began, I was on a layover in Rochester, New York. Denied mechanical services, we were dead in the water, but fortunately there was a nucleus of supervisors and a few other non-union employees to provide for bare minimum operations.

JFK Dispatch wanted us to ferry our 727 to Kennedy. Maintenance supervisors took care of our fueling, and flight dispatch took over administrative duties in connection with our release from ROC. We carried two other deadheading crews who were anxious to get home. We finally pulled everything together to fly back, and on arrival we were furloughed. I drove home with mixed emotions; foremost in my mind was, how long will the strike last? As in previous work stoppages, the company made no attempt to operate any revenue-producing flights.

During my previous visit to Erie, Tom Apple announced his plans to fly his new Trail Air to the EAA fly-in at Rockford, Illinois. I never dreamed that I would be able to go but suddenly, if the mechanics stayed out long enough, it might be possible. Even when they did return, it would take time to get the airline up and running. As of July 8, I was on my own, so until I was called back, I could do as I pleased.

Margaret was very upset about the strike. It was on television, and people all over the country were stranded, unable to get home. They didn't have their own private jet like I did.

She was concerned about discretionary expenditures, and was not at all in favor of my Rockford trip. I tried to get her to view it as an unscheduled vacation opportunity. We could simply lock up the house, and Margaret could visit her folks in Erie while I flew to Rockford with Tom. She eventually agreed provided she could take her convertible, which was fine with me. A few days later, Margaret was on her way, and I went to GLA to pull the Chief out of the hangar for the flight to Erie.

Most of my clothes went with Margaret, so it didn't take long to load up. The weather was perfect, although I had to deal with the prevailing west wind. Using the auxiliary fuel tank I made it all the way to Jamestown, N.Y., and from there it was just a short hop to Erie. Margaret arrived shortly after I did, and we were together again.

Tom was busy preparing his Trail Air for the trip. With an early start, I felt we could easily make it to Rockford in one day. Since my plane had the most space, I carried the camping gear and other necessities for the trip.

EAA Fly-In, Rockford '66

In 1966, EAA (Experimental Aircraft Association) was not yet the gigantic event it would become after its move to Oshkosh in '69. The years prior to the move were known as the "Rockford years," and even by the mid-1960s it was apparent that moving to another location was inevitable.

We departed early to be sure of arriving before Saturday, the most important day of the event. It was a dawn patrol leaving Erie, and our first stop was Findlay, Ohio. We soon discovered that Tom's plane was faster, but he just throttled back a bit so we could fly within sight of each other. For communicating en route, he also had a battery-powered radio. Our next fuel stop was Fort Wayne, Ind., and we arrived in Rockford late that afternoon.

Alas! The Chief was relegated to the modern-aircraft parking area; "It's not old enough [to display], and besides, it has those ugly side numbers," the officials ruled. I was terribly disappointed, but there was nothing I could do about it. However, some appreciated the Chief for the classic it was, so all was not lost. The antique airplane community was an extremely cliquish group, and I would see much more evidence of that in the years to come.

In all other respects, we camped out for an enjoyable stay, and Tom won a trophy for Trail Air at the awards dinner Saturday night. On Sunday morning, we broke camp and took off for Erie. Flying eastbound we made much better time, arriving in Erie by mid-afternoon. The mechanic's strike was winding down, so Margaret and I headed for home.

By autumn, it was apparent the Chief's days were numbered. It was a disappointing outcome for such a demanding project, because it fell so far short of my expectations. Margaret's mom and dad arrived in Ringwood for an extended autumn visit.

The Staggerwing Beech

In 1932, aircraft executive Walter Beech and airplane designer Ted Wells collaborated on a project to produce a large, powerful, and fast cabin biplane specifically for business executives. Their

Beechcraft Model 17, popularly known as the "Staggerwing," made its inaugural flight November 4 of that year.

The Stag on the way to Erie. It was quite a different-looking plane with the landing gear retracted. Note that the tail wheel retracts as well. (Photo courtesy of Gene Olsen.)

All other biplanes of that era were constructed with the top-most wing ahead of the lower. Ted pondered what the outcome would be if you built the plane in such a way that the lower wing projected in front of the upper.

His discovery was astonishing. That radical configuration made it almost impossible to stall the airplane, which was a very good thing. The bottom wing stopped flying first, but the top wing, being further back, was still generating lift, so it became an exercise in porpoise effect. Entering the aerodynamic stall, the plane dipped down as always, but as soon as it did, the top wing that was still flying staged a recovery.

Safety enhancement was not the only product of the design. The efficiency of both wings was substantially improved by the creation of additional lift that resulted in a higher cruise speed. "Staggerwing" simply meant that the wings on that particular plane were radical by design, and placing the lower wing ahead of the upper wing earned the plane its unique nickname.

It was also a large airplane compared to any of its siblings. With seats for four passengers in addition to the pilot, a gross weight of 4250 pounds, and a Pratt & Whitney radial engine of 450 horsepower, it was in a class all its own. The Stag (as it was affectionately dubbed) had a decidedly rakish look that invited closer inspection by anyone encountering it.

I was aware of the Beechcraft's existence from the time I first started flying, but I never dreamed of owning one. Many of those available in 1966 were ex-military models used for high-ranking personnel transport of both services. Approximately 700 were built during WWII, it cruised at nearly 200 mph, and I wanted one.

Hank's Staggerwing

Hank Henderson was a senior DC-8 captain flying out of JFK at the same time I was during the fall of 1966. Hank's Staggerwing, N 75544, was manufactured in June of 1942, and was delivered to the U.S. Navy on June 11 (coincidentally my thirteenth birthday). The butyrate dope finish was the brightest red I had ever seen, with black stripes creating the distinctive Beech color scheme. During its service in the military, the Navy GB-2 version was silver and the Army UC-43 version was olive green.

Hank's plane had been rebuilt in the early 1950s by a restoration shop in Louisville, Kentucky. Countless coats of clear and silver dope were applied to the cotton fabric and then wet sanded to the point where the two-inch reinforcing tapes were virtually invisible. In its present condition it was labeled an older restoration, on its last legs before being a candidate for another complete rebuild.

Restoration of that plane, in comparison with my Aeronca Chief project just completed, would be a bigger project by a factor of ten. In other words, one could figure on devoting over 10 years of one's life to it. In addition, the cost would be colossal.

No, I didn't want to restore the Stag, just fly it for fun. Hank's price was non-negotiable at $8500. That was a lot of money in the '60s, and I wasn't sure I could raise it.

Hank had recently installed a remanufactured P&W R 985-14B engine in the Stag at a cost in excess of $5000. In reality, what I was buying was a very expensive engine, and Hank was throwing in the airplane for $3500. Even though the fabric still passed, in a very few years it might not; that was the risk. The engine had accrued only 45 hours since Hank installed it.

Hank's ad in *Trade-A-Plane* always drew a chuckle. Following the usual information describing the plane, he added, "Kitten in air, tiger on ground; non-tail-dragger pilots need not reply." Several other pilots had looked at it, and some even had the money, but Hank refused to sell it to anyone not having tail wheel experience.

Why am I going into such detail about this airplane? For the next nine years, it had a significant impact on the part of my life that was not spent being an airline pilot. Certain life-altering decisions were made because of it, and Margaret was my partner in the experience of owning it. We will see how it impacted her life the following year. So please bear with me as we unfold this amazing story, along with the airline narrative.

Buying the Staggerwing

While flying with Hank's brother Roy on a 727 trip, we discussed the Staggerwing. "I was up in it once," Roy said. Then I asked him, "Do you know why it needed a new engine?" Roy replied, "Hank brought his wife out for a ride in the wintertime, and she was freezing. The only way to get heat for the cabin was to get into the air, but Hank hadn't warmed it up enough. When he applied full power for takeoff, the engine seized."

Temperatures were critically important to the operation of radial engines. The cylinders were "choke bored," meaning the clearance between the piston and the cylinder wall was critical, and the bore didn't expand to normal dimension until the engine reached normal operating temperature. I guess Hank overlooked his piston engine knowledge, because the same was true for the DC-6's much larger 2000 horsepower engine. Anyway, the Stag's engine was ruined, and that's why he needed a replacement. I asked Roy to inform his brother Hank the next time he saw him that I was interested.

About a week later I received a call from Hank with an invitation to come to Wurtsboro, N.Y., where the Stag was hangared. The airport was in the tri-state area near the Delaware River, about a two-hour drive. Once the arrangements were made, Margaret and I drove out.

I was impressed with the Stag's size and unique design, but it looked more rundown than I had expected. The finish was faded and obviously neglected. Hank saw me looking at the wing and simply said, "I'm not a polisher. Let's go flying."

We pushed the Stag outside and began the preflight. The upper wing was so high we needed a ladder to check the fuel supply. The instruments and radios were far from new, and the panel reflected its WWII vintage. In some ways, it added to the mystique.

The Beechcraft was a complex airplane for the 1930s. The placement of radios and instruments reflects its heritage both as an ex-military aircraft and an antique.

Margaret decided not to go on this flight, saying she was content to watch. Hank demonstrated the necessity of pulling the prop "through" several blades to make sure oil wasn't trapped in the lower cylinders.

The appearance of the new engine was especially impressive because it came with the full dress kit. All the pushrod tubes were polished, and the ignition harness leads were chrome plated. As with virtually all radial engines, a little oil was present; in fact, Hank attested to a small leak in the accessory section that needed attention before it was delivered to its new owner.

The engine ran smoothly, as all Pratt & Whitneys do, and sounded very powerful. The large two-bladed propeller and chrome spinner were impressive. I took the copilot seat for this flight.

Operationally, it was much like a miniature DC-6. Takeoff RPM was low at 2300, but manifold pressure went to 35 inches, indicating the presence of a supercharger (blower).

The Stag sported electrically actuated retractable landing gear — including the tail wheel, which was unheard of in old biplanes. It was necessary to use the hand crank on the left side of the cockpit to complete the landing gear retraction cycle and lock it in the "fully retracted" position. Once that was accomplished, and the engine power was reduced to climb, the cabin became a lot quieter and the airspeed continued to build.

Leveled out in cruise, the airspeed indicator settled down at about 170 mph. Hank said with correction for altitude and temperature and a high cruise power setting, it would true out at nearly 200 mph. He selected a quieter and more economical setting of 1850 RPM and 26 inches of manifold pressure. Hank then suggested I take the controls to check out the handling. Even at reduced power, we still indicated airspeed in excess of 160 mph. We flew to Orange County Airport in Montgomery, N.Y., to practice landings.

At that point, I understood why Hank described the Staggerwing as a tiger on the ground. You really needed to stay on the rudders to keep it straight during the takeoff roll, as the torque effect of the powerful engine pulled us to the left. Even though the Aeronca Chief was not nearly so powerful, the technique was the same. Hank assured me that I would adjust to it in very short order. After a few circuits, it was time to fly back to Wurtsboro.

When we returned, Margaret gave me a quizzical look as if to ask, "Well, how was it, and what do you think?"; she also had a big stake in this decision. I guess my smile said it all — like, "Where do I sign?"

Selling the Chief

Wait a minute. Where's the $8500 going to come from? Obviously, the Chief would have to go, but that would only be a drop in the bucket. I thanked Hank for the ride and his time, and said we would call him with our decision. It was clear that there would be no haggling over the price. I said we were definitely interested if we could raise the money. All of Hank's spare parts for the airplane were included (motors, pumps, engine parts, you name it) — a substantial bonus worth at least $1000.

Margaret and I discussed the Stag at length, and she wasn't opposed to buying it if I sold the Chief, and if we could fit it into our budget. I relied heavily on her in the area of money management. Margaret suggested consulting our banker friend, Gil Brown in Erie, about a loan, but I remarked, "Gil won't like our collateral; planes are not his business." However, she rightly pointed out his satisfaction with the way we had managed the loan for Margaret's illness seven years earlier. "I'll call him on Monday," I said.

Gil agreed to advance up to $5000 on signature only, at attractive terms. What was our collateral? Mainly, it was my rather impressive income at United and my good credit rating. "Okay," I thought, "all I need now is to find a buyer for the Chief." I was hoping to get $3500 for it, and then we would have the funds we needed.

I flew the Chief to Wurtsboro to further check out the Stag. The airport owner was aware that I was trying to sell the Chief and said he knew someone who might be interested. "His best offer is $2500," he said. "I don't think I can sell it for that," I replied, "but I might consider $3000." We left it at that, but I didn't hear from him.

"You better take the $2500," Margaret suggested. It was very difficult for me to consider such a low figure as I had more than that invested in the plane, in addition to which I wouldn't be getting a penny for all my work. Over time, I learned the hard way that's how it worked when it came to restoring planes. You got nothing for your labor and were lucky to get return on investment.

Woe is me! October arrived, and I feared Hank might sell the plane to someone else. I never was good at selling stuff — or waiting, either, for that matter. I called Wurtsboro and told the owner I would accept the $2500 if the offer was still on the table. He responded, "I'll call you back." When I didn't hear anything after a day or so, I decided to fly over there.

My timing was perfect, and the buyer was there. Once he saw the plane again, he bought it on the spot. He got a fabulous deal;

I would never have sold it so cheaply except for so desperately needing the money. But that's usually the case. You always need the money.

When I called Hank, he was out on a DC-8 trip and wouldn't be home for a few days. That meant sweating it out even longer. Eventually, though, we did put the deal together, and the Staggerwing was ours.

"Where do you plan to keep it?" Hank asked. When I told him I had a hangar at Greenwood Lake, he groaned, "That's not a good place for the Stag; the runway is short and there's a hill at the one end."

"I'll just have to be careful," I replied.

"Okay, but we'll do your checkout at Orange County." When that delightful day arrived, I was thrilled — the plane definitely had a heavy feel. There was a tail wheel lock to assist in keeping the Stag straight during takeoff and landing. I soon discovered the main problem with landing was getting the tail down. The solution for that was to retract the flaps immediately after main gear contact, and the tail touched down much more quickly. That's how I managed my landings for the ten years I owned it. We succeeded in landing safely at GLA, but Hank reiterated his dislike of the place.

Approaching a Major Career Milestone

That's enough discussion about small planes; let's talk about the big ones. The airline was in flux, and immense changes were on the horizon. I reminded Margaret that I was reaching the end of my comfortable stint as First Officer, and my professional life was about to undergo drastic change.

The airline seniority system was brutal. You worked your way up the First Officer ladder for ten years or so, and suddenly you were right back at the bottom again as a junior Captain. Not pay-wise, of course; in that respect, I would be due for a substantial raise. It was home life that suffered. It meant, first of all, being on reserve, ready to report for work any time of the day or night, and some call-outs were on very short notice. If a captain got sick, or for a host of other reasons couldn't fly his trip, you were it.

My promotion was no surprise. I knew it was coming, and my plan was to bid DC-6 Captain at Newark. With the jet bidding restriction removed, Capital Viscount captains were now eligible to fly the B-727, and vacancies were being posted on the bulletin board with increasing frequency. Some were moving up to the Caravelle as well.

A few Viscount Captain vacancies had been awarded to pilots junior to me, but I wouldn't consider that because I didn't have the type rating for the Viscount, and the training required didn't justify the short time I would be flying it. I felt quite certain I would be flying Jet Captain within five years.

What is a type rating? Under FAA rules, all planes with a certified takeoff weight of more than 8500 pounds must be specifically listed on your Airline Transport Pilot license, as was the case regarding my endorsement for the Douglas DC-6/7. As of the autumn of 1966, I was still not in a position to fly DC-6 Captain in Newark, but I kept reminding Margaret it wouldn't be long.

A Jet Bridge to the Captain's Seat

A new possibility had just emerged — Denver. It had always been a very senior domicile, and normally the only opportunity to transfer there would be the retirement of captains based there. Any vacancies would promptly be filled by Denver First Officers provided no one bid in from outside.

The FAA, in all its wisdom, issued a mandate that all airline pilots flying in the United States must retire upon reaching their 60th birthday. That regulation had created a few Captain vacancies in DEN, but the biggest shift was in the First Officer ranks. Some DEN B-720 First Officers were senior enough to fly Captain on the smaller jets at other domiciles, so they were leaving Denver in droves and joining the ranks of commuters.

That, in conjunction with ever-increasing numbers of 727 Captain vacancies, created an opportunity for me. I had been watching those bids for some time now, and Denver B-720 First Officer slots were now within my reach.

The B-720 was a lighter version of the 707, with a gross weight of 213,000 pounds, slightly shorter and with fewer seats. The main difference was that the 720 carried much less fuel than the 707, which meant that some components, like the landing gear, could be lighter.

A United B-720 at Denver, 1967. It was my last plane as a First
Officer, and I expected to fly it for five years. Less than a year
later, I was promoted to Captain on the B-737.

In its domestic role, it was still a very competitive airplane and
had tremendous passenger appeal. Coast-to-coast flying was still the
domain of the DC-8, but segments like DEN-CHI-BAL (Baltimore)
and DEN-SFO (San Francisco), and even DEN-Salt Lake-Seattle,
were well within the 720's capability. How about cockpit equipment?
By the latest standard, set by the 727, the 720 was ancient. It reflected
technology of the 1960s, with primarily Sperry avionics and a
primitive flight director and autopilot.

"Hey, Hon, how would you feel about moving to Denver?" It
caught her by surprise: "I'd have to think about that," she replied.
The only time Margaret had ever been to the mile-high city was a
brief visit five years earlier, during my DC-6 Captain upgrading.
I knew she liked it, but I'm quite sure she never considered the
possibility of living there.

Commuting

By definition, commuting simply meant flying out of a crew
base other than the location where you lived. Although it was not
explicitly forbidden, United frowned on the practice. Being a reliable
employee meant availability for work, and that shouldn't be impeded
by living an unrealistic distance from your domicile. As of late 1966,

if you bid a vacancy, the assumption by United was that you would move there. It was really all about seniority. If a pilot bid a vacancy on the B-720 and he had seniority at that base to hold schedule, then he might be permitted to commute by riding on the jump seat or using a pass.

Conversely, a reserve pilot must never attempt to commute, because availability for short notice assignments would be questionable at best. A reserve pilot only had eight guaranteed days off each month, and those were divided into four two-day breaks. Portions of those would have to be allocated for travel, creating a totally unacceptable lifestyle.

Even a pilot holding a good schedule still might have a miserable existence; it would depend on the number of available flights, weather, and a host of other variables, including reduction in flying that might revert said pilot back to reserve. Jump seat availability was contingent on seniority, so that was also a consideration.

Most commuters carried a fistful of tickets, just in case. Riding jump seat usually wasn't a problem unless you traveled a route highly populated with commuters. Moving to a new domicile with low seniority on the equipment guaranteed assignment to reserve. Since I would not be a schedule-holder on the B-720 in Denver, we were definitely going to have to relocate, period.

"That means selling our precious Palo Alto we worked so hard for," Margaret lamented.

"They have nice houses in Denver," I countered. Although I hadn't looked, it was a safe assumption.

"What about 720 pay, assuming you are on reserve?" she asked.

"It should be at least $500 a month more," I replied. "That'll help toward the new plane payment." It was only October, so I said, "Think about it some more."

There was no further discussion for the time being; however, there were two other significant issues I didn't mention. First and foremost, I hated the drive to JFK; the second was Hank Henderson's vociferous objection to GLA as a home base for the Staggerwing.

I was totally immersed in my new toy at the airport. I removed the cowling, looking for that pesky oil leak in the accessory section and familiarizing myself with the engine. When it comes to radials, there was nothing quite like a Pratt & Whitney. Even mine, their smallest version, was built to the same standard as the 2000 horsepower R-2800 I was so used to on the DC-6. In this case, everything on the engine was brand spanking new.

I was thrilled with the front end of the Stag, but the rest of it was begging for attention. I began rubbing out that red dope, and with four wings, that meant a lot of polishing. The lower wing where I began clearly demonstrated the possibilities. Even though the finish was abraded to the primer in certain areas, it looked beautiful after I touched it up. Some enameled parts needed attention as well. It was just an enormously fussy job that couldn't be rushed.

Hank stopped by one day and expressed amazement. "Gee, I never dreamed it could look that shiny again," he said. I had just completed the job when the Olsens paid us a visit at GLA on their way to the American President Lines pier in Jersey City. Gene was just passing through on his way to Panama and San Pedro, Calif. As in my case, Gene was nearing promotion to Captain in the totally different arena of commanding a ship.

Gene was impressed with the Stag and wanted to fly it, but I declined because I had already decided to limit my operations at GLA. "Well," Gene asked, "can we at least pull it out of the hangar and take some pictures?" Gene always carried his Leica camera with him, so we got the plane out and started the engine.

"Hop in and we'll taxi down to the end of the runway where I can do a power check," I said. I hadn't run the engine since Hank and I brought the plane home a month earlier. While we were out there doing the run-up, Gene said, "I'd like to get out and take some pictures with the engine running." Those shots taken that day were the best I ever had of the Stag; Gene was an excellent photographer.

Being off for Thanksgiving, I asked Margaret, "How about flying out to Erie for turkey dinner?" Without hesitation, she said, "Yes, let's."

The day we left GLA was a perfect autumn day. I needed assistance getting the plane out of the hangar, and fortunately one of the guys at the airport was there to help me. While he was admiring the Stag, and in conversation, I mentioned that I had never flown it solo before. He was taken aback by that revelation, and I noticed he stuck around as if he were expecting an airshow of some kind.

RAMAR, the Staggerwing Beechcraft, at Greenwood Lake Airport, N.J., October 1966. Gene Olsen took this photo while I was doing an engine check. We did not fly it that day, but I was able to give him a ride the following year in Denver.

After exiting the plane to take the preceding picture, Gene reboarded and took this photo of me in the pilot seat.

On the way to Erie, we were comparing the Staggerwing's performance to our last trip in the Chief, and shortly spotted a lake ahead. I said, "That must be Lake Chautauqua" (near Jamestown, N.Y.). Suddenly, we both realized it was Lake Erie we were looking at, and we were almost there. After landing, we taxied to Earl's hangar, and all the guys came out. The Stag was a rare sight everywhere we went and always drew a crowd.

We enjoyed a great Thanksgiving with Mom and Dad Taylor, but we ended up staying longer than we thought we would. Our plans called for flying home on Saturday, but we awoke to find eight inches of snow on the ground, and the weather was crappy. Fortunately, the Stag was cozy in Mac's hangar. I had to get back, so we bought tickets on Allegheny to Pittsburgh and then used a pass to Newark. Fortunately, friends picked us up there for the ride back to Ringwood.

Elbert (Bert) Van Doren

We only met a few new people while we were at Greenwood Lake Airport. Bert Van Doren and his wife Joan were two, and we became very close friends beginning in the summer of '66. Bert was well acquainted with Sam Teece, whom I introduced earlier in connection with the Chief project.

Sam maintained Bert's 1964 S model Bonanza, the latest version of that famous plane. Bert owned a sand and gravel business in Ringwood and even had an airstrip on his property. Because of security concerns, he moved the plane to GLA.

I met Bert one day when his Bonanza was in the shop for maintenance. He was already familiar with my Aeronca Chief project, and we struck up a conversation, as all pilots do. Even though the Chief and his Bonanza were miles apart, performance-wise, we had a lot in common.

When Bert learned about my airline flying, he wondered if I would help him with his Instrument Rating. I said, "Sure, I'd be glad to."

One Sunday morning, Bert and Joan invited us to join them for a flight to Nantucket Island, a neat place accessible only by airplane or boat. On the way, I suggested a couple of ILS approaches, first at Providence, Rhode Island, and then another one in Massachusetts. It was quite a day, and a good time was had by all.

When we got home and I called Bert to tell him the Stag was stuck in Erie, he generously offered to come to the rescue with his Bonanza. "It'll have to be next weekend," Bert said.

Sunday dawned clear as a bell, but the temperature was only 10 degrees. I had my doubts about getting the Bonanza started, but Bert nonchalantly said, "Oh, it'll go." Under such extreme conditions it was best to preheat the engine, and with all the cranking we were doing the battery was wearing down, and it didn't appear we would make it to Erie that day. Finally, with the use of booster cables, the engine did start, but we lost two hours of daylight in the process. Sunset was early, so I had concerns about getting home before dark. Regardless, we took off and landed at Erie an hour and a half later.

The Stag needed fuel, and the daylight was rapidly slipping away. Because it had been in Mac's hangar, getting my engine started was not a problem, but it was almost 3 p.m. by the time we took off for Greenwood Lake. Bert went on ahead, and sure enough, by the time we arrived, the sun had set. I considered diverting to Caldwell, N.J. — but no, I insisted on landing at GLA, as there was still a vestige of daylight remaining. However, it was too dark to see the windsock to determine the wind direction and velocity.

I made my approach to the north, but landing in the opposite direction would have been more prudent to avoid the hill at the end of the runway that caused Hank Henderson such angst.

I carried a little extra speed on final approach, and the plane refused to land. I was squandering prodigious amounts of the 2000-foot runway at an alarming rate, but by then it was too late to go around. I forced the Stag onto the runway and applied heavy braking, using up every available foot of runway. Once I stepped out of the plane, I detected a light breeze from the south, reinforcing my suspicion that I should have landed in the opposite direction. At that defining moment I was convinced we must find a new home for the plane.

Denver, 1967

Back at United, I flew 80 hours for December, which necessitated eight trips to the airport. I bid that line to be able to spend Christmas

Eve with Margaret, and visit OV and Mary Pezzi on Christmas Day. When my flight arrived at JFK, a nor'easter was in progress, but because it was mostly rain and sleet it didn't affect our arrival.

After I left JFK for the drive back to Ringwood, I discovered that the weather situation in northern New Jersey was quite different. By the time I reached Ringwood it was snowing heavily, with ten inches already on the ground. I wasn't able to get my car up the hill to Robin Lane, so I parked down below and tramped home through the snow. What a night! What a holiday! When I reached the house, I discovered that Margaret was sick as a dog and hadn't been able to get to the store, or even finish trimming the tree. Enough already! I was totally fed up with JFK and nor'easters, so I said to Margaret, "Is it time to move to Denver yet?" "Yes," she said. "I'm ready."

Bids for the particular vacancy I was interested in closed on December 31. On the chance I wouldn't make it back to the flight office in time, I filled out the paperwork before the Christmas trip and left it in the office with a note, "Submit on confirmation by phone." The main reason for delaying my decision to bid Denver for so long was that I was on reserve during the summer and fall, and only had to drive in to JFK two or three times a month.

I finished trimming the tree and fixed us something to eat; fortunately, by Christmas Day Margaret felt better and the storm had passed. We drove to Matawan for dinner with OV and Mary as planned. Monmouth County Airport wasn't working out for OV's Mooney, either, and they were considering a move to Allentown — attractively priced T-hangars were available at ABE Airport.

Leaving JFK

I submitted my bid for the DEN B-720 First Officer opening, and I was awarded the vacancy. Within just a few short months, we would be relocating to Colorado. It was sobering to contemplate the implications of the step I had just taken. We had to sell our house and one car; move a large biplane, a grand piano, plus all of our belongings two-thirds of the way across the country; and in my spare time, return to Denver Tech and get checked out on another jet. No big deal, right? Since this was a voluntary relocation, all expenses in connection with the transfer were on the bidder — in other words, me.

Denver and the B-720

"What's the training schedule?" Margaret inquired. "January twentieth to whatever it takes," I replied. "How about coming out to 720 school with me? We'll make a vacation of it and go house hunting on weekends." Margaret's response was, "Sounds great, but we've got to put the house up for sale before we go."

We listed the Ringwood house with a local broker, and it was soon time to head for Denver. Margaret rented a machine to work on her sewing projects while staying at the Gotham.

It was the customary three weeks of ground school followed by simulator sessions, with very little time in the airplane. The 720 simulator was fairly sophisticated, reducing airplane sessions to a bare minimum. The hourly cost of operating the four-engine 720 for training was staggering. As it turned out, I was blessed with several unscheduled airplane periods due to limited simulator availability.

Classroom work was mundane by this time; I didn't feel any apprehension in connection with this school, because the 720 was just another member of the Boeing family of jets, albeit an earlier version of the one I'd just been flying. The 720 was my sixth airplane, and its systems were quite similar to the 727 in many ways — just not as sophisticated. To a degree, that made it easier, because the training dealt with many of the technological advances I was already familiar with. Concerning the course of study, however, it was still a lot of work to learn new procedures and numbers. There were always emergency procedures that had to be committed to memory.

What about the 720's engines? Even though they were produced by Pratt & Whitney, they were ancient compared with the JT8D. The JT3 was a spinoff of the old J57, widely used in military jets. As I mentioned earlier, they were not "fan" engines. All the air for combustion came from ram effect. Because the B-720 used these non-fan JT3 engines, and because the wing flap system lacked some of the sophistication of that used on the 727, the 720 required copious amounts of runway during take off. It was definitely a step backward from the engines on the 727 that I was so familiar with.

From a passenger viewpoint, none of that mattered. It was still a Boeing 700-series jet, and once in the air, it could keep up with anything out there. It was a large airplane, and with its four wing-mounted engines it was very impressive to behold.

Margaret's New House

House hunting was on the agenda for our first weekend in Denver, and Margaret liked the Perl-Mack homes best. There were attractive models at two locations, one of which was Montbello, a recently annexed development just northeast of Stapleton Airport. (I say "annexed" because it was incorporated as an integral part of the City of Denver.) Perl-Mack homes were priced around $20,000. Margaret's choice was the Granada, a four-level split with tons of space — a really large house for the money.

The alternate location was in Broomfield, Colo., near the Jefferson County Airport ("Jeffco"). I felt quite certain Jeffco would be our new home base for the Staggerwing, so naturally I favored the models there. Margaret hadn't decided, so a commitment was deferred until later.

While in Broomfield, we stopped at the airport to check on a T-hangar for the Stag. Although none were available at the time, Mountview Aviation agreed to put me on their waiting list. The units were good-sized, fairly new, and the rent was only $55. The manager said they had a fairly rapid turnover and that by summer a hangar would likely be available. I was favorably impressed with Mountview — they were a Cessna dealer operating a flight school.

Margaret liked Denver. I was usually back at the hotel by five o'clock every day, so we soon settled into a comfortable routine. If we didn't want to eat at the hotel, there were plenty of restaurants nearby. Other members of my 720 class also had their wives there, so often we would go out together — it was such a contrast to my experience there five years earlier, fixing TV dinners at Gotham West.

By early February we began simulator training. The schedule varied depending on availability, with sessions occasionally conducted in the middle of the night. Like the 727, this plane had a flight engineer station manned by pilots on our seniority list.

We decided on the house in Montbello, as it was only ten minutes from Stapleton and United flight operations. Perl-Mack promised to have it ready by mid-May, so everything was settled on the Colorado end; we just needed to sell our home in New Jersey.

By the end of February, my training was completed except for the required observer time. Since my activation date wasn't until June 1, 1967, I returned to flying 727 First Officer at JFK.

Our Denver home in the Montbello subdivision. It was a
beautiful house and unbelievably inexpensive at $20,000. No,
I didn't build any planes here. It was home for exactly one year.

Odds and Ends Leaving Ringwood

I was anxious to get the Staggerwing out of Greenwood Lake
as soon as possible. The best temporary base for it was Erie, where
I could rent a T-hangar. OV Pezzi agreed to help — it was simply
a matter of coordinating our schedules and picking a suitable day.

The opportunity came in early March, and the girls went
shopping while OV and I went to Erie. We flew formation, as our
cruising speeds were compatible. By noon we arrived in Erie, put the
Stag away, and had a nice lunch with Tom and Earl. I was pleased to
be free of GLA and its concerns. The flight home in OV's Mooney
went smoothly, and upon our return the four of us went out to dinner.
Needless to say, it was my treat.

Not long after that, we had a buyer for the Ringwood house;
unfortunately, the closing would not be until June. That was okay,
though, as it would provide another opportunity to visit Mary
and OV.

The emphasis shifted to packing. It's amazing how fast one
accrues possessions. Just a few years ago we had virtually nothing,
and look what we were faced with now. Loading day was May 10,

and United allocated seven days for the move. By carefully bidding the May schedule, Margaret and I would be able to stop in Erie for a short visit.

Allied Van Lines arrived on schedule, and it was past three o'clock by the time everything was loaded. Since we could no longer stay in the house, we started out on our journey to Denver. Margaret may have shed a few tears as we left.

Going West

We decided to spend the night near Albany, and Margaret wanted to spend one night in Tonawanda with Nancy, so we didn't reach Erie until the third day.

Coincidentally, Margaret's dad was retiring from his liquor store managerial position on June 1, and he and Mom expressed interest in coming to Denver to visit our new home. Once settled in Colorado, we would be returning to Erie to pick up the Staggerwing, so the germ of an idea began to emerge.

"Would you consider flying back to Denver with us?" I asked them. I knew they had no experience flying in small planes, so I suggested a local test hop before making a commitment. It sounded great to them, so that's how we left it. During our brief time in Erie, I went to the airport to arrange for the Stag's annual inspection. It wasn't necessary for me to be there while the plane was undergoing the maintenance, but I was very interested in the results of the fabric test, which was an integral part of every one of those inspections.

My recent contacts with Mountview Aviation in Colorado led me to believe they would have a T-hangar for me by June 1, so the proposed timetable was working out well.

Leaving Erie in Margaret's convertible, our first overnight stop was Chicago, and the day after that, Grand Island, Neb., finally reaching our destination on Sunday, May 15. Until the furniture arrived, we stayed at the Holiday Inn in Aurora, Colo. — at last we were in Denver.

When United learned I was already there, they advanced my activation date. The Taylors were entertaining Nancy and family in Erie over Memorial Day weekend, so Margaret flew east to be with them; I joined them a few days later. While there, the Olsens visited in their Cessna 180 to discuss their upcoming Alaska trip, and they wondered if Margaret and I could join them there in mid-June. That sounded exciting, so we gave a provisional yes, pending my 1967 vacation assignment at my new domicile.

While in Erie, we took Margaret's parents up for a trial flight in the Staggerwing. It was just a brief flight to Niagara Falls and back, and based on the favorable outcome from that, we finalized our plans for the flight to Denver the end of June.

RAMAR

Margaret had a new name for the Staggerwing: *RAMAR*. No, it's not because of the way it handles, or descriptive of the king of the jungle; it was a blending of RAy and MARgaret.

While the plane was still in the shop at Derion's, I was able to do some work on it. Tom discovered a cracked wheel during the inspection; this could have been a potential disaster if it separated during takeoff or landing. Searching in *Trade-A-Plane*, we found a brand-new wheel still packed in cosmoline at a surplus warehouse in California, and had it shipped by air. All maintenance was completed on Monday following the Memorial Day holiday, so I took the kids up for a ride. The fabric test was marginal, but it still passed.

Margaret and I arrived back in Denver just in time for my Baltimore trip two days later. We checked out the new T-hangar at Jeffco and spent a day cleaning it out. With the upcoming Alaska trip and the pending closing on the Ringwood house, it looked like it would be awhile before *RAMAR* would be able to occupy the hangar at Jeffco.

The Alaska Trip

I successfully rescheduled my vacation, making the Alaska trip with Gene and Jane Olsen possible. On June 17, Margaret and I boarded a DC-8 for Seattle, where we rented a car for a tour of Mt. Rainier. We spent the night on the mountain at Paradise Inn, returning to Seattle the following day to have dinner at the Space Needle's revolving restaurant. What a view! One rotation took about an hour, and we found it to be a very impressive tourist attraction. After spending another night in Seattle, we left for Fairbanks on Alaska Airlines, stopping at Juneau and Anchorage on the way.

We registered at the Golden Nugget Motel in Fairbanks and then drove out to the small airport where the Olsens were supposed to land and learned that they had just arrived. Amazingly, with no specific coordination on their part or ours, we arrived in Fairbanks within two hours of each other.

Gene had the baggage and rear-seat area of the Cessna jam-packed with at least 400 pounds of survival food and high-powered rifles, just in case we decided to go bear hunting. They had sufficient provisions to last a month. All that "stuff" made the plane so tail-heavy, it was difficult for Gene to raise it for takeoff. We piled all of it in the trunk of our rental car so that Margaret and Jane could sit in the back seat of the plane during the excursions we would be taking over the next few days.

Gene wanted to fly north across the Brooks Range to Point Barrow, and our first stop was Bettles, near the Arctic Circle. It was a difficult adjustment to have daylight into the wee hours of the morning. Because it was raining at Barrow, we decided instead to visit Anaktuvuk Pass, an Eskimo village on the south side of the Brooks Range. There were no roads north of Fairbanks; the only access to the outside world for these folks was by air or dog sleds. (Snowmobiles were not widely used at that time.) The airstrip was very rough, used primarily by C-46 (Curtiss Commando) cargo planes delivering fuel oil and other necessities to the Eskimo village.

The locals came out in droves to greet us. Because it was summertime, they were living in tents, but they showed us their winter quarters as well, which consisted of earthen huts. I didn't care to venture into one of the huts, but I think Margaret and Jane did. Throughout the village, caribou hides were hanging out to dry. In the past, the Eskimos migrated with the herd and lived off of it, but now the villagers stayed in the village year-round. Their water came from a fast-moving river nearby that was teeming with fish. The only permanent building was a school, built by the government. The village was seldom visited by strangers, but I'm sure that all changed with the building of the Dalton Highway to Prudhoe Bay.

Returning to Bettles for dinner, we saw a sign at the airport that indicated temperatures fell as low as 60 below in winter. We returned to Fairbanks at midnight, still in broad daylight. The next day was rainy, so our activities were somewhat curtailed. The Alaska A-67 Centennial Exposition was in full swing during our visit, and we had sourdough pancakes and reindeer stew at the Palace Saloon. The Blue Angels Navy Aerobatic Team performed at Wainwright Air Base to cap off the day.

The following day, it was time for us to start back to close on the Ringwood house. We were hoping to see Mount McKinley on the way to Anchorage, but it was obscured by clouds. We had time for a little sightseeing in Anchorage before boarding our Alaska Airlines flight, so we visited the only FAA-tower-controlled seaplane base in the world.

Our final dinner together was at the Captain Cook Restaurant, and then we said our goodbyes and the Olsens flew back to Fairbanks. Unable to get seats on the night flight to Seattle, we overnighted in Anchorage and boarded an Alaska Air Convair 990 flight at 11 a.m. the next morning. We arrived in Seattle at 5 p.m. for our "red-eye" flight to New York, arriving at 7:30 a.m. OV Pezzi picked us up at LaGuardia and took us to their house, where we got some much-needed sleep.

Closing Date in Ringwood

We completed the sale of the Ringwood house as planned, followed by a ride to LaGuardia for the flight to Buffalo. Mom and Dad Taylor picked us up and drove to Erie, arriving at midnight.

By this time we were thinking, "Will this crazy trip never end?" No, not just yet, as we still needed to fly the Staggerwing to Denver.

On June 29, we loaded *RAMAR* for the trip west. We took off at 7:20 a.m. with the intention of flying all the way to Moline, Ill., for our first stop. Unfortunately, that didn't happen because nearing Chicago, I felt a tap on my shoulder — Father needs to go to the bathroom right away. Wow! That was exciting. Our best bet was to land at South Bend, Ind., which was just then passing under our left wing. Because we were at 10,500 feet, I warned everyone to "pop" their ears during the rapid descent. A few minutes later we were on the ground, and Dad was off to the restroom. That was not a fuel stop, but I gassed up anyway in the hope that our next leg would be longer, and we did make it all the way to Omaha in about three and a half hours.

After lunch, we were off again for the final leg to Denver. A little over three hours later, we landed at Jeffco airport. It was a long flight, and my ears rang incessantly for days; subsequently, I always made sure to wear a headset. Margaret's parents survived with aplomb. They were quite relaxed, even nodding off at times.

Since Margaret's convertible was some 25 miles away, I caught a ride to Denver to retrieve the car, while Margaret and her parents waited in the lounge at the airport. Eventually, we were all safely home at 12941 Elgin Place, Denver, Colorado.

With vacation over, it was time to get back to work. Flying the B-720 out of Denver was a new experience for me. My captains were all United types, to a man; I would hate to be starting out there as a new First Officer. I did my best to fit in, but it was an uphill battle for a while, and diplomacy was still the order of the day.

Where did I fly? What were my destinations? Denver was centrally located on United's system, and Baltimore was a frequent layover point for the 720. Most of my flights stopped at O'Hare, which by that time was the principle hub for United. From Denver, many of my flights were to western destinations including Los Angeles, San Francisco, and Seattle.

Washington, D.C., was a case in point for expansion of the "hub" concept. Even though Dulles International Airport had been open for some time, it was slow to achieve the hub status it was destined to attain. Since Baltimore Friendship Airport (BAL) was conveniently located on the parkway between the two cities, it was an attractive destination for Washingtonians.

I'd like to tell a story about flying into Salt Lake City. When flying westbound out of Denver, our flights were required to cross the Front Range of the Rocky Mountains almost immediately. In fact, we flew a circuitous route to climb high enough to clear them. Arriving at Salt Lake, it was the opposite problem: you couldn't descend until clearing the Wasatch Range immediately to the east.

The United old-timers had their own solution for descending into Salt Lake. The first step was to cancel IFR and start a visual descent into Farley's Canyon. It wasn't so bad during the day, but they did it at night as well, and that could be downright *scary*. They obviously knew their way around that canyon, but I remember looking out my side window and seeing nothing but rocks. By doing this, they were able to call Salt Lake approach control and request a right turn for Runway 36. There were all sorts of pilots in the Captain ranks at Denver. Many of United's most senior pilots were based there. One of my captains, Dub Smith, was so short it seemed impossible for him to reach the rudder pedals.

On one of my Baltimore trips I saw a notice on the bulletin board in flight operations. It was official — United had just placed an order with Boeing for 75 737s, with deliveries starting in late 1967.

Boeing 737-200

The Boeing 737 was a shortened version of the 727 with the fuselage retaining the same cross-section, a similar wing and flap system and two wing-mounted JT8 fan engines. Passenger capacity was 100, and it held 22,000 pounds of fuel. That provided for a three-and-one-half-hour range, ideal for the intercity routes being flown by the prop fleet. In two short years, United would become a pure-jet airline.

It was an odd-looking airplane by any accepted standards of the day. Germany's Lufthansa Airlines bought the first ones, 737-100s; those were even shorter and were dubbed "Luftschwein," for "the flying pig." Other disparaging names appeared, like "Fat Albert" and the one that stuck for all time, "The Guppy." We always referred to it as just the '37. The reason I'm spending so much time telling you about this plane is because I would fly it exclusively as Captain for the next ten years.

The announcement of the 737 purchase caught me totally by surprise. Oh, I knew we would be "all jet" soon, but the size of the order and the rapid delivery schedule upset my projected timetable completely. I had expected to be on the 720 as First Officer for five years. The 737 delivery schedule translated into 500 Captain openings within the next two years, and the first bids were likely to be posted by the end of the year.

I was "frozen" until May 1968. (When bidding a new airplane that required training, you were obligated to fly that airplane in schedule for a minimum of one year.) That's okay, though; by the time initial training was completed, and UAL received more planes, it would be late spring '68 anyway.

Who would I be bidding against for 737 Captain vacancies? That would be interesting, because many First Officers immediately senior to me had taken Prop Captain bids, and they would be frozen even longer than I.

The first bids would probably be at O'Hare. That would mean another relocation for us, and we'd have to pay for that one, too. Oh boy, how will Margaret feel about that? I simply couldn't pass up an opportunity to fly Jet Captain. How about the money? My pay would almost double.

In mid-July, we received a surprise call from the Olsens; they were planning to land at Jeffco later that day. Gene and Jane were returning from Alaska, so naturally we invited them to stay with us. We were at the airport for their arrival — it was good to be together again so we could cook up some mischief. I was on reserve, but the crew desk seldom called; I had only flown one trip since we had gotten back from vacation.

Mom and Dad came out to the airport with us, and all six of us piled into Margaret's convertible. I was anxious to show the Olsens our new house in Montbello; we had plenty of room, even with the Taylors being there. The Olsens spent a week with us, and I was finally able to take Gene for a ride in *RAMAR*; a day or so later, they flew home to Kobelt Airport in New York. It was a great visit.

By July 20, Mom and Dad were ready to leave as well, so we put them on a United 727 bound for Chicago and Buffalo. Margaret's sister and brother-in-law, Nancy and Ray Phillips, drove them home to Erie over the weekend.

It was time to consider buying a second car. I discussed it with Capt. Dub Smith on one of my Baltimore trips, and he said he had an almost-new '67 Cadillac Sedan DeVille for sale, and was only asking $5000 for it. After trying it out, I told Dub that we would take it — it was a lovely car with all the goodies, even automatic temperature control. I was spending money in Denver like the proverbial "drunken sailor," and we were now in that precarious realm of deficit spending. Proceeds from the Ringwood house were long gone, and our bank balance continued its downward spiral; I really needed to move to the left seat and start flying Captain.

Margaret Learns to Fly

Referring back to our *RAMAR* trip in early June with Mom and Dad on board, Margaret expressed concern about the trip: "Four of us were on board, but only you knew how to fly the plane. What if something would have happened to you?"

Of course, she was referring to my previous episode on the Swift trip with PG, when I temporarily passed out and he was able to fly until I recovered. Margaret did take the controls on occasion, but the size and complexity of *RAMAR* raised doubt about her ability to fly it on her own to a survivable landing.

"I've been thinking about taking a few flying lessons at Mountview to learn basic flying skills," she said. I told her I thought that was a great idea, and suggested she take the new "pinch hitter" course that Cessna was offering. Margaret enrolled in Mountview's primary curriculum immediately and took her first flying lesson August 11, her second the next day, and her third the following Monday. She really seemed determined to learn to fly.

RAMAR's hangar faced Runway 29, the primary runway at Jeffco, so I would see her taking off in "70 FOX," her favorite Cessna 150 trainer. It only had a 100 horsepower engine, so at Denver's mile-high elevation it rolled a long way down the runway before finally lifting off. All of Margaret's primary training was in the "150," and her instructor, Dale Anderson, was one of Mountview's best. She completed the "pinch hitter" course and just kept going, successfully completing her first solo flight on September 11 after eight hours of dual instruction with Dale.

Margaret with one of the Cessna 150s assigned to the flight school at Mountview Aviation in Denver.

Jeffco was a tower-controlled airport, so Margaret was familiar with proper two-way radio procedure from her very first lesson. Unlike so many hit-and-miss programs, hers was conducted by an approved Cessna Flight School, and the private pilot course she was enrolled in was quite structured. She flew at least twice a week and attended ground school for Navigation, Meteorology, and FARs (Federal Air Regulations). A passing grade was required in all of these to receive her private license. How different it was in 1950, when I got my private license with just 20 true/false questions.

Some requirements remained the same, such as the cross-country flights, although Margaret's dual and solo legs were much longer than mine were. She had to fly over 200 miles to North Platte, Nebraska and back. She begged Dale for permission to take me with her, but he wouldn't allow it; "It has to be solo," he insisted. And so it was, but she found the trip awfully boring. Her destination was in sight when it was still 100 miles away. The trip took five and a half hours round-trip using Omni range radio navigation, as well as visual map reading for identifying landmarks over the route.

Her training continued into December, and by that time she had logged almost 50 hours of flight time. Just as it was for me, she needed a recommendation ride by an independent instructor. Margaret passed, with a notation in her logbook recommending one more session with Dale to hone her landing skills. The following day, December 7, 1967, she took her Private Pilot flight test with FAA Examiner John Smith, and passed with flying colors. The exam lasted one hour, and during the debriefing John paid Margaret a compliment that she always treasured: "I would not hesitate to let any of my family members fly with you." Understandably, Margaret was a very proud girl.

This innocuous piece of paper was very precious to Margaret, and she was very proud of it. It entitled her to act as pilot in command of any single-engine land airplane with proper endorsement in her logbook.

We went out to celebrate her achievement — she had become a licensed pilot in less than four months. Margaret went to Buffalo to spend Christmas with her family. I was on reserve but the crew desk never called me, which was most unusual.

On the way home from one of my Baltimore trips over New Year's '68, Margaret and I met at O'Hare, and flew home together on my flight. It was one of the few times during my career that we were able to coordinate in this fashion. Of course, it wasn't an accident; we worked it out over the phone. "Long distance" was one luxury that I indulged myself in. Margaret and I maintained close contact, no matter where I was. That was long before cell phones, and the pay phone was king. Using my AT&T credit card worked very well for many years.

Thus far, I had flown the B-720 airplane less than 300 hours. I felt semi-retired; such a low activity level was never duplicated in the remaining years of my career with United.

1967 was a standout year — we never did so much in such a short span of time again. As I write this, it seems incredible that we accomplished it all.

Chapter 14

Captain, Boeing 737 — The '60s End With Trauma and Drama 1968-1969

My First Year as Captain — 21 More to Go

Margaret continued her flying at Mountview, checking out in the new Cessna Cardinal and the four-place Cessna 172 Skyhawk. Now I was the passenger, for a change, and she was the PIC (pilot in command). She liked that.

January 1968: This was a brand-new Cessna Model 172, and Margaret was going to take me flying in it. She looked very proud. The plane belonged to Mountview Aviation at Jeffco Airport and was assigned to their flight school.

I was over at the United hangar one day when I noticed a strange-looking jet parked on the ramp adjacent to DENTK. It was B-737, #9002, the first of our order of 75 airplanes — 9002 became our trainer, not just for pilots but for maintenance personnel as well. In fact, it was rather lumpy looking, and this Boeing came equipped with an integral stairway at the front door; that feature soon earned the not-too-surprising name, "Air Stair." Maintenance personnel came over and opened the door while I did a walk-around inspection.

January 1968: United's first 737, N 9002. (9001 was the prototype.) Note "air stair" door. This plane was brand new and just delivered from Seattle and San Francisco. The interior (i.e., the seats) had not yet been installed. This plane became our trainer. (The two people standing by the nose of the plane are Margaret and her mother.)

I showed the supervisor my ID and asked, "Can I take a peek inside?" "Sure, come aboard." Everything was decidedly "Boeing." There was nothing in the fuselage interior except for two rows of seats just aft of the front door. What I was interested in was farther forward, in the cockpit. Everything there was the latest and greatest, including the Collins FD-109 Flight Director that was installed in our newest B-727s and was missing on the B-720. The flight engineer station was conspicuously absent. This was United's first, but certainly not last, two-man jet. All the components once located on the engineer's panel were now overhead.

737 bids for Chicago were posted on the bulletin board. On January 31, I submitted my bid for B-737 Captain, ORD. Life-changing events had been set in motion now, and the logistical nightmare was about to begin all over again.

B-737 Training

My B-737 Captain training was set for April 1 and was projected to take most of the month. I was frozen until May 15, so we had a little time.

I developed a very special friendship with Max Goth at DENTK that lasted for decades. Even though he is gone now, fond memories remain. He was First Officer on the 727 in Denver, moving up to Captain on the 737, as I was. Our closest bond was during the flight-training phase, when we were paired off for the simulator and airplane portion of the course. As of the first day, I was delighted to learn that we would be partners.

Ground school was no problem for either of us because of our 727 experience. There were a few minor differences on the 737 as a consequence of not having a Second Officer station, but for the most part the cockpit was like a late-model 727 but with only two thrust levers.

The makeup of the class was interesting, consisting mostly of flight managers and others in supervisory positions. Ours was class #4, so it was very early in the program; the mood was very relaxed, making it pleasant for those training us. On April 15 we began the simulator phase. They were not the latest full-motion units that permitted flying visually around the Stapleton Airport area. It would be awhile before we would see those at DENTK. Getting a type rating still required seven to eight hours of flying time in the airplane.

I really appreciated working with Max, especially once we moved from the simulator phase to actually flying the plane. He was much sharper than I, which meant it took me a little longer to get up to speed.

Permit me to add a few comments with respect to the flying characteristics of the 737. It was very responsive and, unlike the 727, conventional to land — a very honest airplane in all respects, with no bad habits that I could detect. (Later on, when I was working with new and inexperienced First Officers, I would jokingly refer to it as our "Boeing 150 trainer," alluding to Margaret's Cessna 150 that she and so many other flight school students used for primary training.)

As we neared completion of the flying syllabus, I was concerned about the upcoming rating ride, fearful my performance might not stack up favorably against Max's if he flew first. Sequencing for the flight check was usually resolved by a coin toss because most examinees preferred to go first, if for no other reason than to just get it over with. When rating-ride day arrived, Max graciously offered to let me fly first. Wasn't that nice? What a guy!

The flight test was at the Pueblo Airport, and I did fairly well in spite of my persistent apprehension with "check-itis." My only mistake significant enough to call for a recheck was during the "no flap" approach and landing maneuver.

Instead of flying the constant descent profile of an ILS approach, this maneuver was a non-precision approach broken down into steps based on DME readings (distance measured) from the end of the runway. With no flaps available, the profile was very flat, which made it difficult to descend. Somehow, I missed one of those let-down steps, and it soon became apparent that I was much too high in reference to the runway. To compensate, I lowered the landing gear early to increase the drag, with a subsequent increase in my rate of descent. By doing so, I was able to position the airplane for landing.

Although the procedure I resorted to was unorthodox, the fact that I was able to salvage the procedure safely was to my credit. It was a judgment call on the part of the examiner; fortunately, he ruled in my favor, so I didn't get pegged with a "down."

As predicted, Max delivered a nearly perfect performance. Had I been flying next and made that mistake, the examiner might have ruled differently. Thank you, Max, for letting me fly first.

After completing the necessary paperwork and debriefing, I drove home. When I arrived, Margaret had a big banner strung up in the garage: "Congratulations CAPTAIN Lemmon." She was confident that I would pass. Since my activation date wasn't until June 1, I returned to flying 720 First Officer for the month of May.

The B-737 syllabus I had just completed was my seventh airline transition culminating in assignment to fly seven different airplanes in scheduled service. Six were preparation to fly second in command. The seventh was the fulfillment of every pilot's dream — changing seats to assume the responsibility associated with being "Captain." There would be no more looking to the left for counsel; all I would see on that side from now on was a window, and the empty sky beyond.

Moving Again

During a break in the action, we went house hunting in Chicago. Since we were planning for the short term, we weren't interested in buying anything. We began the search west of O'Hare and found nice apartments in Rolling Meadows, just off the expressway. The $255 rent was a bit of a shock, but we were somewhat prepared, realizing Denver housing costs had been well below average.

We chose Three Fountains at Plum Grove, a Scholz Homes development only 15 minutes from the United employee parking lot at O'Hare. It was a three-story apartment house with garage space in the basement, so our third-floor unit necessitated the use of an elevator. I hated elevators, because they reminded me of countless nights spent in hotels.

The next step was putting our lovely Montbello Granada up for sale. That was asking a lot from Margaret, but she took it in stride by being in my corner all the way. We didn't deal with the *RAMAR* problem immediately, as the rent at Jeffco was reasonable and I wouldn't have time to fly it much during the next few months anyway.

Fortunately, the house sold quickly. It was apparent that all our household goods were not going to fit into the new apartment, so two Allied moving vans arrived simultaneously April 30. One took the essentials to Chicago, and the other delivered the excess to Mother and Dad's attic in Erie. Margaret stayed with one driver and I stayed with the other. What an operation! When the movers finished loading, we locked the house and drove off — again.

When we arrived in Rolling Meadows, we stayed at a Holiday Inn near the apartment. The Allied truck arrived and unloaded our furniture the next day, and after unpacking a few critical items, we left for Erie. It was nice that Erie was only a one-day drive again. Margaret's reward for all her work packing boxes was two weeks at home with her parents, so now I was the one joining the ranks of the commuter — temporarily. I "jump seated" on Mohawk to Buffalo and flew on United to Denver with ease.

While I was in 737 school, I had a fourth stripe sewn on all my uniform coats. When I flew my B-720 trip to Baltimore, the customers thought that, with two captains on board, they were getting a bonus. All three trips I flew in May were one-day turnarounds with over seven hours for the round-trip. Since we hadn't closed on the Denver house yet, I slept there between trips.

Following the last trip on May 13, I decided to drive to Jeffco and fly *RAMAR* to Erie. The sky was getting light by the time the plane was out of the hangar and checked over, so I taxied out, called the tower and left. It was a fine spring day with good weather, so I flew at 11,500 feet to Moline, Ill. to refuel. I stretched out on the sofa in the pilot lounge for an hour or so and then took off again.

Why did I fly the plane to Erie? Quite simply, I couldn't find a hangar for it anywhere in the Chicago area. There were two small airports in the Elgin, Ill. area: One was DuPage County Airport near St. Charles, and the other was Crystal Lake, 20 miles northwest. Both had waiting lists for T-hangars. I did sign up for one, but there was no indication that space would be available anytime soon. My next choice was Erie, especially since *RAMAR*'s maintenance station was Derion Aviation.

Margaret and I returned to Illinois to settle our new apartment. I had flown my last trip on the 720 — with the exception of training, I never sat in the right seat of a United Airlines plane again.

On May 18 I flew my first 737 trip, not as Captain, but in the capacity of Third CM (Crew Member). It was important for new people like me, coming from various assignments, to gain experience with 737 line operations.

You are probably wondering what a Third Crew Member was. A provision of our ALPA contract with United stated that all pure-jet scheduled operations were to be conducted with three-man crews. Even though there was no flight engineer station, a third pilot would be required to be present in the cockpit on all scheduled flights. There was really no place for an additional crew member to sit, and he wasn't required to be qualified on the airplane.

It sounded ridiculous, and in a way it was. It smacked of the archaic railroad rules requiring a "fireman" on diesel locomotives.

Because the Third CM used the main jump seat for his crew position, it created a major problem for deadheading commuters. A second jump seat that attached to the cockpit door was available, but the cockpit was really cramped when anyone used it.

The Third CM had few operational duties. He was primarily a lookout and coordinator for cockpit interaction with the flight attendants. (Crew members assigned for duty in the passenger cabin were no longer referred to as "hostesses" or "stewardesses"; now and forever, they were "flight attendants.") Two other assigned duties for the Third CM were the reading of checklists and preparing the takeoff and landing cards. These plastic information cards, once prepared, were placed on the radarscope for use by the Captain and First Officer. Included on the card were the ATIS (Air Terminal Information Service), weather at the airport including ambient temperature that was used for determining the EPR (Engine Pressure Ratio) values, altimeter setting, and calculation of V1, VR, and V2 speeds.

"V" was for velocity, thus V1 was rejection speed (upon reaching it, the takeoff would be continued even if an engine failed). At VR (rotation speed) the pilot physically pulled the control column back, commanding the plane to assume takeoff attitude. V2 was the speed the plane attained to leave the runway and fly. The Third CM performed these computations using tables from the flight manual. I know it all sounds extremely complicated, but it was a routine part of normal jet operations.

The routes were the jet equivalent of the same structure I had encountered on my first DC-3 trip so many years ago. Specifically, the itinerary might be as follows: Chicago to Washington, D.C.; Grand Rapids, Mich.; Detroit; Moline, Ill.; and back to O'Hare. Some of the legs were longer, but you get the idea: lots of takeoffs and landings. The Third CM assignment differed from my traditional jump seat observation time because this time I functioned as a member of the crew.

The date for my first flight as Captain on the B-737 was June 11, 1968 — coincidentally my 39th birthday. Did I just climb into the captain's seat and start flying passengers? Sorry, that's not the way it worked. I would be supervised by a United "check airman" sitting in the First Officer's seat observing everything I did for 25 hours before being released to the line. It was called "flying shotgun," harking back to stagecoach days, when an armed rider sat next to the driver to ward off Indians or bandits.

This was primarily an extension of the training I had already received for the issuance of the B-737 type rating imprinted on my license. DENTK shouldered the responsibility for certification with the FAA, but United's Flight Standards department exceeded those requirements, calling it "training to a higher standard," and that's why FAA inspectors seldom monitored ATP (new terminology for "Airline Transport Rating" — now "Airline Transport Pilot") certification flights. They knew United's requirements substantially exceeded theirs.

You needed to repeat this "check airman" drill every time you checked out in a different airplane. During the exercise, the pilot being checked usually does all the flying.

I was assigned to a Flight Standards Captain specially trained to aid new captains transitioning to command. In my case, I already had experience flying the 737 airplane, but later on, as the simulators became more and more sophisticated, candidates would not fly the actual airplane until reporting for their first scheduled flight. I only experienced that scenario once during my entire career, and that was for the DC-10 program, twenty years later.

My check airman for Flight 635/11 was Captain Bill Tyndall, a flight manager from Newark Flight Operations. I knew Bill from my years of flying the DC-6 and Viscount while based there. Our flight today was Newark to Chicago, with intermediate stops at Saginaw and Grand Rapids, Michigan.

When we met in flight operations, Bill said to me, "Ray, I'm not sure this is a good flight for your first trip as Captain; the forecast calls for heavy thunderstorms at the time of our Saginaw arrival. How much experience have you had using the radar?" Bill knew it was universal practice for the captain to operate that equipment.

I told him that I was familiar with the unit on the 720, and although the one on the 737 was much more advanced, I felt that I could handle it. "In fact," I said, "I'm anxious to try it out. I think with your help, we can turn this into a teaching moment. Besides, if it gets too threatening, we can always divert to Detroit."

"All right, Ray, if you're game, we'll try it. Some of the guys coming over from the Viscount are having trouble with the new radar." I knew what he was referring to, because on the Viscount the Bendix unit was located on the left side of the cockpit, and difficult to manage.

The flight segment to Saginaw took about two hours, and sure enough, as we crossed Lake Erie, I could see the storm clouds building. The autopilot was on, which enabled me to concentrate on the radar screen. The usable range for planning purposes was about 150 miles, but for storm cell avoidance, the 50-mile range was much more precise.

I was in contact with Chicago Center, interrogating them as to their impression of the line of thunderstorms in our immediate front. ATC radarscopes were not set up for weather depiction nearly as well as ours, but sometimes they had an overview that was helpful. Bill didn't suggest anything, just observing to see how I would handle the situation.

A squall line had passed through the Saginaw area a short time earlier, so the main line of weather was between the airport and us. I requested a clearance for deviation to our right to avoid cells in our immediate front. My choices were to penetrate the line or land somewhere to let it pass.

I had a clear picture of the storm. If I took up a southwest heading, I could parallel the line without penetrating it. But I would need ATC approval to do so, because I would be deviating from our assigned route. Bill had no objection, provided I received the appropriate clearance. The Center concurred, as they were monitoring our discrete transponder code. After ten miles or so, I saw a break in the line, and if I made a hard right turn and flew between two monster cells, we would be clear of the weather in 10 miles or less.

Bill watched all of this without comment. In his role as a check airman, he would not intervene unless safety was a concern.

The controller saw the break too, and encouraged me to try it by issuing the appropriate clearance. When you did something like this, you wanted to be very sure it was prudent. Thunderstorm cells were extremely vicious, some towering to 50,000 feet. The seat belt sign was on, and I made sure the flight attendants were strapped in. We passed through the line without a ripple. When we broke out on the other side and proceeded to Saginaw Airport, Bill complimented me: "Nice job, Ray, I couldn't have handled it better myself."

The rest of the flight to O'Hare was uneventful, and I had just completed my first four hours of "shotgun" time.

I was right back out again the next day with Bob Quinn, one of my old Capital captains. It was to New York again, only this time with a layover. We flew into LaGuardia, and left from Newark on the same Flight 635 that I had flown with Bill Tyndall. There were no thunderstorms that time, so the trip was routine, with another six hours logged toward my 25.

After the New York trip I had a week off, so I went to Erie; Margaret stayed with her folks while I flew my initial Captain trips. It was a welcome break.

On June 18, I flew with a different check airman, Art Bunting, and he was the first captain I hadn't flown with before. The company encouraged new captains to fly with as many different check airmen as possible. Most of the 737 flights at that time were between Chicago and New York with intermediate stops. That sequence yielded an additional 11 hours. A final six hours on June 20 was more than enough to finish my shotgun stint.

Endorsement from Flight Standards certified that all the necessary requirements had been met, releasing me to the line.

Command Decision

My first "solo" flight as Captain was on June 26, and when I arrived in operations, there was a note for me to call Flight Dispatch. "I wonder what they want," I mused. When I called them, I was shocked: "Flare pots at Flint?" I exclaimed. The runway lights were out, and they had 25 passengers for our flight to New York. "Is it legal?" I asked the dispatcher. He assured me it was, pending my concurrence.

"How many flare pots do they have?" I asked. He said there were about 20, spaced out over the length of the 6000-foot runway. By the time of our scheduled arrival, it would be completely dark, and because the sky was overcast there would be no moon.

I asked my First Officer for his opinion, but he was noncommittal. It was clearly up to me to make my first "command decision." I instructed the dispatcher to advise the Flint station personnel to light them just before our arrival so the rain wouldn't snuff them out.

240

"I'll circle the field, and if it looks okay, we'll land." I never used flare pots before or since, but you know, it worked out fine — it was no problem at all. Some had gone out by the time we left, but it didn't matter.

I was on reserve until August 15, followed by two weeks off. Naturally, we drove to Erie again. While we were there, OV Pezzi called to say they were flying out to see us. It had been some time since our last visit, and they had rented an apartment in Bethlehem, Pa. near the Allentown-Bethlehem-Easton Airport (ABE). Their hangar rent was only $27.50 per month. Arriving at Erie in their Mooney, OV said, "Why don't you ride back with us for a day or so?" Margaret and I accepted their invitation and flew back to Allentown with them.

I really wanted to fly *RAMAR* to the '68 EAA fly-in at Rockford because, once again, I had the time off. It was neat having your own plane on the flight line at the greatest fly-in ever. Margaret drove the Cadillac to Rockford, and we stayed at the Holiday Inn for the entire show. Tom joined us there with his Trail Air.

I finally arranged for a hangar at Crystal Lake Airport, so after the EAA convention, I flew directly there and Margaret brought the car. The hangar wasn't the greatest, but it was better than being tied down outside. Mom and Dad Taylor drove to Rolling Meadows that summer, and another time Bert and Joan Van Doren flew out in their Beech Bonanza. We were finally settled in the apartment and able to have company.

At United, I was enjoying my new status as Captain. The flying was a bit monotonous — mostly from Chicago to New York, with stops in between. Many of my flights included the Michigan cities like Flint, Lansing, Grand Rapids, and Detroit. I grew tired of taking maps in and out of my flight bag all the time, so I memorized the radio frequencies I needed most frequently and the courses for the airways, along with ILS, control towers, and approach control. Many have never changed, even to this day.

Later, when I switched to the 727, I included the rest of the country in my repertoire. Some of my First Officers were amazed, but it really wasn't that difficult.

Flying a full schedule, I had already logged over 150 hours of Captain time. That authorized me to revert to regular minimums. As a new Captain, my limits were 400 feet and one-mile visibility; fortunately, being on high minimums was not a problem during the summertime. My flying had been routine so far, but lest I should become lulled into complacency, the reality was that winter was coming — and the challenges of flying in the frigid Midwest would call for resourcefulness on many levels.

TDY San Francisco

I had seen the posting on the bulletin board a few weeks earlier: The San Francisco domicile needed 737 crews to cover west-coast DC-6 schedules while their crews transitioned to the B-737. It sounded like Minneapolis 1956 all over again.

There were similarities. This was a complete restructuring of air service, only this time it was for California and Oregon. Up to that point, the 737 had not been seen in places like Medford, Eugene, and Salem, Oregon and the California Central Valley cities. Thus, many of these 737 flights would be inaugural, with attendant publicity. (Seattle was not involved because it was a separate domicile.)

Margaret and I talked it over, and since she would be able to accompany me, I bid it. Just before Thanksgiving, we were on our way west to San Mateo, California, where United operated its own hotel. Although the location was not as desirable as downtown San Francisco, it was much more convenient to the airport.

My first trip out of San Francisco (SFO) was nonstop to Los Angeles (LAX), returning via Fresno and Stockton, and the following day I flew north to Eugene, Salem and Portland. The inaugural flight to Salem was my first over that route since the Swift trip with PG Fellmeth in 1954; it was hard to believe I had advanced so far since then.

The food was excellent at the Irwin Best Hotel, so we often ate there. When I had a couple of days off, we rented a VW Bug and did some sightseeing. TDY was more like a paid vacation than a job.

Our passengers loved the 737; it was a whole new realm for them as well. By that time over half the fleet had been delivered, and United was finally positioned to replace the prop fleet. On December 1, I had the rare occurrence of a double Pendleton layover, so I took Margaret along. She was a fan of Pendleton woolens, and factory tours were available. We stopped at Medford, Eugene, and Portland on the way, arriving in Pendleton around 8 p.m. Bringing Margaret was a great idea and, fortunately, she didn't get bumped. I had checked the passenger load, so I was quite sure space would not be a problem.

Everything east of the Cascades was dry, so Pendleton was a desert community. December wasn't pretty there, but that didn't matter. We did the tour of Pendleton Mills and bought some blankets. It was one of the few times we flew a trip together, and Margaret thoroughly enjoyed herself.

Factory Delivery

After we got back to San Francisco, I received a message to contact the crew desk; I wondered what that was all about — since we had just gotten in, they knew I was illegal for trip assignment.

"Captain Lemmon, would you consider going to Seattle to pick up a new 737?" That sounded exciting — "When do we leave?" Margaret was there in flight operations with me, and remarked, "What a rare opportunity. Don't pass that up." The airline wanted to get the new plane to SFO Maintenance right away.

"Okay," I said, "Who else is going?" "Just you and Tom Dalstrand; isn't he there with you?" In fact, Tom was still there, as we had just flown the Pendleton trip together. I called him over to see if he wanted to go. "You bet," he said, "sounds great."

Margaret returned to San Mateo, and Tom and I boarded a flight to SEA. No third crew member was required for this trip. When we landed, I checked in with crew scheduling to see what had been set up.

"A car from Boeing will pick you up in the morning and take you out to Renton," the facility where all B-727s and 737s were manufactured. At about 9 a.m., we were advised that our transportation was waiting in front of the hotel. When I asked the driver about the possibility of a factory tour, our hopes for that were dashed when we learned that our plane was at the delivery center, which was located five miles south of downtown Seattle at Boeing Field.

My main recollection of the delivery process was inspecting the new plane, noting how pristine everything was. An airplane's wheel wells are usually messy, but these were immaculate. Our clearance to San Francisco had been taken care of, so when we completed our inspections, we took off for SFO. That's about all there was to it; ho-hum, no big deal, at least not as far as Boeing was concerned; they did it all the time. I'm not sure what I expected, but I guess I was a little disappointed.

Shortly after arriving back at the hotel in San Mateo, I tripped getting off the elevator and sprained my ankle; it immediately swelled up to the point I couldn't put my shoe on. What was the next step? I definitely couldn't fly, and I needed to see a doctor right away. I hobbled to the airport and called in sick. When I reported to United Medical they took an x-ray and announced, "The good news is that nothing's broken, but you'll have to stay off of it until the swelling subsides. It looks like there is a small tear in one of the ligaments, so I'm afraid you're grounded. Call the flight office and remove yourself from schedule."

Oh boy! That was it for our San Francisco TDY.

I cut a slipper open for my swollen foot and then, using one crutch, I hobbled back to San Mateo, where I told Margaret, "Pack up, Hon, we're going home." We didn't dally long in Rolling Meadows, either; shortly after arriving at the apartment, we were off to Erie again. That was the best place for my recuperation.

An Airport Car

Prior to the TDY assignment, we sold the blue '67 Cadillac I bought in Denver; after paying off the loan with the credit union, there wasn't much left. Deficit spending was still a problem, even though I was earning Captain's pay. What I needed was a "beater" airport car like the old '54 Chevy I bought years earlier in Buffalo. Margaret's Pontiac convertible was still okay, but I didn't feel safe parking it in the employee lot; there had been reports of vandalism, so she often took me to work and picked me up.

I checked the bulletin board in Flight Ops for cars advertised for sale. Sure enough, Dick Bunting, one of our crew schedulers, had a '63 Plymouth Valiant listed for only $500. Dick's dad, Captain Art, flew with me as check airman during the "shotgun" phase of my training for the 737.

The Valiant only had 29,000 miles on it, so I decided to check it out. When I saw Dick working at the crew desk, I asked him about it. "Yeah," he said, "My dad bought it five years ago to use for the airport, so when he got a new car this summer, he gave it to me and I've been using it for work; if you would like to see it, we can take the bus over." "Why do you want to sell it?" I asked. Dick replied that it was so ratty looking that his wife wouldn't drive it.

"You're only asking $500?" I queried. "Wait 'til you see it," he replied. It didn't sound very promising but my curiosity was aroused, so we boarded the company bus to the parking lot. The car appeared to be pale blue, although you couldn't be sure with the amount of crud that was on it. "My dad didn't take very good care of it," Dick admitted. When he opened the door, though, I was pleasantly surprised. It was like new inside, except for soil on the driver's-side seat cushion.

"It's still nice inside," he remarked. I started it up and the slant-six engine sounded okay. We took it for a spin around the parking lot and it seemed easy to drive. I agreed to buy it, saying, "I'll take it. I just need a car for the airport for a while." It was almost as bad as the '54 Chevy I bought seven years earlier, but this car wasn't rusty. It was awfully dirty, but somehow I saw possibilities for it. I always enjoyed fixing up derelicts, and we didn't have money for a new car right then. Besides, I knew Margaret would like the clean interior.

"Honey, I just bought a car— do you want to come and see it?" "I was wondering how you got home," she said. Margaret wasn't too impressed with my purchase, but she was relieved not to have to drive me to work anymore. Her only comment was, "That should keep you busy for a while." She knew me so very well.

When we returned from California, I wasn't about to start out for Erie in the untested Valiant. Besides, it was standard shift, and the last thing I needed for my injured left ankle was a clutch pedal. Although it was difficult for me to get around, the ankle seemed a little better already. When we got to Erie, and Mom and Dad saw the crutch, they were somewhat taken aback.

Mostly, I just loafed around the house. After a week or so, the swollen ankle improved to the point I could wear a shoe again. I returned to Chicago, hoping for medical release back to flying status. It was nearing the holidays, so Margaret stayed in Erie. Fortunately, I didn't need the crutch anymore.

Checking in with ORDMD, my ankle still hurt, but I wasn't limping. "Let me see you walk," the doctor ordered. They knew we do a lot of that in connection with our job. His next question was, "Can you fly the plane normally in addition to all the walking?"

"Absolutely," I replied. "Well, okay then; you can return to work, but if that ankle swells, I want you back here." I promised — thank goodness; if there's anything a pilot hates, it's being grounded.

Winter had crept in during my recuperation, and I knew there would be challenges in the months ahead. My first trip back, I flew to New York through the Michigan cities and returned to O'Hare the following day. I had no trouble flying the airplane except for applying the brakes, especially the parking brake.

Normally, when it's the First Officer's turn to fly, the Captain takes over during the landing roll. There were two reasons for this: primarily, it was because the nose wheel tiller (shaped like a miniature half-wheel) was on the Captain's side only. As the plane slowed after touchdown and rudder authority diminished, that device came into play for directional control. The other reason was the First Officer's inability to determine which exit to take leaving the runway. It's just the way it was done.

However, with my tender ankle, I delegated all of the braking, even when it was my turn to fly. Light pressure associated with taxiing to the gate was not a problem, but when it came time to set that parking brake, I needed assistance. I would simply call out, "Parking brake?" and the First Officer would respond, "Set." This procedure was only necessary for a few trips, and then I was able to do it myself.

A Bad Midwest Winter — 1969

The weather hadn't been too nasty so far, but the new year of '69 was still young, and it developed into the worst Midwest winter in memory.

For United, the most serious problem during the winter months was snow- and ice-covered runways. It was customary for planes landing on contaminated runways to give the control tower a "braking action report." Examples were "good," "fair," "poor" and, lastly, "nil." It's the last one that caused a problem, as it was unwise to land on a runway reported as "braking action nil." Doing so exposed the pilot to criticism for exercise of poor judgment, and the plane might slide right off the end of the runway due to inability to stop. With a "nil braking" report, landings were usually suspended until the runway was treated by maintenance crews.

During January, the entire Midwest was a sheet of ice, especially Omaha, where our planes were sliding off runways and taxiways with some regularity. I was very careful there not to become a statistic as well.

A serious problem developed at Muskegon, Michigan. Since the airport was situated near the Lake Michigan shore, it was a frequent victim of lake-effect snow squalls. Muskegon was unique, with 6100 feet of runway and a small lake at the northwest end. Sure enough, in January one of our 737s ended up in the lake.

Allow me to relate a scary experience at Muskegon. I was making an approach to Runway 31, and although there was considerable snow on the runway, it was only partially covered with small drifts and alternating bare spots.

We landed normally, but I just wasn't getting stopped. The anti-skid braking system was cycling on and off between the snow ridges and the bare spots on the runway. The reverse thrusters on the 737 were useless. All you got was noise, and they did virtually nothing to decelerate the airplane.

For a moment, I was apprehensive that I might be a lake victim also, until we reached a larger bare spot where the brakes finally took effect. As we slowed, I did a deliberate 180-degree turn on the runway to avoid sliding off the end. I hadn't done anything wrong, but even "going by the book" could sometimes get you in trouble.

—————

As the dreadful winter progressed, Margaret and I hibernated in the den. Around the middle of January, we took the Valiant on the first of several trips to Erie and beyond. OV and Mary Pezzi had invited us for a visit to Bethlehem, and after returning to Rolling Meadows, we got some very good news! I had successfully bid a 737 vacancy in Newark, so at last we would be returning to the East Coast again. All of the propeller flying in Newark had been replaced with 737 schedules. It worked out perfectly, and I would start flying Newark trips after my first PC (proficiency check) the end of April.

When we had visited Mary and OV at their Stonehenge Court apartment the previous summer, I couldn't imagine driving that far to work, but recent developments shed a new light on it. During our most recent visit in January, we went over to the Allentown airport where their Mooney was hangared, and I was blown away by what was across the taxiway. The Airport Authority had just completed two large hangars with over 2000 square feet of floor space for only $80 per month, and one was vacant. That did it — I was hooked. We decided to move to Bethlehem in spite of the long commute.

As a temporary measure, OV suggested renting a two-bedroom apartment at Stonehenge Court where they lived. Although the units were not as fancy as those in Rolling Meadows, the rent was $100 less. What did it matter anyway, since we didn't plan to lease it for more than a year? Before leaving, we paid our first month's rent for both Hangar #4 and the Stonehenge Court apartment; it was the beginning of a whole new chapter in our nomadic life.

The first order of business was to move the Staggerwing out of Crystal Lake. During days off in mid-March, I flew it to Erie. Fortunately, I retained control of the T-hangar there, suspecting that we might be back. After two major relocations in as many years, we said, "Enough already! We're tired of packing."

You're What?

"Yes, Ray, I'll say it again, I'm pregnant." After 13 years, we assumed we would remain childless. Years earlier, we had discussed adoption, but it never seemed right for us. With Margaret's surgical history, pregnancy was ill advised; most women with ileostomies used birth control. There were successful deliveries, though, so it wasn't impossible. Margaret was very excited about her pregnancy, and really looked forward to being a mother. I can't describe my feelings exactly, except that it seemed complicated, and it was.

———

All that remained was to clear out the Rolling Meadows apartment and drive the convertible to Bethlehem. Allied picked up our furniture and we spent the night at Toledo, driving the rest of the way the next day. We stayed with Mary and OV Pezzi until the van arrived. After one last Chicago sequence at the end of the month, I would start flying my trips out of Newark.

The PC was at Pueblo, Colo., where I had taken my 737 rating ride. All training and checks would be in the simulator in another year or so, but as of 1969 we still used the airplane. The PC went okay, and I was good for another year. My first Newark trip sequence was not until May 11, so we had time to rescue *RAMAR* from the hangar in Erie — and another logistical nightmare would be over.

A Tranquil Summer
Margaret was fine all summer, cheerful and happy in her pregnancy. OV and I spent many of our days off at the airport, and *RAMAR* enjoyed its new home immensely. The hangar was actually roomy enough for two planes and the Pontiac convertible.

Although the Stonehenge apartment was not fancy, the air conditioning worked well and we were comfortable. Bert Van Doren flew in occasionally to visit, and in June we drove to Pine Bush, N.Y. to visit the Olsens. Gene had recently been promoted as well, and was now Captain (Master) for American President Lines. He was still sailing around the world on the same ship, the *President Jackson*.

———

From Newark, I now enjoyed different destinations. Quite often it was an evening departure nonstop to Ft. Wayne, Ind. for the first leg of a three-day trip. We also served Akron and Youngstown, Ohio, as well as "Tobacco Road," all former DC-3 runs. I enjoyed landing at the small stations like Knoxville and Chattanooga, Tenn., and Asheville, N.C.

Followed By Tragedy

Over Labor Day weekend, Margaret was suddenly in deep trouble. Intestinal blockage, the most fearsome side effect of being pregnant with an ileostomy, had occurred. It began with vomiting the Saturday before. There were no doctors available, so we went to the Emergency Room at St. Luke's Hospital. They were rightfully concerned about the baby, and Margaret was admitted at once. They put the customary tube down, and the next day, the blockage was relieved. We were overjoyed; it looked like she might dodge the bullet after all.

But the following day some idiot gave her a tray of regular food, even though the doctor had prescribed "liquids only." The blockage returned, and there was no relieving it this time; now she needed surgery. Unfortunately, that was curtains for the little boy she carried in her womb. She lost the baby and then developed a severe post-operative infection. Margaret was one very sick girl.

Obviously, her case was botched. We discovered later that the primary physician suffered from cancer and was unavailable much of the time. We felt quite certain her surgery had been performed by an intern. It was totally a "gut-wrenching" experience.

We were terribly grieved by the loss of the child, and also by Margaret's perilous condition; all we could think about was saving her. Mom and Dad came to Bethlehem to offer comfort. It was a long siege, and she spent an extended period in the hospital. We felt quite certain Margaret could have carried the baby to term by staying on liquids and receiving supplementary intravenous feeding. That's why it was so difficult: after so many years we finally had a chance to become parents, and it was snatched away by incompetence.

After Margaret's release from the hospital, we took the important step of finding a builder for our next house. Margaret liked a certain design being built in the Chicago area, so when we learned we were moving to Bethlehem we bought a set of "builder's" plans. We submitted these to Thomas Morgan Construction for an estimate. It was similar to the other houses in Delta Manor (a subdivision in

Bethlehem Township not far from the ABE airport). There was no conflict over compatibility with the neighborhood, although this house was much larger, used more brick, and had more generous overhangs. Tom quoted a price of $44,000. We accepted his proposal, and he said construction would begin in the fall.

Near Disaster at Tannersville

It was a ski area not far from the city of Stroudsburg, Pa., about a half-hour drive north of the Lehigh Valley. "Ski area" implies that mountains were nearby, and on top of the highest one there was an Omni Station identified as Tannersville VOR, a component of the FAA airway system. Why am I describing this?

On November 5, 1969, my planeload of passengers and crew almost died there.

The following is a copy of my report to the United Pilots submitted three days after the incident, addressed to Capt. W.E. Arsenault, Chairman of the United Pilots Master Executive Council (MEC).

UAL Flight 285 was a regular scheduled B-737 trip between EWR and DTW; we filed the standard center stored flight plan on November 5, the day of the incident. Clearance was received prior to taxi as follows: Cleared as filed-Tannersville 12 departure-expect FL 310 after TVE. We took off at 1339Z and shortly changed over to New York Center maintaining 7000 feet. We immediately received clearance to FL 240; report leaving FL 230. We made several frequency changes and vacating reports on the climb; the last was leaving FL 190.

At FL 220, approximately over the TVE VOR, the S/O grasped my shoulder and said "Look," at the same time pointing to the 11 o'clock position. I saw a large jet aircraft on a collision course to ours at the same altitude converging rapidly. I immediately applied hard left aileron and back pressure to the extent of 2 g's estimated. The aircraft buffeted considerably, but did not stall. We rolled out on a west heading, having gained 300 feet in the maneuver — the time was 1353Z. The other aircraft appeared to be in a slight nose-down attitude, passed very close to our right side, and was identified as a Seaboard World DC-8. I originally thought we had passed each other

251

with 200 feet of separation, but subsequent testimony by the First and Second Officers causes me to feel it was much closer. The S/O stated he vividly remembered seeing the letters "EA" of Seaboard World framed in the side window, and pilots were visible. I was in a poor position to judge the separation due to the left break. Flight conditions at the time were: on instruments with visibility limited to 1/4 mile in light precipitation. Our heading was 300 degrees and we estimated Seaboard's to be about 060.

I called New York Center and told them we had had a near miss with Seaboard World over TVE at 220 and would be filing a full report. The center acknowledged and changed us to another frequency where I heard the Seaboard flight making inquiries relative to the near miss. I asked him if it looked as bad to him as it did to us and he said we only cleared by 50 feet. Subsequent computations indicate we only had 4 seconds from the time of first sighting to point of impact.

I sent the Second Officer to the cabin to check on passengers and the Flight Attendants. He reported there were no passengers hurt, but the two girls in the aft cabin were "slightly" injured. One had a sprained back and the other received superficial cuts on her right leg and left ankle. They said they wished to continue to Detroit and see a doctor there, so we flew on to our destination and had an ambulance meet the flight. The girls returned to Chicago later the same day.

In looking back over this incident, several thoughts come into sharp focus. Had the Special Review Board ruling on the crew complement issue for the B-737 ruled differently, I don't think I would be writing this letter today. There is no doubt in any of our minds that if the S/O had not seen the Seaboard flight, the result would have been a mid-air collision — not a near miss. In the year and one half I have been on this airplane, it has been my experience that the S/O consistently observes traffic not seen by the Captain or First Officer.

In a crowded airways system understaffed with controllers and overpopulated with aircraft of vastly different performance capabilities operating on a "see and be seen" concept, how can we consider removing a pair of eyes from the cockpit of a jet

transport engaged in short-haul operations — even if we ignore
the other contributions made by the Second Officer.

Sincerely yours,

/s/ R.A. Lemmon, Captain, UAL

That letter stirred up a great deal of controversy in the ranks of
United's top management and the ATA (Air Transport Association).

An independent review board was created (as alluded to in my
letter) to determine if a third crew member was needed. The airplane
was certified by Boeing to be flown by two pilots, as was the case in
the new plane delivery that Tom Dalstrand and I had taken part in
the past December. Management was thoroughly convinced ALPA
was "feather-bedding," as previously described in the railroad-
firemen-on-diesels issue. I did write the letter myself and was sincere
in the statements I made.

Later, I was called to New York to testify at another crew-
complement hearing. We won that one, too, but eventually all jets
became "two-man crew," including the largest intercontinental 747s.

The incident at Tannersville made national press coverage in
newspapers and the weekly business magazines. Even my long-lost
brother Richard wrote to me that he had seen it in the *San Francisco
Chronicle.*

Continuing the story of Flight 285, and the events that ensued
upon reaching Detroit, an FAA inspector was on hand to interview
me. I didn't hesitate for a moment to talk to him, because I knew
we had operated within the parameters of the ATC clearance I had
received.

Then he took me by surprise: "The NTSB wants a hearing as
soon as possible. When will you be available?"

I explained that I was on a three-day trip sequence and,
as of that time, hadn't been relieved. I also expressed concern
about the integrity of my airplane. I felt sure I had pulled at
least 2 g's (twice gravitational pull) and maybe more. I suggested
grounding the aircraft, pending review of the flight recorder tape
and an inspection by UAL maintenance personnel to determine
its airworthiness.

The FAA followed through on my suggestion, and our flight
was delayed an hour before being released to fly on to Chicago. A

conference call between our maintenance supervisor and the Boeing factory in Renton resolved the issue of airworthiness.

Flight Recorders

There are two flight recorders on board every airliner, the so-called "black boxes" referred to in the news of any crash or incident.

One is a voice recorder in the cockpit that runs on a continuous tape, recording all cockpit conversation and radio transmissions for the last 30 minutes. When the near miss occurred, we should have disconnected the power to the CVR (Cockpit Voice Recorder). But no one thought to do it, so the entire incident was erased by the time we arrived in Detroit.

The other recorder analyzes several parameters of flight including airspeed, altitude, time, control movements, etc. — and the piece of data that we were interested in, the "G" load. This recorder also has a feature, called an "event" button, to press when something unusual occurs. I instructed Lars Maher (third crew member) to press it after the near miss. That action was very helpful in locating the incident on the tape later. Since the tape was marked, I didn't expect that it would take long at all to find it and determine the stress level on our 737.

The FAA inspector said he had nothing more for me at that time, and we could continue the flight to Chicago. "I'll be watching for your report," he said in passing.

Boeing's recommended inspection determined that the plane was airworthy, instructing our mechanics on what they should look for and where.

After rounding up replacement flight attendants, we were on our way to Chicago. On arrival, I received an urgent message to report to Captain Luther, manager of Flight Operations, ORD.

"How about it, Ray?" Clark asked. "Are we clean on this, or do I need to get 'Legal' [UAL attorneys] in on it?" I briefly explained the circumstances, that I was fully compliant with our clearance, and that "the ATC tapes should be available by tomorrow."

The FAA inspector in Detroit had said they wanted to convene an NTSB (National Transportation Safety Board) hearing ASAP. Clark informed me, "We've decided to let you complete your trip, and the hearing will be held at Newark on your return."

Amazing! That would be unheard of today. I would most certainly have been relieved in Chicago, "pending further investigation." During an informal discussion some time later, I learned more details concerning the decision to have me continue that trip. It was at DENTK, while we were there for a PC and having breakfast together, so it was strictly "off the record."

Clark said to me, "It was because of your steadfast assurance of our legal position. If you had displayed any uncertainty at all during our discussion, I would have relieved you on the spot. I felt it put a better face on the incident to have you continue flying as though nothing had happened." That was an example of the kind of rapport pilots shared with one another. He was sticking his neck out a mile by allowing me to continue that trip. What a guy!

So, I flew on to our layover point in Ft. Wayne, and shortly after checking in at the hotel, I received a call from Bob Quinn at Newark (yes, the same Bob who flew shotgun with me on one of my first 737 flights). He was a regular Flight Manager now, and he was also "ex-Capital." He just wanted to confirm what I already knew about the NTSB hearing scheduled two days hence. I asked him to contact our local ALPA Safety Rep. "I don't want to be all alone on this," I said.

"Okay, I'll take care of it. Have a good trip." Click — end of conversation. Even in 1969, having me continue my trip in a situation like this was highly unusual, but there was nothing I could do short of calling in sick, and I wasn't about to do that.

National Transportation Safety Board (NTSB) Hearing

When I arrived back at Newark about 6 p.m., Ron Denk, our local ALPA safety rep, met me at the gate and I suggested getting something to eat.

"Oh no, they are waiting for you upstairs in the Flight Office — they want to start right away." I told Ron this was my first experience with NTSB, and I would need his support. "I'm right there with you," he promised.

There were eight of us at the hearing, including my crew, two government investigators, our safety rep, Bill Tyndall (UAL) and a stenographer.

I was instructed to describe the near miss. After a brief statement, I asked, "Did you listen to the tapes?"

"Well, yes, but —" Then I broke in and said, "You know New York Center dropped the ball and I had unrestricted climb to FL 240." At that point it surfaced what this was all about.

"They didn't expect you to be that high at Tannersville. How did you do it?" I explained that my climb speed was 220 knots for best angle, versus the customary 280-300 for best rate. It was less efficient, but I did it because we had been held down so often at TVE, resulting in delay for our climb to cruise altitude. "I fly this trip all the time," I pointed out.

I looked over at Ron, and I could see him squirming in his seat and realized he wanted me to shut up. Continuing my testimony, I said, "I've got nothing to hide. You've seen the 220-knot climb on the tape anyway." The investigator continued, "Controllers get used to handling traffic a certain way, and you surprised them."

I called a halt to this diversion by saying, "The Seaboard DC-8 reported out of FL 210 and the controller read it back as 'leaving FL 230.' That's the problem!"

"How do you know about that?" the investigator asked, but I refused to reveal my source. "It's only important that I do know, and it's on the tape."

That brought the hearing to a rather abrupt conclusion; it had lasted about an hour.

Bill Tyndall didn't say much, but when I got him aside I said, "Bill, I'm scheduled out on 285 again in the morning and I'm really beat. Can you put a reserve on it?"

"Why, sure, Ray, we can do that, but you won't get paid for it." I told Ron what Bill had said, and his response was, "You've got to fly it, Ray. Where do you live?" I told him I had to drive all the way to Allentown.

"Why don't you get a hotel?" he suggested. "No," I said, "I just want to go home." When I got home, Margaret greeted me with a big hug. "I almost lost you," she said. Of course, we had talked on the phone, so she knew everything. I showed up the next morning to fly Flight 285 to Detroit.

That was the closest near miss ever recorded. Timelines from the recorder tapes on both airplanes indicated a separation of about 50 feet. The Seaboard captain had sent his flight engineer back to the astrodome (used for celestial navigation) to inspect the vertical tail. He felt certain we must have hit it. After that close encounter with death, I felt everything henceforth was a "free ride."

The apt description of an airline pilot's life: "Hours and hours of boredom punctuated by moments of sheer terror."

———

The Lemmons and Pezzis celebrated the holidays together. We both had trees in our apartments and mingled. I was home for Christmas, and I think OV was as well.

A Decade of Reflection

As we close out 1969, and the decade, I see it as a time of deep reflection. As a 10-year period of my life, it was unparalleled anywhere, career-wise or otherwise. It included the demise of one major airline and the rise and expansion of another. It saw me personally rise to heights I had only dreamed about. I went from qualifying for command to actually attaining it.

The airline industry transitioned with massive changes, from the type of planes we flew to a complete remake of route structures and the establishment of hubs. I hope I have successfully incorporated these changes in my narrative and illustrated how they affected me. It just so happened that my timing was precise, coming to the airline industry at that pivotal moment when so much would change. I was the last group of pilots to begin their career during the DC-3 era and end with a wide-body "heavy jet," the DC-10.

Geographically, it was almost beyond comprehension. We made more moves over greater distances than at any future time. Recreationally, a whole new field of endeavor surfaced by owning and rebuilding private aircraft.

And tragically, at the end, Margaret lost her baby, and I had my own brush with death at Tannersville. I must not overlook Margaret's significant accomplishment of attaining a Private Pilot License, becoming an aviator in her own right.

———

As we move into Part II of this book, the narrative will change. We have explored a lot of the intricacies and detail of my work as a pilot. I will use more abbreviations, of airports especially, assuming that by now you know most of them anyway. To keep projects and restorations from being too repetitive, I will gloss over much of the detail.

Geographically, we will explore new ground as we move into the realm of dual home ownership and the complexity that entailed. I'll try to cover that aspect of the story without making it more laborious than it really was.

There will be more planes, more houses, even boats in the future. Please bear with me, and I'll try to keep it as interesting as I can.

We must pick up the pace; there are just too many more years to cover. At least I think we are beyond the halfway point. A lot of the story is repetitive, and I apologize. But it was the way we lived it. We come to a new decade — a wonderful time, really, with more challenges and more fulfillments.

I guess the best description of our journey thus far is "living the good life."

Part II

Chapter 15

Florida — The Winds of Change
1970-1973

Lord Byron Drive

The winter of '69 and '70 was exceptionally harsh, with lots of snow lasting all winter. Margaret and I occasionally checked on our new house in Bethlehem Township, Delta Manor subdivision.

Before winter set in, Morgan Construction managed to frame the living room, dining room, and kitchen, but that was it. Footers for the rest of the house were ruined by frost penetration. The small part completed gave no clue as to how much was yet to be done. The house was a four-level split on a Colonial plan.

Adjacent to the area of the house just described was the part I was most interested in: a two-car garage with a large room behind that was suitable for airplane restoration. Yet to be built was the den/family room with a fireplace and a beamed cathedral ceiling.

It was a quiet year, for the most part, with us concentrating on our home-building project. Close supervision was the order of the day, so that mistakes could be remedied in a timely fashion. By late spring the entire house was framed, and the excitement was building for Margaret.

United Hires Private Pilots

What was new at United? Not much; most of the time I flew the three-day Fort Wayne layover because it left late. With only one leg on the first and third day, it was a no-brainer. That trip pairing would never survive the scrutiny of computers, because it demonstrated a total lack of crew utilization. I was paid for being away for three days,

3245 Lord Byron Drive, Delta Manor, Bethlehem, Pa. This
is where Margaret's Colt restoration and some of the PA-12
project took place. We only lived here for three years.

whereas in reality it was only half that. Flying that sequence four
times per month meant there were only eight nights I didn't sleep in
my own bed. I never again had a schedule I liked so well.

The airline was still expanding and in constant need of new
pilots, and there were not many candidates left who met the required
qualifications. The military was United's preferred source, but that
had all but dried up, and many other applicants were too old. The
company was holding firm by refusing to take on anyone over 28
years of age.

The only alternative was to hire private pilots and train them at
contract schools like Clinton Aviation in Denver. They completed
their Commercial and Instrument training there, and then attended
DENTK to qualify on the B-737. Guess who got them after that?
You guessed it: me.

They didn't hire just any private pilots. They selected candidates
with engineering degrees, on the presumption they would be easier to
train and more productive down the road. Unfortunately, that was not
always the case. Prior to flying the line, those new-hire First Officers
(F/O) were required to pass proficiency checks in the simulator.

Observing the proficiency level of the First Officers showing up on my flights, I wondered if they had ever seen a 737 before, and except for observer time, they probably hadn't. Airplane training at Denver Tech had been suspended, and full-motion, high-tech simulators had taken over. Unfortunately, they were a poor substitute for actually flying the airplane.

Field Training New F/Os

I vividly recall one instance. The new-hire F/O sitting next to me had been making hard landings to the extent that I felt it needed addressing: "Mike, when we get down close to the runway, just flare a bit, and let it settle onto the runway."

On his next landing he flared, all right, but he overdid it. Approaching the touchdown zone after pulling the thrust levers back to idle, Mike suddenly yanked the control column back into his lap, and that sent Albert (the airplane) into a 100-foot zoom back into the sky. It was so sudden that it was impossible for me to correct it in time. I instantly grabbed the control wheel and gently tried to ease back down, praying we would land before falling out of the sky. I was able to salvage the landing for the most part, but it was scary to the extent that the tower called to see if we were all right.

It was a quiet walk through the terminal, and Mike thought I would chew him out. It did enter my mind, but then I thought of something better, so all I said at the time was, "Mike, *never* do anything sudden in an airplane."

(Note: Of the many names for the 737, my choice was "Albert," an abbreviation for Fat Albert, just one of the nicknames that cropped up when the 737 first came on line.)

Ascending the stairs to operations to drop off papers and stow our flight bags, there was a decision point at the top of the stairs. Flight Operations was to the right and the Flight Office, home of flight managers and the Chief Pilot, was to the left.

Mike went to the right. I went to the left.

I'm sure he thought I went in to get him fired, but actually I had other business there that had nothing to do with him whatever. By the time I returned to flight ops, Mike had left. That was my inspiration: to let him stew between trips, waiting for a call from the flight office.

263

I hadn't ratted on Mike, but he didn't know that. By the time we met again for our next trip, Mike was noticeably subdued. I felt quite certain his days off at home had not been especially enjoyable.

There were other potentially dangerous occurrences. One new hire was determined to land in the approach lights before reaching the runway. I allowed him to continue as long as I dared, and then I took over at the last minute when it was obvious he wasn't making any correction to his erroneous flight path. It was even an ILS runway with a glide slope, and VASI (Visual Approach Slope Indicator) lights for visual reference. It's stupid to attempt to land staring at two banks of red lights.

At times I prayed for good health and an alert state of mind to be sure the flight would be brought to a safe conclusion. However, the new First Officers quickly learned the ropes and I could relax a bit. That training role took me back to my own humble beginnings so many years ago and the way my captains were patient with me. Otherwise, the job was routine, and now I was making good money; I even had enough seniority to fly a good schedule.

The house in Delta Manor on Lord Byron Drive was nearing completion, and this time the move was local. Since the movers charged by the hour, we moved a lot of the small stuff ourselves. The biggest thing not included in the price of the house was landscaping. I remember spending countless hours watering our new lawn.

Piper PA22-108 Colt

After Labor Day, the phone rang. It was Mac McMillen calling from Erie.

"Are you still interested in the Colt?" he queried. (After Margaret learned to fly, she had expressed a mild interest in it.) "The fabric is bad, and Earl won't pass it any more, so it has to go." "Yeah, Mac, but your timing is awful. We just moved into our new house." He was adamant: "I'll give you 'til the end of the month to make up your mind, and then I'm going to call Arnie." (Arnold Johnson was a junk plane dealer in Falconer, N.Y. with whom Mac had done business before.)

Margaret wanted a plane of her own so she could continue her flying, especially in pursuit of an Instrument rating. The Colt was ideal because, unlike the Swift, it had a "full panel," including an artificial horizon and directional gyro. The price was right and, feeling it was her turn for a change, I wanted to buy it for her.

So, on September 11, I "flew airline" to Erie to pick it up. Mac and I went to the hangar to pull it out — could this wretched thing be it? There were no wheel pants, paint was peeling off the cowling, the interior looked like a herd of elephants had tramped through it, and the radio was missing. The Colt showed almost 5000 flight training hours in its logbook.

"Mac, how can I fly back to ABE without a radio?"

"Sorry, Ray, I needed it for another plane. If you don't want to buy the Colt, just say so and I'll call Arnie." Oh boy, what to do? I didn't expect the plane to be that bad.

"No, Mac, I'll take it, your price is more than fair; I'll manage."

After taking care of the details, I was on my way. I got a green light from the tower, took off, and left Erie eastbound. The weather was good and I had a chart — this trip would be cross-country using pilotage (a sectional chart). The engine was mid-time (halfway through its life cycle) at 1100 hours and ran fine, so that was an important plus.

When I arrived at the Allentown airport, the tower was unaware of my "no radio" status. Perhaps I should have called or filed a flight plan to notify them. I circled the field, and then turned on base leg (just prior to the final approach) for Runway 24 rocking my wings, and then I received a steady green light from the control tower clearing me to land.

Exiting the runway on the way to the T-hangars, I noticed Margaret there to greet me. I said, "I've got to call the tower, Hon, 'cause I had to land without radio." I did call, and the controller said, "It's okay, but let us know next time, and try to get it fixed before you leave." I didn't bother explaining that very soon I would be removing the wings, and the Colt wouldn't be flying anywhere.

"Where're the wheel pants?" Margaret asked, obviously disappointed. I replied, "Mac said they were cracked, but he thinks Earl might still have them." Looking inside, she remarked, "It looks like we need a new seat." "It needs a lot more than that," I said.

"Would you like to taxi it before I tie it down?" Margaret got in and taxied it around the immediate hangar area.

"Visibility is good, and it's easy to steer," she remarked, "but where are the brakes?"

Instead of "toe brakes" at the top of the rudders, the Colt had a handle painted bright red that extended below the instrument panel. Pulling the handle applied brake pressure to both wheels simultaneously, which meant you couldn't swing the plane around sharply, as when maneuvering a tail-dragger. "You'll get used to that; just use the rudders to steer," I told her.

I pointed out that the Plexiglas windows were good and that the engine ran well. "Don't worry, Hon, we'll fix it up good as new." And we did, but it took a precious year out of our lives to accomplish it.

———

Let's leave the Colt at the airport for the time being, and focus on my job. It was Proficiency Check time again — my second, and I scarcely gave it a thought. Oh, I always "cracked the book" on the way to DENTK for review of emergency procedures and to brush up on the numbers, but I didn't commit to any serious study.

Everything went fine, right up to the check ride itself. Due to limited simulator availability, we had to use the airplane. The Denver weather was terrible due to an early snowstorm, and the ceiling was only about 300 feet in blowing snow. These conditions necessitated using Runway 35 at Stapleton, which was not the most efficient for handling Denver's heavy traffic. We struggled through all the delays and finally took off. After some steep turns and simulated emergency procedures we returned to Stapleton for my low-approach certification. By this time I was aware my check airman was a stickler for adherence to procedure and SOP (Standard Operating Procedure).

We were on the ILS with the weather near minimums, and a strong crosswind was blowing from our left. During the descent and now approaching decision height, I noticed a slight "off course" indication on my non-computerized display. I did not want to miss that approach, so I made a positive correction, overriding my flight director to get back on centerline. Since my check airman's information was identical to mine, he detected what I did. We broke out of the clouds at 200 feet and went in to land. Nothing was said until we got back to the office.

"Ray, I'm going to turn you down because you're not following the flight director properly. I saw that deliberate correction near minimums, and it was necessary because you didn't follow the computed commands from the start. You ignored the minor corrections it was giving you all the way from the outer marker. I'm going to schedule you with an instructor for an hour to teach you how to fly the FD-109 correctly and then schedule a recheck. Your First Officer can go home, but I'm afraid you will have to stay over."

A recheck was serious business because it cost the company money, and it put a black mark on my record. Needless to say, I was devastated. The following morning, I was in the simulator at 5 a.m. with Tom Sheeran, my instructor.

"Go ahead, Ray, fly it the way you always do and let me see what's going on." At the conclusion of the practice session he remarked, "I see the problem: you're trying to outsmart the flight director by overriding it, and our flight standards people won't tolerate that. I can see how it works for you, but it's really better to use the computer. That's what it's there for; focus on it throughout the entire approach and follow it all the way in. Just stick the miniature delta-wing plane into those command bars and keep it tight. Don't even look at non-computerized data." So, that was it; I flew three more ILS approaches doing as Tom said, and he gave me the green light for the recheck: "You've got it now, Ray, the problem has been resolved." Later that afternoon, I took my recheck with a different check pilot from Flight Standards, and then I went home.

You know what? I flew better approaches after that, and I was able to impart what I learned to those who looked up to me — my own First Officers.

———

After the PC, I went back to work on the Colt. You know the drill by now: drain the fuel, take the wings and tail feathers off, remove the engine and prop, and take it all home piece by piece. The wings were stored in the basement, and many of the other parts as well. Since the engine wouldn't be part of the project, I left it in the hangar with the Staggerwing, wrapped up for safekeeping.

The Colt was a great at-home project because of its compact size. When we brought the fuselage home, we put it next to the wall and there was still plenty of room. I used rug scraps to protect the new tile floor.

Within a week, everything was at home, so I took a breather and moved on to other things — like a vacation trip to Honolulu, for example. My one and only time there was on my way back from Japan in August 1952, but it was Margaret's first. We had a comfortable room near the Royal Hawaiian, just off Waikiki Beach, and we drove around the island of Oahu in a rental car. We also visited the USS *Arizona* Memorial. We didn't tour Maui or any of the other islands, and we arrived back home by Thanksgiving.

Now that we were back home, I began with the Colt fuselage by removing everything inside the cabin. Most of the instruments cleaned up nicely, but the directional gyro needed overhaul.

Once the fuselage was stripped, I was pleased to find it in excellent condition. Mac always kept the Colt hangared, so rust was minimal. I planned to install a completely new Airtex interior.

———

Mom and Dad came from Erie to spend Christmas with us, and stayed for New Year's.

1971: The Year of the Colt

There isn't much to write about 1971, because all I did was work on Margaret's airplane. I took lots of pictures and made notes, as outlined in my description of restoring the Aeronca Chief. Anything that had a function, or traveled in any way, was badly worn because of the thousands of training hours the Colt had been subjected to, especially the landing gear. It just so happened that Tom Apple happened to have a "like new" replacement unit from a wind-damaged Tri-Pacer.

The present dilapidated condition of the Colt gave no clue to its potential to become a "like new" restoration in just a few short months. All it would take would be time and money--lots of both.

At this point, the Colt was completely disassembled — nothing more could be removed.

This is Margaret's Piper Colt ready for its precover inspection by George Thomas of Reading Aviation. Note pristine condition of left wing — truly "as new." The interior work has been completed and will be protected during the fabric-covering process.

Summer, 1970: This was the plane-building room behind the garage. Margaret was pretending to be flying this skeletal entity. Significant work had been done, but much more remained. However, a few months later, it was completed.

The fuselage frame sat in a cradle made from 2x4s. By spring it was ready for fabric, so I moved on to the wings. Once again, I was pleasantly surprised to find them almost perfect. As I progressed, I realized the Colt had the potential to be like new again. All it took was time and money. Performance-wise, it was hands-down better than the Chief because the engine had almost twice the horsepower, yet the weight was equivalent. The Colt would not be a "dog." I really felt this time I had a project that was worth my effort.

I had an ally in George Thomas, shop manager for Reading Aviation (RAS). George agreed to come over and do the pre-cover inspection, and he also ordered a new set of wheel pants from the Piper factory in Lock Haven.

While working on the Colt in the spring of '71, the Allentown, Pa. *Sunday Call-Chronicle* newspaper called to say they were doing a story on airline pilots living in the Lehigh Valley, and they would like to take a picture of the Staggerwing for the front page of the Woman's section of the Sunday paper. We pulled the plane out of the hangar, and the photographer took this picture.

This photo was taken in the workroom prior to covering the fuselage. Margaret was trying out the new custom seats from Airtex. The seats would be removed, but the new headliner had been permanently installed and I would need to be careful not to spill dope on it during the covering process.

Finally, by the middle of May, everything was ready; George had a few suggestions, but he signed the logbook authorizing me to proceed. A month later the fuselage was recovered and painted, and I was redoing the inside. I bought a complete interior package from Airtex, and shortly after that I was building up the instrument panel. Soon it was time to tackle the wings, and in short order they were painted as well.

Margaret's Piper Colt fuselage ready for transport to ABE Airport for reassembly, August 1971. The double doors ahead of the plane provided access to the main workroom where the Colt was reassembled. This is the Delta Manor house on Lord Byron Drive, Bethlehem.

On a side note, OV Pezzi liked our Colt project so much that he found a plane for himself in New Holland, Pa. It was an all-original PA-12 Super Cruiser, out of license with bad fabric. It had been flying up to the current year, so ferrying it was not a problem. I flew OV there, and soon a deal was made to buy it. The PA-12 was a great project plane for OV, and he planned to rebuild it in his hangar at Penn Yan Airport, near his property on Lake Seneca.

The Piper PA-12 Super Cruiser as OV Pezzi purchased it in 1971, based at Penn Yan, N.Y. (In a few pages you will see a photo from 1972, when we transported the plane's wings to Pennsylvania.)

Except for an occasional trip to Erie, I worked on the Colt all summer. I bought Margaret a brand-new Narco Escort 110 Nav/Com radio as an early Christmas present and the instrument panel sported an ATC transponder with altitude encoder. With a new flat-black paint job, it looked like new. By August the wings were finished, and the Colt was about ready to take to the airport.

Trouble With the Feds

OV was helping me reinstall the engine at the airport when I saw a U.S. Government vehicle come through the north entrance to the airport. I thought nothing of it, since FAA personnel frequently came and went checking their installations. But as the car drove past, I saw the stoplights illuminate, and then the station wagon backed up to where we were.

It turned out to be an inspector from the GADO (General Aviation District Office) on the east side of the airport. The man stepped out of the car and walked over to us while the Colt engine dangled from the chain fall, gently swinging in the breeze. He introduced himself while briefly looking around.

"What's going on here?" he asked.

I explained that I was installing the engine in my airplane — as if that were not plainly obvious. "Let me see your license," he demanded. I explained that I didn't have one and was working under supervision. "And who might that be?" he asked.

I replied that Tom Apple in Erie was my mentor.

"Erie!" he roared. "That's not even in my district." It was evident that he was severely agitated. To reduce the tension, I added, "George Thomas at Reading Aviation is familiar with the project as well." That seemed to mollify him a bit, but then he started making threats pertaining to the Colt's airworthiness certificate, and that really concerned me. He stated something to the effect that he would be contacting George, and then he got back in his car and drove off.

Wow! Now I was in trouble. All these years I'd worked on planes as if I had a license, and now the game was up. I decided I had better stop at the FAA office and try to pacify him, if possible. The inspector had said his name was Bill, so when I arrived there, at least I knew who to ask for.

He invited me in, stating that he had been in conversation with RAS; I guessed George put in a good word for me when Bill remarked, "George says you do good work, Ray, but if you intend to pursue this line of work, you should be certified. It's not permissible for plane owners to perform major maintenance on airplanes in the T-hangars. George says you fly for United, is that right?" When I said yes, he went on, "Dale Ezro runs an A&P school in Quakertown, and he likes airline pilots. How would you feel about working with him for your A&P ticket?" A side note: "A&P" (airframe and power plant) became the current nomenclature for aircraft mechanics in 1958, replacing "A&E" (aircraft and engine).

I explained how difficult it was for me to attend classes due to the demands of my job. Then he replied, "There is another way. If your friend in Erie will write a letter of recommendation attesting to your experience being equal to or surpassing the requirements of Part 61 of the regulations, we can accept that, and authorize you to take the written and practical exams here." I thanked him, and said that I would work on it. He seemed to have calmed down and didn't say anything further about revoking the Colt's airworthiness certificate. The next time I'm in Erie, I mused, I will discuss it with Earl.

I continued the assembly, and by the end of September the Colt was ready to fly. Tom and Earl both knew the plane was nearing completion and, fortunately for me, Earl planned to visit his son in New Jersey. He said he didn't mind stopping by to inspect Margaret's newly finished Colt and provide the paperwork necessary for flight test and issuance of a ferry permit to Erie. An annual inspection at Earl's shop was mandatory prior to returning it to service.

I knew Earl very well, and he always liked to find something when conducting these inspections. I deliberately left a couple of loose wires under the instrument panel. Sure enough, after looking the Colt over carefully, Earl said, "By the way, Ray, I noticed some loose wires under the panel. Be sure to bundle them up before you fly." He seemed happy with everything and signed the logbook.

I told him about my encounter with the FAA inspector and asked if he would write the letter I needed to get started on my A&P. "Remind me again after I get back home," he said.

Margaret and her mother at the new house in Delta Manor during their visit in the fall of 1971. Note Dad's '65 Pontiac in the driveway; we used this car twice to drive to Florida.

Mom and Dad Taylor arrived shortly after that, and one nice evening, we all went to the airport to test-fly the Colt. It did look brand new again and flew very well. After a few minor adjustments, it was ready to fly to Erie for Tom's blessing.

It wasn't permissible to carry unnecessary crew using a ferry permit, so I flew alone. One important component of the airplane had yet to be addressed: the installation of the strobe light system, a safety measure that provided a very intense white flashing light visible from a considerable distance. Since there would be only one, we mounted it on the belly. Strobe lights were more effective when installed on the wing tips, but I didn't provide for that when I re-covered the wings. There were a few other minor glitches, but after a day or so, the Colt was licensed and ready for Margaret. She had been so patient.

Margaret with "Max," her Piper Colt, the day of its test flight
at ABE Airport after complete restoration.

Like everything else we owned that flew or traveled down the highway, the Colt had to have its own name. This time Margaret picked *Max*. Let your imagination run wild determining the origin of that moniker.

Richard F. Lemmon (1919-1971)

Sister Mary called from California informing me that my brother Richard was dying of cancer. I wasn't even aware that he was ill.

"If you want to see him alive, come soon," she said. We were planning a trip to Banff and Lake Louise in the fall, so we decided to stop in San Francisco on the way. He lived with his cat in a little out-of-the-way place on Lombard St. overlooking the bay. I hadn't seen Richard in 25 years, and his appearance was gaunt. He remarked that I now bore a striking resemblance to our father, and that he was disappointed at not being able to show us the sights of San Francisco. I was sorry we didn't make more of an effort to see him when we were on TDY there in 1968.

The visit was difficult, but we got through it, and Mary's assessment of his condition was correct. He obviously did not have long to live. Did we see Mary? No, we called her office in Oakland numerous times, constantly getting an answering machine. Our messages went unanswered, so we left for Canada. Richard died Sunday, November 7, at the age of 52.

———

There was nothing much new at United. The major expansion was over, and the new pilots were trained — the '70s were not projected to be an exciting time for the airline. Fortunately, I was in a good position for that slack period: flying a decent schedule out of Newark as Captain on the B-737. The next major development was seven years down the road.

Super Cruiser

It turned out OV Pezzi didn't care to be an airplane restorer after all. He removed the wings and tail feathers and started the cleanup process, but as time went by he did less and less, and the PA-12 ended up against the wall of his Penn Yan hangar. He called me one day and said, "Ray, would you like to buy the Super Cruiser? You can have it for what I've got into it."

Wow! Take on another rebuilding project immediately on top of the Colt? I wanted to talk to Margaret about it, but he couldn't wait — "There's a guy at the airport who wants it real bad, but I wanted to give you first crack at it."

"Okay, OV, I'll take it." How could I pass that up? He had gotten a really good deal on it. When I told Margaret about it later, she was not enthused. "Haven't you had enough yet? There is more to life than airplanes." End of discussion.

We convoyed to Penn Yan, N.Y. to retrieve OV Pezzi's PA-12 Super Cruiser in the autumn of 1971. The wings were carried on the Pontiac, and we loaded the trailer with the small stuff. Another trip was required to transport the fuselage and engine.

The Taylors came again to visit in October, so I chose that time to retrieve the PA-12 from Penn Yan, N.Y. We used two cars: Dad's '65 Pontiac Star Chief sedan, and the blue Valiant, pulling a U-Haul trailer. We tied both wings to roof racks on the Pontiac, and all the other stuff went in the trailer. We had a full load, but even so, it was going to require an additional trip for the fuselage. The engine was still attached, and that needed to be removed. We put the wings, ailerons and tail feathers down in the basement, and the house was full of airplane parts again. A week or so later, we rented a snowmobile trailer and went back to Penn Yan to retrieve the fuselage. After finding a place for Margaret to stay, I worked several hours getting the engine ready for hoisting the next morning. The folks at Penn Yan Aero stowed everything securely, and by 10 a.m. we were on our way back to Bethlehem, where I put the fuselage in the hangar temporarily.

Margaret started flying solo in her new Colt, and we made a few trips visiting friends in October. All I accomplished on the PA-12 project was to completely strip the fuselage in preparation for the epoxy coating on the steel framework. It was evident this project was not going to be as easy as the Colt. It showed its 22 years, and already I was beginning to have second thoughts about it.

Welcome 1972

As you might suspect, the Super Cruiser project was occupying much of my spare time — far too much. The only fabric I applied the entire year was the small amount that defined the inside cockpit area. It was not going well at all, and quite frankly, Margaret had had enough. I couldn't really blame her, but once I dragged the plane home, there was no turning back. I blocked it up, pushed it over against the wall and covered it up. It was the wrong project at the wrong time for no tangible good reason. Following on the heels of the Colt, it was just too much. Unfortunately, there was much more anguish to come.

We received a Christmas card from the Kanes inviting us to Dunedin, Florida, for a visit in the New Year. At first we planned to fly United, but then Margaret had a better idea: "Why not drive down with Mom and Dad?" An opportunity for her parents to escape the severity of winter in Erie, Pa. was attractive indeed. The Taylors arrived in their Pontiac after the holidays, and since their sedan had more room than any of our cars, it became the vehicle of choice for the trip to Florida. Unfortunately, I wouldn't be going, but while flying my schedule in January, I thought I might be able to catch up with them en route.

Their first destination was Winston-Salem, N.C., where our friends the Hestons now lived. They toured the Reynolds Tobacco factory and Old Salem, and the next day they drove to Atlanta. I had a scheduled layover there the same night, so we enjoyed a nice visit, as well as breakfast together the next morning. Of course, it was all planned in advance, but what wasn't on the agenda was extremely cold weather; overnight, it was down in record-breaking teens. After breakfast, I went to the airport to continue my trip, and they drove to Valdosta, Ga. Thankfully, the weather moderated as they continued south and arrived in Dunedin the following day.

This picture was taken in Atlanta, Ga. in 1972 during a breakfast with Margaret and her parents while they were en route to Florida for a winter vacation. I was flying B-737 Captain at the time.

When I arrived back in Newark at the conclusion of my trip, instead of driving home I boarded a different plane to Tampa. Seeing how easy that had been, I started thinking, "Can commuting really be that bad?"

Margaret picked me up at Tampa Airport, reuniting us once more. It was nice to see Lew and Nat Kane again, and we did a lot of catching up. I only spent one night, but Margaret and the Taylors spent a few more, sightseeing in the Gulf Coast area. Then, they were off to visit friends in Miami and West Palm Beach. I rejoined them there, and we all toured the new Piper Aircraft factory. I stayed with them as far as Jacksonville, where I boarded a United flight to New York. That trip definitely planted the commuting seed, and I started giving serious consideration to wintering in Florida. At that time, however, it was just the germ of an idea. We would have to wait another year for its fruition.

———————

We planned to attend the big Staggerwing fly-in at Tullahoma, Tenn. over Memorial Day weekend, but I had just received word from the Staggerwing Club that the event was being moved to Wichita. Not at the municipal airport, mind you, but at the Beech factory where all the Stags were originally built. Olive Ann Beech, the company President, expressed a wish to bring them back home.

June arrived, and we were ready to fly *RAMAR* to Wichita, but enormous thunderstorms were blocking the way. After waiting one day without significant change, we decided to go on TWA. It was disappointing not to be able to take our plane, but sometimes it just doesn't work out.

Olive Ann Beech inspected each and every one of the 15 planes that attended, and they also gave us a tour of the factory. We all enjoyed their hospitality and I met a very important fellow Staggerwinger there named John Paris from Tullahoma, Tenn., a very enthusiastic Staggerwing Club member. He was in the business of equipping the major leagues with baseball-related material including bats, gloves, and just about anything needed to play the sport.

While we talked about our planes, I mentioned that our interior was shabby, and John told me about his offer to all club members to furnish fine leather to redo their interior free of charge. What a deal! That didn't include the headliner or carpet, but he estimated the entire job could be done at Tullahoma for less than $700.

"How long do you think it would take, John?" "About a month, so you'll need to leave it with us, and airline home," he replied. That introduced a new iron in the fire, but there was no way I would allow such an opportunity slip through my fingers. Besides, Margaret was all for it, too. When we got back home, I wrote to see when we could schedule the job, and he replied that the first opening was in the fall. "Just let me know, John, and we'll fly down."

How was the B-737 flying going at United? I'm afraid there was nothing much new to report on that front. I had accrued almost 2000 hours of Captain time already. The '70s were the doldrums of my career. I don't imply anything derogatory by that statement; it simply means the airline reached a level of stability that I would not have believed possible after the whirlwind of the 1960s. In a sense, it was the calm before the storm.

In September, we finally got word from John to bring the Staggerwing down to Tullahoma; the interior shop was ready. When we arrived, John put *RAMAR* in his hangar and he was decidedly impressed with the airplane, but not its interior. "You were right, Ray, it is bad, but you'll like Bill's upholstery job." I told John we had missed our flight out of Chattanooga and suggested he take us to a motel in town for the night. He replied, "You're welcome to come home with us for dinner, and you can stay in the guest house if you like." That's exactly what we did, and their hospitality was "southern" in all respects. The next morning, John had his driver take us to the Chattanooga Airport for our flight home.

After a month of silence, I called John to check on progress. "Your job is coming along," he replied. I was getting antsy, so before Thanksgiving, Margaret and I flew to Tullahoma to check on it. It was still a work in progress, and I expressed concerns about the onset of cold weather and Bill working in an unheated hangar. Also, we understood that Bill had been ill.

"It should be done soon," John said, but I was definitely getting nervous. Finally, John called in the middle of December to say the plane was ready, so I went to Tullahoma by myself to fly *RAMAR* home. On my arrival in Tullahoma, it was obvious the job was still not finished, and I told John that I was not leaving without my airplane. Actually, the upholstery work was finished; it was mechanical stuff that Bill had taken apart to do the interior that needed to be addressed.

This photo of the Staggerwing's new leather interior doesn't show the elegant tan color of the leather used for the seats, door and side panels. New carpeting and headliner were also installed while the Stag was in Tullahoma, Tennessee.

I reminded John I only had a couple of days, and we should concentrate strictly on airworthiness issues. I would take care of the small stuff once I got home. Finally, two days later, it was finished. Sunday morning dawned cold, very cold, so I told John that we needed to preheat; he produced somewhat of an ancient device for that purpose. *RAMAR* started okay, so John waved goodbye, and I left. I was very pleased with the new brown leather, which smelled great. The flight home was fine, except for being cold and drafty because Bill had failed to seal some of the openings. I flew at 11,500 feet and arrived three hours later. I had furnished Margaret with an ETA, so she was at the airport to meet me with the hangar door open.

What about the PA-12 project? Yes, I had worked on it while the Stag was in Tullahoma. The instrument panel was finished, and much of the pre-cover work had been completed. The elephant facing me now was the engine. I brought it home from the hangar and began disassembly.

Nearing the end of the year, it was time to take a good, hard look at my Cruiser project. I would need to start the fabric-covering process by mid- to late April in order to optimize the good-weather months for doping. All of that had to be completed by fall so that the winter of '73-'74 could be devoted to reassembly. Considering that I had already devoted a year, this was daunting, to be sure, and Margaret was running out of patience.

"What are you trying to do? Where are you going with this project? The PA-12 is no good for the Erie trip — it takes three hours." My reply was, "I wanted to build a show plane, something that would win at Oshkosh."

I guess that was the nub of it; I never had any success there. *RAMAR* didn't win an award, and neither did the Aeronca Chief. "But is it worth it?" she asked.

That was a very good question, and I didn't have an answer. It was quite clear that if I didn't get that plane out of the house soon, I would be in deep trouble. Could I do it? Was it a realistic goal? The truth is, I didn't know. The Super Cruiser had turned out to be so much more involved than the previous two airplanes.

1973: The Winds of Change

A casual observer would have seen the unrest instantly. Oh, not my job with United; that was okay. It was our private life — for all that we had, we were missing out on the annual migration to Florida that some of our friends were enjoying. Margaret, especially, was not content anymore with my constant focus on plane rebuilding; she needed something for herself. "Snowbirding" was the term used for wintering in Florida. I had had itches in the past to be free of winter's grip, and we even traveled south frequently over the years to visit, but it wasn't the same as actually living there. This past winter had been the clincher; when Margaret went to Florida with her parents, and when I saw how easy it was to commute, I could picture myself in that role.

In the New Year of '73, we planned to make the same trip again, only this time all four of us would go. I guess having our friends, the Kanes, there shed a new light on the Sunshine State. Lew was working at St. Petersburg Airport and fantasized about rebuilding a Piper Super Cub for himself.

The Taylors arrived January 8, and once again, the only full-size car we had available was Dad's old Pontiac. Two days later, we were off for Winston-Salem. Does it sound like a rerun? It may, for a while, but trust me, there's new stuff ahead. Another overnight stop put us at the Kanes' home in Dunedin.

Natalie mentioned a new development nearby in Oldsmar, on the way to Tampa Airport, called Green Tree Estates. We liked the Ironwood model, which had three bedrooms, two baths, a nice porch off the living room, and a price tag of only $19,900. All it took was $5000 down to close the deal. Unbelievably, we were able get back into a new house again for less than $20,000. It even came with a tile roof and a washer/dryer. Margaret was delighted, so we bought the house.

Our house on Hibiscus Drive in Oldsmar, Florida. This house was purchased new in 1973, and we owned it for five years.

The next day, we stopped in again to finalize the purchase and iron out (no pun intended) some details. That was all there was to it; we had taken the first step to becoming Florida residents. The rest of the trip was a repeat of the previous year, so I'll return to an old topic, the Piper Super Cruiser.

Since doping in winter was not feasible, I tackled the engine. Teardown revealed an excellent low-time original. Wear was insignificant, so I could see the makings of an inexpensive overhaul. I sent the cylinders out to the Reading Aviation engine shop for honing, new guides and exhaust valves. I cleaned all the parts and did the painting. By the middle of February, the engine job was finished.

Bert and Joan Van Doren stopped in with their new '72 Mercedes 350 SL. I caught Margaret drooling over it. "No, no, Honey, you can't have one; forget about it." For those not familiar with these exotic cars, it was a small sport roadster with two tops. You could drive in three configurations: Hard top in place (as it was for our visit), hard top removed and cloth top up, or as a regular convertible (top down). It was a high-powered car with a V-8 engine, all-leather upholstery, very plush and, needless to say, very expensive.

At this point, I would like to note the passing of my dear friend, teacher, and colleague, C.L. (Mac) McMillen. He died quite suddenly on February 21, 1973, of a heart attack precipitated by emotional issues relating to the renewal of his lease at the airport. He trained over 1000 pilots, but only a few made it to the airlines. I had known "Mac" for over 20 years, and my most recent contact had been in connection with buying Margaret's Colt. I still miss him.

By the end of February, I was ready for George Thomas to perform the pre-cover inspection on the PA-12. There were a few items that needed to be addressed, but he trusted me to do the work. Since it would be to my benefit, why wouldn't I? We had a brief discussion about Bill, the FAA inspector: "I think you better handle this one differently, Ray. That guy's going to be watching. Have you been working on your A&P?" I explained that I was waiting for my letter from Earl in Erie. George suggested I give consideration to moving the PA-12 to the RAS shop for assembly. "We'll see, but it's not likely to be ready this year anyway," I said.

A month or so later, I had everything covered, shrunken, and the first coats of dope applied. Most of the brushing and spraying was done outside to keep the fumes away from Margaret. I was plugging away one day when Margaret suddenly gave me an ultimatum: "Either it goes, or I go, and you have one week to decide." Wow! Was Margaret fed up or what? But who could blame her? It was ridiculous and time to quit, so I called Earl to see if they could finish it for me.

"Gee, Ray, we're pretty busy, and wouldn't be able to get it in for a while. Maybe we can squeeze it in over the winter?" I knew Earl didn't like restoration projects, because invariably they dragged out too long and ran over budget.

"It doesn't matter, Earl, I've got to get it out of the house right now." The next day I went to U-Haul to find something big enough to haul the PA-12 in. The truck of choice was 24 feet long, with storage space over the cab. I made arrangements for a one-way rental to Erie, took the truck home, and started loading it with the Super Cruiser. It was sad; I detested unfinished projects, obvious testimonies of failure. I should have seen it coming, but I think I was in denial. Fortunately, the landing gear was on the plane, so we could simply roll it onto the truck. I packed an overnight bag and kissed Margaret goodbye. Yes, on this trip to Erie, I would be traveling alone. Margaret was crying, and that was the last airplane project.

By the time I arrived in Erie it was late, so I parked the truck at the airport and had Dad come for me. When I went back out the next morning to unload, Earl made room for the fuselage in the machine shop/parts area. It was nice of him to put it there, as that area was heated in winter. After everything was off the truck, I asked Earl for a moment of his time.

We went into the office, and I thanked him again for taking the job, and said I had one more request. "What's that, Ray?" he asked. I continued, "Would you please write the letter I need for the FAA so I can get started on my A&P Rating? I know you're not thrilled, but I really need to get going on that now that the plane project is gone."

AIRCRAFT MAINTENANCE   PHONE (814) 833-0052

PORT ERIE AIRPORT   ERIE, PENNA. 16505

February 2, 1972

To whom it may concern:

I have known R.A. Lemmon since 1949 and during this period
he has worked under my supervision in Aircraft Maintenance
on numerous projects including the complete rebuild of
three aircraft including engine major overhaul.

I hereby certify that he meets the experience requirements
for Aircraft and Powerplant Mechanic outlined in FAR 65-
more than 30 months concurrent supervised experience in
this field.

                                     Signed:

                                     Earl L. Derion
                                     A&E 17164 /A

This is a copy of the letter I needed from Earl Derion in order to
get my A&P license. The FAA accepted this in lieu of attending
the school for a year.

He seemed to understand, and replied, "Okay, Ray, I'll do it. Can
I mail it to you next week?" I said that would be fine, and that's how
I finally got my qualification letter. I returned the truck to U-Haul
and flew home.

The airplane room looked empty now with the PA-12 gone.
Things were a bit strained for a while but, fortunately, we had other

irons in the fire. The house in Oldsmar was finished, and Green Tree Estates wanted to set a closing date.

Earl's letter arrived and, I must say, he did it up proudly. He justified the 30-month, full-time on-the-job qualification certification requirement as having been met, in my case, by a 20-year close association on numerous projects. Then he outlined in some detail the two completed restorations that I had done on my own. It was quite an endorsement, and I felt quite sure it would do the job. He signed the letter as the owner and operator of a designated FAA Repair Station. No wonder Earl didn't want to do it; he was sticking his neck out a mile for me.

The next step was to schedule an appointment with Bill, the FAA inspector. After examining the letter in some detail, he asked, "What took you so long? I had about given up on you. This is okay, so I'll authorize you to take the written and practical exams." In conclusion, he remarked, "Twenty years — that is a long apprenticeship."

I was in for a lot of work before receiving the coveted A&P Rating. I ordered manuals, sample tests, the works. The "A" (Aircraft Rating) was the toughest part. It included studies on metallurgy, steel, and aluminum, and an examination covering the different specifications for using those materials. It also included the different types of aircraft hardware (nuts, bolts, rivets, etc.); working with wood and fabric; welding; sheet metal repair; using approved methods; tools and other shop equipment like shears; aluminum bending and metal fabrication; and more. It's really too involved to cover here, but suffice it to say, it was thorough.

The "P" (Power Plant Rating) was entirely separate, and was not included in the studies outlined above. It involved close adherence to tolerances, complying with meticulous instructions in overhaul manuals, and understanding and interpreting specifications, coupled with a lot of hands-on experience building up complete engines from a bench covered with parts. I will deal with all of this in some detail later, when it is time for my own "practical" exam.

The next step was to schedule a visit with Dale Ezro at the A&P School at Quakertown Airport. Dale managed the facility, and it was approved by the FAA. Dale was a designee, which meant he had the approval from the FAA to conduct the necessary exams for issuance of the A&P certificate. Bill had warned me not to take the exam from the FAA: "It'll take a whole day and I don't like doing them; you're better off working with Dale." 'Nuf said.

I flew the Colt to Quakertown so that Dale could evaluate the quality of my work. It was important to make a good impression, to be sure. He liked the job so much that he remarked, "We can skip the fabric portion of the exam. I've certified several of you guys." (I had explained that my main job was with United as Captain on B-737s.) "I like working with airline pilots, because you guys seem to know where to draw the line — what you can do yourselves, and what to call professionals in for."

Then Dale asked, "How are your written exams coming?" I explained that I hadn't taken them yet, that I was just getting started. "Well, when you're ready, come on down and we'll do the practical exam." I liked Dale, and felt we would get along fine.

Oldsmar

During the summer of '73, we bought a brand-new 1973 Marquis Brougham in connection with the anticipated move to Oldsmar for the winter. That also filled the gap in our transportation needs for a large sedan to travel to and from Florida. We had gone to Oldsmar to close on the house earlier in the fall, but there were no furnishings included, whatsoever.

By now it was November, time for us to be on our way south. Not so fast, you say; where are you going to sleep? Remember when I said the house was unfurnished? "Oh, I know how to handle that," I thought at the time; "we'll just pull a big trailer behind the new Mercury, taking our beds along with us." It wasn't so easy, though, as we were planning to spend the entire winter. We made a list of bare essentials needed to keep house, and we progressed from there. U-Haul said I could tow a 12-foot trailer with the car, so that's what I rented, one-way to Tampa Bay.

I began with the twin beds and dresser, piling things in the trailer until the door wouldn't close, and then we packed the car. It was a load, all right. The things people will do to avoid hiring movers.

The week before Thanksgiving, we started out. What an adventure! We made our customary stop in North Carolina, and spent one other night en route. The house turned out fine, with everything new and the freshly painted tile roof. It didn't take us long to unload and the house looked exceedingly empty — we were due for a shopping trip.

You know, it was sort of fun buying living room furniture and a dinette, plus lots of other odds and ends in the days to come. The kitchen was fitted out with avocado appliances (the rage at that time). We still planned to have Allied deliver a load from Bethlehem.

Our biggest adjustment was having only one vehicle — the '73 Mercury. Margaret would be my chauffeur again, taking me to the airport and picking me up after my trips. She didn't seem to mind, though, and we made do that way for quite a while. Finally, we were in our new house in Florida, and the weather was superb.

We spent both Thanksgiving and Christmas in Oldsmar for '73, and several subsequent years as well. Welcome to Florida.

Chapter 16

Goodbye RAMAR —
Leaving Newark
1973-1977

1974

After the holidays Mom and Dad decided to come to Oldsmar to pay us a visit. They arrived safe and sound for a month's vacation, but they wouldn't be just sitting around. Margaret and I saved some money by doing our own interior decorating, and they agreed to help out with painting the new house. Everyone gradually adjusted to my comings and goings as a commuter — I flew home to Bethlehem the day before my trip, and the same held true for my return to Florida. There was an early-morning 737 flight from Allentown, with a good connection in Pittsburgh arriving in Tampa around noon. It was like clockwork, and I was never in jeopardy of missing my trip.

A&P Ratings

I studied for the written A&P exams. Electrical was the toughest, and the sample tests were most helpful as preparation for the type of questions that would be asked. During my next trip north, I took the tests for both ratings and passed. The final step was to schedule the practical "hands-on" exams with Dale at the Quakertown A&P School. He conducted those in the evening when classes were not in session.

I was a bit concerned about some portions I wasn't too familiar with, such as sheet metal repair, and welding. Fortunately, he cut me a little slack since I worked primarily on fabric-covered projects. It took two nights to complete everything, and we actually spent more time in his office talking than at the workbench. He seemed more interested in getting to know me as a person than in seeing me do the actual work.

"When would you like to schedule the Power Plant exam?" Dale asked. I replied that I didn't have my March schedule yet, and would give him a call. He emphasized that the engine portion would not take nearly as long, and we should be able to wrap it up in just one more evening. The focus was on removal and replacement of a cylinder for a Lycoming engine mounted on a stand. Everything was set up for quick removal, evaluation, specifying the parts needed for reassembly, and installation. Everything was abbreviated for expediency — he just wanted to see how I approached the problem. There again, we spent quite a bit of the time in the office talking about different kinds of propellers and governing systems. That was about it, and I was now a licensed A&P mechanic.

A Journey Into Chaos

During the spring of '74, something snapped. What passed for rational behavior was anything but, and we were about to disrupt, in the blink of an eye, everything we had worked for since we left Chicago. Was it the decision to build a home in Florida? Maybe, but that was only part of it. The unrest was evident in my determination to take on more and more projects, resulting in decisions with far-reaching consequences. From today's perspective, 40 years later, it is easier to grasp. It happened largely because I had the financial means to dig a deeper and deeper pit, continually buying tangible assets in search of happiness. I'm sure you, the reader, have seen it coming. Mom Taylor's diary for that period illustrates the turmoil in vivid detail. On April 2, she wrote, "Margaret called from Florida to say they have sold their home in Bethlehem."

Exactly what preceded this entry, I can only guess. It probably went something like: Why do we need such big house? We're only there part of the year, and it costs us $400 per month. You've given up restoring planes, etc. (By moving to Oldsmar, we did demonstrate our ability to live quite comfortably in much smaller quarters.)

Mom's next entry was on April 24: "Margaret and Ray have rented an apartment in Easton and want to store things in our attic. It is really upsetting to me as to why they would sell their lovely home." Clearly, it made no sense to her. To make a decision of that magnitude after spending only one winter in Oldsmar was irrational. Let me relate how it played out that summer of '74.

The Lord Byron Drive house was on the market for only one day, and the first prospects paid the full price of $49,900. We made a little profit, but obviously, the price should have been higher. We were shocked by such a quick sale and had even considered the possibility that it wouldn't sell, requiring us to stay.

We did rent an apartment in Easton — but before actually moving, we found something better. A new townhouse development was under construction on Grove Road within sight of the airport. The units were priced at only $20,000, and the location was ideal. We could walk from there to our hangar, and in fact we did a few times. It seemed to be the perfect solution, but there was a snag: the townhouses wouldn't be available until the fall. Oh, we would manage somehow, we philosophized. We put large items like Margaret's piano in storage, and moved the rest into the hangar. How did Margaret feel about all this turmoil? She was happy as a clam to be spending all summer with her folks, so it was just a matter of packing her clothes and heading for Erie.

To add to the complexity of the situation, Tom called to say that the PA-12 Super Cruiser was nearly finished, and he was applying the finishing touches. "It should be flyable by Memorial Day," he said.

We had to vacate the premises by July 1, but before that, we finally made it to the spring fly-in at Tullahoma. It provided an opportunity to show off *RAMAR*'s new leather interior, and while we were there, Dub Yarbrough approached me and said, "If you ever decide to sell your Stag, let me know." John Paris, the organizer of the "Tullahoma Bunch" (the fly-in sponsors), had a good turnout, with over 20 planes on the line for the '74 event.

We moved out of the Lord Byron Drive house on July 1, with most of the heavy stuff going into storage and the rest destined for our hangar. That summer, my problem was where to sleep between trips. There was a nondescript motel near the airport that suited my needs, and summer's long days and good weather made commuting to Erie quite feasible. Coming and going in such fashion made me feel like a gypsy.

Margaret's convertible had been relegated to collector status. It was useless for what we planned that summer, so it also resided in the hangar — most of the time while in Erie, she didn't really need a car of her own.

That's how we lived during the summer of '74. As much as possible, I used the PA-12 for the Erie run. Even in those days, fuel was a consideration; *RAMAR*'s thirst for 25 gallons per hour, versus the Cruiser's five, made for an easy choice. Of course the Stag was much faster, but time was usually not of the essence.

Oshkosh '74

This photo was taken shortly after arriving at the '74 EAA convention. It was mid-week and not many show planes had arrived, so I had the field to myself.

It was late July, and time for the EAA convention. I preferred to have company but couldn't find anyone, so I ended up going alone. I stopped on the way to see Dick Berry, my old Staggerwing pal in the Chicago area. Dick was now living in Casa de Aero Estates in

Hampshire, Ill. It was a fly-in community with the hangar attached to the house, and his plane was right inside — every pilot's dream.

I took Dick for a ride in the PA-12, and he was quite impressed. He put me up for the night, and after breakfast the next day I was off on the final leg to Oshkosh. They had special arrival procedures in place because of the volume of traffic, but it was early in the week and attendance was low. I should have come later on Friday or Saturday; it was another example of poor timing.

After a day or so, I was bored and left. The airplane was rejected by hard-core proponents of the classic category because fancy wheel pants, an updated instrument panel, and a slick paint job were not representative of the Piper PA-12 as it was delivered in 1947. Needless to say, I was crushed. Somehow, I just didn't "get it" when it came to EAA judging. Even so, I won the Best Piper award. Jack Cox, EAA's photographer, wrote me asking for pictures and a write-up describing the project for an article in *Sport Aviation* Magazine, and EAA mailed my trophy. That was my final visit to Oshkosh, and my disappointment was profound.

The Townhouse

I was keeping an eye on the Grove Road townhouse, and although construction was proceeding at a good clip, our move-in date would not be until October 1. I was still staying at the motel between trips, and I started getting anxious. Margaret wasn't bothered by any of this, as she was quite content at Mom and Dad's house in Erie. The end of September, we drove back to the Lehigh Valley and stayed with the Pezzis until moving day.

The townhouse was small, but we found it to be cozy in a way. However, it was evident that this would not be a long-term solution — it was more like the Stonehenge apartment we rented for a year.

Was our life as chaotic as I described it in the spring? Probably not, but we still needed to come to terms with the decision to sell the Delta Manor house. There was far more influencing that decision than the impulsive purchase in Florida.

Architecture

When it came to residential architecture, Margaret was not a Colonial person. Even though she liked the Lord Byron house in

Delta Manor, the four-level-split arrangement was really not her cup of tea. She preferred contemporary designs, even A-frames. As we move along with the narrative, you will see the emergence of the true expression of her preference. Our first house in Ringwood, N.J., more nearly met that criterion. I don't remember losing any sleep over selling the Lord Byron house — it was just part of our journey.

Hershey

October was a busy time for us, getting settled in the townhouse, but there were a few other things of note. Every fall, the greatest antique car show and flea market in the country was held at nearby Hershey, Pa. The Hershey Chocolate Company sponsored this meet, and nearby they had their own private airport called Hershey Airpark. You could land your plane there and walk across the road to the flea market and the main car show event on Saturday.

There was an old saying that if you needed a part for your antique car, the one sure place to find it was Hershey. I had always been mildly interested in antique and classic cars, but my preoccupation with airplanes suppressed any tendencies I might have had to gravitate in that direction. Another airport friend, Jim Rossetti, and I flew Margaret's Colt to Hershey for the day. Jim had a Mooney just like OV Pezzi's, but he was a "car guy" in addition to being an aviation enthusiast. That term, "car guy," meant serious affiliation with antique and classic collectible automobiles.

A subtle change was taking place in my persona regarding collector cars; however, my involvement was limited to membership in AACA (Antique Automobile Club of America) and "hanging out" with Tom and other members of the Erie and Bethlehem chapters.

As October gave way to November, it was time for us to fly to Florida, and it was much easier not having to drive. We just went to the airport and got aboard the B-737 to Pittsburgh and Tampa. On arrival, we called Lew and Nat Kane for a ride.

Pivotal Years: 1975 and 1976

Why were '75 and '76 "pivotal"? It was because vast changes were in store that affected both my professional life and my private escapades.

We left Florida for a brief Erie visit in January. We hadn't seen Mom and Dad since we went south, and apparently they were not planning a visit to Oldsmar this year. The flight was nonstop to Cleveland, where we rented a car.

Margaret and I began discussing *RAMAR*'s future at length and decided it was time for the Staggerwing to go. We had been very lucky thus far, and the fabric was still passable; however, Tom had been warning me recently to get rid of it while I still could. If relicensing was denied due to a failed fabric test, the Stag's value would plummet. What was it worth now? With the new leather interior, and a fresh annual inspection, its value should be somewhere in the low twenty-thousands.

I had considered buying a Beechcraft Bonanza, which was faster than *RAMAR* while burning half the fuel. Then, out of the blue, I received a call from Bert Van Doren while we were still in Oldsmar: "Ray, would you like to buy the Mercedes?" Wow — I wasn't ready for that, but I asked, "Why are you selling it, Bert? I thought you loved that car." Briefly, he recounted his troublesome experience with the dealership where he bought it — every time he took it in for service, he found another scratch or some other evidence of abuse. "It makes me crazy, and I don't enjoy the car anymore so I've decided to sell it," he said.

"How much is it?" I asked. His response was, "I'll let you have it for $8500, because I know you'll take good care of it." I suspected that Bert had paid twice that amount when he bought it just two years earlier, and he had only driven a little over 10,000 miles. I remembered how Margaret had drooled over it when they drove to our house on Lord Byron Drive, so I knew I shouldn't pass on this one.

"Sure, Bert, we'd love to have it, if you're sure." "Don't you want to talk it over with Margaret?" he queried. "No need to, I already know her answer. When can I pick it up?" "How about next month?" he suggested. "Okay, but I'll need a loan from the credit union to swing it."

I couldn't wait to tell Margaret, and she *was* ecstatic with the news, especially that it would be hers. The last car of her own was the '65 Pontiac convertible, and she didn't drive that car anymore.

When it was time to take delivery, I drove the convertible over to Ringwood and parked it in Bert's Mercedes garage. "I'll be back for it next month," I assured Bert.

What a car! The Mercedes 350 SL really was special. It was dark blue with a silver hard top, an off-white leather interior, a beautiful sound system, and electric everything. The trip back to Allentown was truly a new driving experience.

Goodbye *RAMAR*

I called Dub Yarbrough regarding our conversation at Tullahoma the previous year. "Are you still interested in buying my Staggerwing?"

"Yes, Ray, how much are you asking for it?" I told Dub the figure I had in mind and he agreed to $22,000, but he had another plane that he had to sell first.

Before long Dub called, saying that his plane was sold and that he was ready to buy the Stag. I turned to Margaret and said, "There it is, Honey, should we let it go?" She looked sad, but resolute. "I think we better — you'd rather have a Bonanza for flying to Erie."

Just like that, *RAMAR* — a plane that defined us for so many years through hardship and plenty — was gone. It truly was a pivotal moment.

"$22,000 it is, then?" I confirmed. Dub once again agreed to the price and said he would arrive at Allentown by airline shortly to fly the Stag back to Tullahoma.

Dub arrived early in May to take delivery. It was too late in the day for him to start for home, so we put him up in the townhouse. I knew he was a heavy smoker from the time we bunked together down in Tullahoma, and I was concerned that he might light up in the house. Thankfully, he didn't.

After dinner, we went over to the airport. Dub knew everything there was to know about the Staggerwing Beech. "Would you mind getting it out so I can taxi it around?" he asked.

"Sure, why not?" I agreed. Afterward, returning to the hangar, we went over everything I was including: all the logs, manuals, etc. He didn't see any of the spare parts across the taxiway in my other hangar, and since they hadn't been discussed, they were not included.

We spent considerable time at the hangar, since he was staying overnight anyway. I think the new leather interior was the clincher; it was so nice. I had mixed emotions about seeing *RAMAR* go but, all things considered, I felt that it was best. Dub indicated that the Stag was going into the museum at Tullahoma, which made us feel a little better.

The next morning after breakfast, it was time for Dub to go. Since he had already checked the plane out, there was no delay. Margaret and I stood by the hangar to watch him take off, and I looked over and saw tears streaming down her cheeks.

The sale of the Stag in the spring of '75 marked the end of my antique biplane era, and a move up to a much more efficient and modern mode of transportation.

Margaret driving her '73 Mercedes 350 SL at the airport in Erie during our spring visit in 1975.

After Margaret and I returned from Florida for the summer, the first opportunity to take her new Mercedes on a little trip was driving it over to Ringwood to pick up the '65 Pontiac convertible that had been stored there. When Bert asked Margaret how she liked the car, she just smiled; did that question really need an answer?

Spring '75 arrived, and I decided to drive the Mercedes to Erie — partly to show it off, but also for maintenance (among other things, a leaking muffler).

I was out on a trip, so Margaret flew the Colt to Erie by herself, and a few days later I joined her with the car.

Debbie

When I drove out to the Erie airport, Earl handed me a message from Red Rhudman, saying he would like to talk to me. I wondered what that was all about.

Red had been the original purchaser of the Swift I flew in the 1950s, and he always owned a plane, including several Beech Bonanzas. His latest was a Beechcraft C-33A Debonair. The Debonair was a lower-priced version of the famed Model 35 Bonanza. Most of the Debonairs were equipped with a smaller 225 horsepower engine and a less expensive cloth interior. To further diminish the plane's visual appeal, it was built with a conventional vertical fin versus a V-tail, the signature feature of the Bonanza.

Both were manufactured under the basic Model 35 certificate, so in a sense Debonairs were also "Bonanzas." The first year Beech offered the Debonair was 1960, and it entered the marketplace as a bare-bones airplane, priced accordingly.

Through the years, though, more and more options became available. What Beech never anticipated was that many customers actually preferred the "straight tail" version. Even though the V-tail saved weight and delivered slightly more cruise speed, there was a downside: that design compromised lateral stability, causing the plane to oscillate left-and-right, especially in rough air. The Debonair completely eliminated that tendency, which provided potential customers with a choice when ordering a Beechcraft.

Red's was a 1967 model, and the C-33A designation proclaimed that it was equipped with the Continental 285 horsepower engine, the identical power plant used in the latest V-tailed Bonanzas. Even with the larger engine, it burned less than 13 gallons per hour. I'm telling you all this because Red was anxious to sell the Debonair to me. As it turned out, I didn't need to call him back, because he arrived at Earl's office shortly after I did.

"Ray, I heard you were interested in buying a Bonanza. My Debonair is virtually the same, and I have to sell it because I'm retiring soon." Cautiously, I began to explore the price issue.

"I've been asking $22,500. It's a fair price, but so far no one seems to have the money. Earl showed me pictures of your Super Cruiser and I wondered if we might possibly work out a trade so I could continue to fly a bit."

I was stunned. "Gee, Red, I just recently got the PA-12 flying, and I hadn't considered selling it." Red again: "I know you'll need some time to think about it. I heard you sold your Staggerwing. You can buy the Debonair outright for $22,500, if you like." I thanked him, saying I would get back to him shortly.

I needed to discuss this with Margaret! We just bought the Mercedes, and now this? It was too much. Of course, I still had the *RAMAR* money, and it was almost an even trade, airplane for airplane. What should I do?

There were other considerations. The Debonair was eight years old, and although it had less than 800 hours total, it was far from a new airplane. On the plus side, Earl had maintained the Debonair its entire life, and Red purchased it new.

"Let me show it to you, Ray; the paint is still good, and the interior is nice. Of course it's not leather, and I know you like leather." We went to his T-hangar and I looked the Debonair over carefully. I acknowledged that the plane was exceptionally nice.

"What about the engine, Red? I see it's never had a top?" By that, I was referring to intermediate removal of the cylinders for reconditioning of the combustion area. Red responded by saying, "Compression is right up there in the 70s, and Earl says the engine should be okay for the foreseeable future."

Opening the engine cowl, I remarked, "It sure runs dry; I don't see any sign of oil leaks." The Debonair *was* in excellent condition, no question about it. Can I, or should I, pursue this? I needed to talk to Margaret.

"How much is he willing to allow for the PA-12?" Margaret asked. "I don't know; we didn't discuss that." "Well, don't you think we should get $10,000 for it?" This was followed by Margaret's next question: "Are you really willing to part with the Cruiser? It cost us dearly, in more ways than one." With that, I replied, "I better talk to Red some more, and get all the numbers." Continuing the inquisition, she probed, "How does the Debonair look? I think you should fly it before going any farther." Margaret's pretty sharp, I thought to myself; maybe I should let her handle the negotiations.

It was all catching up with me now — the hard choices I should have made in the past about putting so much of myself, and Margaret, into those projects. There were commitments for the *RAMAR* money, other than airplanes, and I had just recently borrowed from the credit union for the Margaret's Mercedes. I was completely overwhelmed. I liked the Debonair, and I wanted it. Even though I hadn't owned a Bonanza myself, I had flown them on occasion. Some said the 285 horsepower Debonair was faster because it was lighter.

I called Red back to arrange for further discussion and a demonstration flight. "Sure, Ray, how about meeting at the hangar after supper? And be sure to bring Margaret along." We met as planned, and Margaret saw the Debonair for the first time. "Can we fly it?" she asked. Red offered me the left (pilot's) seat, and talked me through the engine-starting procedure. It was my first experience with a fuel-injected engine, and different techniques were required. After the preflight, Red said, "The first start of the day is the easy one, but when we get back and try to start it hot, you'll see how the procedure varies." Margaret seemed more interested in the interior appointments than in what was going on up front.

I was amazed at how low the noise level was. Headsets and intercom were best for engaging in cockpit conversation while airborne, but they were not widely used in the 1970s. But even without them, we were still able to talk over the engine noise without shouting.

My log showed only 20 minutes for that demonstration ride. When we returned and shut down the engine, Red said, "Now let's try a hot start: Mixture idle cut-off, throttle wide open, and just a touch of fuel boost. When it fires, immediately go to full rich, and be prepared to pull the throttle back." At first, when we started cranking the engine, nothing happened; then it fired, and I did as Red instructed. "It's kind of a pain — just a quirk peculiar to fuel-injected engines. Hot weather aggravates it even more, but you'll soon get used to it," he said.

It was time to talk business, and I wanted Margaret to be a part of the conversation. Red began by saying, "I'd really like to fly the Super Cruiser before committing to a deal, but for the purpose of defining an agreement, let's assume that I'm as pleased with your plane as you are with the Debonair. How much would you ask for the PA-12 if you were selling it outright?"

"Somewhere between $10,000 and $12,000," I replied.

Red countered that the book value on the Debonair was $25,000; so, proportionately, the difference was $15,000. "Could you live with that?"

I looked at Margaret, and she nodded in agreement. "Yes," I said, "We can live with that. It looks like I need to get the Super Cruiser up here."

Red concurred: "I think that's the next step. When can you have it here?" "After my next trip, I'll fly it up from Allentown," I said.

The drive back to Allentown in the Mercedes was a blur. I just couldn't wrap my mind around the immensity of it all. The need for a decision on the Debonair didn't exist just one week ago. We had never bought anything that expensive, except a house.

Driving southbound on I-79, I was so engrossed that I missed my turn to the east on I-80. I wasn't about to go back, so I just took the Pa. Turnpike instead. That evoked memories of my trip to IGMR in the '36 Pontiac over 20 years ago.

As promised, I flew the PA-12 to Erie, and doing so aroused more confusing emotions. It was my last flight in a plane I had invested so much of myself (and Margaret) into. However, if it would be an avenue to more excitement, and especially a better plane for the Erie mission, it would be worth it. I couldn't have it both ways.

Red climbed into the PA-12 and flew it around awhile to make sure that it met his expectations. In spite of his extensive flying experience, I chose to go along in the rear seat. Red was a Navy pilot in WWII and threatened to do some slow rolls. "Not with me in here," I announced — I assumed he was joking.

Red seemed agreeable to complete the transaction as we had proposed. Finally, everything was finished, and the Debonair was ours, and I couldn't wait to fly it to Allentown. It took exactly 1 hour and fifteen minutes — 30 minutes less than an average trip in the Stag. Over the next two years, I made that trip 25 times.

1967 Beechcraft Debonair. *Debbie* was purchased from Red
Rhudman in Erie in 1975. We used it primarily to fly between
the Lehigh Valley and Erie. With this plane, the car trip of
seven hours was reduced to less than two. With the prevailing
tailwind, our speed eastbound was nearly 200 mph. We only
owned *Debbie* for two years, selling it after transferring to
Cleveland in 1977. (Photo by Gene Olsen)

During the summer, we made one last trip to Tullahoma. It was
special because they had recently finished the Staggerwing museum
hangar, and Olive Anne Beech was to attend the dedication. We were
pleasantly surprised to see *RAMAR* sitting right in the middle of the
display area. Dub was there and asked, "Would you like to fly it? We
can roll it out if you want to." That was kind of him, but I declined,
and he seemed to understand. We only stayed for the dedication
ceremony and left immediately after. That was the last time we saw
the Staggerwing Beech.

Goodbye Colt

In July of that tumultuous year, I sold Margaret's Colt without
any logical explanation. I guess I thought she had lost interest in

it, since she didn't fly it much. My justification was that we owned this wonderful Debonair, so what did we need that little puddle jumper for?

That decision to sell the Colt stemmed from my purchase of the Debonair in Erie. It turned out that Red didn't fly the Cruiser as much as he thought he would, so he put it up for sale. Earl had a Canadian customer named Chuck Cox and, knowing he was in the market for a PA-12, Earl immediately called him. Chuck said he would be right over. The next day, Chuck and his wife Peg arrived at the Erie Airport, and although he loved the Cruiser and wanted to buy it, the timing was not right for him. Red gave Chuck the impression that time was not of the essence and that he would hold it for him. In due time, though, Red received another offer, and since Chuck still was not in a position to buy, he had to let it go. Chuck was devastated. At that point Earl spoke up: "I know of a Colt refurbished by the same guy who restored the Cruiser. Ray might be willing to sell it now that he has Red's Debonair. I can give him a call if you're interested." Chuck asked about the price and Earl replied, "I have no idea, but I'm willing to call this evening."

So that's how it came about. When Earl called, I was totally unprepared. We had not taken a single step to sell Margaret's plane and hadn't even thought about it. The proposal came out of the blue and without thinking, I turned to Margaret and asked, "Do you want to sell the Colt?" I felt certain she would reject it out of hand, but instead she started feeling me out, answering a question with a question: "How do you feel about it? We could use the money." That's where I made my mistake. Instead of having her answer first, I replied, "Now that we have the Debonair, we probably won't fly the Colt much anymore." From that response, she deduced that I preferred to sell it, and she wouldn't stand in the way.

From there, it was all downhill, opening discussion with Chuck Cox about the money. I suggested something in the $5000 range, which was exceedingly low. It was a disaster from start to finish, and that's how it progressed until the little Piper was gone. Everything except the Debonair was gone now — all my blood, sweat and tears over the past three years. How could I do it?

Soon Chuck Cox and a friend were on our doorstep, and the Colt flew away to Canada. I don't remember whether Margaret cried or not, but she probably did. Barely halfway through 1975, I had sold all three airplanes that I dearly loved and had slaved over. What was wrong with me? Was I crazy? The circumstances may have been extenuating to some degree, but could I really justify such behavior? At the time it seemed perfectly rational, because I loved the Debonair that much.

How were things at United? I was still flying the B-737 to the same places, so very little if anything had changed during the year so far. United had transformed our entire operation into a jet-age airline with a network of routes enlarging the hub-and-spoke system. Passengers accustomed to nonstop service between principal cities now found themselves going through O'Hare, and recently Dulles International had become a hub as well. The system worked great until it snowed, and then schedules simply fell apart. Concerted efforts were made to move planes out of the path of East Coast blizzards and hurricanes.

We were gradually moving into the computer age. Again, we were on the cusp of something major. We started seeing the effect it was having on crew utilization, with many cushy trip pairings being eliminated. Efforts to make as many combinations as possible fit acceptable parameters were called "crew homogenization." It was like an undercurrent; on the surface things seemed much the same, but an inescapable shift was in the wind.

Deck House

Margaret wanted to build again, but first we needed to find suitable property. She saw an ad for an interesting building site located in a development called Spring Lake Farms, an affluent neighborhood at the extreme northern edge of Bethlehem, bordering Monocacy Creek. The lot was of a generous size, but the land rose steeply at the rear. It represented a challenge to build on, and might require a very special plan. Rock Hill Circle was our proposed new address.

On one of my trips I flew with Joe Gates, a First Officer who was building an interesting home in Hamburg, N.Y., a suburb of Buffalo.

It was designed and built by Deck House, of Massachusetts, and the more he described it, the more my interest was piqued.

Joe's house was designed using post-and-beam construction that accommodated a wide range of interior room placement. The home was designed for a hillside lot, similar to our Ringwood Palo Alto, and included abundant windows on the lower level. The most striking architectural feature was a cathedral cedar ceiling throughout the main level. Large windows and sliding glass doors opened onto spacious decks that surrounded the house, and all window and door frames were constructed of mahogany.

The main entrance door was also mahogany, and very special. It was called a "waffle door" because it was built up from many smaller mahogany blocks (actually scrap), which suggested the texture of a waffle iron. Those doors were handcrafted, very labor intensive, and expensive. It all sounded very interesting, and I told Joe that I wished I could see his house.

His reply was, "Deck House is building a new model home in West Chester, Pa. You can go down there and check that one out. I'll give you the 800 number for the home office and they'll provide directions." "Sounds great, Joe. Thanks a lot."

When I got home, I told Margaret what I had learned and she was all ears. After hearing that there was a model home in West Chester, she was even more excited.

"Let's go see it," she urged. We got directions and headed for West Chester without delay. It was a hillside home and looked very rustic, sitting there in the woods. Margaret took it all in — the western red cedar siding, beams, glass and, yes, the waffle door. When she saw it, she said, "Look at that door! It's beautiful." At that point, I knew I was in trouble.

When Joe Nangle, the sales manager, learned that we already owned a wooded lot in Bethlehem to build on, he was like a bulldog — in a nice way, really, and not pushy. We spent most of the afternoon there, and by the time we left, Margaret had written a deposit check for $500.

Dad Taylor was recuperating from hernia surgery, so the Debonair got some exercise. In keeping with Margaret's fetish for naming our toys, the Debonair now became *"Debbie"* — so from now on, I'll refer to her by that name.

That trip to Erie was my first opportunity to fly IFR. *Debbie* was an excellent instrument platform, and the single-axis autopilot made a big difference. The "wing leveler," as it was called, was worth its weight in gold and almost a necessity for single-pilot instrument flying.

In November, Margaret drove the Mercedes to Florida by herself — I wasn't able to accompany her, but she didn't seem to mind traveling alone. She made the usual stop at the Hestons' in North Carolina, and included a visit to a high school classmate in Atlanta. After three days, she arrived in Oldsmar, and the Mercedes never left Florida again while she owned it.

Nearing the end of December, I rented a shelter for *Debbie* at the Clearwater Airport. I couldn't leave Allentown until 1 p.m. on December 29, but I still hoped to make the trip to Florida nonstop. The forecast was excellent, with light headwinds, and I planned to fly VFR at 12,500 feet. However, I was getting really low on fuel as I approached Orlando, so I decided to land there instead of continuing all the way to the Tampa Bay area. I only had eight gallons of fuel remaining, and that was cutting it a bit too close. The flying time was just over six hours from ABE — a personal nonstop record in any plane, private or commercial, up to that time.

Except for a few hours of local flying, *Debbie* just sat, so there was little point in keeping her in Florida. We made plans to fly north before the February rent came due.

Margaret and I made several trips to Erie that spring. Mom and Dad were always glad to see Margaret, but I'm not so sure about me — I was just part of the package. The focus for the remainder of that summer was flying frequent trips to Erie and back in *Debbie*. Remember when I alluded to an undercurrent at United? Well, hold your hat.

Cleveland

"Hon, it's official; the Company is closing the Newark domicile and opening a new one in Cleveland." "You're kidding," Margaret responded in disbelief. "I wish I was," I said, "but look at the good side. Now we can move to Erie to be near your folks."

There had been rumors, but there were always rumors at work, and I never gave more than passing consideration to that one. United unveiled a grand marketing scheme for capitalizing on our Great Lakes-to-Florida route. Deregulation of the airline industry didn't take place until later, during the Carter administration, so in '76 the CAB was still king. By markedly increasing our service to the Sunshine State we would have a much more dominant presence, and the 737 was the perfect instrument.

Margaret asked, "How can we live in Erie when you're flying out of Cleveland? What if you're on reserve?" Those were good questions, but things had changed since our Denver days. United gradually accepted the inevitability of pilots commuting, and had established the four-hour-reporting-time rule as standard. The distance from Erie to Cleveland Hopkins Airport was 110 miles, almost precisely a two-hour drive. "I've worked it out," I said. "It's just barely doable using I-90. In the winter I might occasionally have to report the night before."

Margaret continued asking the hard ones: "What about our building plans for Rock Hill Circle?" By that time we had made a major commitment to the Deck House project in the form of deposits for drawing up blueprints, etc. that were specific for that site. I replied, "I better give Dave [Dave Mitchell, Deck House V.P.] a call and explain the situation. I'm sure we can work something out."

Then she asked the big one: "How much time do we have? When's the first trip out of Cleveland?" "The Company is targeting June 1, 1977," I said, "but that's only tentative." We've been flying to Erie in *Debbie* with ever-increasing frequency, I thought, so why not just move there and be done with it? The Taylors were getting up in years, so it might be advantageous for us to be living nearby.

What about *Debbie*? Moving to Erie would eliminate her main mission, so we wouldn't really need an airplane any more. If we sold her, it would provide a $35,000 nest egg for the new house.

Sell *Debbie*? Forget it. Everything I had worked for in planes over the past ten years was invested there. Did I say $35,000? Yes, *Debbie* had appreciated. Since the price of new planes was rising dramatically, older ones had increased in value.

When I spoke with Dave Mitchell at Deck House, he was clearly upset about canceling our building program but he seemed to appreciate, at least to some degree, the extenuating circumstances. "You will forfeit your deposit unless you build at another location within a reasonable time. Have you considered building in Erie? We ship everywhere." I explained that we just found out about the transfer and hadn't had a chance to look. "We're willing to work with you, but don't take too long," he cautioned.

We lucked out with disposing of the Rock Hill Circle lot when Harold Campbell agreed to take it back and refund our purchase price minus closing costs. The property had appreciated during the short time we owned it, so he stood to make a profit by releasing us and reselling it. It was expensive, but we dodged a bullet on that one. With that taken care of, we left for Florida. After the holidays, I said, "Well, Hon, it looks like we better get to Erie and look at property." From that point on, we could no longer ignore the elephant in the room with us: the imminent transfer to Cleveland.

Chapter 17

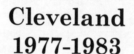

Cleveland
1977-1983

1977: The South Shore of Lake Erie, Fairview, Pa.

We were quite content in Oldsmar; Christmas and New Year's had come and gone. For once we were in the right place at the right time. Snow blanketed Pennsylvania to a degree not seen in decades — especially Erie, the "snow capital" of the state. The tally was 86 inches as of the first of January.

I had vacation the last half of January, and shortly after, we were going to have to leave our cocoon and face the real world. Of course, I faced it daily flying the B-737, and United Airlines experienced the usual flight delays and cancellations.

We flew to Erie and used Dad's car to look at property — luckily, we timed our visit during a lull between storms. The quest began with Mary Kern, a Realtor we had known for many years.

"What are you looking for?" she asked.

"Lakefront would be nice," I said, almost in jest. She immediately responded, "You know, I do have a listing in the Colony subdivision just west of the airport. If you would like to see it, we'll need boots for the trek through deep snow."

What a gem! I couldn't believe such a beautiful offering existed in Erie County; it was a pristine wilderness. Trudging through the snow and woods finally brought us to the edge of a bluff looking out on Lake Erie. We were at least 150 feet above the frozen lake, and the view was spectacular. There was no sign of open water as far as we could see, and it was totally silent.

Margaret and I were blown away. We just had to have it for our Deck House, so naturally, the next question was, "What's the price?" "They're asking $39,900 for it, but I would offer considerably less." "How much less?" I probed. Mary suggested something in the low thirties. Almost two acres on the south shore of Lake Erie that could be had for less than forty thousand dollars? Unbelievable!

It was a perfect winter day for our first look at this amazing place, and we were very excited about it. I tried to hide my enthusiasm, but I'm sure Mary saw right through me. We tendered an offer of $33,500, and our bid was accepted. I immediately notified Dave Mitchell at Deck House, and he agreed to send their district representative in the spring for an onsite inspection. We were concerned about the ramifications of building a Deck House on the perfectly flat Colony site. Deck House architects assured us it would be fine, with minor adjustments. It wasn't fine at all, and it took a *major* adjustment to fix it.

Raising the Money

The proceeds of the Rock Hill Circle property in Bethlehem would cover half of it, and we would be selling our townhouse as well. Other financial good news was that United was picking up the tab for everything, including storage for our goods while the house was under construction. With the purchase of the Colony lot, it was time to head back to Florida. The famous blizzard of '77 was on the way, with wind gusts of nearly 70 mph.

Early in February, I sold Margaret's Mercedes, the car she loved so much — a terrible decision. Why would I do such a thing? To raise money for the Deck House, of course. She agreed to the sale — but then, if we look back, she also agreed to sell her plane, and look what a disaster that turned into. I just couldn't or wouldn't learn from my mistakes. We didn't have to sell her car, but the $3000 profit it brought was an enticement. I had no idea how badly hurt she was until the man came to pick it up, and then Margaret broke into tears and went into the house. I considered chasing after him, but it was too late — the Mercedes was gone.

I sold *Debbie* as well. Gut-wrenching as it was, the $35,000 it brought was sorely needed, and that did turn a substantial profit. Realistically, with the move to Erie, we wouldn't need a plane

313

anymore, and by the middle of June *Debbie* was gone — for the first time in 13 years, I was without an airplane. Around the same time, we also sold the townhouse on Grove Road, so everything was falling into place. All of our household goods went into storage, including Margaret's grand piano. At least I didn't sell that.

Flight schedules for the Newark domicile were being pared down and flown by other crew bases, all in anticipation of the transfer to Cleveland. We were allotted nearly two weeks for the move, and once *Debbie* was gone, I vacated my precious hangar at ABE.

It was truly sad eradicating so many years of commitment and hard work, but in due time it was over. Mom and Dad invited us to move in with them for the summer, and before long we were settled in at 720 West Seventh, Erie, Pa. Our entire focus for the next five months was building the Deck House in Fairview.

The Deck House on Lake Erie

By March the lot was clear of snow, and I made a brief visit to meet with the Deck House representative and our builder, Mike Lewandowski. Mike had previous experience building a Deck House in Meadville, Pa., so we were indeed fortunate to find someone familiar with the product so close by. The plans were finalized, and the "package" went into production during April. The cost of $46,000 was payable in full prior to delivery. Mike brought his crew in to clear the building site and carve out the driveway. Drainage was a major issue because the lot was so flat water wouldn't run off, so a great deal of stone was trucked in to combat that problem.

It was exciting when the trucks carrying building materials arrived, and the delivery was spread out over several days. An inventory was provided for checking everything as it came off the truck. The wall sections were prefabricated with cutouts for the window units, so everything went together like a giant jigsaw puzzle. Surprisingly, the house was under roof within a week. Unlike the "glue-lam" beams used today, the precut structural beams were solid Douglas fir. They were sawn to exact size, stained, and then set in place just the way they came off the truck.

Philippine mahogany was inexpensive, and Deck House used a lot of it. In a way, it was the opportunity of a lifetime to build a house out of such high-quality materials. Even though the framing went quickly, it seemed like an eternity for Mike to finish the job. There were snags, such as bringing in the water, gas and electric from the road, 500 feet away. Separate trenches were required for the utilities, so double-digging was necessary. We did what we could to cut costs by staining the cedar and mahogany ourselves. The wood was gorgeous and had a rich look about it. I stained the exterior siding, and Margaret did windows.

Deck House #1, 1977, on the south shore of Lake Erie. Located about seven miles west of the city of Erie, it was built in a pristine wilderness overlooking the lake. Note extensive work to create a suitable entrance. Margaret designed this on her drawing board. The entire structure was over 100 feet from the master bedroom to the far end of the garage.

The building was over 100 feet long, including the attached three-car garage, and the basic width was 30 feet, with a four-foot bump-out for the living room. The main waffle-door entrance door was in the middle, opposite the living room, looking ridiculous standing there four feet above grade with a wooden ramp leading to it. When I called Dave Mitchell to complain, he simply said, "Truck in some dirt and shape it." "Yeah," I said sarcastically, "won't that look great?"

We hired an architect, but we didn't like his solution either. Margaret was good at the drawing board so, in the end, she redesigned the entry herself. When finished, it was an asset, but it cost a fortune. Work continued all summer and into the fall. Finally, in mid-November, the moving van arrived from Allentown.

United spent millions establishing the Cleveland domicile. Everything was new, including a massive hangar on the south side of Hopkins Airport. The south finger of the terminal was extended to create more gates, and the space below was used for our dispatching requirements. A separate operations building was constructed adjacent to the hangar, and that was where I reported for work. Bus service to the terminal ran on a schedule, as was common at other domiciles. The project never worked out as planned, and eight years later CLEFO (UAL lingo for Cleveland Flight Operations) closed — a victim of deregulation.

What about my friends at the Erie airport? Tom Apple lived only 10 minutes away, and his interests had recently gravitated to antique cars. When I last visited him, Tom's project was a '35 Hudson Terraplane rumble seat coupe. He built a two-story garage behind his house with a big sign advertising it as "Tom's Garage." I joined a group of old-car nuts that met for lunch every Saturday at Hoss's Steak House. They owned various makes of collector cars, and I was making a gradual shift toward that venue myself. Nature abhors a vacuum, and I created one for myself with the sale of my airplanes.

Thanksgiving at the Taylor's was once again a family affair. The meal was festive, but it was becoming more difficult for Mom and Dad each year, as they were approaching their eightieth birthdays. Our presence in Erie would prove to be a godsend.

Even though we were barely moved in, it was time to head for Florida. Erie was due for an exceptionally snowy winter, but lake-effect blizzards were nothing new for the snow capital. The man I hired for snow removal plowed our driveway four times in December.

Tom Apple working on his '39 Lincoln Zephyr in his garage shortly after we moved to Fairview, Pa.

One positive aspect of our new location was air service to Tampa. Flights were frequent and nonstop from Cleveland, so we commuted with ease. Everything in Oldsmar was fine; however, we discussed the future of the house there. Since the neighborhood was in decline, we considered selling it with the prospect of returning later to join a seniors-only community. Because of the project in Fairview, we couldn't afford a change anytime soon. We returned to the Deck House for Christmas but didn't stay — early in the new year, we were headed back to Florida.

We invited Mom and Dad to join us for a month, and we provided tickets for them on United. I drove the three of us to Cleveland, and we flew nonstop on a DC-10 to Tampa, where Margaret picked us up. Everything was fine until Dad was ready to deplane. He could scarcely walk and needed my assistance. It appeared to be some kind of neurological event, but apparently it was not a stroke because his speech was not impaired. We finally got him to our house in Oldsmar, where we suggested a trip to the emergency room.

Naturally, we were alarmed, but Dad refused to go, insisting he would be okay if I would bring his cane down next trip. During the course of their visit, he slowly recovered, but he just wasn't the same old Dad he used to be, and from that point on he complained of occasional dizzy spells. That had a direct bearing on a decision Margaret and I had been wrestling with. Shortly after they returned to Erie, we put the Oldsmar property up for sale.

Up north, a new pattern was emerging. When I was out on trips, Margaret frequently went into town to have supper with Mom and Dad, sometimes staying overnight. I enjoyed maintaining a close relationship with Margaret's parents as well — even when I was home, we exchanged frequent visits, and during the winter they enjoyed coming out to the Deck House for pizza and a fire in the fireplace.

Living by the Lake

What was it like, living on the south shore of Lake Erie? Was our initial assessment accurate? Yes and no — Lake Erie had many moods. During the summer months the lake was often smooth as a millpond, but from late fall to freeze-up, it often became a roaring physical being, throwing its fury against the cliff outside our living room.

1977-1981: Behind the Erie Deck House, this was our panoramic view from the precipice 200 feet above Lake Erie at the north end of our property.

Dense foliage prevented us from even seeing the lake during the summer, and we were cautioned not to disturb the trees (with their established root systems) to improve our view. We located the house well back from the brink as further insurance against weakening the bank. The only thing preventing further erosion was a layer of shale that the waves crashed against. Occasionally we climbed down to the lake level, but there was very little there resembling a beach. While going in swimming during the summer, we wore sandals as protection against the sharp rocks.

Once the leaves were down in the fall, we could see the ships carrying iron ore from the Mesabi Range in Minnesota. We had great views from both the living room and the master bedroom; however, by early December all shipping ceased.

The freeze-up was dramatic. During a typical late autumn day Margaret and I would be aware of the normal roar of the lake, but by the next morning we might be greeted with absolute stillness. Huge dunes built out from the shore, and beyond them lay an endless expanse of ice. One winter I ventured out onto the ice to take pictures looking back toward our house. Movement beneath the surface caused all sorts of weird, grinding noises, making it a bit scary. It was a beautiful place, but there was also an inescapable lonely aspect to it. I wondered about Margaret being in the Deck House alone while I was away on trips. Apparently, she felt at least some concern as well. We had good deadbolt locks, but at that time there was no alarm system — ADT home security systems did not yet exist.

Winter also had a severe impact on our new domicile in Cleveland. Returning from a trip, we would often find a foot of snow on the cars in the parking lot. The right-of-way would be plowed, but our cars would be buried. It became a ritual, going to the office where the brooms, shovels, and brushes were kept, and then starting to dig. Once, after an hour's work, I discovered to my dismay that I had dug out the wrong car. Oh my!

1978: A Spate of New Cars

Everyone in the family got at least one new vehicle in '78, and I got two. In February I bought a new short-bed pickup from Hallman

Chevrolet in Erie. It was a Custom 10 model with hubcaps and white wheels, a white front bumper, and a rubber floor mat. What really got my attention was its V-8 engine and automatic transmission. Since Dave was an airport friend and owner of the dealership, I got a special price break at $4400. Why did I want a new pickup truck? The old '68 I bought from Jim Rossetti was difficult for Margaret to drive, and I did enjoy having a truck. I also bought Margaret a '78 Volkswagen Scirocco so she could have her own car again. She loved it, almost making up for the Mercedes fiasco, but not quite.

Margaret with her new '78 VW Scirocco at the Deck House in Fairview.

The last was a new Buick LeSabre for Dad Taylor. His old '65 Star Chief Pontiac was shot. The LeSabre cost $5500, including freight. and no prep. I promised Dad I would take care of the prep for him.

1978 turned out to be my last year on the B-737. There were a number of reasons for making a change. Primarily, it was just time since I had been on the same plane for ten years — that was just too long, partly because it bred complacency. Even though I had flown Albert for ten years as Captain, it didn't guarantee immunity.

My 5000-hour experience with the small Boeing demonstrated that it was a good aircraft with very little downside. Oh, yes, there was the scare at Tannersville in '69, an occasional brake-and-tire issue, and even an engine failure flying into South Bend, Indiana.

I craved a change of venue — flying different routes and seeing familiar places from a new perspective. I couldn't wait to get back on an airplane with a genuine Second Officer — I had sorely missed that ever since leaving the B-720. And, of course, the money would be better, and in the end, it's always about the money.

By that time, many of our 727s were the "advanced" model. That signified that they were the latest "stretch" model of the 200 series, with increased performance for cruising at FL 410 with the same agility the very first "sport" models did. Don't hold your breath just yet, because the move to the 727 won't take place until the end of the year.

Did the Deck House ever get finished? Not quite. We were fortunate to find a local contractor named Morris Powers to build the front entry I referred to earlier. He was excellent, and we couldn't have been happier with his work.

This is the front entrance area that Margaret designed. It was quite impressive, with mahogany railings that matched those on the main house.

The last major improvement was paving the driveway. The Township resurfaced Bonaventure Drive in front of our property, so we made a deal with the contractor to include our driveway with the job.

We sold the Oldsmar house mid-year — we wouldn't be going to Florida anymore. I bought a 10 horsepower snow blower for our driveway.

When October arrived, it was time for B-727 school, and Margaret accompanied me. It was my second assignment at the new training center — a beautiful facility, to be sure, with all the latest full-motion simulators and great classrooms and mock-ups. They even conducted guided tours for the public.

As before, ground school was simply a refresher course. I had been flying Boeing airplanes for the past 15 years, but I did need to reacquaint myself with the engineer's panel and working with a real Second Officer again. That was a distinct pleasure.

I could still expect to spend five to six weeks at DENTK, but the course schedule was much more predictable now that flight training in airplanes had been eliminated and type ratings were issued in the simulator. The new simulators were much more demanding than the airplane — examiners knew that a newly certified Captain would find the airplane to be a delight. The only thing lacking was the perspective of actually sitting in the seat and looking out the window.

December arrived, and it was time for my rating ride. The training had gone exceptionally well, and my instructor had no reservations about recommending me. However, my old "check-itis" nemesis surfaced. After turning me down, the flight standards examiner was furious with me. He said, "I know you can do it, Ray; your instructor insisted that you were ready. Why did you screw up that low approach? The FAA inspector saw it too, so I can't let it go. I'm going to assign a simulator period with an instructor, and then we'll do a recheck. Everything else was fine."

During my simulator session with Tom Sheeran, after takeoff I was vectored for the ILS approach, and after completing it Tom said, "Ray, you're doing it again, still refusing to fly the flight director properly. I don't know how you've been getting away with it on your 737 PCs. You have to fly the command bars all the way in, as we discussed before." I flew two more approaches with diligence, and Tom seemed content to have me fly the recheck.

Amazingly, my old friend Gene Olsen was in Denver having warranty work done on his new Aerobatic Bonanza. I invited him to accompany me during the training session with Tom, who said, "Why don't you go get a cup of coffee, and we'll let Gene have a crack at it?" So that's how Gene got to fly the 727 simulator. He was ecstatic; he never dreamt of having that opportunity.

The recheck went fine, and I was out of the "box" (jargon for simulator) in nothing flat. The FAA inspector didn't show up, since he told the UAL Flight Standards examiner that my initial approach was satisfactory for him. We saw this repeatedly — where United Flight Standards was so much tougher than the FAA. I could never figure out why that unsatisfactory practice of mine wasn't detected and corrected during training.

Back to the 737

When I returned to Cleveland from 727 training, I resumed flying my 737 schedule for December. That practice of reverting to previous equipment resulted in some compromise of safety, and the practice was discontinued shortly after that. The planes were vastly different, and the slightest distraction caused by unfamiliarity could lead to trouble.

My first trip back on the 737 was a case in point. The flight was from CLE to EWR, and when we arrived, Newark was landing to the south. At that time there was no ILS approach for Runway 22, and since the weather was excellent, there was no need for it. It was a visual approach, with no radio aids required.

The problem was daylight, or more specifically, the lack of it. It was precisely twilight, too dark to see the airport clearly but too light to discern the runway lights. I should have asked the tower to turn them all the way up to step 5, but I didn't. As I continued the approach, everyone detected my error at the same time — I was lined up with the parallel taxiway. We were too close in to transition over to the runway, so I directed the First Officer to notify the Tower that we were executing a missed approach.

"What's wrong, United, why are you aborting?" I took over the mike and said, "We were out of position for safe landing." The tower didn't ask for details and seemed unconcerned. I directed the Third Crew Member to make a PA announcement to the effect that the plane ahead of us had failed to clear the runway. As we pulled up, I noticed the runway lights were brighter, so I think the controller caught on. The misalignment would have been obvious on radar, but apparently no one was watching the scope.

I thought I had put an end to it, until suddenly the New York Manager of Flight Operations showed up at the cockpit door. "Okay, Ray, now tell me what really happened." I outlined as tactfully as possible the nature of the runway misalignment.

"Why didn't you ask for the lights to be turned up?"

I explained further that none of us detected the problem until it was too late, but what I didn't tell him was that it was my first trip back from 727 school. He said he didn't intend to pursue it further, but hoped I would be more vigilant in "twilight" conditions. My activation date was January 1, 1979, an interesting time of year to be starting out on a new airplane.

1979: A New Year and a New Plane

Well, sort of. Returning to the "three-holer" in my present capacity as Captain, it was almost as if the 727 was brand new to me again — my situation being so vastly different now than it was at JFK back in 1966.

The time finally arrived for the "shotgun" phase of my training. Just as it had been ten years earlier, a United B-727 check airman was required to assess my performance from the First Officer's seat for 25 hours before releasing me to the line. Each time when checking out in a new plane, in addition to earning the "type rating" imprinted on your pilot's license, supervision during regular line operation was part of the equation. Flight managers specifically trained to familiarize Captains new to the airplane were delegated. This time, because of my extensive first pilot experience on the 737, the same check airman was assigned to me for the entire session.

We only flew the most desirable trips. My mentor had the authority to displace any Captain and First Officer of his choosing. "Displacement" simply meant involuntary removal of a pilot from his bid schedule — the regular Second Officer flew his assigned schedule. Pilots so notified received full pay and credit, just as if they had flown the trip. I had experienced it a number of times, and objection was futile. Training and supervised flying, such as I was engaged in, had top priority.

The first flight was nonstop to San Francisco. This was new for the Cleveland domicile and had only recently been added to our schedule. Although it was winter in Cleveland, they were very proficient at keeping the runways clear; while assigned to the 727, I seldom experienced snow-covered runways. It was only during storms that I encountered slippery conditions.

The San Francisco flight took about four hours, and then we were guests once more of United's Best Hotel in San Mateo. It was my first layover there since my TDY assignment with Margaret ten years earlier. The next day we flew the return trip to Cleveland. Not bad — I already had eight hours.

The next sequence was a doozy: from CLE, nonstop to Las Vegas, with an hour to play the slots and then off again nonstop to Milwaukee. That was nearly eight hours for just one day. The reverse trip the following day provided an additional seven hours. On our arrival back in CLE, the "shotgun" was almost over. We finished it with a turnaround to O'Hare, and then I was on my own with the 727. While flying those trips, it was evident that not all flights were routed through Chicago anymore; in fact, O'Hare was becoming so congested that United considered adding even more direct service.

Handling the 727

By now, I was well aware of the responsibilities of command, so it was just a matter of getting used to the new airplane. In a way, it was always like that; DENTK training and certification provided only the first step for attaining the feel necessary to be successful in all the various conditions encountered while flying the line.

I've known pilots who flew strictly "by the numbers" their entire career, and built their security in that fashion. Many others, myself included, had roots in what was called "seat of the pants" flying, and found our comfort level exploring the envelope a little more deeply. You needed to be careful and acquire that "feel" for the airplane over time, because any time you deviated from SOP (standard operating procedure), you were on your own.

The B-727 was a case in point. Due to the aft placement of the wing necessitated by the rear-mounted engines, it had some unique handling characteristics. Who would design an airplane with three heavy engines mounted at the extreme rear of the fuselage?

There were advantages, to be sure — primarily the absence of engine noise throughout most of the airplane. In the cockpit, there was little engine noise at all, and the first class section was equally quiet. Another advantage was the extreme cleanness of the wing. Even though engine pods didn't impede lift, the wing looked so much better uncluttered. The Douglas DC-9 was similarly constructed.

One serious compromise with rear-mounted engines was the way the airplane responded to reverse thrust on an icy runway. In any significant crosswind, the plane tended to weathercock into the wind. When this occurred, the only way to regain control was to get out of reverse immediately and use the rudder and brakes to maintain directional control — a small price to pay for the other immense advantages.

The only way Boeing could keep the center of gravity within acceptable limits was to move the wing back. Since the landing gear was mounted in the wing, the main wheels were a considerable distance behind the pilot. An attempt to flare the plane for landing might accelerate the sink rate of the plane approaching the runway. To reduce the likelihood of a hard landing, the accepted technique was to begin a flare at the point of throttle retardation, but once the descent was checked, initiate forward pressure on the control column to lower the nose. In the process of exerting that forward pressure, the main landing gear usually contacted the runway. Then, the spoilers in the wing deployed and canceled any residual lift, increasing the weight on the landing gear to help slow the aircraft until the nose wheel touched down. At that point, reverse thrust was applied to provide additional deceleration, resulting in considerable noise and vibration.

There was nothing wrong with that method, until winter came. Using the above technique, there was still a lot of forward speed to dissipate, because the airplane was still traveling at over 100 knots. There were two ways to deal with that inertia in a timely fashion: wheel brakes and reverse thrust. A crosswind might limit the use of reverse thrust, and adverse runway conditions could reduce the effectiveness of wheel brakes. That's one reason jet airplanes sometimes went past the end or off to the side of runways. It was really about physics and kinetic energy: an object in motion tends to stay in motion unless acted upon by an overriding force.

Pitch sensitivity was evident on takeoff as well. Again, especially when flying a stretch model, the rate of rotation to takeoff attitude had to be somewhat delayed to keep the tail skid from contacting the runway. It wasn't difficult; you just needed to pause at the plus-five-degree point to allow the plane to lift off before assuming normal climb attitude.

There were lots of new places to fly to. Deregulation had become law the previous year, which meant that now United and all the other carriers could schedule flights anywhere they chose. For us that meant invading American Airlines territory in the great Southwest: Texas, Arizona, and New Mexico. New destinations included Dallas/Ft. Worth, El Paso, Tucson, Phoenix, and Albuquerque. On the main line I now flew regularly to Portland, Seattle, Boise, and Salt Lake. It was a whole new world for me, and I loved it.

This photo was taken by a flight attendant at FL 410 (41,000 feet) on the way to Las Vegas. For public-relations purposes, United furnished instant cameras that the flight attendants could use to take keepsake pictures of passengers.

Why did it take me so long to move up to the 727? Primarily, it was a seniority issue. Until the past year, I would have been relegated to reserve much of the time. The dynamics changed when new nonstop flights, like I had just flown, were added to our schedule. But there was also some vertical movement on the seniority list through retirement of more senior pilots.

What had Margaret been up to? She liked to visit her mom and dad on a daily basis, and I hung out with Tom Apple. Tom's Garage was the focal point for old-car activity in the area, and you could always count on John Ropel or Doc Higbee to show up. Tom removed the engine from his '39 Lincoln Zephyr for overhaul and I, being a "motor-head," became intensely interested in that project. Tom was extremely cramped for workspace and needed more room.

Deck House Questions

We kept trying to make the Deck House work for us. The rec room was downstairs, with its fireplace and the organ we brought from Florida, and Margaret's grand piano was upstairs in the living room. We bought sectionals, which were ideal for company. The color TV set was downstairs in the rec room also. So what was the problem?

We were constantly running all over the house just to live in it. If we went downstairs to watch TV, and then wanted a drink or a snack, it meant a trip back upstairs to the kitchen. That was fine when the Taylors came for a fire in the fireplace, but on a daily basis it wasn't working out well at all. The TV problem was relatively easy to fix by building a furniture wall in the middle upstairs bedroom, converting it to a den. It was still a trek to the kitchen, but at least it was on the same level.

To provide the drinks and snacks when Mom and Dad came to visit, we put in a downstairs kitchen, complete with sink, cupboards, fridge, cooktop and microwave, at the far end of the utility/walk-through area adjacent to the family room.

Okay, now we've got it covered, right? Wrong. Margaret's laundry room ended up halfway down the stairs on the way to the garage, at the opposite end of the house from the master bedroom. As a result, she had to truck the dirty clothes and bed linen 100 feet through the house, and after taking it out of the dryer, truck it all the way back to the master bedroom where she did her ironing. For all our scrupulous planning, we ended up with a house that was difficult to live in. What a shame.

1979 was still a construction year, as the front-entry work and concrete for the garage apron was still not finished. Would the parade of trucks never end?

During vacation in October, we decided to fly to Florida to look at houses again. We contacted Marion Daniels, the agent we had used for the sale of the Oldsmar house, and she suggested a seniors-only community in Palm Harbor. At age 50, we were barely eligible. It was a nice place, but we couldn't decide which model to buy. In any case, '79 would likely be our last winter up north for quite some time. The last entry in our check register for 1979 was a $500 deposit for a house in Highland Lakes. We were going back to Florida.

Highland Lakes

We really liked Highland Lakes' location because it was equidistant from Dunedin, where the Kanes lived, and Tarpon Springs, the Greek sponge-fishing center.

U.S. Home, a well-respected presence in the homebuilding industry, sponsored the development. All the amenities, such as the large swimming pool and clubhouse, were included in membership. On January 18, we submitted the balance of the down payment due on our new Florida home.

That raised issues about the validity of keeping the disappointing Deck House in Fairview. Even after all we went through, if the price was right, we might consider selling it. Mary Kern, our Realtor, planted the seed even before the house was completed: "If you ever want to sell, call me; I know I can get $250,000 for it." It was a wonderful place, but we seldom even looked at the lake anymore. A smaller place nearby would suffice just as well. By the middle of March, we had talked ourselves into selling and contacted Mary, who promptly listed it for $249,900. It was a good time to sell, but interest rates were through the roof at more than 10%. We told Mary we might consider holding the mortgage.

One of the great advantages of living adjacent to Lake Erie was the availability of fresh Lake Perch. The fish market was just a few miles down Route 5, and we frequently invited Mom and Dad to our home for a Perch dinner. Even after we left the Deck House, we continued to enjoy that tasty cuisine.

We made a series of inspection trips to Florida to check the progress on our new home in Highland Lakes, and by the last trip in May, the house was virtually complete. The closing was in June, and with payment of the final installment, we were Floridians again.

It had been nearly a year since I checked out on the B-727, and it really was a new world for me — flying to so many new and different places, with much longer segments. Many of my flights were through Denver to the Pacific Northwest, including Portland and Seattle. There were nonstops to San Francisco and Las Vegas as well.

Jane Olsen posing with the new B-727-200 Advanced in the background at Sarasota, Florida.

Gene Olsen called to say he and Jane were vacationing in Florida, and it just so happened I was on a trip to the Sunshine State that included several stops. One was Sarasota (SRQ), and we agreed to meet at the airport so I could show them my new airplane, the B-727-200A (stretch, advanced), our newest and longest version. SRQ was just one of several stops on the way to Cleveland, so our visit was brief. I conducted a tour of the outside, the passenger cabin and then, of course, the cockpit, where I introduced my crew. All too soon, it was time to take off for Orlando.

We were lightly loaded for that short flight, so I demonstrated the short-field capability of our latest 727. Since the runway was fairly short, I could justify using the 25-degree flap takeoff procedure. Gene was impressed as he watched us take off and climb like a rocket — so unlike the usual mundane climb angles of jet aircraft.

I did have an opportunity to fly one brand-new 727. No, I didn't pick it up at the factory in Seattle but, other than the test flights at Renton, it had only made two previous flights before reaching me. The first was the factory delivery flight to the San Francisco maintenance base, and the second was its first line trip, SFO/Portland, where I picked it up. Boy, was it nice! Just like the 737 I delivered in 1968, the wheel wells were spotless, as was everything else. This new 727 also was equipped with previously-used avionics supplied by the San Francisco avionics department. It was the last of our order for those planes, and its service life would be brief. Before long, three-man crews were a thing of the past at United. I flew that gem to O'Hare, where I handed it over to the next crew.

Charm School

The Command, Leadership, Resource Management (CLR) program was driven by industry executives. Some learned psychologists concluded that it would be perfect for the airline cockpit, because the basic tenet embodied was synergism — to the effect that, in times of crisis, two or more insightful professionals could collectively make better decisions than any of them could individually. It took a totally unnecessary accident for United to embrace CLR or its twin, the CRM (Crew Resource Management) program designed for industry.

The accident that precipitated inauguration of CRM at United was tragic indeed. One of our DC-8 flights inbound to Portland, Ore., had a problem with its landing gear indicating system — displaying only two green lights instead of three — and that led the crew to question whether the landing gear was safely down and locked. All troubleshooting measures, such as changing light bulbs and resetting circuit breakers, were in vain, so the decision was reached to go in and land, but not immediately.

The captain had announced publicly on numerous occasions that if he was faced with a similar situation, he would "land on fumes," clearly stating his intention to dump or burn off all excess fuel to reduce the fire hazard to a minimum, just in case a belly landing occurred. He went too far, though, and ended up with insufficient fuel to make it back to the airport. After turning on final approach, the engines flamed out, one by one, and he was faced with two choices: land either in the Columbia River or in the midst of a housing development. He chose the housing, and people died.

The tragic irony was that the Flight Engineer was keeping the Captain fully informed of the low fuel state at all times, but his warnings were ignored. Post-crash investigation revealed that the landing gear was safely down and locked, and a normal landing would have resulted without incident, since the failure was in the indicating system only. After that totally unnecessary accident, United elected to embrace the crew resource management program.

All United flight crew members were required to attend a special class to form a new understanding of Captain's Authority. Gone were the concepts of autocratic and dictatorial power of one person. Was it an assault on a Captain's implied authority? Actually, very little of that behavior was evident in the 1980 airline cockpit. Oh, I observed it on rare occasions — and I had experienced it myself as a new copilot with Capital Airlines so many years ago — but the complexity of airplanes like the Douglas DC-8 demanded at least some level of crew integration for safe operation.

The special training was perceived as a joke by many of our pilots but, in fact, synergy worked. There was no better demonstration of its effectiveness than United's DC-10 accident involving Flight 232 at Sioux City, Iowa, in 1989. All hydraulic power was lost as a result of the catastrophic failure of the tail-mounted, center (#2) engine. The giant fan disc at the front of the engine separated because of an undetected crack that progressed to the point of allowing this enormous component to exit the aircraft.

Once released from containment within the engine, the disc sliced through hydraulic lines common to all three systems, which meant the control column and rudder pedals were useless for controlling the aircraft. Those controls could be moved through their full range with absolutely no effect on the flight path. Denny Fitch, a deadheading instructor pilot from the training center, was summoned to the cockpit to function as an integral member of the crew.

Fitch's contribution to survival was vital because he managed the only remaining resource to control the plane: regulating the power of the two remaining engines, according to the Captain's directions. Synergy was instrumental in enabling the flight to make a successful crash landing at the Sioux City airport. Of the 296 people on board, 185 lives were saved.

What CRM accomplished was to bring the crew into a collective huddle anytime an emergency arose. The program was fully integrated into our six-month training syllabus. Margaret attended Charm School with me, as she often did for my training programs. It was like a vacation, as we always enjoyed Denver.

Fall, 1980

We attended a wedding in the fall of 1980. My sister Peg's oldest daughter, Janet, was getting married, and it was great to be back with the Balanoffs again.

Back home, the Deck House had been sold, provided a very complicated contingency deal was successfully consummated. We were fourth in a long line of transactions ending with the sale of our home to a local doctor and his wife. At first I didn't think Mary Kern could pull it off, but she surprised us by closing the deal in early 1981. She delivered on her promise, and we netted $150,000.

That meant finding another place to move into, and we didn't have enough time to build one — but, fortunately, Mary had that covered as well. A local contractor had built a small ranch house on Lakeland Drive, just off of Route 5, also known as the Lake Road.

The contract with his clients had fallen through, and he was anxious to sell the house to recover his investment. It was only $49,900.

We waded through deep snow just to get in for inspection. It was small but, with a few modifications, adequate for our needs. Margaret loved modifications, and I knew just the guy: Morris Powers. The house wasn't air-conditioned, so that would need to be added come summer. I told Mary we would take it with the stipulation we could move in as soon as the Deck House sale was finalized.

1981: Sadness and Transition

'81 became the year of real estate transactions, car shows and family crises. It was evident Dad Taylor was failing; this included his increasing difficulty with walking. In addition, his doctor discovered an undetected collarbone fracture. Somehow, he managed the trip to Tonawanda and back for Christmas while we were occupied with our new home at Highland Lakes.

The move to Lakeland Drive in Fairview reduced my garage space to two cars. I had an ambitious plan for solving the garage dilemma, but I needed advice from Morris to determine its feasibility. The house had a full basement and the lot sloped gently to the rear — sufficiently, I believed, to excavate the dirt away from the foundation and install an eight-foot overhead garage door. That would make it possible to use part of the basement as a garage and/or a shop for projects.

Family Realities

While we were in Florida, Margaret got a call that her father was in the hospital and not expected to live. He had been diagnosed with stage 4 prostate cancer that had metastasized to his bones. That explained his walking impairment and the undiagnosed collarbone fracture. There was no hope for him, and Mom was devastated.

Margaret immediately went to the airport to fly home, but was not able to get on the flight. She arrived in Erie the next day to provide aid and comfort for her mom. A week later, Dad died at the age of 78.

It was a somber funeral service, and we Lutherans always bring the casket right into the church. Mom and Dad were members of St. Matthew's Erie for many years. Burial was on the family plot in Erie.

The death of Margaret's father had a profound effect on our life in Erie. The immediate question was whether her mother would be able to continue living by herself in the large house on West Seventh Street. Dad's Buick LeSabre was not a problem, since I immediately expressed my desire to buy it for our use in Florida. No one else expressed any interest, so I paid Mom full market value for it.

Margaret and I were more than willing to assist Mom, but now we were committed to spending winters in Florida again. For the time being, at least, we tried to make her journey as easy as possible and, at least for the short term, would see to her needs.

Modification: 1890 Lakeland Drive

Shortly after Dad's death, Ryan Moving and Storage moved our household goods to Lakeland Drive. Our plans to upgrade the house were finalized; the bedroom end was okay, but extensive changes in the family room/kitchen area were in store. Counter space was severely limited, so we extended it. Since this was not an "eat-in" kitchen, we built a booth at one end of the family room to create a breakfast nook.

After selling the Deck House on the lake in Erie, we bought this home on Lakeland Drive in Fairview Township. This photo reflects the additions and changes we made. Note large porch to the right and overhead door for access to the basement.

Margaret wanted a porch for summertime, and I wondered what Morris thought about converting the basement into a garage. His answer was mixed: He didn't completely rule it out, but he wanted me to be aware that it went beyond the realm of accepted construction practice. Drywalling the ceiling would be a positive step toward fireproofing.

I gave the go-ahead to work up a proposal for the job. In the city, an inspector would have been called in, but in Fairview Township requirements were less stringent, and all I had to do was apply for a building permit.

The Collector Car World and Flea Markets

Moving ever deeper into the old-car hobby meant obligatory attendance at more and more shows and events. The season starter was Dunkirk, N.Y., always held the weekend prior to Memorial Day. It was a local show, only 50 miles from Erie, and Tom found lots of parts for his cars there. Prices were much more attractive than at big events like Carlisle and Hershey. In the early '80s, there were still many NOS (new old stock) parts for the '60s cars.

Vendors displayed their wares on 20'x40' rectangles laid out in a systematic grid for identification and location. Small items were often on tables, but larger and heavier parts would likely end up on the ground. Some parts had prices marked in crayon while others didn't, but everything was negotiable. And so it went, hour after hour: looking, haggling, buying and hauling. Transporting the precious finds was an art form in itself, and all sorts of conveyances were used: wagons, backpacks, shopping carts, you name it.

Sleeping arrangements were just as varied, including motor homes, tents, trucks, and motels. Toilets were primarily portable units serviced by a contractor, but at Dunkirk they had inside flush toilets and running water in the old grandstands.

Many hobbyists bought tires, still wrapped in cellophane, for their antique cars, and it was a common sight to see them moving through the aisles. It was lots of fun, and these diversions were eagerly anticipated by all the old-car nuts.

The best and last meets were Carlisle and Hershey in October. Carlisle was the first week, followed by Hershey the second, held consecutively so that vendors from afar could attend both shows during a two-week vacation. Tom and I religiously attended both in the '80s, often sleeping in his little 15-foot trailer. The classic car event at Carlisle began as a flea market focusing on postwar cars, including the '50s, '60s, and '70s. That changed over the years to include an auction of huge proportions, but the postwar flavor still remained.

For issues pertaining to the early cars, you still needed to attend Hershey. The number of flea market spaces at both shows was awesome, and it took days to fully cover everything. Most attendees focused on filling their individual needs rather than trying to cover the entire show. By any measure, Hershey was the king of all car events. It took hours on show day just to direct the cars to their class location. It was a fine demonstration of efficiency and a marvel to watch.

Hundreds of people would stand, or sit on blankets, at the main entrance where the show cars entered the judging field. It was a special treat to watch these marvelous machines actually being driven, as opposed to simply seeing them parked on the show field. Tom and I witnessed it so many times that, in a sense, we became immune to the special nature of what we were experiencing.

By November it was time to journey south, and for '81 Margaret and her mother drove Dad's Buick LeSabre to Highland Lakes. Margaret was able to stay in the driver's seat for long stretches, and I admired her for that. It took them three days to get to Highland Lakes for Mom's first visit. She stayed well into December, returning with me on my deadhead flight to Cleveland. It was nice for her to escape her painful memories for a time. It appeared she would be okay remaining in her house after all.

Even though Florida was our winter home, I made frequent visits to Erie between trips. I liked checking in with Tom, and I also needed to keep an eye on our house. While there, I would check on Mom, and often that resulted in a trip to the County Home to see Aunt Hazel. I urged Margaret to hop a flight to Buffalo to be with the family but she chose not to, so we spent Christmas in Highland Lakes. In the spring, Margaret and Mom closed up the new house in Palm Harbor and headed for Erie; Dad's Buick stayed behind to be used as our Florida car.

Bow Wow — Gretchen

We bought a Dachshund puppy. Margaret had loved them from the time she was a child. She located a breeder in our area who came highly recommended. A new litter had been born recently, and both males and females were available for only $300. In no time flat, we were off to the kennel and bought a little female that we named Gretchen. She was a miniature, guaranteed not to weigh more than ten pounds when fully mature.

Margaret holding Gretchen on the porch at Mom and Dad's house on West Seventh St. in Erie, Pa.

Thus began a 16-year commitment to something other than ourselves. We were unprepared for the ways dog ownership would change our life. Mom realized immediately that it was going to adversely impact her, because Margaret's freedom to travel was suddenly being impaired. Previously, we made several trips north during the winter to visit, and now there would be none.

At first, Gretchen rode on the plane in the passenger cabin with us, but that became marginal after she reached maturity. Margaret didn't seem to mind the inconvenience, as she adored Gretchen. Weighing in at only three pounds at first, she was so tiny I could almost slip her into my pants pocket. I soon learned whose needs came first. In early November we all flew to Tampa together. It was a big load, with the dog stuff in addition to our own, but somehow we managed. Suddenly, life for the Lemmons was profoundly altered.

Because Margaret stayed in Highland Lakes, I had to help Mom that winter. Fortunately, it turned out better than I thought; Mom was able to visit Jane in Mansfield, Pa., for Thanksgiving, and Nancy in Tonawanda for Christmas. In Erie, Judy Shanahan, her next-door neighbor, took her grocery shopping and put up her hair.

Chapter 18

Deck House II —
McDonnell Douglas DC-10
1983-1986

1983: Major Decisions

During the winter of '82/'83, I divided my time off to spend some of it in Erie helping Margaret's mother (and, of course, I would visit Tom as well). At the conclusion of my United trip sequence, instead of simply boarding another flight back to Tampa, I often drove to Erie for a day or so. Margaret didn't seem to mind, especially since I would be looking after her mom.

Before coming north for the summer, Margaret and I discussed my equipment options at United. As much as I liked flying the 727, I was going to have to leave it and move up to the DC-10. It was of prime importance to earn as much money as possible during my last few working years, because those earnings defined the amount of my pension check for the rest of my life. United would average my yearly income for that period to determine my retirement benefit, and that number would never change.

The pay difference between narrow- and wide-body jets was substantial. It was important for me to bid a DC-10 vacancy as soon as I could, probably within a year or so. Since wide-body flying was not available at the Cleveland domicile, there were only two crew bases I could realistically bid into: either New York or Chicago. Since we have already noted that Chicago was not our cup of tea, New York was the remaining choice.

The DC-10 flying at New York was unique. Technically, my assignment would be JFK, but I would seldom be required to drive there. All JFK DC-10 trip pairings originated and terminated at Newark, so flying out of there would be a return to my roots of the 1960s and '70s. Other than reporting for my annual physical or attending an occasional meeting, I would seldom go to JFK. It had been that way since the DC-10's inception.

"Hon, how would you feel about moving back to Bethlehem?" Much to my surprise, Margaret burst into tears. "Could we? Are you sure? I wouldn't want to get my hopes up."

"Does it really mean that much to go back?" I asked her, to which she replied, "I never wanted to leave." I had no idea she was that unhappy in Erie, but I think Dad's death affected how she felt about living there. So that was it, the die was cast — we would be returning to the Lehigh Valley.

Once we came north for the '83 season, we looked forward to a quiet summer on Lakeland Drive. We had company occasionally, and the time quickly passed.

Bierys Bridge Road

During my vacation, we drove to Bethlehem to check out property. We took our time and looked at various sites, but we kept returning to Spring Lake Farms and Bierys Bridge Road. The property we previously owned there had been sold, so Rock Hill Circle was out. In retrospect, we probably should have kept that lot, but we never expected to return.

There were still a few building sites on the north side of Bierys Bridge Road, but they were on a steep downhill slope. The only reason they were still available was because prospective buyers considered them too difficult and/or expensive to develop. In addition, Harold Campbell, owner of the subdivision, pointed out the lots were too small as drawn on the original property development plat from the 1950s. "We'll need to redraw the map, so there will be a price increase," Harold said. "What kind of house are you planning to build?"

We wanted another Deck House, of course. The slope was perfect for the design, provided it wasn't too steep. Most assuredly, a lot of backfill would be required to create a parking area for our cars, and we would be looking for a totally different house plan this time around. Hindsight was always 20/20.

Our next call was to John Pearson, the current Deck House representative at the model home site in West Chester, Pa. When I briefly described our dissatisfaction with the Erie design, John urged us not to be discouraged: "We've got some new offerings that weren't available five years ago." We couldn't wait to see those new designs. We still loved the product — the mahogany windows, railings, the vaulted ceilings with cedar facing, etc. We just needed a plan that more nearly met our needs.

"Let me show you what we've got. You might like Model 7184, a combination of two of our basic 28'x40' platforms arranged 90 degrees to one another." The front entry, living room, enclosed porch, dining room, and kitchen comprised the basic structure. The bedroom/garage unit was set at 90 degrees and arranged so that two of the bedrooms projected beyond the kitchen, facing the street. The remaining space was used for two more bedrooms, two full baths and the laundry.

When Margaret studied the plans, she was visibly impressed. It was crystal clear how that arrangement would work for her, especially with the inherent flexibility of relocating interior walls. The hallmark of Deck House post-and-beam construction was that many modifications to the plan were possible without appreciable increase in cost.

"I really wish you could see the plant, and meet with Dave Mitchell regarding your specific needs," said John. I replied that maybe we could — perhaps OV Pezzi might fly us there in his Mooney. A phone call confirmed OV's willingness to do so.

If we expected a modern manufacturing plant in Acton, we would have been sorely disappointed. It was located on a railroad siding, since much of the incoming lumber arrived in boxcars. The entire Deck House complex spanned many acres, a maze of ancient sheds and cutting mills. Stockpiles of cedar, mahogany, and Douglas fir originating in the Pacific Northwest arrived by train, with most of the rough cutting accomplished in Oregon. Much of the mahogany came from the Philippines and was purchased at scrap-wood prices. (Today it comes from Honduras, and it is expensive.)

Most impressive were the workers. The ones manufacturing windows and doors were seasoned veterans — New England craftsmen with a heritage dating back generations. That was especially true in the shop that produced the famous waffle door. We watched while small individual mahogany blocks were glued into a frame of larger mahogany stock using a special fixture that could be set for various dimensions. The enormous Douglas fir beams caught our attention, and Dave told us, "We'll only have those for another year, and then it will be all 'glue-lams'." What Dave was alluding to was that the trees producing those beautiful beams that were so characteristic of Deck Houses were disappearing at an ever-increasing rate, and the Douglas fir beams would soon be replaced by laminated ones built up from 2-inch-by-6-inch stock.

"Western red cedar siding is also getting scarce. If you build by next year, I think we can still provide you with the good stuff," Dave said. There was an assembly line of sorts to build the interior and exterior walls. Those pre-manufactured sections were assembled on-site for rapid erection. We had seen that system at work in the construction of the Erie Deck House.

Everything supplied was top quality, including hinges, locks and other hardware. You really got your money's worth. We observed "packages" being loaded on flatbed trucks destined for delivery all over the U.S. Huge tarps were used to protect the shipment.

After touring the facility, Dave took us to his office to discuss business. "John tells me you like the 7184. Are you sure you want the entire lower level of the bedroom section for garage? It's going to be a big one at 28x44; are you sure you wouldn't like an office at one end?" We also discussed the lower level of the kitchen/living room end normally used for a rec room. I told Dave, "I might be restoring an antique car, and I'd like to have the option of bringing it inside." Dave gave me an uncomprehending stare.

We talked for a couple of hours before returning to the airport. Dave was very congenial and exceedingly generous with his time. His parting remarks were, "Not many of our clients come here, and I wish more did. Addressing our customer's concerns firsthand would hopefully prevent thorny issues from cropping up down the road. I'm quite sure your unpleasant experience with the Lake Erie house could have been avoided."

That concluded our spring visit to the Lehigh Valley. Suffice it to say that we agreed to purchase Lot Three, 267 Bierys Bridge Road, with the understanding that we would return within 60 days to close. It looked like *déjà vu*, but our circumstances were much different this time around; we were older now, and hopefully wiser. We needed to be very careful from this point on. Mistakes were bound to be made, but because my remaining working years were few and finite, our ability to repair financial damage would be much more limited.

We also thought about the effect on Margaret's mother, but we really couldn't let that influence our decision, since it was our life and we had to live it for us. Margaret wanted to return to the Lehigh Valley, and nothing would stand in the way. Now in her 80s, Mom's options were even more limited than ours. If she couldn't manage in Erie anymore, perhaps we should move her to Bethlehem, near to us.

At the pace things were escalating in Bethlehem, my plans for transitioning to the DC-10 needed to be re-examined. The Deck House project in Bethlehem was progressing at a faster clip than my seniority for assignment to the DC-10.

The Bridge

Clearly, Margaret did not want to delay our move to Bethlehem for another year, so I needed a bridge, and that would be in the form of a B-727 Captain slot at LaGuardia. A recent retirement there opened up a vacancy, so I decided to try for it.

I was reasonably confident of successfully bidding it because by that time I was fairly senior. However, moving to La Guardia on the 727 would not increase my popularity there. Pilots were sensitive with regard to outsiders bidding in on top of them, so to speak. Awards usually went to lower-seniority pilots within their own domicile, but hopefully they would understand the temporary nature of my presence there.

How did Margaret feel about the LaGuardia option? She was grateful that I would do that for her, since she knew I could have continued to fly out of Cleveland while waiting for an opening on the DC-10.

The effective date of the LaGuardia opening was still months away, so hopefully the timing would work out. With a little luck, I should be able to start flying 727 trips out of New York by June '84.

Mary Kern suggested listing the Lakeland Drive property in the fall. She thought most of the improvements we made would boost the value. As to the "improvement" downstairs, Mary was quite explicit: "Get those cars out of the basement before I start showing the house."

After the Fourth of July, we returned to Bethlehem to close on the Bierys Bridge Road property. Campbell & Company redrew the subdivision, reducing four lots to three, and the new price was $39,000. While we were in the area, we touched base with Deck House in West Chester. I told John Pearson we wouldn't be able to sign a contract yet, since our building plans were contingent on selling the house in Fairview. "Where will you live in the meantime?" he asked. "In Erie with Margaret's mother," I replied.

We spent the rest of the summer of '83 doing our usual things. Margaret and her mom went off to Chautauqua, and Tom and I did the car-show circuit. We also celebrated a wonderful gathering of the entire family at our house for Lake Erie Perch.

1890 Lakeland Drive went on the market after Labor Day, with prospects showing up almost immediately. In Mary Kern's opinion, it wouldn't take long at all. You know, she was right; a month later, it was gone.

Our furniture went to a warehouse downtown, except for Margaret's grand piano, which we moved to West Seventh Street. Later Mom remarked how wonderful it was to have music in the house.

The movers cleared out 1890 Lakeland Drive, a house we had owned for less than two years. We cleared about $30,000, but we didn't make any profit. That was partly my fault with the basement garage.

We moved in with Mother in Erie; I paid her gas bills in lieu of rent and donated our new side-by-side fridge. It was nice for Mom to have Margaret and Gretchen at home with her. She never minded dog-sitting duty when it was needed.

By then it was November, and time to wrap up the Deck House purchase agreement, so we drove back to the Lehigh Valley once more. We spent an entire day with John Pearson, drawing our specific plans and circulating various suggestions and ideas back and forth. "Who do you recommend for a builder?" I asked John.

In anticipation of that question, he had already invited Ray Norton to our meeting. Ray was young and very sharp. "Ray is your man," said John. "He just completed a project in West Allentown that another builder gave up on." You didn't want to pick just any framer to build a Deck House. A certain level of engineering expertise was important to interpret the special drawings.

While we were all gathered there, we went over the plans and discussed the steep terrain. John began, "It all starts at the front-door elevation, and you have to work up and down from there. I'll tell you right now, it's going to require a lot of fill in the back." He suggested that Ray verify the grade for himself. Based on John's recommendation and our favorable impressions, we hired Ray Norton on the spot. We also talked about the site preparation and oak tree removal. Ray thought he might know someone interested in buying the logs.

We spent an enjoyable day with John and his wife at their Deck House. It was a done deal, and we were all set to start building in the spring of '84. From there we journeyed south to Highland Lakes.

1984: Deck House #2, Bierys Bridge Road

Ray Norton's foreman, Shefford (Sheff) Webb, was exceptionally talented when it came to working with wood. He proudly proclaimed, "If it's made out of wood, I can fix it." I got a call from Ray regarding his plans to break ground in mid-March, and inquiring if we were planning to be there. Since I hadn't seen my March schedule yet, I wasn't sure but said I would come as soon as possible.

By the time we arrived, the trees were gone and the foundation had been poured. At the northwest corner (down the hill), the cement was eight feet high, and I observed that the sill for the man-door to the garage was well over my head. The entire wall that I was looking at would be below grade and out of sight.

A Conrail spur line to the old Bethlehem Steel Works bordered our property to the north. There was one train a day in each direction during the week, and neither caused us any concern. Beyond the railroad track was Monocacy Creek, the northern boundary for Bethlehem, so we were just barely within the city limits.

Margaret and Gretchen had arrived in Erie from Florida. Once Margaret and I got to Bethlehem, we planned to stay with OV and

Mary Pezzi until we found suitable quarters for the summer. That scenario firmly established me in the role of a commuter until I started flying out of New York.

Our timing was perfect; we arrived just after the first Deck House truck had unloaded, and two more were expected shortly. The shipping schedule was structured so that the first materials needed for the job would be on the first truck, etc. The entire package cost $72,000, payable in full prior to any materials departing Acton, Mass. It was encouraging to see the shell going up, and Sheff seemed quite competent in his role as superintendent.

At the end of June, it was time to say goodbye to the Cleveland bunch. It had been an incredible seven years — and ages ago that I dug the wrong car out of the snow when I returned from my trip. As I said, I wouldn't be missing the snow and cold of Cleveland.

OV knew about a place not far from Nazareth that might work as a lodging for the summer. It was called Ye Olde World Inn on Airport Road, west of Bath, and I went to check it out. Their main business was a restaurant, but they also had a few motel units in the back. It would be perfect, and they didn't mind Gretchen. The cost was reasonable at $166.95 a week, and if we wanted a snack in our room, I just could meander over and order take-out.

One of us tried to visit the building site every day; if I was out on a trip, Margaret went alone. She had already caught some mistakes — Sheff did his best, but he couldn't be everywhere. Improper use of material resulted in shortages, and on one occasion Margaret and I drove our truck to Acton to pick up replacements. I explained the shortages to Dave Mitchell, and he agreed to make good on some of them at their expense. I had to pay for a few items, but the trip was definitely worthwhile.

As summer gave way to fall, the basic house was complete, and it was time to address the kitchen and bathrooms. We contracted the kitchen job with Quaker Maid of Allentown. They drew the plan and provided all the cabinets, including a large island with a Jenn-Air range. The top of the island was finished in tile, and the cost of the kitchen alone was $15,000.

Deck House #2 at Bierys Bridge Road, Bethlehem, Pa. This house was built in 1984 on a very challenging piece of land. The Annex is barely visible down the hill at the right of the photo.

This photo was taken in 1994 when we considered selling Deck House #2 in Bethlehem. However, we did not leave there until 2010. The Annex is barely visible at the right side of the picture. We initially asked half a million dollars for the property, but ended up selling it for much less.

By November everything was finished except for the carpeting, and that wouldn't arrive until January. At that point I informed Ray Norton of our intention to move in. "You can't, because we don't have an occupancy certificate," he said. "We'll deal with that later," I replied. "We're checking out of Olde World Inn on the twelfth." There was no refrigerator or washer/dryer on the premises, but we would get by with a cooler out on the porch and the Laundromat. Tension was building between Ray Norton and the two of us; we couldn't fathom how it was feasible for him to keep Sheff on our job for over six months.

We drove the Chevy truck and a small U-Haul trailer to Erie and loaded them with a bed and other essentials. Now I would be able to bunk in the new house between trips.

With that accomplished, it was time to make our plans for Florida, and Mom, Margaret and Gretchen left shortly thereafter — this would be an extended visit for Helen, lasting through Christmas. I spent part of the holidays with them, but I was out flying much of the time. It was the end of a traumatic year, to be sure, but '85 will provide its own measure of turmoil of a kind we haven't seen thus far.

1985

The Floridians returned in Margaret's Scirocco in early February and camped with me in the Deck House for a few days, and then we all departed for Erie. What we needed first for the new house was a refrigerator, washer, and dryer, and all three were installed and operating before the week was out.

We parked Margaret's Scirocco in the garage and drove the truck to Erie to pick up another load. I was concerned about slick road conditions, because the truck didn't have snow tires. It was treacherous, but we made it okay. While we were in Erie, in addition to loading up the truck for the return trip, I terminated our warehouse agreement with Allied and arranged for them to deliver everything to Bethlehem.

DC-10 School

Great news: I finally got a DC-10 bid, but it was for Chicago, not New York. After completion of training, I would have to revert to being a commuter for a while, until I could successfully bid an opening at Kennedy.

My reporting date at DENTK was April 1, and this time Margaret decided to stay with Mom while I was in school. That was just as well; I would have to work a lot harder to get up to speed during this program, because the Douglas DC-10 was totally different from the Boeing family of airplanes I was so used to.

For those not familiar with the DC-10, let me provide a brief description of this wide-body jet transport.

The DC-10 was identified by the air traffic control system as a heavy jet because its gross weight exceeded 300,000 pounds, and all radio calls to and from such aircraft were prefixed by the word "heavy." Some of the DC-10s I flew weighed in at over half a million pounds. Fuel capacity was in the thousands of gallons, giving it a range of over 7,500 miles. (One of the routes I flew, Chicago-Honolulu, was just barely within range.)

Passenger capacity on average was about 300, divided between first class and coach. The DC-10 had two aisles, the distinguishing feature of wide-body jets, as opposed to a single aisle on smaller planes like the B-727.

Cruising speed was about 600 mph (Mach .83), the same as for most jets. Exterior dimensions were impressive, with a wingspan of 160 feet, length of 182 feet, and height at the tail of almost 60 feet.

Power? Three GE CF6 turbofan engines, each rated at 50,000 pounds of thrust.

The DC-10 was an impressive aircraft by any measure. Can you imagine the cost of training pilots in it, as was the practice in the old days? Luckily for United, the entire program, including final certification, was accomplished in the simulator. My first experience flying the actual airplane would be on a regular scheduled flight with passengers.

Ground school was the customary three to four weeks, followed by an intense simulator syllabus. The DC-10 simulator was one of the most sophisticated at DENTK, capable of full motion and incorporating a computerized flight management system. It also had the capability of flying visual traffic patterns in the Denver area, displayed as a night presentation. You could clearly see your position in relation to the mountains and the entire Stapleton Airport complex.

While we were in the midst of the simulator portion of our training, rumors of an impending pilot strike circulated. My flying partner was Ray Engel, an old friend from Capital days, and we had a lot to discuss concerning past experiences and the present situation.

The simulator training went very well, and my instructor, Dick Burton, seemed well satisfied with my progress. Some procedures in connection with programming the FMS (flight management system) were totally new; for instance, protocol called for the pilot to make the following announcement after taking off: "Positive rate, gear up," followed by "vertical speed 1000, flaps zero, climb thrust." Those commands indicated how you wanted the First Officer to set up the FMS. After only a session or two, I realized that it would be imperative to commit those commands to memory, so I memorized all of them. That simple step expedited my training immensely.

"Terry McNulty will be your examiner," Dick announced. "How is he?" I asked. Dick replied, "Oh, Terry is great; you'll get along fine with him, I'm sure." As it turned out, we didn't get along at all, as Terry was terse, abrupt, and in some ways hostile. Terry and Dick were both DC-10 instructors, so there was nothing special about his status at the training center, except that he had been authorized by the FAA to issue type ratings for the DC-10.

The FAA notified us that they would not be present, and in fact they seldom showed up for wide-body type-rating issuances. They knew all the candidates for wide-body jet ratings were experienced captains with many years in the left (captain's) seat.

A Dark Day at DENTK

With that background, let me relate my experience on Friday, May 13, 1985.

It started out okay; the oral portion dealing with airplane systems was fine. In fact, later, during our flight review with Hank Denton, Terry acknowledged that my oral was excellent. It was after getting into the simulator that Terry became unhappy with me.

We started with the steep turns exercise. That consisted of entering a 60-degree bank at exactly 250 knots; then, after turning 360 degrees, roll out, and immediately enter a 60-degree bank the opposite direction for another 360 degrees; then roll out on the original heading. You must do all of that without losing or gaining more than 50 feet of altitude and without gaining or losing more than five knots of airspeed.

As the plane banked to enter the maneuver, it tended to lose altitude and airspeed. That had to be compensated for by back pressure on the control column and a touch of power to maintain the airspeed. On rolling out on the desired heading, the opposite took place to reverse the turn. It was an instrument scan exercise, for the most part, to see how quickly the student observed the changes and took appropriate corrective action.

My instructor, Dick, spent very little time on these during my training. Of course I did them, and my performance must have been satisfactory, or we would have spent additional time practicing until they were.

When Terry asked me to repeat the maneuver, I got that old check-itis feeling. I looked over at Dick in the copilot seat with a questioning look, and all I got back was a blank stare as if to say, "What do you want me to do about it?"

At that point, I should have simply gotten up out of my seat, saying that I didn't feel well, and ended it then and there, but I didn't. Terry had me repeat the turns again, and once more after that, for good measure, until he was finally satisfied.

All of those repeats depleted my allotted time for the check. Terry's only remark was, "I'm not here to give instruction." It was all downhill from there, and it seemed like nothing I did was satisfactory. Dick sat in the right seat like a dummy. It was my worst experience ever at DENTK.

Finally, we simply ran out of time and I hadn't completed all of the required maneuvers, most particularly the "no flap" landing — making an approach and landing without any flaps, as might be the case if hydraulic fluid was escaping.

As we left the simulator, we were greeted by the unhappy faces of the next crew that had been patiently waiting for us to leave. Tension was at a high level indeed. Terry led the way to Hank Denton's office, but we were not accompanied by Dick Burton, my instructor/First Officer.

Captain Henry (Hank) Denton headed up the DC-10 section at DENTK. Hank and I had been best friends, dating back to the 1960s and Greenwood Lake Airport. He based a small plane there at the same time I had the Staggerwing Beech. Hank worked his way up the corporate ladder starting as a flight manager at Newark, and later in Cleveland after the Newark base closure. His latest promotion to department head, DC-10 training, was fairly recent. We were closest in Cleveland, in his capacity as my flight manager.

"What happened down there, Ray?" asked Hank. "I know you know how to fly these airplanes." I replied, "Why don't you ask Terry? He's the one who seems to think I don't know what I'm doing." I noticed Terry squirming in his chair a bit. Then it was Hank's turn: "Terry, how was the oral?" Terry acknowledged that the oral was above reproach. "Well," continued Hank, "what was the problem? I wanted to get Ray finished up today."

Terry proceeded to tear me apart, saying that my steep turns were sloppy and out of limits, and my certification low approach was marginal at best. However, he wanted to make clear to Hank that he was not failing me: "We just ran out of time and we couldn't do the 'no flapper.' If we would have had another half hour, I could have finished it." Terry continued, "I'm writing it up as incomplete, with the recommendation of more work on steep turns, low approach, and of course the 'no flap' that we didn't have time for."

Hank was not at all happy with Terry's response, so he called his secretary into the office and said, "See if you can find Dick Burton, and have him come to my office." It looked like Hank wanted to probe deeper into that "incomplete" check ride of mine. Then the secretary returned: "I'm sorry, Captain Denton, no one can locate Dick; I'm afraid he left for the day." So, that's how that episode ended, and no one understood the reason why Terry failed to complete my DC-10 check ride.

A side note: Some 20 years later, when Margaret and I spent winters in Tucson, Ariz., I visited Hank at his home there. He definitely recalled the incident and was sorry it happened, and followed up by saying, "Terry had a brain tumor and died while I was still heading up the DC-10 section, and I was a pallbearer at his funeral service. There were other instances similar to yours, so we stopped having him do check rides. Terry was only 50 years old." I asked Hank if he thought the incomplete check ride had any connection with the impending pilot strike. Hank replied, "I don't think so. But along that line, I questioned Dick Burton later, and he thought you were tense, under pressure, and rushed. That was the reason why your performance was below par." When I visited Hank in 2005, he was suffering from Parkinson's disease; he died a few years later. Hank was a real gentleman.

After the debriefing with Hank and Terry, I packed up and flew home to Bethlehem, and Margaret had to drive all the way to Newark to pick me up. She sensed my solemn demeanor, and I explained, "I just don't know what's ahead; I never should have taken that rating ride." It was a long ride to Bethlehem.

The 1985 Pilot Strike

May 17 arrived, and we were indeed on strike — but prior to that, I had a few days at home to validate my status at Kennedy as a B-727 Captain. A fellow pilot living in the Lehigh Valley had the quiz for a pilot's "renewal of qualification" that I filled out and submitted to JFK so that, on paper at least, I was still qualified.

I received two calls: The first was from the JFK Flight Office inquiring about my availability for work, to which I responded, "As a dues-paying member of the Air Line Pilots Association, having withdrawn our services to the company, I would not be available." The person on the other end of the line made it quite clear that if I remained steadfast in that position I would no longer be in the employ of United Airlines. In other words, I would be fired.

CEO Dick Ferris intended to play hardball with an attempt to break ALPA at United. He lured weaklings and the money-hungry back to work as strikebreakers, crossing our picket line to fly the planes. He succeeded in getting about 500 union pilots to fly, and with the plethora of non-union DENTK staff — flight managers, instructors, and Flight Standards people — he was successful getting some United jets into the air. It was the first time during my entire career that the company made an attempt to operate during a valid union work stoppage, and it was ugly.

The other call was from Pete Singer, our local union representative, to confirm my availability for picket duty, first at the ticket office at ABE and later at the United passenger terminal in Philadelphia.

At that point, it got worse after the Company hired security personnel who attempted to restrict our access to United's portion of the terminal, denying us access to the bathrooms. They also sent photographers to take our pictures as we picketed on the sidewalk outside, presumably as proof of our refusal to work and fodder for future separation proceedings. We laughed at them and made faces.

When I returned home, Margaret and I had a long and serious discussion. We had invested everything we had into our new home, and now we wondered if we were going to be able to keep it. To retain our sanity, employees living in the Lehigh Valley banded together for picnics and other unification activities. We even attended a combined rally of New York employees at one of the major well-known Manhattan hotels with a national TV hookup, including big-name supporters like F. Lee Bailey.

The mechanics (IAM), flight attendants, and ticket counter people all supported our cause, but they continued to work. We received troubling rumors that the Denver pilot domicile was caving in, with threats to return to work en masse. Anything on that scale would be disastrous, and we feared for our jobs.

However, there were other forces working in our favor. The State of Hawaii was up in arms over the lack of air service to the mainland. Other communities and organizations were putting the heat on Ferris and Company. He just didn't have enough pilots to make a meaningful dent in the schedule. In the end, it was the flight attendants that saved our bacon when they exhibited their solidarity by calling in sick.

I didn't spend all my time during the strike walking the picket line. We drove to Erie at least twice for Margaret to see her mom, and for me to visit with Tom.

Finally, on June 15, the strike was over and we had won a major victory — and a historic one, in the sense that no airline has since ventured into such a vendetta against union workers.

As a result of the strike, we had a problem at United. About 500 of our pilots made the very bad decision to cross our picket line and report for work. During the strike some of the strikebreakers, in places like Denver, woke up to find nasty graffiti on their driveways and windows. It was Halloween taken to a much higher level.

All of the New York Captains were instructed to report to the JFK flight office prior to returning to work. Specifically, the company wanted clarification of the ALPA position regarding the strikebreakers by interviewing each captain for a statement of intent.

They made it quite clear that abuse against those pilots would not be tolerated. When it was my turn, I simply reiterated my intent to follow the ALPA policy of extending courtesy insofar as getting the job done without compromising safety.

To wit: The cockpit would be sterile at all times. Conversation would be limited to the performance of SOP (standard operating procedure), and company business and efforts to engage in day-to-day conversation would be futile. In other words, all the social graces that were commonplace in the pre-strike cockpit would be denied.

A thorny problem existed at DENTK. All of the instructors, flight standards pilots, and managers were strikebreakers by definition. Since I expected to return to the DC-10 program, I would find myself on the cusp of that problem. Not so fast, though; I had just learned that the bid openings authorizing my initial training had been canceled, so I guessed I wouldn't be returning to DENTK, at least not anytime soon.

The situation was extremely confusing. Nothing resembled the pre-strike United. What was my status at Kennedy? I had been fired, remember? Because of the confusion, the flight office seemed content to have me return to B-727 flying. That quiz paper I submitted just before the strike seemed to have done the trick, at least for now. Almost immediately, I was back on the San Diego trip as if nothing had happened.

At first it was very challenging, because during the course of DC-10 training I deliberately attempted to erase the 727 from my brain to make room for the new DC-10 data. It was always like that when transitioning from one plane to the next. Especially troubling was the vastly different cockpit orientation. The DC-10 cockpit was fifteen feet above the ground, and the nose wheel was 50 feet behind me. Even though we trained in the simulator and not the plane, it was still a problem. I was very careful at first not to level out too high on landing. Before long, though, everything returned to normal, and I erased everything pertaining to the DC-10.

After the Strike: B-727 Proficiency Check
Around the middle of July I was flying my regular San Diego trip pairing. While passing through Chicago, I stopped by the flight

office to talk to one of the flight managers I knew from my B-737 days. "What's new with the DC-10 program?" I asked.

"I hear they're reinstating the bids that were canceled after the strike," he replied. "By the way, what's your status? Did you finish your training?"

I briefly explained the events that took place at DENTK in May, including the part about not being able to complete my DC-10 flight check, and that I just needed a recheck.

"Oh, no! It's too late now," he exclaimed. "You had to complete that within 30 days. You did schedule a PC [proficiency check] on the 727 before returning to work, didn't you?"

What have I done now, I conjectured. Can't I ever learn to keep my mouth shut? I admitted that I hadn't taken a PC, and didn't know that I needed one, etc. The flight manager couldn't figure out how that slipped through the cracks. DENTK should have notified JFK that I had an unsatisfactory flight check in May, and would require a proficiency check prior to returning to work. Continuing, the flight manager stated emphatically, "You should have come out during the strike and gotten that out of the way. Now, I'm afraid, you will have to start over with a new instructor, and repeat the complete syllabus. I'm calling the director of training immediately."

I didn't bother to explain that it would have been impossible for me to come to DENTK during the strike or I, too, would have been a strikebreaker. While he was talking on the phone I could only hear his side of the conversation, but it went something to the effect that, "I don't care how it happened. Captain Lemmon is grounded pending satisfactory completion of a PC on the 727." That dreaded word, "grounded," was a nightmare for any airline pilot's ears, but at least I was still on the payroll.

"Go home, Ray, DENTK will be in touch with you." "What about my trip to San Diego?" I asked. "Who's going to fly that?"

"It's not your concern anymore. I'll take care of it."

It was a lonely deadhead flying back home, and I was terribly depressed. Getting recertified on the 727 would not be easy, because in my mind I had deliberately wiped that slate clean during the DC-10 program.

When the call came, it wasn't DENTK calling; it was the Kennedy Flight Office, with the date for my B-727 proficiency check. Since I was on non-flight status, they wanted me to report as soon as possible. However, they realized that I might need some time to prepare, so a contingent date was set for the following Monday. My flight manager was courteous and considerate: "Ray, I know you didn't expect this and if you like, I can set you up with a ground instructor to help prepare for the oral." "Thanks, that'll help," I replied. I had already retrieved my 727 manuals as soon as I got home.

The PC went pretty well; the check airman was aware of my situation and tried to cut me some slack. The most difficult maneuver was the single-engine approach and landing. Yes, the 727 would fly on only one engine. Fully loaded, you couldn't maintain altitude on a pod (outboard) engine; they always performed the maneuver that way, never with the center engine. Sustaining flight required sacrificing some altitude. Usually the examiner failed the second engine somewhere in the early stages of a two-engine approach, so that you would have time enough to set up the correct profile. The key to avoid crashing was to maintain a clean (no-flap) configuration and 200 knots until assuredness of reaching the runway was beyond question. Then you would gradually add 15 degrees of flap.

I did that pretty well, and the check pilot remarked after we finished that I had more difficulty with easy items, and excelled on the hard stuff. We had just come out of the simulator, and were in the cafeteria before the oral, when Hank Denton came to our table. Hank begged me to return to DC-10 school.

"Your bid has been reinstated," Hank said, "and we desperately need DC-10 Captains. We'll set up a special syllabus for you — ground school refresher, our best simulator instructor, and all the time you need. We want you back."

"Gee, Hank, I don't know. I had just about decided to stay on the 727." "Oh, don't do that, we'll get you through just fine. Think about it and get back to me as soon as you can."

After the oral, I asked the check pilot I was working with for his opinion as to what I should do. His reply was immediate and unequivocal: "Go for it; you'd be crazy not to. You can do it, it's just another airplane. It's a fact that United is very short of DC-10 Captains."

I was relieved to be back on flying status, and I wanted to discuss Hank's proposal with Margaret. She had a big stake in my decision as well. The pay increase would really boost my pension earnings.

"How soon does Hank need an answer?" Margaret asked. "Within a week," I replied. It was gut-wrenching, so I decided to call Ray Engel, my ex-flying partner in Los Angeles. He had completed the rating ride, so his circumstances were a lot different than mine.

I dialed his number: "Hi, Ray, how's it going?" I knew he had returned to the 727, as I had, but because he passed the course, he didn't need a PC.

It turned out that Ray Engel knew a lot more than I did: "I just talked to Hank, and I'm set up next week for a refresher course. Why don't you come and we'll fly together again? Hank mentioned that you might be coming."

So, I caved in and returned to DENTK. Ray Engel agreed to use my simulator instructor, Tom Brown. Ray Engel's instructions read, "Simulator time as needed for instructor sign off, no PC required." His program was a free pass.

We attended the ground school refresher together, and then moved on to the simulator. After just a few sessions, Ray was gone and I was just getting started. I repeated the entire syllabus. Tom Brown, my new instructor, was very good and, unlike Dick Burton, took nothing for granted. Tom had me doing steep turns until I could do them in my sleep.

One day, Tom said, "We've got extra time, so I'm going to let you try something no students going through here ever get a chance to do. It's a confidence-building exercise for instructors only, but I believe with your extra training, you can handle it." Tom explained that we were going to take off, fly a visual circuit of Stapleton Airport, then come around and land. I said, "What's so hard about that? We do that all the time."

"This time," Tom said, "the instrument panel lights will be turned off and your only reference will be outside." I looked at him incredulously and said, "It can't be done. I've got to have airspeed indication or we'll stall out."

"Just do what I tell you, and try it," Tom insisted. We lined up on Runway 35, and started our takeoff roll. The instrument panel was useless — completely blank. Tom continued, "When it feels 'right,' apply gentle back pressure to raise the nose and just let it fly off."

We lifted off, retracted the landing gear and left the flaps in takeoff position while I looked out the window. When I estimated we were at about 1500 feet or so, I leveled off and pulled the thrust levers back to the mid-point.

We seemed to be flying just fine, even though I had no idea how high we were or how fast we were going. I noticed Tom taking notes, checking readings on the copilot side, and also on the engineer's panel.

Now on downwind leg and past the south end of the airport, I called for gear down and started a descending turn to final, adding more flaps until 30 degrees were extended. I knew once I had extended landing flaps, my airspeed had to be somewhere between 120 and 150 knots. It was all visual, so when it looked right I simply retarded the throttles and landed.

Tom was pleased with my performance, and after we set the brake on the simulator, he showed me what my altitude and airspeed were at various stages of the circuit. It was amazing how close I was to acceptable values all the way around.

It really was a confidence builder. Tom said it takes a student with a fair amount of time in the simulator to pull it off. In the end, I had more time in the DC-10 simulator than any student ever, up to that time. I guess it was time for the check ride again.

Naturally, after all I had been through, my old "check-itis" nemesis was lingering in the background. However, this time I was so well trained that I could almost perform it by rote. During the briefing my examiner said, "You'll be pleased to hear that there won't be any steep turns in the program today. Tom tells me that you can do them in your sleep."

It was a grind, though, and this time there were no time constraints; we could stay in the simulator all day if need be. Actually, the check ride took less than two hours and after the last maneuver, as I set the parking brake, the examiner leaned over to me and said, "Congratulations, Captain Lemmon, and good luck with the DC-10." It was finally over; all I needed now was 25 hours of shotgun time in the airplane.

Shotgun Tension

At first, I was apprehensive about the shotgun phase of my training, because all of the instructors and check airmen had worked during the strike. Since my bid award was in Chicago, it was the ORD staff's responsibility to complete my line certification.

Harry Hopkins, an ex-Capital pilot whom I had known for years, had been assigned to check me out. Actually, Harry supported the strike right up to the last few days. I never knew why he had crossed our picket line, but I felt sorry for the position he was in. Harry was quite frank and declared openly at our first meeting that he had worked during the strike, and asked me if that was going to interfere with the work we had to do. In this case, I couldn't invoke my inflexible position of no interaction beyond the requirements of SOP. The shotgun phase of training required the closest possible working relationship throughout the entire process. I simply replied, "Harry, for the next week let's pretend that there never was a strike."

"That'll work for me," he said. So, that was it; we had just put the elephant back in the closet.

Our first leg of the trip was O'Hare to Boston. When we entered the cockpit, I looked around and remarked to Harry, "Everything seems normal until I look out the window, and then it's like we are on the second floor of an old two-story house."

"You'll soon get used to the height; in fact, you're going to enjoy the panoramic visibility compared to the 727. Taxiing is going to be more of a problem, so take it slow and remember I don't have a tiller [power steering for the nose wheel] over here. Also, keep in mind while turning that the nose wheel is 50 feet behind us."

Jokingly, I ventured, "Should we make an announcement to the effect that the Captain has never flown a DC-10 before?"

"Better not, or we'll lose all our passengers and maybe the flight attendants as well." Harry introduced me to the flight engineer, who seemed totally unconcerned. Apparently he was used to these qualification flights. I did have a brief conversation about my incipiency with the flight attendant in first class, and she didn't leave.

Taxiing was awkward at first, so I took it slowly while Harry talked me through it. The sounds and environment were all strange and new to me, but it was no big deal. Takeoff was a joy compared to the simulator and performance was awesome, as we were lightly loaded. When I commented on that, Harry replied, "Wait until we fly the Honolulu trip next week and you'll see the other side of the coin." He was referring to the overwater qualification portion of my checkout, Chicago-Honolulu nonstop — over eight hours of flight time.

We were approaching Logan Airport (BOS) for my first actual landing in the DC-10, and I don't recall being apprehensive. I was so well trained that it was almost like I had landed the plane before. It was such a joy to fly, not nearly as sensitive on the controls as the simulator. In every respect, the "box" was more demanding than the airplane, and that made this first flight a very enjoyable experience. Harry talked me through the first landing at Boston. Eventually I would apply my full-flare landing technique that I had developed for the Boeings. The DC-10 was a much more honest airplane regarding its landing characteristics by virtue of having two wing-mounted engines versus all three in the tail, as on the 727.

Harry and I flew together the better part of a week. He selected trips that had as many landings as possible, and that was not easy because the DC-10 flew only our longer segments. In fact, that was a problem for First Officers as well — some captains appropriated all the landings.

By week's end, I was closing in on the magic 25 hours needed for my release. The trip to Hawaii didn't count, because the overwater qualification was a separate requirement. It involved the use of special navigation equipment called INS (Inertial Navigation System). Waypoints, defined by latitude and longitude, were entered into the system one by one, and then all the data came up on the screen pertaining to each leg of the trip. It was the predecessor for GPS (global positioning system). Pilots who flew overseas routinely became very adept at using the INS.

Harry was right: the DC-10 was a different animal when fueled for its flight to Honolulu, with a full load of passengers and bags. Our ground run was noticeably longer, and it took longer to reach V-2 (takeoff speed). After liftoff, climb rate was also compromised by our combined load of over 250 tons.

Other than that, it was just a long, boring ride. Several hours after takeoff from Chicago, I saw the Golden Gate Bridge slip under our wings — and we were only about halfway there.

Our arrival at Honolulu was timed for mid-afternoon. It was beautiful flying past Diamond Head on our way to the airport. Other than our brief vacation in the '70s, my only visit to Hawaii was in 1952, returning from Japan on emergency leave. Once we arrived in Honolulu, jet lag was a problem, and I found myself wandering about on Waikiki in the middle of the night. However, it was nice to have breakfast on the beach.

My United DC-10 after arrival in Honolulu in 1986. This "overseas" model was larger and heavier than the standard model, grossing out at over half a million pounds. We had just arrived nonstop from Chicago.

After completion of my overwater qualification, I was finished with supervised flying; I was finally on my own with the DC-10. In a way, I can understand why the Company was so very careful checking out Captains on wide-body jets. They were not only entrusting us with a plane worth millions of dollars, but with passengers by the hundreds. Responsibility was ratcheted up enormously from what it had been in the piston days, or even the B-737. Flying the DC-10, my pay increase was sizable. Only one more increase was possible, and that would be the B-747. OV Pezzi, recently retired, was on it for several years.

Just prior to the strike of '85, UAL acquired Pan American World Airways' Pacific division for $750 million. The sale included 18 jets (B-747 SPs) and landing rights in 13 more cities in Asia and the South Pacific, along with absorbing the 2700 Pan Am workers included with the sale.

As a result, United was now a major presence in the rapidly expanding trans-Pacific market known as the "Pacific Rim." Unfortunately, as part of the deal the pilot seniority lists of the two airlines were merged, basically according to "date of hire," and the majority of the New York-based Pan Am Captains were senior to me.

It was not my intention to bid the 747 anyway, as it would entail flying out of JFK. With the DC-10, I had made my final transition up the equipment ladder at UAL. However, I did successfully bid a 747 vacancy in Chicago during the summer of '88. Because I had less than a year left to fly, UAL paid me 747 pay rates in lieu of sending me to school. Of course, I knew about that provision and capitalized on it. It increased my monthly benefit by $200.

Harry ended the shotgun phase of my training with the recommendation that for the first 100 hours I should do most of the flying myself. I ignored his advice because that was not the way I ran my cockpit. First Officers got every other landing when they flew with me — and besides, I could learn a lot just by observing them.

The training was over, but not all the problems. I was flying out of Chicago again and because I was on reserve, I had to be there much of the time. I rented a room near the airport and even drove one of our cars out so I didn't have to rely on the motel courtesy car. My hours were not exactly nine to five.

I hung out at the crew desk, just in case a trip became available. I wanted to build up my flying time for two reasons: One was to get used to the new plane, and the other was to deliberately build up my 30-hours-in-seven-days limitation, so I could go home early.

I picked up a Honolulu trip just by being at the airport. The captain became ill after reporting in, and they needed a replacement immediately; I was Johnny-on-the-spot.

I only had eight guaranteed days off each month, but by closely watching the unassigned flying I was sometimes able to leave early and then fly back to ORD my first day on call. It was a calculated risk, but I always had the option of calling in sick. The commuting from Chicago was excellent, because we had B-737 nonstop flights in both directions from Allentown.

During this fiasco, Margaret was in Erie with her mom some of the time. Mostly, though, she busied herself in the Deck House, making drapes and doing other sewing projects.

Sadly, we reached the decision to sell the house in Highland Lakes. Margaret said it was too much hassle going back and forth, but I think it was really about Gretchen, as air travel with a dog in tow was difficult. In any case, the decision had been made. We listed with Marion Daniels, our Florida Realtor, and by September it was sold.

The closing date was October 1, and luckily I was able to bid reserve lines that would give me the four consecutive days off I needed to clear out the house and drive north. Fortunately, the only car there was Dad's old Buick LeSabre. Allied came, and suddenly our snowbirding days were over. It was sad, and I hated to do it, but maybe now we could settle down to a more conventional lifestyle. If I could just land a DC-10 bid in New York, we would be able to enjoy some measure of stability.

The lion's share of the excess goods from Florida ended up in the garage, so I rented a storage unit to get some of it out of my sight. We hesitated to dispose of the furniture, as most of it was only a few years old and some things, like the IKEA dining room set, were nicer than what we had in Bethlehem.

So it was just a matter of moving things around, keeping the best for our new home and storing the rest. I discovered that storage units were not cheap, and the pressure for that and shop space was certain to affect future decisions.

Mom Taylor came down from Erie to spend some time with us after Halloween. More painful decisions lay ahead for 1986.

Chapter 19

Mom Taylor — The Annex
1986-1987

It was Christmas time again, and with my lowly status on the DC-10, be assured I would not be home for the holidays. It was our first year not to be wintering in Florida for quite some time; when I asked Margaret if she had missed it, she replied that so far, at least, she hadn't.

1986

The big news for the New Year was that I finally did get a DC-10 bid to New York. At last, I would be flying out of Newark again. There had been notable improvements to I-78 — it finally was finished all the way to Newark Airport. The driving time from our house to the employee parking lot was reduced to only one hour and fifteen minutes.

With the arrival of spring, we had a lot of outside work to do. Concrete work and landscaping were in the forefront of our plans for the immediate future; however, the big question mark was on the north side, where extensive filling was going to be required in the near future. At some point, I hoped to build a garage/workshop back there.

Mom Taylor — Erie

We were increasingly concerned about Mother Taylor. We had observed her decline and mounting listlessness.

Going to Erie in late February, we found Mom in a state of depression, and it wasn't just emotional support that she needed — her health was also going downhill. At the core of the problem was her failing heart, although at that time the medical community failed to diagnose it as such. They kept trying to medicate her for peripheral ailments.

On arrival, we noted that she was despondent and melancholy. Even though she knew we were coming, nothing had been prepared. We found her sitting in a chair, head in hands, and as soon as I saw her I knew we were in trouble. I immediately called an Italian restaurant and ordered takeout. That seemed to perk her up a bit; I think just having someone there was the key. We only stayed a day or so because I was due to go out on a trip.

When we went to Erie again for Easter, I returned to Bethlehem by myself because Margaret finally shared my doubt about Helen's ability to manage on her own anymore. A few days later Margaret called to say she was coming home and bringing Mom with her for an extended visit. I was relieved, and she could stay as long as she liked. Also, Margaret wanted her to see our family physician, Dr. Snyder.

It was becoming quite clear that Mom could not continue living alone on Seventh Street. She had to sell the house and either move to a care facility, or live with us. A third option was to find a condominium close by in Bethlehem, where we could keep an eye on her. In any case, Helen finally signed the listing agreement, but instead of taking her to Bethlehem immediately, as Margaret and I should have, she remained there and suffered with prospective buyers traipsing through her house. That step led to the inevitable sorting, packing, and general upheaval that Helen certainly didn't need.

Margaret and I also endured some pain. The Pontiac convertible Margaret purchased new in 1965 was in Mother's garage. We paid rent for the past five years and had even taken it to a few local car shows. However, at the time it was excess baggage, so we sold it to Tom Apple for $5000. Just in case he ever decided to sell the car, I had Tom sign an agreement that we would have right of first refusal to buy it back for the same amount. That seemed so unimportant at the time — why would we ever want to buy it back? Tom and Alice drove home with it the middle of June.

Margaret and I had not been idle in dealing with Mom's housing problem. New condominiums were being built less than ten minutes from our house, and we felt one of those would be perfect for Helen. Estimated completion date for the first units was the fall of '86, and even though Mom hadn't seen it, she agreed to buy one.

Helen came to Bethlehem a week or so later to see the model. Measurements were taken for furniture placement, and then the two of them returned to Erie. The closing date was July 29, leaving Mom just two weeks to vacate 720 West Seventh Street.

It was just too much, and Helen collapsed with a heart attack and ended up in Hamot Hospital in Erie. Perhaps it was just as well that she did not have to endure those chaotic last days. I loaded the '78 Chevy truck to capacity. A junk man came and was throwing trash out the attic window. We were certainly thankful Helen didn't have to endure that.

At the conclusion of the ordeal, Margaret and I took one last nostalgic tour of the attic that had held our treasures and theirs over the years, now empty of everything except storm windows and a few other things that went with the house. It was a sad day indeed. I left 720 West Seventh Street for the last time with a heavy heart. As I drove home, I pondered the history there; closing that chapter of our lives, and realizing I would never return, was almost too much to bear. There were so many memories.

There was a new chapter in the offing provided Helen survived and, in fact, her attack was mild, as heart attacks go. Once her electrolytes were stabilized, she was well enough to leave the hospital. It was decided to take her to Nancy's for recuperation and then, when she was able, to our house in Bethlehem. For the next three months, Mom would be our guest.

She bought her condo in early November, but moving in was a gradual process, beginning with the arrival of her household goods from Erie. We didn't push her, since traveling between our houses was so easy. Margaret and I helped by unpacking boxes and putting things away, and before long she commented that the place was beginning to look like home. Having her own furniture there made a world of difference.

Early in the fall, John Pearson came to our house with a proposal to build a garage out back that would mimic the Deck House. As drawn, it was all on one level and I pointed out the impossibility of building in that location: "John, there's nothing back there to set it on, unless we build it down next to the railroad track."

John countered my objection by saying, "Have you thought about a two-story building? That way you could have a 'showroom' upstairs and your shop underneath." Wow! That would be neat. I asked John, "Do you know how much it will cost?" "I'll get back to you with drawings for that," John said.

Now it was November, and John had returned. As he unrolled the drawings, he commented, "I did a lot of work on this; I hope it meets with your approval." I replied that I was confident that it would, depending on the cost.

"The Deck House package will run about $60,000, but you will need to meet with Ray Norton for a quote on the rest of it." John was referring to the cost of all the site preparation, foundation, retaining walls, and basically everything not made of wood.

"You must have some idea as to the total," I said. "Can you give us a ball park figure?" "It might run upward to $100,000," he replied. Margaret and I rejected it out of hand as being ridiculous — but somehow he left our house that day with a deposit check, and I don't understand to this day how that transpired. Margaret and I had discussed it before he came, and decided on a cap of $50,000 total for the entire project.

Of course, nothing was carved in stone, but we had just laid the groundwork for a project that was to have horrible consequences for us. I wish I could do that one over; of all the construction mistakes I ever made, that one tops the list. The next step was to contact Ray Norton and Sheff. Ray wanted the job, so I couldn't look for any objectivity there. "Let me call Trunzo," Ray said. Anthony Trunzo was the concrete contractor who would pour the foundation walls.

When Tony arrived, Ray and I were there to greet him. By the time we got Ray's estimate, and Trunzo's, plus Deck House, it was well over $100,000. Why didn't I put a lid on it right there? Stop! Stop! Stop! I just don't know; all I really do know is that I didn't stop. The "Annex" project became a major focal point for 1986.

My first winter on the DC-10 was just fine, as most of my trips were to LAX (Los Angeles). It was a different world flying a wide-body jet. Whenever we encountered snow in Chicago, the runways were cleared immediately, unlike the old days at places like the Michigan cities and Akron/Canton. Even Cleveland was not kept as clean as Chicago and, of course, there was never any snow in the L.A. basin.

The worst downside was boredom; it just wasn't fun anymore. It got even worse later on, when all my trips were coast to coast, flying all night. At least in the winter of '85 and '86, we had some Tampa and Miami layovers. Tampa, especially, evoked memories of the many winters we spent there.

Bierys Bridge Road: The Annex

Now that spring had arrived, Ray Norton and Sheff came with their transit to survey the new building site. They discovered more bad news: My two-story garage, which Margaret had named "The Annex," had just grown to three stories. Wow! This *was* getting complicated.

The lowest level would only be 20'x32' because of the slope; there was no use cutting deeper into the bank to gain space we didn't need. From that point, it was money, money, and more money going down the drain. Oh, it was impressive, all right, but I didn't really need three stories.

After the forms were set, the expensive concrete pumper appeared on the scene. It was the only way to span the distance from the supply truck to the farthest forms, which were over 50 feet away. If it weren't costing so much, it would have been fun to watch.

Arrival of the Deck House trucks produced another round of entertainment. Tractor-trailers couldn't negotiate my driveway, so everything had to be hand-carried to the site or, in the case of heavy items like the two main structural beams, by machine.

The two main beams were a sight to behold. They were 24 inches high by 8 inches wide, 20 feet and 32 feet long, respectively. We needed a crane to set them into place. Fortunately, Trunzo still had one on site from setting and stripping forms, so I got a break on that. As before, construction moved at a good clip due to Deck House prefabrication.

Installing the cedar siding was terribly labor-intensive. The walls were covered by individual 3/4-by-3-inch strips up to 16 feet long. It took forever, especially working on the north side, which was over 30 feet high. It became apparent we wouldn't finish that year because everywhere I looked, we needed retaining walls, and that meant buying railroad ties — more than 100 of them.

We needed staircases for the new three-story building, and the best solution for that was two sets of spiral stairs, one on top of the other. The upper set required a six-foot opening. The other, to the lower level, was smaller and required only a 5-foot opening. Doing the math, we could see that with 13 stairs for each flight and 8-inch risers there were almost nine feet between levels. Then, how many stairs was it from the very bottom of the Annex to the main floor of the house? Answer: 43; I climbed them thousands of times.

The Annex at the Deck House on Bierys Bridge Road, Bethlehem, Pa. This building was erected in 1986. Because of the terrain, it was incredibly expensive to complete. The Annex was three stories tall.

Ray Norton was fed up with the building out back, and frankly, so was I. It sat there like an island in the sky. There wasn't any decent access to it, and you had to walk a plank over an abyss 15 feet deep just to get in, and I was afraid of someone getting hurt. I'm not going to go into all the detail that went into dealing with the onerous grade issues. Suffice it to say that it took scads of railroad ties and concrete retaining walls to make it usable.

Trailers

Shortly after Hershey, Margaret and I were discussing our travel plans for retirement, and I was quick to point out that hotels and motels held no appeal for me. At the car show we had been looking at some of the recreational vehicles that most vendors traveled with — both motor homes and trailers. Margaret suggested we attend the RV show opening the following weekend at the Allentown Fairgrounds.

Margaret fell in love with a 31-foot Starcraft fifth-wheel trailer. I tried to convince her that it was too big and heavy to tow with our little truck, but she kept going through the unit and inspecting it for the best part of an hour. Naturally, we picked up a brochure, and after we got home I noticed it on the table next to her chair.

The dealer was Colonial Woods Campground, located at Upper Black Eddy, a little town by the Delaware River. We had never camped before, and I didn't know anything about the RV lifestyle, but I figured it couldn't hurt to drive over and talk to them.

It was a pretty place, and very rustic. By then it was November, and the leaves were down. Margaret looked at the trailer again while I went to the shop to talk to Russ Jones, the shop manager. When I told him about my truck, he assured me that with certain modifications it would be fine for pulling the Starcraft. "What you need is a 'big block' 454 engine — with that, you should have plenty of power." By the time we left, we had placed a deposit on the Starcraft for early '88 delivery.

A New Engine

After a few calls to auto shops in the area, I discovered that the 454-cubic-inch engine Russ alluded to was not readily available, so I called him back. "You should get in touch with Jim Tote at Superior Automotive in Allentown," he said.

Superior's specialty was building "race engines." As part of that business, they also did machine work for customers like me. Following up on Russ's lead, I met Charles (Butch) Spencer and Jim Tote, co-owners of the shop.

Jim offered me a tour. I was fascinated with the work they did there, converting old, rusty hulks into gleaming works of automotive art. They had all kinds of special equipment to achieve that goal — Jim's specialty was operating a massive machine that ground crankshafts to very close tolerances. Then I continued my discussion with Butch, who said, "I'm sorry we can't help you out, but to change to a big-block 454, you'll need much more than a junkyard core. The radiator, transmission, and many other components are all different from the small-block engine you have now. What you need is a parts truck, because you really can't afford to buy everything new."

The Junker

I got a call from Russ Jones at Colonial Woods soon after: "Ray, there's an ad in the *Reading Times* for a '76 Chevy 3/4-ton truck with a 454-cubic-inch engine; would you like the number?"

"I'll say — let me have it." I called the seller in Reading, the owner of a service station with a parking lot. He readily admitted that the truck was basically junk — far too badly rusted to pass inspection. He just used it in the winter to plow snow. I told him I only had two questions: Does it run, and what's the price? He answered affirmatively to the first, and the price was $800 firm. I asked for directions and told him we would be right down. Margaret needed to come along so that, hopefully, we could drive it home.

It was bad, all right, with over 100,000 miles. There were holes where there shouldn't be any, and when I started the engine, a dark blue smoke plume belched from the tail pipe. The owner agreed that it was in sorry shape and explained, "That's why the price is so low. I'm basically selling it for parts." I told him it was exactly what I was looking for, and wrote out a check.

"How far are you going?" he asked. When I replied, "Bethlehem," he wished us luck. I just made sure there was adequate oil in the crankcase, and we headed for home.

I drove the scrap heap down to Superior to show it to the guys. They thought it was just the ticket and inquired about my plans for it. I told them the small-block V-8 that came with my truck was not powerful enough to pull the 31-foot Starcraft we had just bought and I would like them to rebuild the worn-out engine and install it in my '78. I left the junker with them, and Butch said they would take care of everything.

I made somewhat of a nuisance of myself while the engine was going through the shop, and I was most persistent when Butch began assembly of my 454 engine. It was fortunate I was there on at least a couple of occasions. Butch asked me, "Do you want to use forged pistons? If you are towing a heavy trailer you should have them so the motor doesn't get 'black death'." As Butch explained it, "black death" occurred when the stock aluminum pistons failed due to high internal temperatures generated by heavy loads.

"You should also use an RV [recreational vehicle] camshaft as well, for better low-end torque," Butch advised. Even with all my experience building aircraft engines, I was discovering a whole new world at Superior. The total cost of the engine rebuild was only $1500. Welcome to the automotive world, where parts and labor were much more reasonably priced.

Butch also sent the transmission out for overhaul; he said I shouldn't take a chance on a Hydramatic with over 100,000 miles on it. Altogether, the bill for the truck came to about $5000, and I was very proud of the way it looked under the hood with that big 454 engine installed. Everything bolted up without modifying the engine/transmission controls, and Butch even transferred the "454" emblem off the '76 radiator grill for a nice, custom touch.

Chapter 20

Welcome to the RV World
1988

Starcraft Time, 1988

Colonial Woods RV called in early April to announce the arrival of our new Starcraft trailer. Margaret couldn't wait to rush right over, and when we arrived it was sitting out front — looking great, but enormous. A fifth-wheel trailer required a special in-the-bed hitch located precisely over the truck's rear axle. The "fifth-wheel" terminology was borrowed from the over-the-road semi-trailer rigs that dominated our highways. The cab and trailer were separate units, and the truck backed under the front of the trailer to hook up.

I told Russ Jones, the shop manager, about the steep hill leading to the parking area between the Deck House and the Annex on Bierys Bridge Road. "Sounds like I better come down and have a look," he said. Russ showed up a few days later, and he agreed that the route to our parking spot was pretty tight. He also checked out my Chevy truck, and although he liked the engine installation, he recommended heavier springs — "Stengel Brothers in Allentown is your best bet for that." This project *was* getting complicated. I went to check on the heavier springs right away, and then brought the truck to Russ's shop for the hitch installation. In addition, I needed a brake control unit for the electric trailer brakes. The RV lifestyle sure required a lot of special equipment.

Finally, by the middle of April, everything was set. When we arrived at Colonial Woods, the truck and trailer were all hooked up and ready to go. It was an imposing sight. Russ let me drive the truck and trailer on our way to Bierys Bridge Road and then showed me how to navigate our driveway. We finally reached the parking spot, but would we be able to get out? We took a short break before tackling that.

The Starcraft looked stunning sitting there. Russ thought this would be a good time to teach me how to unhitch the trailer. It wasn't difficult, and he explained the intricacies of the procedure. Exiting the parking area was easy, because the driveway on the west side of the house was wide and there were no obstructions. "Now you try it, Ray. Just take it slow and don't hesitate to get out and look around at any point." I drove in and out twice, just to make sure I had it down pat.

Everyone wanted to see the new trailer, so Margaret brought Mother Taylor over first. Bob and Colleen Berry came last, because we wanted to discuss our vacation plans with them. The Berrys were our neighbors on Rock Hill Circle, dating back to the time we owned the building lot there. When we built our house on Bierys Bridge Road, we renewed our friendship and have remained close friends ever since. Bob and Colleen spent summers at their "cottage" located in the Upper Peninsula of Michigan. It was near the town of Cedarville, approximately 30 miles from the Mackinac Bridge connecting the upper and lower peninsulas. Cedarville and Hessel were the focal points for a group of 36 islands lying along the north shore of Lake Huron, just east of the Mackinac Bridge. They were named Les Cheneaux, French for "The Channels."

We gladly accepted Bob's invitation to visit them during our June vacation, and that tied in nicely with our plans to try out the new trailer. Bob assured me they had lots of room to park. It sounded very enticing, and we looked forward to seeing their place. Margaret's mom would accompany us as far as Tonawanda to visit her daughter Nancy; it would be cozy in the truck with three people and a dog.

The Starcraft was parked behind the house for a few weeks before the start of my vacation. On the appointed day I picked up Mom at eight a.m. sharp and brought her over to our house, where everything was in readiness. The trailer's refrigerator was a godsend, and we had it turned on early in preparation for our trip. It reminded me of the 1953 movie, *The Long, Long Trailer*, with Lucille Ball and Desi

Arnaz. In the movie, Lucy piled her rock collection into every nook and cranny of their trailer. Fortunately, Margaret wasn't that bad, but we did have a load. One problem with RV living was a tendency to take too much stuff.

Leaving the parking area and going up the steep driveway turned out to be a cinch. Our first challenge was "Five-Mile Hill," west of Stroudsburg on I-80. I had plenty of power, but the coolant temperature kept inching up toward the red line. I feared the radiator might boil over but it didn't, because the pressure cap elevated the coolant's boiling point. We rose almost 1500 feet from the Lehigh Valley floor to the Pocono plateau on the way to Scranton/Wilkes-Barre. It was up and down mountains all the way to the New York State Thruway — fortunately, there was a rest area on I-81 where we could pull off and relax.

Joining the New York State Thruway at Syracuse we found a whole new world, sailing along at 65 mph with the engine temperature in normal range. We arrived at Nancy's around five o'clock, dead tired and needing a break. While parked on the street, our friends the Koenigs, who lived two doors down from Nancy, came over to check out the trailer. We had known them casually for years, but from that point on our friendship grew much closer, since they also owned a trailer.

First Night Out

In our campground guide, we located a KOA at Grand Island, N.Y., and it was almost dark by the time we registered and parked on our assigned space. My initial mistake was wasting precious daylight trying to extend the awning, and it became abundantly clear that I didn't know how to do it. Thankfully, my neighbor recognized my ineptitude and came over to assist. When I explained it was our first night out, he pitched in to help hook up the water, sewer and electric. Setting up after dark was difficult, and we took steps to avoid it in the future.

Boy, were we tired. That queen bed really felt good. We slept like proverbial logs that night. You know, though, it was fun being out on the road — really an adventure, in a mundane way. It was readily apparent Margaret made a good choice in choosing the Starcraft, as it was very comfortable. I was sick and tired of hotels and motels, and I hadn't expected that extensive travel would be a major feature of our retirement. I was certainly wrong about that.

The next morning dawned bright and clear, and we crossed the border into Canada at Niagara Falls. We didn't do much sightseeing because we had been there many times before. Crossing the U.S./Canadian border in those days was not much different than going through a tollbooth on the N.Y. Thruway. After a couple of routine questions, the lady in the immigration booth waved us on.

Instead of taking the direct route to Sault Ste. Marie, we chose a more roundabout route. After traveling west to Lake Huron's eastern shore, we followed Ontario 21 north along the lake. We passed through the quaint towns of Kitchener and Stratford and had lunch at a park near Goderich, overlooking Lake Huron. It was very pleasant there, with a breeze coming in off the water, but we wanted to reach Port Elgin before nightfall. Our campground guide told us we would find a nice park there for our second night out.

The weather was gorgeous, ideal in all respects. However, unbeknownst to us, it was about to change. We didn't listen to the radio and just meandered along, enjoying the day. We bypassed the Bruce Peninsula to our north and proceeded east, past Owen Sound to Collingwood Park on Georgian Bay. It was a perfect place to have lunch, and Gretchen had fun exploring the beach while we ate our sandwiches.

It was so perfect that we decided to spend the night. Since the few sites with electric were already taken, this would be our first night "dry camping." There was a good selection of sites with nothing on them but a fire pit, so we picked the best one we could find. Since we were "on battery," I cautioned Margaret to be frugal with power use.

We carried a lantern that was powered by "D" cells. The term "dry camping" meant we weren't connected to city water or electricity. It was delightful, and very relaxing. We turned everything off to save our battery, and since we didn't need to unhitch, the setup for the night was simple— except for the awning.

Never leave an awning out when you turn in. I forgot about it, and in the middle of the night we awoke to thunder and lightning and wind rocking the trailer. I could hear the canvas flapping in the wind, and realized I was facing a major challenge. Fortunately, the camper in the trailer next door heard me yelling and came to my assistance.

What wonderful people you encountered in the RV world. Without his help, we would have lost the awning.

We awoke to a dismal scene, and our idyllic world had changed. I examined the trailer for leaks, but except for a few traces around the windows, there weren't any. Quality trailers and motor homes were "leak tested" at the factory. The rain had stopped, but the murkiness persisted. We were lucky to have selected a pull-through site. (That meant you didn't have to back up to leave the campsite.) Backing with a long trailer is not fun.

Continuing east around the foot of Georgian Bay, we joined Route 400, the main north/south artery from Toronto. Studying the map revealed how much we could have shortened our journey by using the faster highway. But we were on vacation, so it didn't matter if we lost a day en route.

The countryside around Midland and Victoria Harbor was exceptionally scenic. Our destination for the day was Perry Sound. We were old hands at setting up camp now, considering ourselves pros. The following day, we could have made it all the way to Bob's cottage on Mackinac Bay, but we would have arrived late, so we camped at Blind River instead. It was very pretty, being right on Lake Huron.

Crossing the border at Sault Ste. Marie was a breeze, and the Customs officer didn't give us a second look. Ho-hum, just another tourist towing a trailer. Finally, we saw the sign for Cedarville, but the town was not our destination. We were going to Mackinac Bay, in the midst of the Les Cheneaux Islands, about five miles west.

Bob's instructions were: "When you intersect Route 134, turn right and drive west, watching for Rudd Road on your left, and then proceed south to the end of the road." Rudd Road was not paved, but it was kept in excellent condition by the borough maintenance crew. The distance was greater than expected, and I started to worry. I wouldn't be able to turn our rig around if we came to a dead end. There was no need for alarm, though; before long, we passed through a gate, and quite suddenly, we had arrived at an idyllic spot.

We could see the water of Mackinac Bay through the trees, and right in front of us, as Bob had promised, was a large open area with plenty of room to maneuver our trailer. We parked in what once was the front yard of the Rudd home. There was a rock-lined path to the dock, where Bob moored his Chris-Craft 16-foot runabout. (The name of their boat was *Mackinac Bayberries*.) It was a wonderful place, with a gentle breeze coming in off the bay. With a wave, Bob was there to greet us.

After a bite of lunch, we backed the trailer into a shady spot next to the old well house. Since we would be driving into town, I unhitched the Chevy, freeing it of its load for the first time since leaving Bethlehem.

We followed a meandering path to the Berry Cottage, an alpine structure much like a Swiss chalet. Bob and his son had built it from a kit during a summer vacation some years earlier. It was perched on stilts that elevated the main floor for a spectacular view of the bay. Recently a large screened porch was added, and that became the focal point for most of our visits to the Berry Cottage. Margaret and I spent many delightful hours on that porch, observing boats transiting the main channel to Hessel.

The "Berry Patch." This is the Alpine cottage that Bob and Colleen Berry built in the late 1980s on Mackinac Bay in the Les Cheneaux Islands near Cedarville, Mich. Margaret and I spent copious amounts of time on their front porch over the years.

Boats

Hessel, Michigan, was the home of the famous Mertaugh Boat Works and the annual Les Cheneaux Islands Antique Wooden Boat Show. Margaret and I attended most of them during our ten-year residence there. I had the distinct privilege of attending the boat show's 36th edition in 2013 with old friends.

I would like to say just a few words about the Mertaughs. Gene Mertaugh was the patriarch and two of his sons, Jim and Jack, were also active in the business. Jack managed the store in Hessel, and Jim did everything else, including running the shop and boatyard. We became exceedingly close friends.

Jim had two sons, Tommy and Danny, and all of the Mertaughs were experts in the field of maintaining and restoring mahogany boats. Danny could replace planking with precision unrivaled anywhere, and Tommy could apply varnish with such expertise that it never ran — he made the application of the varnish look easy. Their whole life, all of their life, revolved around mahogany boats.

The main boathouse was a wonder to behold, and the dominant structure on the Hessel waterfront. It was huge, perhaps 100'x250', with a domed roof to ward off the heavy snows of winter. Incorporated inside was a long pier to tie up boats undercover, out of the sun and rain. Also, there were chain hoists dangling from a huge I-beam overhead for lifting boats out of the water for winter storage or maintenance. The long 100-foot beam provided the means of transport to a large storage area beyond the slip.

———————

We really enjoyed our visit with the Berrys. Cooking was mostly barbeque out on the deck. Inside, the cottage was very cozy. It had a main living area with stairs to a loft over the bedrooms for the children when they were visiting or for overflow guests. Beneath the loft were two small bedrooms. Later, in the '90s, a large master bedroom and bath were added to the east side. A wood-burning stove, which had originally been the only source of heat, dominated the living room. Next to the living room was a small, efficient kitchen, and there was additional expansion in that area over the years to create a dining room.

The next day, Bob offered to take us out in his Chris-Craft. It was small, but it could accommodate four people. Our ride was local, staying in the main channel through the islands. An hour later we were back at the dock; that was our introduction to antique and classic boating.

All too soon, it was time to start back to Bethlehem. We said our goodbyes and hitched up the Starcraft. Margaret and I were very impressed with Les Cheneaux, and we planned to return again in the fall for another visit.

Route I-75 ran all the way from the Canadian border to Florida, and an important component of the interstate highway was the Mackinac Bridge. Built in 1957, it earned the distinction of being the longest suspension bridge in the country. Since it was only 34 miles from Mackinac Bay, we reached it within the first hour. It was an impressive sight when we first saw it — a thing of magnificent beauty to behold. I had observed it under construction during my first months with Capital while flying the DC-3 to the "Soo" (jargon for Sault Ste. Marie).

There was an observation point on the north end of the bridge, and we stopped to take advantage of it. Our camera was out while we parked and enjoyed the excellent view. Driving across the bridge was a memorable experience; at the highest point, we were 150 feet above the water. The bridge, including its approaches, was five miles long.

Our 1987 Starcraft trailer and Chevy truck at the Mackinac Bridge in 1987. Note how the 31-foot trailer towers over the short bed Custom 10 pickup. It was feasible only because of extensive modifications converting our half-ton pickup truck to a heavy-duty tow vehicle.

Continuing south on I-75, at the intersection of I-69 in Flint, we turned left 90 degrees and proceeded east to Port Huron, for the border crossing into Canada. From there, our return to Bethlehem was the reverse of our outbound trip, and we picked up Margaret's mom in Tonawanda. That trip was our introduction to the RV lifestyle, and we were active in it for the remainder of Margaret's life.

Having some vacation time remaining in September, we decided to take another trip to Mackinac Bay. We were smitten with the possibilities there, especially the chance to visit at a different season of the year. Bob said it was a unique experience after Labor Day, when all the summer people had left. After thoughtful consideration we wondered about the possibility of finding a place there of our own. The likelihood of that seemed remote, but Bob suggested we talk to John Griffin, of Smith & Griffin Realtors, anyway. You never know.

We arrived early in October, and it was beautiful. The leaves were falling, and it was eerily quiet, since the boating season was over. Well, not quite. Duck hunters were on Mackinac Bay, and we were awakened with the crack of shotguns discharging their loads. We did contact John Griffin, and he said he had a few properties to show us; however, nothing caught our fancy. Toward the end of our stay, we woke up to find snow on the ground. I told Margaret that it was time to pack up and leave.

———————

After our return to Bethlehem in late October, Tom arrived with Margaret's '65 Pontiac convertible to store it in the Annex over the winter. Finally, we had a car in the showroom (the top story of the Annex). I asked him if he was ready to sell it back to us, but he said no, he wanted to keep it for his daughter, Mary, to drive. After we got it safely tucked away, I drove Tom back to Eric.

Chapter 21

The End of My Flying Career
1989-1993

The Final Months

Flying the DC-10 coast to coast, nonstop, was a boring job. It was nothing like the old days, when there were multiple stops to break the monotony. I flew the afternoon trip to Los Angeles and returned on the all-nighter, arriving back home two days later at six a.m. At times I longed for the B-727 days, when I had enjoyed going to work.

The day to hang up my uniform was drawing near. There were times I thought I would never make it: thirty-three years and two months — 28,000 flying hours, equating to having spent over three years above *terra firma*. However, I wasn't quite there yet, as my last proficiency check was scheduled in February. Since I had accrued more than a year's sick leave that I would not be reimbursed for, it did occur to me to just stay home.

As it turned out, though, it wasn't all that bad. The simulator instructor was aware that I only had three months left to fly, so he cut me some slack by having me do only a few certification maneuvers — no high dive or engine fires. After only 30 minutes, he shook my hand and wished me well in retirement. The abbreviated PC was a pleasant and unexpected surprise, thank you very much.

With the focus on myself, I haven't mentioned Margaret lately. For some reason, she had become intolerant of the glue that attached her ileostomy appliance to her abdomen, allowing toxic bowel discharge to damage her skin. She had tried many different adhesives in the hope of finding something suitable, but to no avail. Her surgeon wanted to operate to relocate her stoma, but how long would it be until that skin was ruined as well? It was a very trying situation.

Margaret was under the care of a dermatologist who tried various preparations, but nothing worked. For the next six months, she suffered with a level of misery ranging from discomfort to out-and-out pain. It was impossible for her to wear most of the clothing she preferred, so our lifestyle was severely compromised. Since the final chapter of this story is many months away, I'll cover other topics to keep the narrative on track.

New Opportunities

After flying my last trip, we planned to return to Michigan, this time for the entire summer. Cedarville RV Park and Marina would be our new summer home. The park consisted of 50 sites and was owned by Red and Til Beukema. The choicest spots were out on the point, with frontage on the main channel that wound through the islands. We definitely wanted one of those, so we placed a deposit on site #27 well in advance of the '89 season. We would have been welcome at the Berry Patch, but there weren't any utility hook-ups. Camping in the park would be fine, and we were looking forward to our first summer of retirement.

I met Jim Coates on one of the LAX trips and discovered that he also was an RV enthusiast, owning a site in an RV park near the Sarasota, Florida, airport. Jim said he had no plans to use his spot during the upcoming '89 winter season, so Margaret and I considered renting it. Margaret liked the idea, so a phone call and a deposit check sealed the deal.

The last few months of my flying career had slipped away, and the day of my final flight was at hand: June 2, 1989. In exactly eight days I would no longer be permitted to act as pilot in scheduled airline service in the United States. To continue airline flying some pilots went overseas, beyond the jurisdiction of the FAA. In fact, I got a call from Saudi Airlines offering me a DC-10 Captain position, but because of Margaret's problem it was out of the question.

No, this was it. We planned for it, and because of the mandatory age-60 retirement regulation, Margaret and I would be able to enjoy some very special years in the Upper Peninsula (UP) of Michigan.

Oh-oh, a snag: there was no room for Margaret on my flight. United policy granted a retiring pilot the privilege of inviting his spouse and children to accompany him on his final sequence of trips, so when the flight office called me the day before my retirement flight with this news, I quoted chapter and verse from the policy manual.

"Furthermore," I informed them, "If you can't find room for Mrs. Lemmon, then you don't have room for me, either." To wit: I won't be flying the trip. "Let me call you back," was the reply. "Okay, you do that," I said.

Somehow, they managed to find a seat for Margaret after all, and she came to the cockpit during the boarding process to meet my crew and take some pictures. Soon we were off for California. On arrival at LAX, I instructed the Second Officer to request a closer gate to the terminal so we wouldn't have to walk as far. "Sorry, unable," was the response. I was denied even that simple courtesy.

At the hotel we had dinner with the crew, and that was about it. We spent the next day together in a leisurely manner — nothing special, just relaxing for the all-nighter ahead. Preparatory sleep was the order of the day, but it was seldom successful.

My retirement flight on the DC-10, June 1989. Margaret had a seat in First Class for the flight to LAX and back.

Reporting in at 8 p.m., PDT, everyone in LAX operations seemed to be aware that it was the Captain's final flight. After boarding the plane, the "A" flight attendant came to the cockpit with a cake and a note from UAL flight operations: "Congratulations to Captain and Mrs. Lemmon; our best wishes to you for a happy retirement." There were several other teletype messages from flight operations execs and the President of UAL.

My First Officer could scarcely believe it when I offered to have him fly us home. It was his turn, and at that point, I wasn't about to change what had become my lifetime pattern of cockpit discipline.

When we arrived at Newark the following morning, the airport was fogged in, and the ceiling was so low we were unable to land. At that time, there was no ILS for Runway 22, and the non-precision approach restricted us to 400 feet and one-mile visibility. We descended to our minimum altitude, flew out the computed time to the end of Runway 22, and being unable to establish visual contact, we pulled up and executed the missed approach.

Oh boy! What a way to end a career — with a diversion to Baltimore, our alternate airport. No, not this time — I requested a vector for the Runway 4 ILS, accepting the eight-knot tailwind. Again, the First Officer offered to have me take over.

"No thanks, you can handle it." We broke out at 250 feet for a routine landing. It was no big deal, just everyday stuff. We taxied to the gate and I set the parking brake for the last time. There was no welcoming committee, no company rep, no ALPA rep — nobody, period. I had cleared out my mailbox before we left, so I didn't bother to go to flight operations, either. Margaret and I just walked off the plane together into retirement.

During the drive home, Margaret didn't say much, sensing my depressed demeanor. We had left Gretchen with Mom, so we stopped there to pick her up. We gratefully accepted Mom's invitation to come for dinner that evening, and then we went home to bed. My new title at United was "Captain R.A. Lemmon, Ret."

Retirement Syndrome

Since we intended to stay in Michigan all summer, we allowed a week or so to prepare. Now that I was retired, everything seemed new, with many adjustments to be made. Change was the order of the day, for a while at least. By the middle of June, we were ready to start out.

We planned a different route this time using the Pa. Turnpike, I-80 and I-79 to Erie. The long climb into the Poconos could not be avoided, but using the Turnpike made the ascent a bit more gradual, and we didn't encounter a serious overheating problem. Three hundred miles later, we arrived at the KOA in Erie.

Our friends Ken and Jackie Michaels expected us, and hosted a surprise party to celebrate my retirement. It was very nice, and a memorable occasion. Being in Erie precluded our usual route through Canada, so we traveled west on I-90 and the Ohio Turnpike to Toledo. From there, we proceeded due north to join I-75 to the Mackinac Bridge.

After a couple of overnight stops, we arrived in Cedarville. Entering the RV Park, Red and Til Beukema welcomed us and showed us around. Site #27 was delightful; a gentle breeze was coming in off the water, so there was no need for air conditioning.

Even Gretchen loved it, running around sniffing and checking everything out. Before long, I had everything set, with the awning out and the truck unhitched. Margaret was tired, so she went inside to stretch out while I checked out Mertaugh's boatyard.

Bob had introduced me to Jim Mertaugh during our brief visit the previous summer. I told Jim I had just retired and would be spending the summer there. I asked if it would be all right to look around in the boathouse. He replied, "Sure, let me know if you see anything you like."

An hour later, my next stop was the Berry Patch (we often referred to Bob and Colleen's property by that name). The Berrys and I had a nice chat, and I said I had been over to see Jim and check out the boathouse. I returned to the park and told Margaret about what I seen, but she was not overly impressed and wondered what I was getting into now.

Margaret's abdominal skin problems were putting a serious damper on our vacation. She felt okay but was limited as to the clothes she could wear, and riding in the truck was not pleasant. She was most comfortable wearing a robe or loose-fitting clothing. Because Margaret didn't leave the trailer very often, Til was concerned and looked in on her frequently.

My daily routine became a ritual of getting up, preparing breakfast, letting Gretchen out, unrolling the awning, and then going to Mertaugh's to have coffee and doughnuts with the guys.

Sitting on blocks at Mertaugh's was an old Chris-Craft cabin cruiser that was a derelict destined for the burn pile. The name on the transom was *Fudgie*. For something to busy myself with, I began to dismantle it piece by piece for Jim. He was mostly interested in the engines, but I saw a lot of other goodies worth saving — like the forward hatch, for instance. I enjoyed being at the yard and working on it. Why the name *Fudgie*? For the famous Mackinac Island fudge sold on the island.

Even though Margaret was confined to the trailer much of the time, we visited with Bob and Colleen at the Berry Patch. We frequently dined at the Freighters Restaurant in Sault Ste. Marie, where we watched the ore boats transiting the locks. Occasionally we would take a cruise through the channels on a charter boat. At the park we would often have a bonfire and socialize with other park residents. The summer passed quickly, and at the conclusion of the Labor Day Weekend we began packing for the trip home.

The trip took three days, as usual. We were concerned about Margaret's mom being alone in her condo, but that turned out not to be the case — she spent much of the summer with Nancy and Jane.

Hope for Margaret

Margaret's skin problem was becoming a crisis; something had to be done, and soon. Her surgeon wanted to operate to relocate her stoma to the other side of her abdomen. Margaret steadfastly resisted, and just before submitting to surgery, a glimmer of hope appeared on the horizon. One day, while buying surgical supplies, Margaret was talking to a nurse she knew quite well, and they were discussing her problem.

"Have you heard about the Continent Ostomy Center in Florida that is doing the internal pouch?" her friend asked.

BCIR: Barnett Continent Intestinal Reservoir

No, Margaret hadn't heard about it, but she was all ears. The nurse really didn't know much more, but she provided a phone number. Margaret couldn't wait to get home and call the Palms of Pasadena Hospital in St. Petersburg, Florida. Naturally, she was curious but afraid to get her hopes too high, only to have them dashed by another dead end.

I made the call and talked to Susan Kay, head nurse and administrator. I immediately sensed we were in good hands with Sue. When I explained the severity of Margaret's problem, she was very sympathetic and pointed out the advantages of the internal pouch reservoir.

"No more bags, ever," Susan proclaimed. Further, she said, "Not wearing an appliance means no need for cement anymore, and eliminating the glue would put an end to the excoriated skin problem." That sounded almost too good to be true. I then asked her if she knew anyone in our area who had undergone the operation. Susan didn't have that information at her fingertips. "Let me check, and in the meantime, I'll send you some information," she said.

Was it the work of the Lord? The Holy Spirit? I don't know, but that timely intervention was a godsend. Looking back on it, I think it *was* divine, but at that time I never thought of such things.

Susan called back a day or so later to say that the earliest they could fit Margaret into their schedule would be early the following year. "If we get a cancellation, perhaps we can do the operation sooner," she said. I replied with a rather desperate plea: "Margaret mustn't be made to wait that long." "Let me talk to Dr. Pollack, but for now, please fill out the paperwork I sent you," Susan replied.

Dr. Jason Pollock, MD

Dr. Pollock studied under Dr. Barnett, the creator of BCIR. Margaret had the good fortune to meet Dr. Barnett while she was at Palms Hospital. At that time, Dr. Pollock was the only surgeon in the east who could perform the operation. Let me briefly explain exactly what BCIR is, and how it evolved.

An internal waste reservoir was not a new concept, as its history went back many years. The problem with the early procedure was leakage at the outlet, due to rejection by the body of the different closure materials that were used. Since foreign materials were used, the results were unsatisfactory. What Dr. Barnett did was to create a living collar out of the patient's own bowel tissue to eliminate valve failures.

For emptying the pouch, a special catheter was used to breach the seal. That required the use of mineral oil to lubricate the catheter. The reservoir (pouch) was also made from bowel tissue, so it wouldn't be rejected, and held up to a quart of liquid waste material.

It was crucial for people with ostomies to drink lots of water. Not having a large intestine meant that the body's main source of hydration had been eliminated. Those with a Barnett reservoir needed to be especially vigilant, because only liquid could be expelled through the catheter's small opening. Any degree of solidification would plug it, requiring repeated irrigation.

Along with filling out the paperwork Susan requested, I decided to enclose pictures of Margaret's excoriated skin. That did it. When Dr. Pollock saw those pictures, our phone was ringing off the hook. "Get her down here immediately," he commanded. "I'm scheduling her surgery for Monday, November 13; can you make it?" "Yes, doctor, we certainly can." Finally, we had found someone to help Margaret.

Our appointment gave us just over a week to prepare for the trip. Since I had Jim Coates's campsite in Sarasota available, we wanted to take the trailer. A facility closer to St. Pete would have been nice, but RV parks were not a part of the crowded downtown area. Sarasota would be just fine; after all, Palms Hospital was only a short drive over the bridge.

The Sunshine Skyway, bridging Tampa Bay, was built in the 1930s and had recently added a companion span to make it a modern connecting link between the two cities. I drove over it numerous times during Margaret's hospitalization.

Fortunately, the weather cooperated, and although it was very cold outside, we were snug and toasty in the truck. We traveled our familiar route of the 1970s, even stopping for a night with the Hestons in North Carolina. A day or so later, we were down south where it was warm, and the only trouble we had with the truck was a broken speedometer cable.

The RV park was just east of the Sarasota Airport and it was very nice, with a palm tree on the site (I mention this only because we had never encountered flora adjacent to our hook-ups before). I drove Margaret to the hospital on a Sunday night for admission, and Dr. Pollock stopped in to see her. While sitting on the bed, he outlined the procedure in detail. We were very impressed with his caring nature and felt blessed to be there. Parting was difficult for us, and Gretchen and I were already missing Margaret by the time we returned to the trailer.

Margaret's Recovery

Margaret came through the surgery in fine fettle. The BCIR wing of the hospital ran like a well-oiled machine. It was much like an assembly line, in the sense of evaluating a patient's progress; you could look at a patient 10 days post-op and reasonably project yourself to be at that point of recovery on your own tenth day.

The hospitalization period was projected to be 21 days, which meant Margaret would be spending Thanksgiving there as an inpatient. Gene and Jane Olsen flew in to visit, and to take Gretchen and me back to Allentown. We were already anticipating Margaret's needs after leaving Palms Hospital — we had been advised to stay in the area until late January, so having a car would alleviate being restricted to the Chevy truck for transportation.

The trip to Allentown went fine, and Gretchen and I started back almost immediately with Margaret's car. The return to St. Pete was a long first day; I finally called it quits somewhere in Georgia, where I found a motel for some much-needed sleep. I returned to I-95 fairly early in the morning and arrived at the hospital by noon. Margaret was ambulatory by that time, and since it was almost a month since she had seen Gretchen, I suggested coming out to the car for a reunion.

Guess what? Gretchen wanted nothing to do with her mommy, and would barely acknowledge she knew her. I was shocked, and Margaret was keenly disappointed. Animals are strange and unpredictable. We didn't stay long as I wanted to get to Sarasota, where Gretchen and I could catch up on our sleep.

After a few more days, Margaret was released to return to the trailer, with instructions to see Dr. Pollock in two weeks. She was delighted to be out of the hospital and back home in the Starcraft. I had a phone installed in the trailer so we would be able to talk to Mom back in Bethlehem.

Margaret was doing well with her new BCIR, although it would take time to manage it effectively. It was a gift of inestimable value for

Margaret; truly, it was a new lease on life. In a sense, she was "born again." She gained strength every day, and soon was helping with the cooking and shopping. Bringing the car solved our transportation problem, and I moved the truck to the public lot and we seldom drove it.

Christmas in the trailer was a novel experience. I bought a little tree and some other decorations, making the trailer quite festive. Margaret's demeanor had changed completely, and her depression was gone. I was so delighted with this change in her.

When we went in for Margaret's two-week post-release visit with Dr. Pollock, he was very pleased with her progress. He knew we wanted to go home, but wisely pointed out that it was best to wait a bit longer before leaving the area, just to be sure there were no complications.

Nearing the end of 1989, and also the decade, was another time for deep reflection. We were exceedingly thankful for our blessings, especially Margaret's BCIR. We were also accepting the realization that my flying career was over, and making adjustments to a newfound freedom that had been unknown to me up to that point in my life.

Exploring possibilities in the Les Cheneaux Islands would not have been possible during my flying career. Overall, rather than being overcome with the sadness of not being able to fly anymore, I had a feeling of excitement and optimism regarding what lay ahead. Of course, everything hinged on Margaret, and on her being able to enjoy retirement with me. It looked like we had just taken a giant step in that direction with her BCIR.

Return to Bethlehem

1990 presented new and different challenges and opportunities. With the cessation of those big paychecks, I needed to curb my impulsive spending a bit, but don't hold your breath.

Margaret had her final checkup with Dr. Pollock, and he gave her the green light to travel. That was wonderful news, and we thanked him effusively. In conjunction with receiving her BCIR, Margaret became an active member of QLA (Quality of Life Association), a group formed by BCIR recipients. They met once each year in St. Pete, and Margaret planned to attend.

We prepared our trailer for the trip — Margaret was well on the road to recovery, and quite capable of driving home. She would follow me with her car, as she had done so many times before, and we had portable CB radios for short-range communication.

We stopped overnight in South Carolina, and again in Virginia. With a snowstorm pressing in, we canceled a planned stop at Gettysburg and continued all the way home. I was concerned about overexerting Margaret, and we did receive six inches of snow overnight. It was good to be back in Bethlehem.

1990: Cedarville

After Memorial Day we returned to Michigan once more, dropping Mom off in Mansfield, Pa., where she planned to spend time with her daughter, Jane. We arrived at the Cedarville RV Park, and the breeze blowing in off the channel felt wonderful. It was good to be back with the Starcraft again, and we were anxious to attend the annual Antique Boat Show that we missed the previous year.

The second Saturday of August had been the date set for the event since its inception. It covered the entire area between Mertaugh's and the Hessel Marina, and on the water it utilized the piers and facilities of both. Almost 100 boats arrived by water, with many others sitting on trailers in the area. Marine flea market spaces were provided, and other goods and equipment were spread out on the grass.

Bob Berry customarily entered their *Mackinac Bayberries* Chris-Craft, in which we had a ride the previous summer. Boats of the same type were grouped together for judging, and it was a challenge for the docking crew to get all the boats spotted where they belonged.

People came from far and wide to experience the wonderment of Hessel's beautiful mahogany boats. It was an all-day event, usually ending with parties and cookouts. We attended as many of the shows as possible during the summers we lived there. It was the climax of the season, although many events were held right up to Labor Day weekend. After that, it was lights out in the islands; all of a sudden it became very quiet.

During the boat show, Margaret and I stopped by the Berry Patch, where we met Tim and Sylvia Lyman. They were also mahogany boat enthusiasts and had entered their *Miss Sylvia* in the Hessel show. Toward the end of August, we rendered our deposit on site #27 for the '91 season and departed. We planned several stops on the way, including Erie, Tonawanda and, lastly, the Labor Day car show at Olean, N.Y., so we were on the road for about ten days. From Olean, it was only a one-day drive to Bethlehem, and we were glad to be home again.

The classic mahogany boats were lined up for judging at the E.J. Mertaugh boat works in Hessel, Michigan. This annual boat show is the most prestigious event of its kind anywhere in the U.S. The most desired "classics" featured barrel-back sterns, white-caulked decks, and gleaming chrome hardware. Note the boat on the left with its hatch open for inspection of the engine compartment.

In the middle of January, I received word that Tom Apple was retiring after being with Earl for 35 years. Tom had recently been honored by the FAA for his long continued service as an aircraft mechanic and inspector for licensing planes. The *Erie Times* newspaper covered the party that was held in his honor, and more than 50 people attended.

In April, Margaret purchased a new '91 Toyota Camry station wagon with a V-6 engine. She was delighted to have a new car that she had selected for herself. Mom had one ride in it, just before going to the hospital for the last time.

Helen Harshaw Taylor (1902-1991)

Margaret's sister Jane and Rich McGee came for Mother's last birthday in March. Just prior to their visit, Mom improved on prednisone. But the improvement didn't last, and she wasn't able to come to our house for dinner as planned. Mom was able to mind Gretchen while we attended the New York Auto Show, and in connection with that, she was required to go up and down the stairs to let the dog out. After we returned, she never climbed those stairs again. On April 10, Helen walked out of her condo on her own two feet, and after a brief hospitalization, died peacefully. Margaret and I spent a few precious moments with her the evening before, talking openly about her impending death, and she seemed to be fully prepared. "Pretty soon I'll be with Jack again. It's been such a long time." Dad had been dead for 10 years.

Now she was gone, and the loss was extreme for both of us. The funeral service was somber, as all are. A post-service gathering of at least 20 of our closest friends was held at our house on Bierys Bridge Road. Her graveside service in Erie was well attended by friends, including Judy Shanahan, who had so tenderly cared for Helen during her final years on West Seventh Street. And then, it was over; our life would never be quite the same again.

A New *RAMAR*

By the end of May, we returned to site #27 at Cedarville RV Park, ready for another enjoyable summer season at Les Cheneaux.

Early in the evening of June 7, 1991, a 30-foot, twin-engine 1973 Chris-Craft Catalina cabin cruiser named *Popeye* tied up in the marina next to our trailer. It had just arrived from Charlevoix, Michigan, and there was a "For Sale" sign in the window. The Stapletons were sitting in the cockpit of the boat, enjoying the lovely evening, when I stopped by. *Popeye* looked impressive, and after a brief discussion about their trip, I asked them the price. $17,500 was the reply, and then I went to find Margaret.

"Hon, come see the boat," I announced, to which Margaret answered, "What boat?" and it proceeded from there. The next morning, Jim Stapleton, *Popeye*'s owner, offered to take us out for a sea trial. I invited Bruce Glupker from Mertaugh's to join us for a professional evaluation.

Boy, what a boat. Those 307-cubic-inch V-8 engines really sounded great.

"Do you think we could swing it?" I asked Margaret. We agreed on a price of $16,500. Then I asked Bruce, "Should we take it over to your place for a haul-out inspection to check the bottom?" Bruce replied, "That won't be necessary. They wouldn't be driving it all the way from Charlevoix with bottom damage." The only stipulation was that Jim's wife insisted that *"Popeye"* be removed from the transom at the first opportunity. We changed it to *RAMAR* anyway, the same name we had used for the Staggerwing.

We enjoyed several nice rides through the channels, quite often with Bob and Colleen. On one occasion we struck a sunken log while returning to the dock, which damaged one of our propellers. The fix for that was a premature haul-out at Mertaugh's. Fortunately, the boat came with spares to remedy just such a mishap.

We lifted the boat using a watercraft transporter with rubber tires called a "Travel-all," and while it was still over the water, we scrubbed the bottom in preparation for brushing on special anti-fouling paint. From there, it was taken to a maintenance building to do the work. After painting the bottom, both propellers were exchanged and the take-offs were sent out for repair. When all the work was completed, we took the boat back to the launching site and put it back in the water.

DeTour Village

The narrow waterway from the expanse of Lake Huron to the Soo Locks began at an inlet called DeTour Passage. Bounded on one side by Drummond Island and on the other by DeTour Village, a giant ferryboat shuttled across the isthmus on a regular schedule. Margaret and I frequently drove there to eat and watch the thousand-foot ore carriers transiting the Soo Locks on their way to Lake Superior. Even Gretchen loved to go; all I would need to say was the word "DeTour," and she got very excited. Dogs really do understand English.

Around that time, Bob Berry reported trouble with his Chris-Craft. The engine started and ran, but it made a terrible noise, and the boat refused to move no matter which gear was selected. Further investigation revealed that the input shaft to the transmission was not turning, so *Mackinac Bayberries* didn't make it to Hessel that year.

The boat show may have been repetitious, but we wouldn't think of missing it. Tim and Sylvia Lyman were there with their children, and we all convened on the porch of the Berry Patch. On Sunday morning following the show, we were invited to a breakfast hosted by the Les Cheneaux Yacht Club on Marquette Island. It was a very prestigious event, and everyone looked forward to it. Because it was on Marquette Island, the only access was by boat, and many of the show participants attended with their beautifully restored classics.

We had just finished mooring our boat to Bob Berry's dock at the Berry Patch in preparation for attending the annual Sunday breakfast at the Les Cheneaux Yacht Club on Marquette Island. We were a party of ten for the event.

RAMAR was selected for the run, as our boat could accommodate 10 people. To shorten the trip on Sunday morning, on Saturday after the boat show we drove *RAMAR* to the Berry Patch and tied up at Bob's dock overnight. The kids, Sylvia, and Carolyn (Bob Jr.'s wife) rode down below in the cabin, and the rest of us were in the cockpit. The ride from Mackinac Bay was only thirty minutes, so no one was uncomfortable. The island setting was beautiful, and everyone had a great time. Those Yacht Club breakfasts were a wonderful climax for Boat Show weekend. After breakfast and dropping off our guests, Margaret and I took a two-hour cruise through the channels.

After Labor Day, when it was quiet again, we decided to remove *Mackinac Bayberries'* engine for transport to Ray's Marine in Bethlehem. I suggested that Bob try to find a replacement Model "B" 60 horsepower engine to bring along, just in case his was damaged beyond repair. Red Beukema, at the park, just happened to have one and agreed to sell it to Bob. When it was time for us to leave, I loaded both of them into the bed of my truck.

Margaret and I were just driving around the area, as we often did in the evening. Just by chance, we found ourselves on Hill Island Road: "Hey, Hon, I see a 'For Sale' sign there on the left — let's stop and take a look."

Hill Island

If it was an island, how were we able to drive out there? There was a bridge, of course, but there hadn't always been one. Like many of the 36 islands that constituted the Les Cheneaux group, Hill Island had been inaccessible by car before the turn of the century. At that time there was little interest in tourism; the islands were all about lumber.

Hill was a narrow island, and we were able to see water on both sides of the road while transiting much of it. Out at the tip, where we were, it widened a bit and was quite wooded. The house was situated near the water, so the driveway was nearly 200 feet long. The ranch-style house appeared to be fairly new and sat on a bluff; the land beyond sloped gently down to the water, providing a magnificent view. The portion of Lake Huron in front of the house was named Moscoe Channel. How wide was it? Perhaps three-quarters of a mile, and the open water of Lake Huron was clearly visible in the distance, off to our right.

It was an exceptionally warm August day in the islands, and a gentle breeze drifted in off the water. After we had walked around the house and absorbed all of this, I simply stood back and said to Margaret, "This is it, Honey; we are home," even though, at that time, I had no idea how much it was going to cost.

Smith and Griffin had the listing, as they did for most of the available property in the area, so the next day we stopped in to see John Griffin: "Hey, John, how come you didn't tell us about the Hill Island property?" "I thought it was out of your price range. I've been showing you less expensive listings," he replied.

"Well, how much is it?" I asked. "$165,000, and the price is firm. We've had several offers in the 150s, but Harry Kapp, the owner, won't budge." "Can we look at it? We're about to hook up our trailer and head for Pennsylvania." "Sure, I'd be glad to show it to you. I only wish I had known."

The house was about 60 feet long, with the bedrooms at one end and an eat-in kitchen and two-car garage at the other. There was a low wall between the living room and kitchen and it was one step down to the living room. Overall, the house was quite plain. The hot-water heating system originated from a very small and efficient boiler in the garage. It was a well-built house, but cost-cutting measures were evident everywhere. Being a schoolteacher, Harry's funds were limited — he didn't even have a window in the garage.

The major attraction was not the house, but the property. It had over 150 feet of prime lakefront exposure. There were two mature cedars down by the water, but for the most part the view was unobstructed from the living room. We bought the place a few days later, and the closing was set for October. So, during the summer of '91, we managed to buy both a boat and a house, and the year was still young.

Our Hill Island home near Cedarville, Mich., after extensive changes in the mid-1990s. We summered here for almost ten years.

After Labor Day weekend, it was time to put *RAMAR* in lay-up, so Bob and I drove the boat over to Mertaugh's for haul-out.

We loaded Bob's two Chris-Craft Model "B" engines in the bed of the truck and secured them well. During the ride back to Bethlehem, our conversation centered on all that we had done during that past fantastic summer. We didn't regret any of it, but certain things had to be done as soon as we got home. Foremost on the agenda was selling our trailer. Now, as owners of lake-front property in Michigan, we wouldn't be traveling much anymore. We advertised the Starcraft and within 10 days, it was sold.

Sault Bank notified us that the closing for Hill Island was set for October 15. We wanted to take the bare essentials to set up housekeeping with us, so we rented a U-Haul trailer to tow behind our Chevy truck. We still had a lot of our Florida household goods left, so we were in pretty good shape. We took the twin beds, two gold La-Z-boy chairs, TV, and kitchenware.

Snow was a problem north of Saginaw-Bay City, but we finally made it to St. Ignace, where we spent the night. By the next morning the weather had improved, so we continued on to Cedarville. The closing was still two days away, but John Griffin was kind enough to let us unload our trailer contents into the garage so we could turn in the trailer. While there, we inspected the house again. Thankfully, the heat had been turned on, and we found a business card taped to the boiler: "Kester and Son, Plumbing and Heating." Keith Kester would be our caretaker to open and close the house for each of the ten years we lived there.

We overnighted at a motel in Sault Ste. Marie that would accept Gretchen. Fortunately, we only spent one night there, as John moved up the closing date to accommodate us. Then we returned to Hill Island to spend the first night in our new home. While we were looking around outside, I said to Margaret, "There's something missing." "What's that?" she asked.

"There's no dock for the boat. Where will we keep *RAMAR*?" When I went to see John Griffin in the morning, he suggested we consult Dan Carmichael at Flotation Docking Systems, right there in Cedarville. Dan showed us around his shop, asking a few questions about our boat. "You'll need a slip so you can tie off on both sides. Would you like a roof over it?"

Boy, that was a lot for a landlubber to digest. I explained to Dan that I was new to boating, and would appreciate all the help we could get.

"Let me show you some of the jobs we've delivered recently, and we'll go from there." That sounded like good advice, so we went into his office to see what he had to offer. Those docks were beautiful, and I couldn't imagine being able to afford what he was showing us. To set up a roofed-over "boat shelter," big enough for *RAMAR*, at our Hill Island property would cost about $15,000. The price included all required drawings and permits.

Dan provided us with some material for home study, but it was really pointless. I knew then and there, we had to have it — "Where do I sign?" We wrote out a deposit check, and we were on the schedule for spring delivery of one of the largest covered boat shelters they had ever built.

It was time to close up and head home, so I called Keith to come over and winterize the house while we were still there, but that was not the way he worked. He suggested that we be on our way, and he would take care of everything. In effect, he was telling us that now he was the caretaker, and we needed to trust him to lock up and take care of our place. "Just call me a week before your arrival next spring, and the house will be ready." Keith provided that service for many island residents. On the way home, we discussed our car situation and concluded we would like something more suitable for traveling to and from Hill Island.

Back at Ray's engine shop in Bethlehem, the *Mackinac Bayberries* engine had been sitting in the garage up against the wall for some time. When all of us had returned to Bethlehem for the winter, I invited Bob to come down to our house to observe the teardown. Once the gearbox was removed, we discovered that we could turn the rear of the crankshaft without turning the engine. That discovery could only mean one thing: The crankshaft had broken in two, a catastrophic failure.

If it had failed on their run to or from Mackinac Island, they would have been dead in the water — very serious indeed, especially with no radio. Luckily, it separated at the dock and, incredibly, the engine still ran, even though the boat refused to move. I told Bob that in order to return his engine to service, we needed a replacement crankshaft. I set up a model "B" engine assembly line, of sorts, in the rec room on sawhorses; I might as well be comfortable while I worked. I discovered a man in *Classic Boating* magazine who dealt in Hercules engine parts and who had most of what I needed: piston rings, bearings, valves and gaskets. What he didn't have was main bearings for the Model "B" engine; they simply didn't exist.

I was able to locate a used crankshaft for Bob's engine, but it was in poor condition and needed to be reground. Fortunately, it was standard (original dimensions), which meant it was a viable candidate. Because of the lack of new .010 undersize main bearings, we had to use the standard ones that Bob already had. Of course, they were worn, but Jim at Superior Automotive reconditioned them to usable condition and reground the crankshaft to the specific dimension of the worn bearings. Overhauling those old engines was not cheap, and I worked most of the winter reconditioning the two of them.

The holidays were somber without Margaret's mom, but we put up a tree and observed the Moravian custom of a candle light in each window of the house. We also hung a Moravian star in our entranceway.

By spring, the two model "B" engines were ready for transport back to Cedarville. As a token of his appreciation, Bob assembled and refinished the Emperor School Clock kit that I had given him years earlier, and he returned it in running condition.

We worked in the Annex on nice days, selecting things for Hill Island. Much of what we chose came from Florida and would be used to furnish the Michigan house. Margaret saw an ad in the paper for a 1990 Lincoln Town Car just coming off a two-year lease with only 15,000 miles on it, so we decided to drive to Emmaus to check it out. Off-white in color, it had all the Lincoln bells and whistles, and the ride was superb — just what we needed for the trip to Hill Island. The leather interior was spotless and still had that "new car" smell. Since everything seemed to be in order, we bought it. That Town Car turned out to be our best car purchase ever, for both satisfaction and price. We bought it for one-half of new-car invoice.

Allied Van Lines picked up our shipment in mid-April, and then I loaded Bob Berry's Model "B" Chris-Craft engines in the Chevy truck and left immediately after the movers. I had agreed to meet the van at Hill Island two days later.

When I arrived in Cedarville, Bob was already there. After unloading the household goods, he helped unload his engines that were still in my truck. Bob suggested I keep his spare in my garage, and we dropped off the *Mackinac Bayberries* original engine at Mertaugh's. Bob and Colleen drove me to Tri City Airport, near Saginaw, where I boarded a flight for Chicago and Allentown. Now that I was a retiree, jump seating was no longer an option for me. Space usually wasn't a problem, though, as I had over thirty years' seniority.

We departed Bethlehem mid-May in our new Lincoln Town Car. Margaret and Gretchen spent a couple of days with Nancy in Tonawanda while I drove to Erie for a quick visit with Tom Apple.

Completing the last leg of the trip to Michigan was awesome; we covered the entire 525 miles in one day without excessive fatigue. The Town Car was the only vehicle we ever owned that made that long one-day run an enjoyable experience.

We stopped at Mertaugh's on the way to Hill Island and, much to our dismay, Bruce Glupker had already launched the boat, ignoring my instructions to the contrary. When I went out to inspect it, I discovered *RAMAR* was banging into the dock from not being tied off properly. With that discovery, my dealings with Bruce were at an end.

The Boat Dock

Our next stop was Flotation Docking Systems, where I spotted our new boat shelter tied up in the slip. Built entirely with pressure-treated lumber for long life in the water, I was impressed with its size and construction. We went inside, and Dan Carmichael said the dock was ready for delivery.

"How do we get it to Hill Island?" I asked. Dan replied, "Goose will tow it behind the barge tug. Would you like to ride along?"

Goose (Dave) Windsor was the man in charge of dock repairs, maintenance, and new installations for Flotation Docking Systems. A massive barge was used in conjunction with this work, and we would be using its source of power to deliver our dock.

"Gee, Dan, thanks, that would be great." I told him our boat was tied up at Mertaugh's, and I suggested bringing *RAMAR* over to Cedarville to check the fit. I further directed him to keep the boat at Cedarville Marine until the dock was in place — "*RAMAR* won't be returning to Mertaugh's."

The next day I met Goose in town. I was excited to be a part of the dock delivery. There were two other men in the crew, but I was the one who got to ride in the tug's pilot house. We had a fairly long tow line strung out behind, with a bridle to the front corners of the dock. It was slow going, and the tow took almost an hour to reach our house on Hill Island. Margaret was there to greet us, and as we neared shore Goose asked, "Where do you want to place it?"

"Right off the end of the launching ramp," I replied. The old boat launching ramp, dating back to the days when our property was part of Hill Island Resort, projected out from shore about ten feet. I assumed that would be a good starting point, and Goose agreed. Dan was aware that we required a custom boarding ramp to be built on site. In fact, Jim Bohn, the shop foreman, came out to see what would be needed.

Fortunately, the water deepened sharply from shore, allowing the ramp to be fairly short. Since the dock was free-floating, it needed to be pinned in place. Steel sleeves were mounted on each corner to accept 6-inch-diameter steel pipes (called spuds) up to eight feet long. When the dock was in position, the crew simply dropped the pipes through the sleeves and they anchored themselves in the lake bottom. A tap or two with the sledge ensured that the dock would not shift. Once placed, it was unable to move laterally, but was still free to raise and lower with changing lake levels. By lunchtime everything was set, and it was time to bring *RAMAR* home.

RAMAR the Chris-Craft's new home at Hill Island. Note that because of the rapidly deepening lake, only a short boarding ramp was required.

The new dock was beautiful, and we were so pleased. Now the boat was right out front, readily available for evening rides or anything else we wanted to do. The roof was a distinct asset, because it kept the boat out of the rain and the direct rays of the sun. We added an owl at the edge of the roof. Hopefully, that imitation creature would deter the gulls from roosting.

This view of the boat shelter shows the Hill Island house in the background.

Dan Carmichael recommended pulling the pins on the new dock and relocating it closer to shore for the winter; he feared ice moving in and out of the channel might damage it. Since I had no expertise in that area, there was little I could do but follow his seasoned advice. "It will cost $500 for that service," Dan said. Usually I had it taken care of before we left for the season, but that wasn't always possible.

When haul-out time for *RAMAR* arrived, I contacted Chuck Lindberg at Cedarville Marine. He would now take care of the layup, storage, and the spring refit. Chuck seemed more than happy to have our business, and Cedarville Marine was much closer than Hessel to Hill Island. Their storage building was just a short distance north on M-29, which meant a short run down the highway. Their equipment was different than Mertaugh's, but the end result was the same.

Summer, 1993

In the spring of '93 we all returned to Hill Island, again enjoying a much smoother ride than when I drove the truck. It became a ritual, repeated time after time: have Keith Kester, the plumber, come and open up the house; arrive and unpack; and when we left in the fall, it was the reverse procedure.

Cutting the grass was a lengthy chore. We didn't have any in Bethlehem, but the Hill Island property more than compensated for it. At first, I used a walk-behind power mower, but I soon reached the conclusion that something more efficient was needed. At a neighborhood garage sale, I bought an ancient Snapper riding mower, and although it was a bit dilapidated, I fixed it up and was then able to ride instead of walk. It served me well all the summers we lived there.

RAMAR out on Moscoe Channel.

Frequently we used *RAMAR* for evening rides so we could enjoy a sunset on the water, and Bob and Colleen often went along. (We couldn't see the sun set from our house because it faced east.) Bob Jr. and Carolyn arrived to spend their vacation and to complete the dining-room project at the Berry Patch that Bob had started the year before.

One day, we watched as a beautiful wooden yacht passed by our house on Moscoe Channel. It was a 1964 46-foot Chris-Craft Constellation, just arriving from Traverse City. *Sand Castle III* was owned by Dale and Betty Sheldon. It was the most beautiful, stately yacht I had ever seen in our area, and they were docking just a few houses north of us.

I was aware that Dan Carmichael's crew had built a finger dock there the previous week. Margaret and I went to meet them and extend our welcome to Hill Island. "Maybe they will show it to us," I said, somewhat expectantly. How exciting! *Sand Castle* was one gorgeous boat. That was how we met the Sheldons, and we became much closer friends than I ever could have imagined. And yes, we did get a tour of *Sand Castle*.

When Dale and Betty came to visit, I showed them Bob's spare engine out in the garage. Dale was restoring a postwar Chris-Craft 21-foot Express Cruiser powered by a Chrysler Crown 115 horsepower engine that needed overhaul. During the tour of our house, Margaret said she would like to improve the kitchen, and in almost no time at all, we struck a deal that Dale would do the kitchen job in exchange for me rebuilding his Chrysler engine. That simple arrangement laid the foundation for a friendship, both personal and professional, that has lasted to this day.

Boat show time reunited us with the Lymans, and we attended the traditional Les Cheneaux Islands Yacht Club breakfast on Marquette Island.

That wound up the '93 season up north. After laying up *RAMAR* at Cedarville Marine, we returned to Bethlehem.

Shortly after arriving home, I got a call from Tom Apple in Fairview with the news that Margaret's '65 Pontiac convertible was up for sale, because he had no place to keep it anymore. Tom had a local buyer in the Erie area who really wanted it, but pursuant to our notarized agreement, he contacted me first.

Did we really want it back after so many years? "You bet, Tom. Margaret's convertible was like one of the family; don't even think about selling it to anyone else. I'm on my way."

Tom met me at the airport, and I detected a note of sadness in our conversation while discussing the car. I didn't dally long, as it was early December and I didn't want the car exposed to salt on the way home. It turned out okay, though, and I made it all the way on dry pavement. The car ran fine, but it seemed to be running hotter than normal. Margaret was delighted to have her convertible back.

Investigation of the overheating problem revealed that the heat-riser valve on the exhaust manifold was stuck closed. It was a small thermostatically controlled plate in the manifold that hastened engine warm-up during cold weather. Being stuck closed, the exhaust gases could only escape from the left side of the engine, increasing the operating temperature. I was unable to free up that valve, no matter how much I soaked it with penetrating oil.

The next step was to remove the manifold but, unfortunately, some of the bolts broke in the process. Now I really had a problem, and I ended up removing the engine. One thing led to another, and the first thing I knew, I had it all apart.

The assembled '65 Pontiac convertible engine and transmission ready for installation.

I decided to rebuild the engine because, after nearly 30 years, it was time. Suddenly, I was back at Superior Automotive again, getting Jim Tote involved. In terms of outlay, it was a cheap overhaul, and I was able to make some beneficial changes to lower the compression ratio. It really did give the convertible a new lease on life.

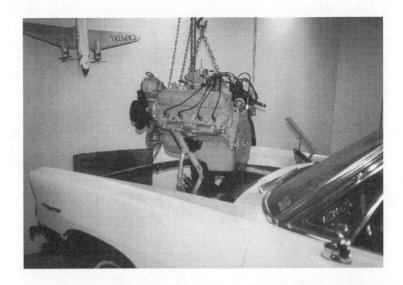

To reinstall the engine and transmission, I had to separate them. I lowered the engine into its place and then, with the car jacked up high, I was able to roll the transmission underneath and bolt it to the engine.

The convertible out for a spin with the top down. At that time, the car was almost 30 years old, but it still looked like new.

Chapter 22

The Michigan Years
1994-1998

Repetitive Years

Early '94 was extremely snowy — we had 13 nor'easters in a row. The pattern was set and regular as clockwork: twice each week, one came through and deposited an additional six inches or so. It was so bad that I gave up trying to keep the front driveway open; I simply ran out of space to blow the snow.

In the spring, on the way to Michigan, I accompanied the Erie Antique Car Club members attending the Dunkirk car show. I wasn't looking for anything specific, but was always watching for '65 Pontiac stuff. Now well past its 25th birthday, the convertible was eligible for judging at Hershey.

Jobs for Hill Island

On arrival at Hill Island, Dale was ready to start on the new kitchen. I also asked about the feasibility of enlarging the ancient log garage I had used for overflow storage. He didn't think it was worth saving; some of the foundation might be usable, but that was about all.

In addition to the garage, Margaret wanted a porch added to the front of the house to give us a better view of Moscoe Channel. Since the land sloped gently away from the house, we needed help with the design.

The kitchen job was progressing nicely. We needed new base cabinets for the large island that was part of the plan, and we also purchased a new range in Bethlehem that would need to be transported to Hill Island.

To comply with my part of the kitchen agreement, we loaded Dale Sheldon's Chrysler Crown marine engine into my truck for transport to Bethlehem. I would fulfill my part of the bargain by rebuilding it next winter. We delayed our departure for Bethlehem until the new garage was closed in. When we finally left after Labor Day it was in Margaret's Camry station wagon, which I had used to deliver the new range for the kitchen.

1995

There were a host of projects scheduled for the '95 season, and at one point I thought the agenda was far too ambitious. However, I underestimated Dale's capabilities; he was very resourceful.

Dale Sheldon's overhauled Chrysler Crown marine engine, ready for delivery to Hill Island.

By early spring, Dale's engine was finished. The Chrysler Marine engine sported quite a bit of brass, which polished beautifully. I also reconditioned all of his instruments. Keeping the Chevy truck in Bethlehem for the engine's delivery to Hill Island really paid off, and I was off to Hill Island shortly after Easter. On arrival, Dale and Betty's inspection produced favorable comments regarding the appearance. "Will it run?" Betty asked. "Maybe, with a little luck," I quipped.

We were late arriving at Hill Island and Dale was chomping at the bit, anxious to break ground for the house addition. The backhoe was out front the very next day. Along with the house project, we needed to finish the garage we had built the previous year. Dale was not amused when I remarked, "Gee, Dale, you could have poured the garage floor while you were waiting."

Our "porch" became the new living room. The trusses were special-order because of the cedar cathedral ceiling. With demolition of the original "window-wall," the new addition created one huge room, measuring almost 50 feet from the lakeside windows to the low wall dividing the living room from the kitchen. It was an impressive space, especially after Bob Smith laid the carpet. I said to Dale, "All we need are a couple of hoops and we could play basketball."

We were so busy, *RAMAR* didn't get launched until it was almost too late to be worthwhile, and once we did, we only used it a few times. It just wasn't the same anymore — most of the time the boat just languished out there in its covered dock, looking pretty. I recall one instance when over two weeks elapsed without taking it out even once.

1996: Paradise Lost?

It was becoming apparent that the Upper Peninsula was not the paradise we once thought it was. There was, as it turned out, such a thing as too much tranquility. Over time, *RAMAR* didn't turn out as expected, either, and again in 1996 the boat just sat there for long periods of time. In fact, you could predict our boating activity based on the company we had.

The Sheldons seemed to be similarly affected, as they sold *Sand Castle III*, and concentrated all their boating activity on Dale's recently completed Chris-Craft 21-foot express cruiser.

We were so busy with the house that *RAMAR* was late again getting launched, barely in time for the Boat Show. Our fascination with boating was waning, and Margaret deferred to my likes and dislikes along those lines. It was just that boating never truly captured my imagination to a significant degree. However, we weren't ready to sell *RAMAR* just yet, especially since we had spent all that money for a dock.

Because of the intensity of the previous winter, Margaret and I discussed the possibility of spending some time in Florida. For something different, we left the Lincoln Town Car in the new garage at Hill Island, with plans to depart from there for our visit with the Kanes. Although we could certainly expect lots of snow, Keith Foster, my next-door neighbor, agreed to keep our driveway open for our return in January. As there were no serious projects lined up for winter, '97 would be a good year to go south.

1997

There was a lull in the nor'easters around the middle of January, so we packed Margaret's station wagon for the trip to Michigan. Never having been there in winter, we were anxious to see Hill Island under vastly different conditions than we were accustomed to.

Driving was no problem, as the Interstates were clear; even M-134, the side road to Cedarville, was in good shape. However, as testimony to the tough winter the area was experiencing, there were high snow banks on both sides of the road. We arrived at Hill Island just in time to see men from McMaken Carpentry shoveling snow off the roof. Keith Kester, the plumber, called them after he came to open the house and decided the amount of snow on the roof was beyond acceptable limits. That activity blocked the main entrance to the house, so we had to wait until they finished. We walked around to the lakeside and discovered a winter wonderland. Moscoe Channel was frozen solid, and our boathouse, moored close to shore, was covered with snow; it was an impressive sight to behold.

Once inside, the house was quite comfortable. We patronized the Landings Restaurant in town for our evening meal, and made a brief stop at the Red Owl for groceries. Lights were on at the RV Park, so we stopped in to see Red and Til Beukema.

Keith Foster had done an acceptable job of clearing the garage-door area so we could get our Lincoln out. Unfortunately, the temperature plummeted as our departure drew near, and I began to question the wisdom of my decision last fall to begin the Florida trip from Cedarville. It was too late now; we drove west on 134 to the Interstate and headed south.

On the way, we struck a patch of "black ice," and I nearly lost control of the car. That experience was very unnerving, so I drove with utmost caution the rest of the way. Even after getting on I-75, only the right lane was clear of snow, and that provided us with a messy salt bath on the way to St. Ignace, where we spent the night.

A day or so later we finally reached Florida's Gulf Coast beaches, where we spent a few days near Panama City. We then followed the coastline to join Route 19 south to New Port Richey to visit with Lew and Natalie Kane.

The QLA convention Margaret customarily attended in St. Petersburg was being held in Vail, Colorado, in October '97. At first, she planned to fly to Denver and rent a car, but I suggested driving out so that we could do some sightseeing on the way. We had always wanted to visit Mount Rushmore, and from our starting point in northern Michigan, it would be almost a straight shot on I-90 to South Dakota. Margaret heartily agreed, so that was our plan for October.

Realizing that we would return before winter, we left Hill Island without winterizing the heating system. Of course, we alerted Keith Kester of our plans. Snow was possible in October, but unlikely.

Off to Colorado

After only a short stay in Pennsylvania, we returned to Cedarville again. After packing the Lincoln, we left Hill Island early in October, and spent our first night at Green Bay, Wisconsin. The shorter days reduced the distance we traveled each day, typically only 350 to 400 miles.

On our second day we barely made it to the Minnesota/South Dakota border at Sioux Falls. Pulling into Rapid City, a strong, steady wind began to blow, causing us some concern about the weather. By the next morning, though, the wind had subsided, and we awoke to a beautiful autumn day for the drive to Mount Rushmore. I had seen the monument so many times from seven miles up that I wasn't prepared to experience it "up close and personal."

We drove across the entire state of Wyoming to Ft. Collins, Colorado without seeing a single tree. I remember pulling off the road for a break and being able to see forever in all directions, our view unobstructed by any signs of civilization. It truly was a different perspective from the one I was used to from 37,000 feet.

Once we crossed into Colorado and the front range of the Rockies came into view, we were back in familiar territory. Memories of our life there, thirty years earlier, came rushing back. It was less than 100 miles to our next stop at Golden, Colorado, where we planned to spend the night. Golden, located in the foothills of the Rockies, was an excellent jumping-off point for destinations to the west.

We spent a day in the Denver area driving to familiar places like Montbello, where we had lived for a year. The development was completely changed — so much so, in fact, that we could not find our home that had been brand new in 1967. After a few minutes of fruitless searching, we found a mailman and asked directions.

Jeffco Airport, where Margaret learned to fly, was also on our itinerary. It, likewise, was very different. The control tower was still there, but not Mountview Aviation. It turned into a day of sadness, in a way, which was something neither of us had anticipated. Gretchen, sitting there on Margaret's lap, was oblivious to all of it. She had not existed in 1967.

Since we arrived in Colorado a week before Margaret's convention, we decided to cross the Front Range of the Rockies and visit Max and Darlene Goth at Montrose, Colorado, in the inter-mountain region. A quick phone call was all we needed to set it up. Actually, they weren't totally surprised, because Margaret had written to Darlene about the possibility of a visit before leaving Michigan.

Leaving Golden shortly after 9 a.m., we drove west into higher and higher terrain. We encountered the long steady climb to Eisenhower Tunnel, almost 10,000 feet above sea level. It took quite awhile to reach the tunnel entrance, and we were still at least 4000 feet below the mountain peaks all around us. It was very impressive indeed. When we exited the tunnel, we were treated to a spectacular view to the west, and it was all downhill from there. Margaret paid close attention to our route, as she was going to make the identical trip by herself a week later, on the way to Vail.

Grand Junction, Colorado, was situated on a 7000-foot plateau between two mountain ranges, and that was the point where we turned left on Highway 50. We continued south to Montrose, arriving at 5:30. There was a nice motel right in town where we had planned to stay, but then I talked to Max and he invited us to come out to their place to stay with them. I was concerned about Gretchen, but Darlene said to bring her along.

Max and Darlene suggested we visit the Black Canyon of the Gunnison River. We began by stopping at a viewing point at the top of the canyon, and from there we drove down into the canyon itself. It was one of the most popular tourist attractions in the area.

Our last day in Montrose was a Sunday, and Max wanted to show us the Telluride ski area, a popular winter destination in the mountains to the south. We had a great visit with our friends, but now it was time to leave for Denver. We arrived back at our Golden, Colo. motel by day's end. Gretchen was not welcome at the host hotel for the convention, so Gretchen and I stayed in Golden while Margaret drove to Vail.

After Margaret returned from the convention, it became apparent that the fine weather we had been enjoying was not going to last much longer. In fact, we were cutting it close, in the sense that we would be heading home just ahead of the inclement weather. Margaret had been watching too, with growing concern about the forecast for snow — the kind the skiers love. It was imperative for us to get out ahead of the storm so we wouldn't have to deal with it all the way across the country.

After breakfast, we headed east. It was already snowing in the mountains where Margaret had been just the day before. We made 500 miles each day for the next four, reaching Cadillac, Mich. on day five. Unable to find a motel, we climbed back into the Lincoln and continued on to Hill Island, arriving at midnight. What a trip! We had covered more than 4000 miles in just two weeks. It was wonderful, but unfortunately it was one of the last times we saw Max; he died of cancer ten years later. I mourned his passing, along with Darlene and her family. We all loved and admired Max for the special man he was.

The winter of '97 and '98 was a quiet time, and the first time in years that I was not engaged in engine work. We returned to Hill Island for the summer of '98, just in time for the Fourth of July parade.

The Boat Show was now only a few weeks away, and we prepared for company to arrive. We knew the Olsens were coming, as well as

Tim and Sylvia Lyman and their children. Also, the Berrys would be there in full strength, so we planned to have quite a gathering in mid-August.

There were nine people on board *RAMAR* for the traditional Marquette Island breakfast, and it turned out to be our last. The weather was foggy on the way over, but improved for the ride back. By Monday morning everyone had gone, and our life was mundane again.

August 12, 1998: Goodbye to Our Little Brown Friend, Gretchen

Jerry Dutcher and I were reviewing proposed work at Hill Island when Margaret rushed out of the house, screaming that Gretchen had fallen down the spiral stairs in the living room. Margaret was crying when I came into the house. She said she couldn't bear to go downstairs, where Gretchen had struck the cement floor. I found her standing but immobile. She was wailing in pain, and when I picked her up she cried even louder. It was obvious she was seriously hurt, and I could feel tears welling up in my eyes as well.

I suggested we call our veterinarian in Pickford at once. After making sure he was in, we were on our way. I held Gretchen all the way there, trying to comfort her, but was not very successful. I carried her into the examining room, where the doctor began a thorough evaluation of her injuries. When we arrived, we were asked to sign a euthanasia permission form, so I was somewhat prepared for what was ahead.

The doctor was sympathetic, but focused on Gretchen's advanced age and failing health, both physically and mentally. Even before the accident, she had been weak, and we had to carry her outside for her toilet. In short, he felt it was time to say goodbye. I couldn't bear it any longer, and left the office for our car.

When we got to the car I told Margaret flat out that I could not go back inside, and she agreed that I should stay. Margaret went back in and stayed with Gretchen until it was over. The doctor's staff took care of the cremation and other details. We simply drove away, petless, for the first time in 16 years.

Any pet owner would sympathize with the adjustments we faced. It may explain some of the erratic decisions we made in the months ahead. I really don't know. What I did realize was that our life was just a little different after August 12, 1998. I do not mean that in an entirely negative sense, just "different." On the positive side, we now had options for doing things and going places previously denied us.

Boats, Meets and Trips

Once Labor Day weekend arrived, the boating season was over for us. I decided it was time to put the boat in lay-up, and afterward we returned to Bethlehem. The date for the big antique car show at Hershey was approaching, and Margaret decided to enter her old '65 Pontiac convertible for judging, vying for the First Junior award. I didn't think she had a chance, because there were point deductions all over the car. Basically, it was an untouched original, with the underside cleaned up a little. Margaret and I drove to the meet with Bob Berry and a friend. She was in luck; it had rained, and consequently the show field was quite wet.

Margaret's judging card clearly indicated the car was owned and had been entered by a female entrant. Sometimes that could be a good thing, sometimes not. Water was standing on the car, and the judging crew didn't seem anxious to spend much time on it, so the car's underside received what we called a "one knee down" look. Margaret was fortunate indeed.

Tim Lyman always attended Hershey, and we frequently saw lots of familiar faces; we even ran into Bob Heston and his son, Bobby Jr. By three o'clock they began releasing cars from the show field, so there was always a massive traffic jam that affected the surrounding area. For that reason some people delayed their departure, preferring to wait for the congestion to ease up. I asked Jim Rossetti to pick up our trophy if Margaret won, and we then packed up and drove home.

Believe it or not, Margaret did win First Junior with the Pontiac. Maybe there was something to the myth that women got special treatment at Hershey.

Chapter 23

Goodbye Hill Island
1998-2000

Earl Derion

I received word from Tom that Earl Derion had died. He had suffered a debilitating stroke a few years earlier that had confined him to a nursing home. Earl went back to the very roots of my flying. He had been central to everything I did aviation-wise in Erie for so many years. I keenly felt the loss. It was difficult saying goodbye to my old friend.

1999: The Last Year of the Decade — The Last Year of a Millennium

We enjoyed a quiet winter in Bethlehem, with minimum snow. We received an invitation to visit the Kanes in New Port Richey, and we agreed to come in early March.

I still liked the Lincoln Town Car for long trips, even though by that time it was showing its age. Also on the agenda for our Winston-Salem stop was buying a few more pieces of furniture for the living room.

We left March 1, arriving at the Hestons' just in time for supper. The next day, after we did some shopping we continued our journey to Savannah, Ga., where I had always wanted to visit the Eighth Air Force Museum. We arrived with just enough time for the tour.

The following day, we drove straight through to New Port Richey. It was during our visit there that we began discussing the possibility of selling Hill Island. John Michaels, our next-door neighbor, had been bugging me for some time: "Ray, if you would ever consider selling, please let me have first chance."

Leaving Hill Island

Did we really want to stay on Hill Island? What about the boat? We'd been using it less and less; on and on went the discussion. With John we might have a ready buyer and not have to pay a realty commission. I knew lakefront property prices had been steadily rising, but how much? What price would we ask, if we did indeed decide to sell? Margaret and I had never discussed selling Hill Island — should we call John Michaels, just to see what he might offer? We did contact him, and John replied, "What would you say to $199,900?" I didn't have a specific figure in mind, but I knew it wasn't that high. "Let me call you back, John. Margaret and I will discuss it."

That we did, back and forth, even though we knew it was unwise to broach the subject at all *in absentia*. Then I said, "Let's call John Griffin; we can count on him for some sound advice." John didn't provide anything, and was miffed at being bypassed. He wasn't really concerned about what was good for us at all. The conversation ended on an advisory note: "If you are truly motivated to sell, you might want to give serious consideration to John Michaels's offer."

Instead of calling Smith & Griffin, I should have consulted our close friend, Tilia Beukema. Til knew more about the Island real estate market than anyone in town. For some reason, it never occurred to me to call her. After thoughtful consideration, we decided to accept John Michaels's offer of $199,900. There was nothing in writing, but I gave John my word.

John kept pressuring us to close: "Take as much time as you need to vacate," he kept saying. Since he had nothing in writing, he was afraid we would back out of the deal.

Our decision to sell Hill Island sent us scampering back north — so much for our Florida vacation. John Michaels kept pushing us to close, and yet I still didn't get it. Even if I did, it was too late. (We later realized that the selling price was too low; we could have easily realized $250,000.)

Moving out of Hill Island was not easy due to our accumulation of stuff over the years. Some household furnishings went to John

Michaels, and the remainder was either disposed of or sent to Pennsylvania.

At the closing in mid-May, we walked away with $150,000 in cash. It was a sad day, as it always was, and yet we kept doing it. At least I don't recall Margaret breaking out in tears.

Much of the magic that brought us there in the first place was gone, so it was probably best to move on. It was not our intention to discontinue our visits to Les Cheneaux; we would just revert back to camping in the RV park, as we had done 10 years earlier. You can never really go back, though, as we soon discovered. Fortunately, we were able to rent a trailer for the summer, so we parked it near the house at first, and moved our clothing in there. We stayed for a few days, but before long, we pulled up stakes and went to the RV park. That was it. Quite suddenly everything had changed, and ten years of effort was obliterated. By the first of June, Hill Island was history.

An Ontario Cruise

During the winter, we made a deposit to Ontario Waterway Cruises for a five-day summer excursion on Canada's inland waterways. We signed up for the western portion terminating at Big Chute near Georgian Bay.

After setting up in the park, it was time to drive to Peterborough in the Lincoln and board the *Kawartha Voyageur*. Crossing the border at Sault Ste. Marie, we retraced the route of our first trailer trip of '88 as far as Manitoulin Island, where we turned south to Baymouth, the northern terminus for the Tobermory ferry. From there, it was a 40-mile boat ride to the Bruce Peninsula and Owen Sound.

The Tobermory ferry was a gigantic ship, and carried all sorts of vehicles. I can't imagine what the fare would have been for an RV. It was a perfect day, and much of the crossing was over open water, out of sight of land. Once we docked at the southern terminus, it was just another car ride. We spent one night at Owen Sound, and the next day drove to Peterborough, where the *Kawartha Voyageur* was docked. Everything was very relaxed, and we were welcomed aboard.

The cruise ended at Big Chute, where a bus returned us to Peterborough. The cruise encompassed 150 miles of waterway, including 22 locks. Often we would be in canals or rivers; other times we were out on the open water of Lake Simcoe or many smaller lakes along the way. It was a relaxing vacation, and something totally different from anything we had previously done. We were looking forward to next year's cruise with Rich and Jane. It would be more fun traveling with another couple.

She was not much to look at, but the *Kawartha Voyageur* was comfortable. We frequently sat out in the prow where the people are standing.

Reflections

At the end of the cruise, instead of driving back to Cedarville, we returned to Bethlehem. It had been such a whirlwind pace the past two months; we needed the comforts of home to catch our breath. During the cruise we had tried not to dwell on Hill Island.

That intermission in Bethlehem gave us time to reflect on the ways our lives had changed. With respect to Michigan, a vacation home on wheels would give us much more freedom of action. We were no longer obligated to go to Cedarville every year; we now had flexibility. In the meantime, we planned to spend the winter at home in Pennsylvania.

After the Fourth of July, we drove the Lincoln back to Cedarville and resumed trailer living at the park. The Koenigs came for a week.

The pace was slow and relaxing, and we visited DeTour Village quite often. Another diversion was dinner at the Freighters Restaurant in Sault Ste. Marie with Bob and Colleen. The cuisine was excellent, and the dining room looked out on ore boats transiting the waterway. It was a very special place.

We attended the Boat Show as usual, but there was no breakfast at the yacht club. *RAMAR* was up on blocks at Cedarville Marine, its future uncertain. With the sale of our dock, owning *RAMAR* no longer made sense. Before heading home, I posted a "For Sale" ad on Mertaugh's bulletin board, with a picture of *RAMAR* and instructions to contact Jason Bohn at Cedarville Marine.

After the Boat Show, we vacated our rented trailer and returned to Bethlehem. We left behind just one thread of our life in Michigan: a Chris-Craft named *RAMAR*.

Nancy Ann Taylor Phillips (1927-2000): Margaret's Older Sister

Instead of going through Canada as we usually did, we stopped in Erie first and then went on to Tonawanda. Margaret's sister Nancy was fighting terminal colon cancer. Emergency surgery had been only partially successful, as the surgeon was not able to "get it all." We knew what that meant: Nancy's days were numbered. Margaret spent time with her in Tonawanda, and I drove to Erie for a couple of days to visit Tom Apple and the Michaels.

―――――――

I had just received word from Jason Bohn in Cedarville that a man named Eddie Ernest, from Ohio, was interested in buying *RAMAR*. He said my asking price of $17,900 was ridiculous, but he did offer $15,000. Margaret thought I should accept it, and just let it go.

I called Eddie back and accepted his offer. Launching and delivery was tentatively set for mid-June, at which time I agreed to come to Cedarville to deliver the boat. That was inconvenient, being 1000 miles away, but I really wanted to get rid of it.

Chapter 24

Welcome 2000 and the Winnebago
2000-2003

The Great State of Maine

We desperately needed a change of pace, so we decided on a trip to Springfield, Maine to visit our friends, Helmut and Frances Kaffine, at their cabin on Bottle Island. It took awhile to get ready, but eventually we were on our way. We stopped at Shushan, N.Y., to visit Bert and Joan Van Doren, and rested there for a day or so before driving the rest of the way to Maine. There were no motels in the Springfield area, so we stayed at a bed-and-breakfast Helmut recommended.

Contact with Helmut and Frances on the island was via marine radio, with its base station at Bill Settles' camp on the mainland. There were no utilities of any kind on Bottle Island. Electricity was provided by batteries that had to be charged periodically. Gas for cooking and hot water came from propane. Transportation to and from the island was by outboard motorboat; Helmut enjoyed the isolation.

We were anxious to see their place and, after coordinating with Bill Settles, Helmut arrived by boat to pick us up. On the way to Bottle Island, two loons surfaced just ahead of us. Helmut cut the engine, and we just sat there observing them. It was a real treat to see them that close. When we got to the island, Frances greeted us and helped tie up the boat.

Helmut kept busy with projects to improve their life on the island. While we were there, he was repairing the deck used for the guest

426

tent, and on the way to the sawmill to pick up some deck planking, Helmut told many stories of transporting challenging loads in his small boat. Large and heavy items were transported over the ice during winter. We succeeded in getting our load of wood to the island, and I helped install the planking. Helmut had plans to build an outside shower, and to install solar panels on the roof to charge the batteries.

On the way back from the sawmill, we went to the top of Bowers Mountain for an excellent view of the lake country. Frances prepared dinner, and then we returned to our car parked at the Settles camp. It was a special day, filled with memories that endure to this day.

Helmut Kaffine took this photo of Margaret and me during our first visit to Bottle Island, Maine.

The following day, when we got to the Settles camp, we received good news. Bill had offered to take us for a ride in his pontoon boat to Junior Lake. Junior was a much larger lake accessible via a narrow, winding channel. The two-hour ride was very scenic, although it was somewhat difficult to navigate the shallow waterway between the two lakes. After supper, it was time to say goodbye, and we returned to the B&B.

We wanted to include the Maine coast on our trip, so we headed for Eastport, Maine, the most easterly point of the U.S. We spent an extra day touring the Roosevelt summer home at Campobello. Even though Campobello Island is part of Canada, there were no issues with Customs because the only way off the island was to return to Maine.

Margaret loved lighthouses, so we never missed an opportunity to visit those we encountered in our travels. After we left Eastport going south on Route 1, we followed the coast most of the way to New Hampshire. There were several lighthouses along that route, including our favorite at Cape Elizabeth, aptly named "Portland Head." Everyone visits that one.

Eventually, we found ourselves back on I-95. For the return trip, we joined the Mass Pike to New York and Connecticut. Margaret and I traveled much farther than planned, arriving home a day early. It was a marvelous trip, and the first summer in over ten years in which we did not go to Michigan.

Motor Home Time

Our friends, Butch and Dee Stevens, had just bought a motor home. It was a leftover 1999, 33-foot Forest River "Windsong" that was for sale at the Allentown RV show. Surprisingly, it had a living room/dining room slide-out. (Yes, slide-outs had finally come to the motor home world.) Butch invited us out for a ride, and we never thought it would progress beyond that. As it turned out, though, the Windsong was not exactly their motor home of choice; their sights were set on an even larger and more expensive unit, a Monaco diesel pusher.

"Diesel pusher" simply meant the motor home was powered by a diesel engine that was mounted in the rear of the coach, instead of the engine's customary location up front. With respect to noise, that configuration produced an extremely quiet ride. In fact, they had already purchased the Monaco and needed to sell the Windsong. Were we interested?

Margaret and I hadn't considered another RV, least of all a motor home. Maybe it *was* time to try something new. Thinking about it from the perspective of potential ownership, we examined the Windsong again. But wait, there was a snag. With a motor home you needed a "toad" (towed vehicle), a small car to hitch behind the coach so you had transportation when the motor home was hooked up in a campground. It was very inconvenient to unhook utilities just to go shopping.

This was our first motor home, which we purchased from our friends, Butch and Dee Stevens. We only owned it for a year or so — it was not entirely satisfactory.

Of the small cars available, many were not suitable for that role. You needed one with the capability of disconnecting the drive train from the transmission, and those were few in number. The one I selected was a Chevy Tracker, a derivative of a Suzuki SUV. The Tracker was equipped with a transfer case; when the selector handle was positioned in neutral, it disconnected the drive train from everything else, including the speedometer. You didn't want the toad racking up miles while you drove your motor home down the road. Buying the Windsong brought us into an entirely RV lifestyle.

2001: The Year of the Windsong

By early April, we were anxious for our first trip in the Windsong. Driving a large Class A motor home was not akin to pulling a trailer. The driver sat up high with a panoramic view. Reliance on mirrors was necessary to determine what was going on around you.

Overall, the move was a positive one, and we felt safer. For my checkout, Butch and I took a 20-minute drive down Route 29. "You'll get the hang of it," he said.

Our first outing involved the four of us. Butch and Dee were in their Monaco, and we drove the Windsong. We camped at a park west of Allentown, where they had based their unit after returning from Florida. It was an excellent opportunity to check out all the systems before starting out on a long trip.

Motor homes were equipped with onboard leveling jacks, something not found on trailers. While sitting in the driver's seat, you were able to raise and lower all four corners of the coach to make it perfectly level. The refrigerator was quite sensitive in that regard. We only camped for one night, but we had fun with our new toys.

The First Windsong Excursion

After that, we were ready for a trip to North Carolina to visit the Hestons. Everything went fine until I pulled into a rest area for lunch near Roanoke, Va., and discovered a soft tire on the right-side inboard wheel. Being near Roanoke, I decided to drive carefully to a truck service station there. With a motor home, it was a good idea to find "big rig" service facilities. The tire was ruined from being run underinflated.

Unable to locate the correct tire, we used our spare. It was dark by the time we arrived at Tanglewood Park, where we had previously stayed, only to discover it was closed — so we spent the night at a nearby Walmart. We didn't find that very satisfactory, as bright lights burned all night and cleaning machines roamed the lot before daybreak. However, we were very tired and just wanted to get off the road. The nearest suitable park was west of us, almost to Statesville, which meant a 30-minute drive each way in our Chevy Tracker. We sure missed Tanglewood.

That was our first excursion in the Windsong, and it had other issues, mostly relating to the suspension. The Ford chassis was just a bit inadequate for the 33-foot coach.

Our primary destination for the summer was Cedarville for a three-week stay. Having missed the previous summer, we were anxious to camp out on the "Point" again. We sent a deposit for site #27, but this time the parking would be different. Because we were in a motor home, we would face the water instead of backing in. The view of the channel out our front windshield was spectacular. Motor homes came with a curtain to cover the windshield, but since we only had the waterway in front of us, privacy was not an issue. Sometimes we just left the curtain open to let the moonlight shine in.

Much of our time there was spent visiting the Berry Patch and other friends in the area. While there, we drove past our house but weren't inclined to stop in. We frequented DeTour Village, and the Freighters Restaurant in Sault Ste. Marie as well.

The vacation soon came to a close, and we headed home. Our overall assessment of motor home living, compared to the trailers we had owned, was a positive one. The motor home was better, but mainly because it had a slide-out. Those were definitely a game changer for the RV industry.

We made a few other short trips in the fall, and soon it was time to consider our options for winter layup. I mentioned to Butch my previous satisfaction with Cherryville Storage. Early in November, we took both units there, and parked one behind the other.

Once we bought the Windsong, we were anxious to join Phyllis and Forest Koenig in Arizona for the winter. They had found a really nice RV park on the outskirts of Tucson.

2002

Christmas in Bethlehem, with the extensive light displays all over town, was always a treat. It may have been a bit somber with the knowledge that we faced another snowy winter up north, but hopefully we might get a break.

During Margaret's last physical exam, the CBC (blood count) had indicated that she had way too many WBCs (white blood cells). At the time her doctor was not concerned, as a host of factors could be responsible. However, he recommended an appointment with a hematology specialist to look into it further.

Spring arrived, and Butch and I took our motor homes out of storage at Cherryville. Our next trip was to attend my 55th high school class reunion in Erie at the end of July. Arriving in Erie, we stayed at the KOA campground just off I-90. I visited Tom Apple and the Michaels, as well as making our customary trip around the peninsula. We had a nice time, but it was announced that this would be the final reunion for the class of 1947.

———

Word arrived from my niece Janet, in Chicago, that they were coming east on vacation. It was a camping trip at a place called Confluence, near Pittsburgh, and she wondered if we would like to join them for a tour of Frank Lloyd Wright's Fallingwater. That sounded interesting, so Margaret and I dragged out our Pennsylvania maps. We were familiar with Wright's architecture, and Margaret especially had always wanted to see Fallingwater, so the invitation was most welcome.

After considerable searching, we found Confluence and noted that the nearby Keystone State Park offered camping by reservation. The whole program sounded great, so we wrote Janet to confirm the dates, and made our reservations. On arrival, after getting set up, we called to let her know where we were, and then she, and her husband Michael and son James, came to our campsite. We hadn't seen each other since they were married in the late '70s. We went out to dinner together and made plans for our visit to Fallingwater the following day.

It was only a half-hour drive, and we joined a group already touring the property. Water flowed right through the house. It was a memorable visit to an architectural wonder. After another great dinner together, we said our goodbyes and returned to the Windsong.

Motor Home Storage: Birth of the Pole Shack

Butch and I had been notified that our space at Cherryville Storage would no longer be available for winter motor home storage. As it was virtually impossible to rent reasonably priced storage for motor homes, Butch Stevens and I discussed the possibility of putting up our own building. We were even discussing buying land when Rob Stevens (Butch's son) offered to let me build on their property. My original plan called for a 40'x40' structure with sufficient height to accommodate 12' overhead doors. That would create sufficient space for three motor homes. I intended to use one of the spots and rent the other two.

Pioneer Metal Buildings, located 40 miles west of Allentown, came highly recommended by the pole-building fraternity, and a phone call brought a sales representative in short order. They were running a special on their 40'x60' unit that was almost the same price; it was like getting 800 square feet free. I opted for the "special deal" at the end of September, and the building permit was issued shortly after.

As Rob prepared the site, it became apparent how wet it was; the whole area was a network of springs that percolated down the nearby hillside.

The building package arrived on two tractor-trailers, and once the crew started working, the site turned into a sea of mud. An auger was used to bore holes for the treated poles that supported the building. I was amazed at how they could place those poles with accuracy in all that mud. The mucky conditions didn't seem to bother the crew, and it only took one day and part of the next to erect it. It looked great, until you got up close. We dug a drainage trench and placed a pipe that led to the creek, fifty feet away. Then we began bringing in stone by the truckload to stabilize the ground where we planned to park motor homes.

Eventually we won, but the site stayed moist; it was much too damp to consider storing vehicles over the winter. The only solution was to pour a concrete floor — an expensive solution, to be sure. However, the concrete slab had to wait for spring's warmer and drier weather. With the stone down, the ground was stable enough to bring the Windsong in temporarily. At least it would be inside, and out of the weather.

The Last RV

Margaret noticed an ad in the paper for Winnebago motor homes on sale in Easton, so we decided to check them out. We were impressed with their superior quality compared to the Windsong. The 35-foot Adventurer model we were looking at came with two slide-outs and a rear-view camera. That was a miniature TV camera, mounted up high at the rear of the coach, that monitored the tow-car status as well as traffic coming from behind. It was a wonderful device, and I wanted one.

The Adventurer's chassis was a notable improvement over the Windsong's. Rated at 22,000 pounds, it had adequate reserve capacity.

Built by a company called Workhorse, the chassis incorporated many desirable features including 22-inch tires, a 500-cubic-inch engine, and a six-speed Allison transmission. The Winnebago truly had it all; the inside appointments were luxurious and tasteful in all respects. It came with two slide-outs, one in the living room and the other in the bedroom. The Adventurer had just arrived at All Seasons RV in Easton a few days before, and the plastic sheeting protecting the carpeting was still in place.

"Would you like to try it out?" the salesman asked.

"Yes, that would be great." He warned us that it was windy for a test drive, and that we might be adversely affected. We ventured out on Route 33 and headed north towards Stroudsburg. I drove out a few miles, and Margaret drove it back. Since taking a motor home driving course in Florida, Margaret was frequently behind the wheel, and she was an excellent driver. She really liked the Winnie and remarked on how well it handled in the wind.

Margaret had taken a motor home driving course in Florida. She was an excellent driver and often gave me a break from driving duties.

We traded the Windsong in on the Adventurer. The terms were very attractive. Even though the Winnebago listed for over $120,000, we were able to drive it home for less than $50,000 cash. We never dreamed we could be the owners of such a beautiful motor home.

This photo of our new Winnebago was taken at the Berry Patch in 2003. Note TV antenna on the roof.

Margaret and I were floating on air as we drove the new Winnebago to the pole barn. The four overhead doors had been installed only days earlier. We expected a big snowstorm, but "Winnie" was snug as a bug in a rug.

When Butch and Dee saw us drive in, and we told them about our pleasant buying experience, they were off to Easton. Within a week they traded their unit in on a 33-foot Adventurer as well.

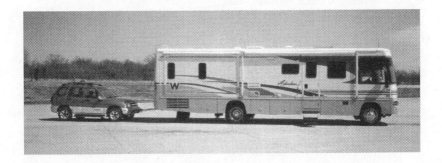

This view shows the extreme length of our rig as we cruised down the highway — well over fifty feet.

435

That was the major excitement for 2002, and it came at the very end of the year. Naturally, we were focused on our new toy, and already making travel plans for the New Year.

2003: New Horizons and Winnebago Travel Plans

Beginning with the snowstorm at the time we bought the Winnie, it had been a fearsome winter with extremely cold temperatures affecting not only our area, but reaching all the way to the Gulf States. Dee Stevens suggested a trip to Summerland Key, Florida, with our new Winnebagos. Of course, our units were winterized, and we would leave them that way until we were far enough south to avoid frozen water lines.

The temperature was in the low teens the morning we left, and I wondered if Winnie would start. It did, but I got a red warning light that stayed on for quite some time. The motor home's computer was fickle (you never knew exactly what was going on with it unless you plugged in a system analyzer), but eventually the warning light went out. We drove east of the Appalachians to reach moderate temperatures in the shortest time possible. In that expectation we were only partially successful; it was barely above freezing when we reached a campground in southern Virginia at the end of the first day.

We were really enjoying our first trip in the new motor home — it was such a pleasure to drive. Instead of a motel, we wanted to stay in the Winnebago that first night out. We managed without our onboard plumbing system by using bottled water and antifreeze for the toilet; the furnace worked fine.

We had no idea where Butch and Dee were — our first contact point was the KOA Kampground in Florence, S.C. When we arrived there, I checked at the desk, but there was no word from them. Since we arrived in mid-afternoon, I had time to activate Winnie's onboard water system, enabling it to function normally. As long as normal temperature was maintained in the coach, freeze-up of the water system was unlikely as long as the inlet hose was disconnected and drained overnight.

After supper, a park attendant stopped by with a message that Butch and Dee were on their way and planned to arrive later that evening. They had left home that very morning, and driven straight through in one day. Spending excessively long days on the road was not our style, so there was no way we could convoy together. When they arrived, they parked a few sites down from us and we discussed our plans for the morrow.

As it turned out, we weren't far enough south yet. Six inches of snow fell overnight, which was unheard of in South Carolina. Margaret and I stayed over an extra day to avoid driving through salt on the highway, but our friends left in spite of the snow. We were separated once more; they were anxious to reach Florida as soon as possible, and our next contact point was St. Augustine.

The following morning we left Florence for points south. When we reached the Jacksonville area, we placed a call to the KOA in St. Augustine. Butch and Dee were already there and encouraged us to join them. It was already late afternoon, but since it was only another 200 miles we continued the rest of the way. We could scarcely wait to cross the Florida border into the Sunshine State.

On arrival at the KOA, Butch was busy removing salt from both the motor home and his towed vehicle. The high temperature for St. Augustine was only in the 50s, so it was indeed a cold January.

We stayed over an extra day for sightseeing, but we were anxious to press onward to the Keys. The next night we camped west of Miami, and the following day we reached our destination at Summerland Key, just west of the seven-mile bridge. The weather was finally perfect, sunny and warm. Only essential goods were available at Summerland; for any serious shopping, we needed to continue on to Key West.

We did just that on a number of occasions. We enjoyed the fabulous sunsets at the pier and had fun shopping at all the tourist traps in town. It was a very relaxing week, but all too soon it was time to start back.

On our way north, it was showtime for the Adventurer at the Hestons' in North Carolina. By the time we put Winnie back in the pole barn at Emmaus, the weather had moderated and spring was not far away.

With the arrival of temperate weather, I was anxious to pour the concrete floor in the pole barn. It was perpetually damp in there, and nothing but a concrete floor was going to fix it.

George Fegley, a friend of Rob Stevens, poured the slab. To this day, that floor has never developed a crack. We also installed gutters, and with those improvements the pole building was finally complete.

We considered going to Cedarville again, but an invitation from Helmut and Frances Kaffine to visit them again at Bottle Island, Maine, changed our minds. They offered us a parking spot at the church in Springfield, provided we didn't stay over the weekend.

On August 10, we left for Maine. As before, we stopped at Shushan to visit Bert and Joan Van Doren for a day or so. We overnighted at Bangor and drove on to Springfield the next day. Everything went like clockwork at the church; we were even able to plug into the building for electric service. We always had a good time there, enjoying our boat rides to and from Bottle Island. Helmut had installed the new outdoor shower, and the solar panels on the roof kept the batteries charged.

Chapter 25

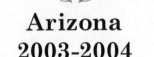

Arizona
2003-2004

Margaret's Diagnosis

Somehow Margaret bumped her elbow, and shortly after that her entire arm suddenly turned black and blue from subcutaneous bleeding. I suggested she see Dr. Martin immediately. He wasn't in, so another physician examined her. Although no specific cause for the hemorrhage was evident, they drew blood for a CBC (complete blood count). The hematoma gradually receded, and Margaret heard nothing more from Nazareth Family Practice.

A month later, Margaret had an appointment with Dr. Martin for something totally unrelated, and while examining her record he noted that she had an extremely low platelet count, as reported on the CBC from her previous visit. She also still exhibited the high white blood cell count noted earlier.

Since a finding of 40-50,000 platelets was well below the normal range, someone had erred by not bringing it to Dr. Martin's attention. Like many doctors, he did not exhibit any outward alarm. He examined Margaret's arm, which had been the focus of her previous visit, and noted that it had returned to normal. In view of the abnormal findings, Dr. Martin recommended that Margaret schedule a visit with Dr. Steven Volk, a hematologist and specialist in abnormalities of the blood, at the earliest opportunity.

Margaret took an immediate liking to Dr. Volk. When she visited his office, she noted that it was not just a doctor's office but a complete laboratory and treatment center for all blood disorders, including leukemia. She expressed concern reading the sign on the door, specifically "Oncology/Hematology." Margaret knew the word "oncology" was a reference to malignant tumors. The doctor attempted to allay her concerns by noting the fact that as yet she had not been diagnosed with anything, and the main purpose of her visit was to determine the cause for her low platelet count.

Prior to seeing Dr. Volk, Margaret had blood drawn for more blood counts and other studies. I always felt concern for her when a blood sample was required. She had the most elusive veins of anyone I ever knew, and we always asked for the most experienced technician to work on her. Being an old lab rat myself, I knew exactly how serious the problem was; but, of course, Dr. Volk's technicians were tops in their field. In a brief discussion, Dr. Volk outlined some of the possible causes for her low platelet count.

He suspected Margaret's spleen might be the culprit, and if so, removing it was not a big deal. You didn't need a spleen to live a normal life. Dr. Volk's surgical associate was right upstairs on the fifth floor. Dr. Thomas performed splenectomies on a regular basis using laparoscopic procedure, but it was much too soon to discuss surgery. Dr. Volk advised Margaret to return for another visit in a month or so, and in the meantime he suggested going about her business in a normal fashion.

As summer gave way to fall and the leaves began dropping, our thoughts drifted toward our plans for the upcoming winter. We had already decided to join Phyllis and Forest Koenig at Cactus Country RV Park in Tucson, Arizona.

Since the Koenigs were spending the holidays with their family in the Niagara Falls area, we also delayed our departure until after Christmas. We placed our reservation with Cactus Country for a New Year's Day arrival. We just prayed the weather would cooperate with our mid-winter departure plans.

Dr. Volk's office scheduled a follow-up appointment for Margaret. We hadn't thought much about our previous visit, since Margaret felt fine, but Dr. Volk didn't pull any punches. Although he had concerns about her persistent high white-cell count, he pointed out that getting her extremely low platelet count under control was most urgent, and he was confident that removing her spleen would restore her platelets to a normal level. He emphasized the urgency to correct her condition by saying, "As it stands now, if you were involved in an auto accident or other trauma, you might bleed to death. We'll start with an infusion of platelets immediately, followed by a splenectomy at the earliest possible date."

It was difficult for Margaret to grasp Dr. Volk's urgency, given the fact that she felt quite normal. However, she knew she could not dismiss his concern. He didn't think the surgery would interfere with our plans for Arizona at the end of the year.

Dr. Thomas also reassured us by declaring that Margaret's prognosis was excellent, in view of her current state of health, and that using the laparoscopic procedure would expedite her recovery.

"Okay, we're convinced — when will it be?" The operation was scheduled for November 4, 2003.

Margaret should have been out of the operating room and into recovery within two hours, but instead it was closer to four. Something went wrong, but what? Customarily, the surgeon came to the waiting room to brief family members on the procedure, but Dr. Thomas did not. When I finally got in to see Margaret later that evening, she was deathly pale — about the same shade as the bed linen. I was alarmed beyond description.

When I finally did get a report from Dr. Thomas concerning the operation, I was blown away. He freely admitted that the spleen had been dropped during its withdrawal, which necessitated opening her abdomen to retrieve it. So now we were dealing with open surgery, with its inherent blood loss as well; what a mess. Even when I accosted him about her deathly pallor, he was reluctant to transfuse her. I begged him to get some blood into Margaret, as I truly feared for her life. Later, I learned her hemoglobin was less than nine, compared to the normal range of 14 to 15.

Thankfully, when I returned to Margaret's room, she was receiving blood, but it was not prescribed by Dr. Thomas. Margaret was truly fortunate that Dr. Volk had stopped by and intervened. She was scheduled to receive three additional units of whole blood, and her color was already improving. Later on I had reason to believe that Dr. Thomas directed his assistant to perform Margaret's surgery, and that is why it was botched.

Margaret was hospitalized for nine days, and she was weak as a kitten. It took months for her to completely recover. Dr. Volk was reluctant to let her travel, but in late December he issued a conditional release with the stipulation that Margaret receive periodic blood tests at a laboratory in Tucson, with reports sent directly to him.

Off to Arizona

We celebrated a quiet Yuletide for '03, with the Christmas-light festivals so unique to the Bethlehem area. By leaving between the Christmas and New Year holidays, we experienced a quiet time to travel. We motor-homed due south to Florida before heading west. Traveling via I-10 added mileage to our 2500-mile journey, but it was worth it to escape the land of ice and snow. Proximity to the Gulf usually precluded accumulation of snow.

In deference to Margaret's weakened condition, we traveled at a leisurely pace. She spent much of the time on the sofa with a blanket, and quite often she was fast asleep when I checked on her. One of the advantages of motor home travel was the convenience of retreating to the living quarters to relax. If we were still in the Starcraft trailer, I would not have attempted the trip.

While driving across much of Louisiana, I-10 was elevated on stilts above miles and miles of endless swampland. We were pleased to see a sign informing us that we had arrived in Texas, but close examination of the mile-marker posts indicated that it was still 850 miles to El Paso. Our drive across Texas brought back memories as we passed near San Antonio, where Margaret and I had landed in *Debbie* 25 years earlier, and Midland, where PG Fellmeth and I had stopped overnight almost 60 years ago.

It took us two more days to reach El Paso and the New Mexico border. The weather remained pleasant crossing the Texas plateau. I noted huge expansion at El Paso; it was no longer just a cow town. More mountains and more deserts finally led to Tucson, and Cactus Country RV Park — just off I-10 at the east end of town. The name for the park was quite appropriate.

Site #184 was reserved for us, right next to the Koenigs. We had finally arrived for a three-month stay. We celebrated the arrival of 2004 a long way from home.

Forest and Phyllis were delighted to see us, being well aware that Margaret had been through some difficult times. They had been uncertain for a while if we would be able to make the trip at all.

Enjoying Tucson

First, we wanted to explore the park. It was very nice, with lots of amenities including a large room adjacent to the office in which the proprietors could hold dinners and other activities for the guests. Our hosts were most cordial, welcoming newcomers like us and making us comfortable in a strange land. Everything was extremely neat and clean. The area we were in allowed guests to have pets, and that was because Phyllis and Forest had a cat. It was a beautiful white Angora that we had met before, during their visits with us at Hill Island.

Everyone was there to have a good time, and many guests had been coming for years. The occupancy rate was high, so there were few empty sites. Forest was anxious to drive us to Mt. Lemmon, northeast of Tucson, nearly 10,000 feet above sea level. On our way to the summit we toured Saguaro National Park, with its distinctive species of cactus.

Other attractions included aviation-related landmarks such as the Davis-Monthan Air Force Base and the Pima Air & Space Museum. Tucson itself was the major attraction, with many drawing cards of its own. There was much to investigate, and plenty of time to absorb it all, so there was no rush.

The weather was superb, with clear, sunlit days and starlit nights. However, it was much colder in the wee hours than we expected, with temperatures frequently falling below freezing. In the morning I often saw Forest lugging a portable propane tank to the fill station. We rented a larger supplemental tank that was exchanged on an as-needed basis by the propane company. It was easy living, with the Koenigs frequently driving into town for breakfast and Margaret and I often accompanying them.

The daily newspaper was delivered each morning, and other services were available as well. Fortunately, Phyllis knew the location of a medical laboratory where Margaret could have her blood tests done.

In case we needed anything for our motor home, there were extensive resources all along I-10, providing parts and service for all makes. In fact, the local dealers for all the major manufacturers, like Winnebago, brought new units to the park for the residents to inspect. Checking out the new models was always a pleasant pastime. Most were motor homes, but occasionally they would bring trailers.

The Koenigs were more interested in trailers, and there was a huge dealer for them as well.

I also checked out the Pima Air & Space Museum, where I ran into Captain Hank Denton, who had been my boss while training on the DC-10. He welcomed me as an old comrade. Hank suffered from Parkinson's disease and would soon have to give up driving. I also met another one of our retired pilots from the Cleveland domicile, now living in Green Valley. Both acted as docents for the museum, conducting tours there.

Special dinners were served in the main dining room — that space was also used by sales reps for motor homes, and for raffles and other promotions. These events were also a good way to meet other residents living in the park. Often Cactus Country hosted ice cream socials in the afternoon — always a big hit.

We were able to have Margaret's blood work done as required, but we didn't know the results because they were forwarded directly to Dr. Volk in Bethlehem. She seemed fine, gaining strength each day. She and Phyllis regularly attended a "Curves" exercise class, and that was also helpful. Sometimes she would accompany me to the camp exercise room to use the treadmill or ride the bike.

Our lease was up March 15, and that date was rapidly approaching. Before leaving, we learned of a change in the camp's policy concerning pets. Effective for the 2005 season, guests with cats would be permitted to occupy sites at the front of the park, as well as some of the more desirable spots along the edge of the desert. I think they agreed to this change for the simple reason that cats don't bark, and they stay indoors much of the time. We reserved sites eight and nine.

Our route home was somewhat different. This time we followed I-10 into New Mexico, where we turned sharply north to Albuquerque and then headed east on I-40 to Amarillo and Oklahoma City. We made it to ABQ the first day, and the descent to the Texas/Oklahoma plain the next day was very dramatic; it was one long downhill run of 6000 feet. From there, our route was primarily easterly to Little Rock, then east on I-40 to Memphis, Nashville and Knoxville. Then we picked up I-81 all the way to Pennsylvania. The mileage was still approximately 2500 miles.

Leukemia

Although Dr. Volk indicated he wanted to see Margaret as soon as we returned, there was nothing in his letter denoting urgency. We were aware Margaret had problems with her blood, but even so, we weren't prepared for what he was about to tell us. He began, "First, let me give you the good news: the removal of the spleen has largely corrected your low platelet count. It varies somewhat, but I no longer have a problem with that. Now it's your high white-cell count [leukocytosis] that concerns me. We need to do a lumbar puncture [spinal tap] and analyze your spinal fluid."

A spinal tap was no everyday procedure, so something was definitely afoot. Dr. Volk continued, "Your persistently high white count is worrisome, and requires further study. It's been creeping up ever since I first saw you."

He had Margaret undress and don a hospital gown and then return to the waiting room until she was called. During the procedure, Dr. Volk had trouble accomplishing the tap. He said he encountered such masses of packed white blood cells that he had trouble withdrawing a clear fluid sample. He submitted some of these packed cells to the technician for microscopic examination, and they were primarily monocytes.

There are several types of white blood cells in the bloodstream. The majority normally are lymphocytes and neutrophils with a smattering of others, including the monocytes that Dr. Volk found in such abundance, as well as eosinophils and others. Not only was he finding monocytes in great quantities, but further study identified a proliferation of blast cells straight from the bone marrow.

After the spinal tap, we were in the waiting room for quite some time before Dr. Volk returned. "I'm sorry to keep you waiting so long; I know you must be anxious, but I wanted to confirm my diagnosis. Although you have leukemia, it can be treated with chemotherapy."

Leukemia — one of the most dreaded of all diseases and, until recently, a fatal one. But wait — let's hear Dr. Volk out first. The full description for Margaret's diagnosis was CMML: chronic myelomonocytic leukemia. It sounds like a mouthful, but broken down it simply meant that her disease was chronic as opposed to acute (which would be a virtual death sentence); myelo (consisting of early marrow-produced blast cells); and monocytic (describing the type of white blood cells involved); and, of course, we all know that leukemia is essentially cancer of the blood.

Dr. Volk continued, "Your WBC count is fast approaching 80,000. We must reduce that as soon as possible, because of the packing nature of the large monocytes. In sufficient quantity, they could clog minute arteries in the brain, causing a stroke. I don't want to alarm you, but I must stress the need to begin your chemotherapy immediately."

From that day on, Margaret was no stranger to the oncology/hematology office of Dr. Steven Volk. The frequency of her visits was on the order of once or twice a month, and she took oral chemotherapy for the rest of her life. Dr. Volk assured Margaret that she could live a normal life with leukemia, provided it was managed properly.

Margaret's life was changed forever. In addition to managing her ileostomy, she now had another cross to bear — sobering, to say the least. During the summer of '04, she was able to reverse the trend, and her blood parameters began moving in a more positive direction. None of the treatment caused Margaret to feel any better; she had always felt fine, even while the disease was running rampant.

In early August, we attended the last Capital Airlines Picnic under the bridge at Jones Point in D.C. Since it was the last, there was an exceptionally large turnout. It was sad, but the organization just couldn't keep going. Everyone seemed to realize we were seeing one another for the last time. I was outliving our reunions — first the high school event in Erie, and now the Capital reunion as well.

Chapter 26

An Anniversary —
Our Last Good Year
2005-2009

Most of the remainder of '04 was spent quietly at home in Bethlehem, and Winnie was little used. Being away for extended periods of time was just not feasible with so many visits to Dr. Volk's clinic; besides, Margaret was not anxious to go anywhere. It was encouraging to see that her blood count was stabilizing; however, discussion concerning spending the next winter in Arizona did not seem to be reaching a favorable conclusion — after giving it a long, hard look, we decided to cancel the trip. We called our friends, the Koenigs, with our decision, and Forest called back shortly after to announce that they also had decided not to trailer to Cactus Country.

Since Forest and Phyllis Koenig were not planning to go to Arizona either, we decided to squeeze in an autumn trip to the Buffalo/Niagara Falls area to visit with them there. Even so, we spent the bulk of our time with Nancy's children, who were still living in the Tonawanda area. That was our last trip in Winnie for '04. Margaret continued to be monitored quite closely at Dr. Volk's clinic. We observed Thanksgiving and Christmas in Bethlehem — it was nice just to be home for a change, and count our blessings.

2005: Our Fiftieth Anniversary

Medical issues seemed to be ganging up on Margaret, and I wondered how much longer we would be able to continue the RV lifestyle. Margaret had recently become quite hard of hearing, and she seemed reluctant to do anything about it. By March of '05 I was repeating myself with increasing regularity, and I finally convinced her to schedule an appointment with Dr. Greenspan, an ENT physician who shared his office with an audiologist.

She certainly did need hearing aids, and was fitted up for them. Her hearing loss compromised our communication for the remainder of her life. Her decline in so many different areas was beginning to take its toll, and Margaret used phrases like, "I'm falling apart."

I bought Margaret a sapphire ring for her birthday on May 26, and immediately following that, we celebrated our 50th wedding anniversary. Since it didn't appear that the family was planning a celebration of any kind, I took the bull by the horns and made arrangements myself. The festivities began with me giving Margaret a gold watch.

The logical place for the party was in the Buffalo area, home for most of the remaining family. We selected a Greek restaurant on Niagara Falls Boulevard that was easy to find, and sent out about 30 invitations. Some were out-of-town guests, including Margaret's sister Jane, Gene and Jane Olsen, OV and Mary Pezzi, and a few people from Erie as well. It turned out fine, and everyone had a good time. We arrived in our Winnebago and camped at our usual spot in Niagara Falls. In retrospect, it is amazing how many of those who attended are no longer with us, specifically Ray Phillips (sister Nancy's husband) and the Koenigs.

After that, we made a rather hasty decision to pack up the Winnie and drive to Cedarville for a couple of weeks, just to relax and visit friends.

We decided to return to Cactus Country, in Tucson, this time for Christmas. The trip out would be tough, but once we got there it would be fun, as we had heard that Christmas was special in the park.

The weather in early December was terrible, and we wondered if we would be able to start out. We finally did, but there was snow on the ground, with more predicted. We decided to visit the Hestons in Winston-Salem, and then proceed through the mountains of North Carolina to pick up I-20 across Tennessee to Memphis and Little Rock. From there, we stayed on I-20 all the way to the junction of

I-10, and the remainder of the trip duplicated our first trip. A day or so later, we pulled into Cactus Country RV Park. This time, our arrival was like old-home week. Even though we had skipped the previous season, everyone welcomed us back. Forest and Phyllis said they were received enthusiastically, as well.

It was the week before Christmas, and our new parking spot at site #8 was a vast improvement. Immediately behind us was the open desert that had a rather mystical look. It was nice being back, and we enjoyed being there. As before, Margaret had to make periodic trips to the lab downtown for blood tests.

We brought our little RV Christmas tree with us, along with a few other decorations. The park was festive, and we were looking forward to the much-touted Cactus Country Christmas dinner. It was an enjoyable way to end a year dominated by Margaret's health issues, but the New Year was to have its own issues.

2006

Much of our time that winter was spent on joint activities with Forest and Phyllis, including eating out, shopping, or just being together in the park. Frankly, by early February I was bored, and I convinced Margaret to let me fly home for a two-week break. By the time I returned, our Tucson visit was winding down, and at the end of March we left for Bethlehem.

Arriving home, we discussed how to spend the upcoming summer. We decided against returning to Cedarville because it just seemed too far, and we were uncertain about a trip to Maine. The things we had liked for so many years had lost much of their appeal. Even our annual trek to Arizona was coming into question, but we decided to make one last trip. There were changes in the wind, and Margaret's difficulties exacerbated the problem.

We took the Winnie to the Sentimental Journey fly-in at Lock Haven, where they provided an excellent field for us to camp in. Of course, there were no facilities there, so we had to be careful of our water usage. Running the onboard generator was okay during the day, so we kept the batteries charged. We heard the land we were parking on had been sold and would not be available next year.

Margaret enrolled in a physical-fitness program at St. Luke's North. She went for an hour three times per week, and it seemed to be helping her retain her strength. I was so pleased that I enrolled myself in the program a little later on. We attended on a regular basis for the next three years.

Our traveling that summer was limited to what I have outlined so far, plus our usual visits to Erie and Buffalo. During that trip, we stopped to see Forest and Phyllis, discussing our plans for Arizona. It was clear we were all nearing the end of wintering there. We were figuratively running out of steam, and it really didn't have anything to do with Margaret's leukemia — she was remarkably resilient at that time.

Margaret wanted a new car. She was tired of the Camry and had recently asked me to bring the Chevy Tracker home, preferring to use that for her errands. So we started looking at SUVs, and since we liked Toyotas, that meant either the RAV4 or its larger brother, the Highlander. The RAV4 seemed a little small, so she opted for the Highlander, and she wanted the hybrid version. With navigation system and all the goodies it was a bit pricey, in the neighborhood of $38,000. But I thought to myself, "Oh well, if she wants it, why not?" We ordered the '07 Limited model at the end of October.

We left for Arizona after Thanksgiving, but both of us were exhausted by the time we reached Winston-Salem. We needed minor repair on the motor home, so we spent an extra day there. We recognized that it was ill-advised to continue westward, but we went anyway.

We had just arrived at Cactus Country when we received word that Margaret's new Highlander had come in. We were aware that might happen, so I told OV Pezzi to handle the delivery for us and put the new car in our garage.

I stayed through the holidays, but early in January I was on a Continental red-eye flight to Newark, where I boarded a Trans-Bridge bus to the Lehigh Valley. I just had to see Margaret's new Highlander. I didn't return to Tucson immediately, as I should have, and Margaret was fed up with being left alone at Cactus Country. She caught a bad cold due to her lowered resistance, and was miserable. Dr. Volk warned Margaret to avoid exposure, and she insisted that I return to Tucson immediately.

Upon my arrival, we packed up early and returned to Bethlehem, terminating our lease effective February 1. Forest and Phyllis hated to see us go, but I think they understood. That was it — the conclusion of the Arizona chapter of our RV experience.

It was a shame to return early, but we knew in our heart of hearts that we shouldn't have gone in the first place. Margaret was able to see Dr. Volk in early February, so we arrived just in time to enjoy a little Lehigh Valley winter.

Margaret was very excited about her new Toyota Highlander. As we got closer and closer to home, I could tell she was anxious to see it. I had taken an album of pictures to Tucson with me to whet her appetite even more. She finally had a car of her choosing again.

Margaret lost no time resuming our exercise routine at St. Luke's Fitness Center, and we attended Monday, Wednesday, and Friday each week. That program was an excellent regimen for both of us, and I'm sure it helped Margaret to keep active.

Since we were home so early, Margaret decided to fix up the house. She ordered new carpet for the bedrooms, new La-Z-Boy chairs and sofa for the den, and a new mattress for her bed.

We didn't go to Michigan that summer, either, and I'm not quite sure why. Most likely, we were tiring of the RV lifestyle; nothing lasts forever. It was nice just to stay home and relax. Margaret's health in '07 was remarkably good, to the extent that we considered the possibility of a remission.

Hershey, in October, was fun. Bob Berry and I went out as usual to visit with Tim Lyman.

2009: Our Last Good Year Together

2009 began with sadness. Forest Koenig called to say that his wife Phyllis had died suddenly at their home in Wheatfield, N.Y. This was shocking news, because we had thought she was in good health. There would be no more trips to Cactus Country for Forest; he gave their new trailer to a friend in the park.

In August, we took a break and drove to Tonawanda by car to visit family. We stopped at Wheatfield to see Forest Koenig, now living alone after Phyllis's death. He looked lost. We spent about a week there and then returned home.

The New Year started out like so many others, and yet something was different. Margaret tired more easily and was much less active. Even though she still exercised, she became unsteady on her feet, and I feared she might fall, especially on the treadmill. The change was slow and ill-defined — at times she even seemed like her old self.

Unbeknownst to either of us, Margaret was displaying early symptoms of Parkinson's disease. Dr. Martin, our family physician, saw her frequently but was not aware of it either.

In early May, Margaret's sister Jane called from Mansfield to announce the graduation of her grandson, Martin Sexton, from Valley Forge Military Academy. It was on May 15, and she wondered if we would like to join them as they celebrated this special event. "Absolutely," we replied. They planned to come the day before so that we could drive to Valley Forge together.

VFMA was a very prestigious college that prepared students for service in the U.S. Army. The graduation was very impressive, and it was followed by a pinning rite where, by custom, Jane pinned Martin's Second Lieutenant's bars on his jacket. The uniforms were stunning, and the entire ceremony was formal. Martin's father Dale, a Lieutenant Commander in the U.S. Navy, was standing proud in his dress blues by Martin's side.

The graduation was followed by dinner at a local restaurant, and a good time was had by all. The building where the pinning took place was down a fairly steep incline, and Margaret struggled with the climb back up after the ceremony.

For a change of pace, I suggested driving Winnie one last time to Niagara Falls to visit my nephew and niece, Scott and Celia. So far, it hadn't been out of the barn at all that year. Margaret was in favor of the trip, so I called the campground to make our reservation.

I also put through a call to Forest Koenig to alert him of our plans. When I got no answer — not even a recording — I was puzzled. I tried a couple more times the next day or so with the same result.

"Maybe he's away with family," I ventured. Margaret suggested calling his son John in Lockport, N.Y.

I did reach John, who relayed the tragic news that Forest had died at home, suddenly, several months earlier. I was stunned, and blurted out to Margaret, who was standing nearby, "Forest is dead." I didn't press John for details, but he did say that his father had suffered a heart attack and ended up on the kitchen floor, unable to get up. Somehow, he managed to reach the phone to call his neighbor across the street. On arrival, the neighbor could see that Forest was in dire straits and called 911 — but by the time help arrived, Forest was dead.

What a shock—both of our dear friends dead within a year! Just a short time ago, we were enjoying life in Cactus Country; life is short.

We decided to go to Niagara Falls anyway, our last time there together. On arrival at the campground, the proprietors welcomed us enthusiastically. Later on, though, when I was in the office by myself, the receptionist commented on Margaret's frailty and asked about her health. I was struck by this observation, as it confirmed my own assessment of Margaret's condition. Of all the adjectives that might be used to describe my Margaret, "frail" would certainly not be one of them. And yet, during the summer of '09, it was very appropriate.

We stayed more than a week, but I didn't get to Erie to visit Tom, as I customarily did. Margaret didn't want to go, and I preferred not to leave her alone. Also, in a recent phone conversation with John Ropel, I learned that Tom was suffering from Alzheimer's and I didn't know if I could handle that.

John Ropel Gets the Pontiac Convertible

John Ropel seemed determined to buy a '55 Thunderbird in Florida. The price was in the $20,000 range, and I was quite certain he was making a serious mistake. To divert his attention, I offered him Margaret's '65 Pontiac convertible on a conditional-loan basis. Based on an agreement I made with Tom Apple 20 years earlier, John was to inherit the car after Margaret and I died. When Tom returned the convertible to us in '93, I had told John he was next in line.

The car sat dormant in the pole barn for months at a time, without exercise of any kind. We didn't take it to shows anymore, and I toyed with the idea of taking it out of service and pickling it for long-term storage.

I discussed John's Thunderbird fixation with Margaret, and asked her how she felt about turning the Pontiac over to John to use for shows and other classic car events. She didn't really care about it anymore and had no objection.

We stopped in a rest area on I-80 and I took this photo of the
'65 Pontiac on the way to Erie.

John jumped at the offer; the problem was how to get the car to Erie. I rejected his suggestion of driving it there for a number of reasons, with its aged tires being my chief concern. I rented a U-Haul trailer in mid-July and trailered it to Erie behind my Ford truck. Chet Cline accompanied me on the trip. We arrived in Erie without any problem, and John and his wife Dianne were delighted with the car. John loves the convertible and, fortunately, it got him over his T-Bird fever.

Thomas P. Apple (1924-2009)

John Ropel called to tell me about Tom's passing. He died August 18 in the hospital, but his wife Alice had cared for him at home from the time he was diagnosed with Alzheimer's. John stated further that I was lucky not to have been in Erie during his long downward spiral. What an ending for one so brilliant; Tom could fix anything. We were as close as friends ever get for over 50 years, and I was extremely saddened by his passing.

We were obviously approaching that point in life when we needed something more than just a roof over our heads. We were aware of Moravian Village in Bethlehem as a final destination for folks like us. We didn't know anyone there, but we did hear favorable comments around the time of its inception from Ken Smith, ex-mayor of Bethlehem. In the fall of '09, we didn't feel any urgent need for a continuing care facility; however, we did accept Valerie Stumer-Heller's invitation to come and check it out. After a free lunch and a sales pitch, we were invited to inspect the apartments and cottages. We were favorably impressed with their program, but it was costly. We would need to sell our house on Bierys Bridge Road to swing it.

Chapter 27

Margaret
2010

Losses And Illnesses

Acting on an invitation, we enjoyed a great Thanksgiving dinner at Moravian Village, and I thanked Valerie for her generous hospitality.

The year ended with more tragic news. Yet another death, and this time it was our dear friend and neighbor, Bob Berry. We knew Bob had suffered from ill health since he had surgery to replace a heart valve. Prior to that Bob's health had been excellent, but he experienced a brain hemorrhage while vacationing on Mackinac Bay and very nearly died. He did recover from that, but never completely. We were friends for so many years, including our very close association during the Michigan years. He was only 81, and his passing came as a shock.

In the New Year of 2010, Margaret had grown so weak that she needed to hold onto me when we walked together. Margaret's downhill slide precluded doing much more than just living day by day. My new role from that point on was mostly "caregiver."

2010: Yet Another Devastating Illness

It is with a deep sense of sadness that I embark on the task of writing about this final year of Margaret's life. By the New Year of 2010, she had already become so weak that she needed my support, and a cane was being considered.

She no longer worked in the kitchen, so my culinary skills were taxed to the limit and beyond. Much of the time we ate frozen dinners or rotisserie chicken. Wegman's Market offered prepared food that I would serve on occasion. It was a challenge, but somehow we managed.

Margaret continued to do the laundry every Saturday, so I asked her one day to teach me how, while there was still time. I encouraged her to keep at it as long as she could.

At the first signs of spring, I broached the subject of selling the Deck House. That upset Margaret immensely, but it was unavoidable. It was important to list property early in the year when the buyers began to stir. Spring of 2010 was a terrible time to sell; the housing market was especially weak in the wake of the deep recession of '08. I naively believed our house was special and would have irresistible appeal to a certain group of buyers, such as car collectors who might need extra room for toys. We were going to be hurt financially; of that I was certain. I had over $150,000 invested in the Annex alone.

Mary Gedley, who had been our Realtor fifteen years earlier, was still in the business, working under the Re/Max umbrella out of the Allentown office. I thought we should start with her, since she was familiar with our property. All it took was a phone call and Mary was there, and an irreversible process was underway.

She was pleased to have the first opportunity to list our home, but was quick to point out that our house was 15 years older than when we had tried to sell before. Although we had taken good care of it, things like the dated kitchen were detrimental. She was pleased that I was making improvements like re-roofing and re-staining the house. We had just put an expensive carpet in the sunroom at a cost of $3000. Money spent like that was wasted, a total loss.

I cleaned and waxed the expansive garage floor that I had tiled back in 1985 during the pilot strike. That was a humongous job, but it was well worth it. Mary encouraged me to continue making improvements: "Buyers in this price range are not looking for fixer-uppers," she said. After looking at the comparables, she recommended an asking price of $495,000. She also pointed out that there really wasn't anything like our house on the market. It was unique. That can be a good thing or sometimes a bad thing, depending on the buyers. Some prospects viewed the Annex out back not as an asset, but as a liability.

Mary also pointed out another advantage of listing with her. We would have additional resources available in the persons of her daughter Beth and son Jim. They, and an army of other Realtors, would be going through the house shortly. We signed the listing agreement later that day.

———

Margaret wanted to visit the Hestons in North Carolina. I questioned the feasibility of such a trip, but she insisted that she would be okay. She seemed fine on our arrival and for the remainder of the evening, but by morning at breakfast, it was evident that we were in trouble. Walking unsteadily, and having slight speech impairment, I feared she might be on the verge of a stroke. I told Ruth we best return home immediately, and she agreed. Ruth donated a pillow and blanket to make a bed for Margaret in the rear seat of the car, and we headed for home.

Margaret tolerated the trip without incident, and on occasion, I looked back to see her sleeping. By the time we arrived back home, she had recovered. So much for trips — but wait, there was still one more: her class reunion in August.

———

Mary hosted a party for the local Realtors' walk-through inspection of the Deck House. That was the customary procedure for new listings, and Re/Max footed the bill. I met Mary's daughter Beth and son Jim, who were part of her team. We discussed the huge job we were facing in relocating, and Beth recommended a friend who offered an organizing, sorting and packing service for clients.

"That sounds great," I said, "what's her number?" Beth kindly handed me Erin Gruver's card. "Life STYLE, defeat chaos and clutter," I read from the card to Margaret. "I think Erin is just what we need around here."

We had deferred the problem of packing; it was just too overwhelming with all the stuff we had accumulated over the years. And it wasn't just ours. The deaths of family members, and the consolidation of two homes into one, were also major contributors. Perhaps, with someone like Erin, we could at least make a dent in the job. Margaret suggested I call her immediately. Thus began a professional and personal relationship that endures to this day.

After a tour of the premises, Erin said we should tackle the most difficult area first: the Annex behind the house. There were three stories of problems, and Erin thought we should start with the lowest level first. That was the worst of the worst. I was a great believer in the adage, "Out of sight, out of mind." Obviously, there were issues there that Erin couldn't deal with, but she had an amazing list of providers that could handle almost anything. That included a junk dealer who could make anything disappear.

The lower level took over a week to clear out. With that accomplished, we had 13 fewer stairs to climb. In addition to working with me, she assisted Margaret with evaluating and sorting through her clothes. There were enormous quantities of everything a woman could wear. Margaret loved clothes, and they were her hobby. Another solution was simply giving stuff away.

"Why not try a yard sale?" some people suggested. We considered that, but we felt that the amount of work and time necessary to set it up would outweigh any financial benefit, so we didn't have one. We just donated things to our friends and to good causes, like the Salvation Army and American Family Services, that plied the neighborhood on a regular basis. We made progress, but with Erin working only three days per week, the job took most of the summer. We could only handle two or three hours per visit as the work was very tiring, especially for Margaret.

On July 15, Margaret fell. It happened while she was writing a check for the replacement of defective windows. She stood up from writing the check and suddenly and inexplicably collapsed. The person waiting for the check was frightened and rushed outside to get me. Margaret tried to get up, but she was just too weak. When I got back inside I helped her up and, fortunately, she wasn't badly hurt. I felt that it was a very significant event, and I worried even more.

The inspection required by the city for reissuance of the occupancy certificate revealed some noncompliant items, such as railings and electrical GFIs not up to code. The problems were mostly in the kitchen and bathrooms. I fussed about adding the additional railings but I found them useful, even for me, during the remainder of the time we lived there. There were so many requirements just to sell a house.

Suddenly it was August, and decision time for Margaret's class reunion in Erie. I hated to say no, so I gave in. She was diligent in arranging her things for the trip, and we stopped in Mansfield, Pa. to visit her sister Jane and Rich McGee. We got to their place okay, but the stairs were a problem. Margaret had not been going up and down many prior to the trip, but she managed, and the next day we drove on to Erie. Arriving in mid-afternoon, I encouraged her to lie down for a nap while I made some calls and visited John Ropel.

One of the phone calls was to Ken and Jackie Michaels about having dinner together at Serafini's Restaurant. They agreed, so arrangements were made to meet them there. Margaret's nap was beneficial, and we had a nice dinner and then spent the rest of the evening visiting with our friends. I hoped the reunion dinner would go equally as well.

The event was held at the Erie Maennerchor Club, a fancy restaurant in downtown Erie that we had been to before. About 30 people attended, and Margaret enjoyed being with her classmates for one last time. It was decided to terminate future reunions, so this was the last. She was proud not to be wheelchair-bound, as some were. However, David Palmer, a very close classmate of hers, told me later he was shocked at Margaret's appearance.

She managed quite well, in fact, and we were able to stop in Meadville, Pa., to visit Esther Wollman, a close friend and classmate who was unable to attend the dinner. I think Margaret enjoyed her visit with Esther as much as the reunion itself.

On to Moravian Village

When we returned home, I decided it was time to begin the application process with Moravian Village. That required a substantial deposit and didn't specify any particular unit; it was just to initiate the paperwork. An important part of that process was a physical exam by our family physician certifying Margaret's ability to live independently, and the expectation of being able to do so for at least a year.

We didn't anticipate any problem having Dr. Martin sign off on Margaret and, in fact, he didn't have any problem doing so. However, as part of the exam, he asked Margaret to walk to the end of the hall and return. Watching her, Dr. Martin exclaimed, "That looks like Parkinson's disease. I can't be sure, but I think Margaret should see a neurologist." Making that observation, he wrote out a referral. Parkinson's was a terrible diagnosis because of the diversity of ailments it implied. It is defined not just by tremors, as many people believe; it can also involve balance problems, debilitation, and even dementia. If Dr. Martin's suppositions were true, I thought to myself, it would explain a lot of what had been going on with Margaret this past year.

After I retired, I became a fan of crossword puzzles. Margaret had been much more adept at solving them than I was, but gradually I improved to the point we enjoyed an equal level of expertise. For years, it was a daily ritual in the afternoon to sit down together with the daily paper and "do the puzzle." This past year Margaret had displayed a sharp decline in her ability, so we stopped doing them together because she wasn't able to participate at my level anymore. I made a copy of the daily entry and put it by Margaret's chair for her to solve at her leisure. But as the months went by, she accomplished less and less. Was it Alzheimer's? Later on, the definition of her disease included "dementia" as part of the Parkinson's diagnosis. The hardest part of my journey was to watch my lifelong friend disappearing before my very eyes.

Margaret was not happy with her new oncology physician who had taken over Dr. Volk's practice, so she decided to get a second opinion. She respected the new doctor because he took the time to carefully study her case and explain the details in layman's terms. He acknowledged that Margaret was at an advanced stage of monocytic leukemia, but he felt different paths of treatment were worth consideration.

A Moravian Village Apartment

There were two distinct types of accommodations available at Moravian Village: cottages and apartments. Up to the point of Dr. Martin's suspicion that Margaret might be suffering from Parkinson's we had intended to move into one of the cottages, but after the diagnosis the focus changed to an apartment in the main building. The neurologist confirmed that Margaret did indeed have Parkinson's. With that diagnosis a host of other considerations came into play, such as whether it was safe for Margaret to continue driving and, if so, for how long.

Moravian Village had their own evaluation system, and Kristel Seagraves (NHA) spent time with Margaret, making her own assessment. She concurred that an apartment would be best.

October 10 was an important day, although not a pleasant one. We had been advised to attend to Margaret's funeral arrangements. We chose Long's Funeral Home. It was an easy choice for us, as they had taken care of her mother's burial. The salesperson was very tactful, and she made every effort to keep the necessary decisions on a pleasant plane. Margaret indicated which casket she preferred, plus other selections; it was all straightforward, and didn't require much more than an hour.

If there was an upside to all this negativity, it was called L-DOPA. As a medication specifically for Parkinson's disease, it could produce a remarkable turnaround in some patients. By the time Margaret started taking it in late October she was using a cane, and because of her unsteadiness I accompanied her to church on many occasions. I think most of the parishioners knew why I was there.

Since a cottage at Moravian Village seemed ill advised, we told Valerie we would like an apartment in the main building but, unfortunately, none were available at that time. It was all quite complicated because the Deck House still had not been sold, and there were no prospects in sight.

Not long after that, I reached the decision that we must make the move irrespective of finding a buyer. That was difficult, because over $200,000 cash would be required at the time of finalizing our deal with Moravian Village. By marshaling all our resources and using the Deck House for collateral, I could close with a small bridge loan. It was a frequent problem for people desiring to move to Moravian Village, and First Star Bank, with a branch office on the premises, was very helpful. They provided funds for the short term without imposition of any fees.

David Roth, the Executive Director of Moravian Village, called to ask if we were interested in a fourth-floor two-bedroom "B" unit that was being created by downsizing one of the larger apartments. He indicated that it would take several weeks to complete the changeover. The apartment faced south on the Market Street side, with a nice view of South Mountain. Apartments facing Market Street cost an additional $10,000.

I said definitely yes, pending another look. He invited us to come at our earliest convenience. "Work has already begun," David said. A day or so later, Valerie escorted us to the fourth-floor apartment. I preferred living on the top floor, and of course there were elevators to take us there. After renting the apartment in Rolling Meadows so many years earlier, I swore I would never again live where an elevator was part of the equation. Never say never.

It *was* a nice view. Actually we had seen the apartment before, on our initial tour, without any consideration that we would ever live there. In its original configuration it was just too large and too expensive.

The alterations were extensive: the kitchen was moved to where the dining room had been, and everything on the north side of the apartment was being restructured to include a large walk-in closet and guest bath. The original apartment guest bath became the master bedroom bath.

What had been a den with cherry cabinets became the master bedroom. It was a bit small, but adequate. The original massive living room was cut in half to provide space for the guest bedroom. There was a small balcony off the living room that was accessible by a sliding glass door. Both bedrooms ended up with electric fireplaces. They were largely for visual effect, but they did have heating elements incorporated into them. Lastly, there was a stacked-unit washer and dryer in the guest bath. Valerie also agreed to include a small pantry off the kitchen in the entrance closet.

In a nutshell, that was our new home. Compared to the homes we had enjoyed over the years, it wasn't much, but we had to view it from the perspective of our current circumstances. Margaret needed to be in a facility that could provide continuing care. Moravian Village could provide whatever level of care might be required.

We signed up that day for apartment 414, with agreement to move in after completion of the renovation. Valerie recommended we begin making our financial arrangements and have our attorney review the agreement.

One day in early November, I awoke with the conviction that I needed to act decisively to sell the house. We were nearing the time of year when there could be no reasonable expectation of finding a buyer. We had already made several price reductions and were currently at $429,000. Suddenly, it struck me like a bolt of lightning that we must reduce it below $400,000 to avoid being stuck with it all winter.

Much of current real estate strategy relied on computer advertising. By dropping the price below $400,000 we gained access to a whole new spectrum of buyers in the $350,000 to $400,000 range. At breakfast I ran my idea by Margaret, but at that point she was beyond caring. All of the tension associated with moving preparations, and chasing all over town for doctor appointments, was taking its toll.

I called Mary Gedley for her reaction to such a drastic reduction. It would reduce her piece of the pie, but in a minor way compared to the hit we would be taking. Surprisingly, she was all for it, and admitted the alternative was to wait for 2011. "What price did you have in mind?" she asked. I gave her my figure of $389,000, and she replied, "That just might do it." "Okay," I said, "Let's give it a try."

We had two serious offers almost immediately, and the highest was from Erin's father, Roy. She had mentioned that her dad was in the market for a house, but he had never seen ours, and Erin was vague about his intentions. I never gave it a thought, because she could have brought him over anytime, informally. Roy countered our $389,000 with $10,000 less, and we accepted his offer. The other offer was lower than Roy's, so it was a no-brainer. Even though we ended up much below the original asking price, we rejoiced at having it sold. Most sellers could not afford to take a hit of that magnitude but, thankfully, we could. Don't misunderstand; it hurt — a lot. I put my heart and soul into Bierys Bridge Road. Margaret also acutely felt the pain, but we would survive.

The changeover at Moravian Village was proceeding steadily, and the apartment was ready for occupancy on December 1. Because the closing on the Deck House was still more than a month away, we needed that bridge loan to move in.

December 6, 2010: Moving day

Shively Moving and Storage of Bethlehem was a company Erin had worked with satisfactorily on a number of occasions. Paying for moving services by the hour was a new experience for us, and the bill ran high because everything had to come through a side door at Moravian Village, and then be brought up the elevator to the fourth floor, and finally brought down a long hall to our apartment. In fact, more help had to be recruited to finish the move in one day.

Because space was at such a premium, we were limited as to how much we could bring. Erin created full-size templates for the large furniture pieces to aid in their placement. Using a floor plan drawn to scale, she was able to calculate exactly what would fit, and where. That saved both time and money. It was still an all-day affair, though, with the clock nearing 4:30 by the time the movers finished. The cost was almost $2000, and a lot of stuff was still at Bierys Bridge Road. We would need Shively's assistance again for a second move to the pole building in January.

Getting Acclimated

Erin stayed just long enough to make up the beds and unpack the kitchen sufficiently to prepare breakfast, but needless to say, the place was a mess. She returned the next day to continue unpacking and arranged furniture to help us get settled.

Our apartment included the use of a large storage compartment in the basement. That helped immensely with the overflow, and

Erin made numerous trips down there during the unpacking phase. Fortunately, sturdy utility carts were available for transporting excess items to store there.

Inside parking was available for $55 per month, so I decided to rent a space for my Avalon. Unlimited parking was available outside. Margaret was still driving, and one day she took my car to the hairdresser, stopping at the Giant for groceries afterward. When she returned, she was confused, and came up to the apartment where I was working. She was crying, telling me that she was unable to get the groceries out of the trunk of the car. It was as simple as pressing a button under the dash, but she thought she needed the key to unlock the trunk. I told her to relax, and I would go down.

"Where's the key?" I asked. She fished around in her purse and pockets, but she couldn't find her car keys. I went down anyway, and found the keys in the passenger side door. Margaret was trying to open the trunk by inserting the key in the car door. I'm not writing this to ridicule her in any way, but to illustrate the confusion issues connected with dementia. It was clear to me at that moment that her driving days were over, and they were; she never drove a car again.

Remarkably, Margaret exhibited steady improvement from the special Parkinson's medication, L-DOPA. Shortly after moving into Moravian Village, she was able to dispense with the cane. She really enjoyed the dining room and seldom missed a night there, right up to the time of her death. She was meeting new people, and a welcoming committee headed up by Nancy Young stopped by for a visit. Nancy's husband David also had Parkinson's, and she suggested we accompany them to a meeting of others living with that disease.

I was determined to have a nice Christmas for Margaret, and decorated the apartment. I even put up the little train she liked around the coffee table, and hung the Moravian Star on the balcony. I had to write all the Christmas cards, setting a few aside for her insertions. I only confided her true condition to our closest friends, those whom I felt needed to know. I'm sure the fact that she was not sending the cards spoke volumes.

Margaret still went to church regularly, really enjoying the close proximity of St. Matthew's, less than five minutes away. The Christmas Eve candlelight service was her favorite, and I was pleased she was able to be there. That was one of the few church services I attended regularly.

From our apartment we had a nice view of the Christmas lights on the south side of Bethlehem. Numerous friends stopped by to visit, including OV and Mary Pezzi. Margaret was much better physically than I would have believed possible. Mentally, though, she was on a downhill slide — thoughts of her slipping away into obscurity were devastating to me, and I tried not to think about it. We had an excellent Christmas dinner in the dining room, and welcomed the New Year watching the ball drop at Times Square on television.

Chapter 28

Alone
2011

The Calm Before the Storm

The focus now was on vacating the premises at Bierys Bridge Road for the closing January 19. Erin helped me pack up what was left at the Deck House so the movers could come a few days before closing to finally empty the house of everything (except for the items purchased by the buyer). It was cold when we arrived at the pole building in Emmaus and unpleasant to work outside, but it didn't take long to unload the van. We filled two bays, so I had my work cut out for me.

Margaret was quite stable the first half of January, and much of the time we discussed the upcoming settlement on the house and how nice it would be to get that behind us. I recall how pleased she was to be able to go down to the dining room every night for a good meal — so different from my efforts of the past year. I look back on those few weeks as a treasured period of calm before the storm.

Finally, closing day arrived, and I tried to convince Margaret not to go — she could sign the necessary papers without leaving the apartment. But no, she wanted to go because it was her house, too. I reluctantly agreed, but reminded her that walking was treacherous and she would need to hold on to me. The closing was at the Re/Max Allentown office, about a half-hour drive, and Mary Gedley led the way.

Margaret was extremely frail, and had not left Moravian Village for some time. Her signatures were barely legible, but she provided her own. After about an hour, it was over and we headed for home. On the way, I was aware that Margaret's speech was abnormal and that I was having trouble understanding her.

Before returning to our apartment, we dropped the proceeds check off at our brokerage office. Margaret spoke with Carol, the receptionist, while I met with my financial advisors. Carol had not seen Margaret for some time, and she was shocked by her appearance.

By depositing the check into our investment account, we said goodbye to the Deck House on Bierys Bridge Road. It was the grand finale of so many property-closing transactions.

My World Crashes

Margaret seemed tired, but otherwise all right, or so I thought. A lot of what I observed in her that evening was fatigue — not unexpected after such a day. It was the next morning that our world came crashing down. At first I didn't notice anything unusual, but then I realized Margaret was not preparing her breakfast; she was not even able to peel a banana for her cereal. When I attempted conversation with her, she was incoherent, and then I sensed that she was very lethargic in all respects. I immediately called the health care unit for assistance.

The nurse took one look at Margaret and called for an ambulance. Alarmingly, she said, "I think she's having a stroke." She asked for Margaret's driver's license so she would have ID on her person. It all happened so fast; in almost no time, Margaret was on a gurney on her way to St. Luke's Hospital, never to return.

The EMTs denied permission for me to accompany Margaret in the ambulance, so I drove to the hospital, where I provided information needed for her admission. I wasn't permitted in the ER, either, as they were doing tests and administering anticoagulants. The first information I got was that her white count was through the roof at 80,000 — all monocytes. With that report, I suspected the new lab was not as thorough managing her leukemia as the oncology/ hematology department at St. Luke's had been.

Eventually I did get in to see her, and she seemed to be recovering. When I consulted the ER doctor, he felt all of those monocytes might have clogged minute arteries in her brain, causing the stroke symptoms. He said they were transferring her to a room shortly; I breathed a sigh of relief that possibly she might pull through yet. I stayed with her the rest of the day, leaving only briefly to return to our apartment. Margaret asked me to bring a few things, and while there I had dinner in the dining room.

When I returned to the hospital just before 7 p.m., I discovered Margaret was not in her room, and the place looked like a cyclone had hit it. On the way to the nurse's station, I ran into Pastor Mauthe, who had also just arrived.

"They've taken her to ICU," the nurse announced. The intensive care unit? Why? I told Pastor I wanted to find out what happened before going there. I approached a nurse's aide who was working in Margaret's room, and she blurted out information that she probably shouldn't have: "The patient choked on her dinner, and by the time someone got here, she had turned blue and was unconscious."

I raged at her, "Are you telling me she was eating unsupervised?" The aide said that she didn't know, but that obviously considerable time had elapsed before her choking was discovered, or someone would have performed a Heimlich maneuver. Pastor was there with me, and just shook his head.

Anyone diagnosed with Parkinson's should never eat alone, because the disease sometimes impedes one's ability to swallow. I should have gotten the aide's name, but I didn't. The appearance of the room was testimony that extreme measures had taken place in a flurry of activity. While I was having dinner at Moravian Village, Margaret was choking to death in her room at St. Luke's. I could never forgive myself for not being there with her. If I had, would she still be alive today?

When Pastor and I arrived at the ICU, Margaret was on a ventilator, with IV's using the newly created port in her chest. I'm sure they discovered that her arm veins were useless. She was very drowsy, but would feebly squeeze my hand. Pastor Mauthe provided prayers. Her color was good, and the nurse confirmed that she was heavily sedated.

I didn't know what I should do, except to sit with her in that dismal room. She never turned her head to look at me; she just stared ahead into nothingness. I couldn't just stay there. I had obligations to the family and others, especially Scott and Celia, her nephew and niece and, of course, her sister Jane. So, as bedtime approached, I kissed Margaret good night and relinquished my vigil.

The following days and nights all ran together. The only difference was the people who came to see Margaret. The hospital staff kept telling me she was improving, but it wasn't apparent to me. Scott Phillip's arrival on the weekend was one of the few times I detected a reaction from her. It was in Margaret's eyes after Scott first arrived; they followed him as he moved about the room, almost not believing he was there. She seldom moved her arms, and her primary means of expression was gently squeezing my hand. Did she understand when I spoke to her? I'm not sure.

Rich and Jane McGee arrived about the same time, and stayed in the apartment with me. Scott had a room at a nearby motel. Pastor Mauthe was faithful to Margaret with frequent visits. Others came, but I was in a daze much of the time. The weekend was long but it finally passed, and then discussion began to center on Margaret's living will. It clearly stated that she didn't want extraordinary measures to prolong her life.

What was a reasonable time to keep someone on a ventilator? The only consensus seemed to be if the patient was responding, it should be continued. Her doctor insisted that she was benefitting from it, and would eventually be able to be taken off and breathe on her own. So, we waited. Monday became Tuesday, with no perceptible change, at least none that I could detect.

Fortunately, others were intervening on my behalf — someone called for a hospice doctor on Tuesday the 26th, and he arranged a meeting for the following day. Margaret's doctor, Pastor Mauthe, myself and, of course, the hospice doctor himself, would attend. When I learned about the meeting, I asked Pastor about its significance. He replied that it was time to make a decision about removing the ventilator. There was a difference of opinion as to whether she could breathe on her own, and the only way to find out was to remove it. That action was supported by her wishes not to keep using extreme measures.

The meeting took place as scheduled, and I requested that Scott and Rich join us as well. Margaret's personal-care physician was the only one in favor of continuing the status quo, so it was decided to remove the ventilator later that evening.

I was at Moravian Village that evening with the full intention of going to the hospital, but a snowstorm developed that made travel difficult. I called the hospital and the doctor assured me that Margaret would be okay to breathe on her own overnight. The doctor didn't think I needed to be there, and promised to notify me if Margaret took a turn for the worse. The doctor was wrong, and Margaret died at 2 a.m., Thursday, January 27, 2011.

The Transition

I felt terrible for not being by her side, bad weather or no. Fortunately, though, Pastor Mauthe was there, and I asked him why he didn't call me. He replied that it was quite sudden and unexpected, and insisted that Margaret would not have known of my presence anyway, as she was unconscious. "Don't beat yourself up over it," he said; but I did, and still do — I can't help it.

Thursday was a blur, and I really don't remember much of my first day without Margaret. Fortunately, I was not alone. In addition to Rich and Jane, I also had Jo Ann Smith. She was one of Margaret's closest friends and they did lots of things together, including participation in the Bible Study group at the church. I knew Jo Ann from her frequent visits to our house in connection with their activities. During the calling time at Long's Funeral Home, she approached me with an offer to help me in any way she could.

The funeral home experience was barely tolerable, and many people came to pay their respects. Besides the family, we had about ten very close friends attending, some local and some from out of town, like Jane and Gene Olsen and the Pezzis. I invited everyone to join me for dinner at Moravian Village, only a short distance away. Of course, Cindy, our dining room supervisor, knew we were coming and had a huge table specially prepared for us. It was a very intimate dinner, and I was indebted to Cindy for the way she accommodated us.

I still had to suffer through the funeral service at St. Matthew's and the interment at Girard Cemetery near Erie, Pa. Somehow I would survive; I had to. Our dear friend and retired pastor, Helmut Kaffine, spoke eloquently at Margaret's funeral service, followed by a nice luncheon downstairs at the church after the service. We were watching the weather, as I planned to drive to Mansfield, Pa., later that day to spend the night with my in-laws, Rich and Jane. On Tuesday, I drove to Erie for the graveside service. Pastor Mauthe offered to ride to Erie in the hearse, officiate at graveside, and then return to Bethlehem with me. It sounded complicated, but it would all work out if the weather cooperated.

Unfortunately, the weather didn't cooperate, and we were forced to reschedule the graveside service for Wednesday, a day later. I stayed with Rich and Jane Monday night, and the next morning I was greeted with six inches of fresh snow on my car. I cleaned it off and left for Erie about 8 a.m. At first the roads were treacherous, but they improved when I crossed the Pennsylvania/New York border to reach Route 17 (the New York Shortway — soon to become an Interstate highway). This was a slightly longer route to Erie, Pa., but it was more practical for the snowy conditions I was encountering.

After registering at the Erie Hampton Inn, I drove to Girard Cemetery to check on the burial site. There was at least a foot of accumulated snow on the cemetery grounds, and I didn't see how they could possibly dig Margaret's grave. Shortly after my arrival, I encountered an old friend from long ago named Ed Erickson. Ed had been the man in charge of Girard Cemetery for decades. He even knew my Uncle Dell, and was a member of Grace Episcopal Church in North Girard.

Ed clarified the agenda for the following day. The snow had already been cleared adjacent to the gravesite in preparation for the tent they would erect. Margaret's grave was to be dug early the next morning, intentionally leaving the snow on top of the excavation site to prevent frost penetration overnight. Ed said the burial vault should arrive later that day, so everything had been arranged. The forecast was for temperature near zero overnight, moderating to 10 above during the day. No additional snow was expected.

When I returned to the motel, Rich and Jane had just arrived. We all went to Serafini's for an Italian dinner. I filled them in on my cemetery visit and they were pleased that everything was set. "Ed said to dress warm," I said facetiously.

It was very cold when Pastor Mauthe arrived with the hearse the next morning. The burial vault was placed before we arrived, the grave had been opened, and all the earth taken away. Ed did a magnificent job under extreme conditions. Many northern cemeteries suspend burials during winter, and I considered it a stroke of very good fortune that we were able to lay Margaret to rest.

Although the delay of the interment had been posted in the Erie newspaper, we only had about a dozen brave souls at the graveside. Besides family, there was John Ropel and his wife Dianne, Ken and Jackie Michaels, plus a few others. As promised, the service was brief; it was really tough for me to see the casket sitting there with the realization that my Margaret was inside. I was resolute by necessity. Soon it was over, and we dispersed.

Pastor Mauthe and I drove back to Bethlehem in my Avalon, and I returned home to my empty apartment. It was my first time being truly alone since the day Margaret had gone to the hospital. Now it was my turn to grieve. The people at Moravian Village were exceedingly compassionate. I was so much better off being around people. It would have been terrible to be alone at the house on Bierys Bridge Road, with all its memories.

————

Rob Stevens approached me some time later on to say he had a prospective buyer for the Winnebago if I was ready to sell. Since I couldn't think of any good reason to keep it, I let it go. That created space in the pole building to set up tables for sorting through the many things I needed to dispose of.

Margaret's Spirit

I gratefully accepted Jo Ann Smith's initial offer to assist with selecting Margaret's burial clothes and jewelry; however, she did much more by sticking with me through the exhausting process of donating Margaret's clothing and personal effects. She was also with me as I became more aware of Margaret's presence. At that time I wasn't into "the spirit" much, and I just considered the unusual things that were happening to be "influence," but these experiences were powerful enough to change who I was into a completely new and different person.

At least one encounter with Margaret's spirit involved Jo Ann. We were downstairs in the storage locker sorting through items to donate, when I abruptly opened a cabinet that had nothing to do with her wardrobe.

I took out a chest containing Margaret's sterling silver service. The reason for doing that is beyond explanation, because we were there to work on clothing. When I opened it to show Jo Ann, she became very red in the face, and I feared she might faint. The silver pattern was called "Rondo" by Gorham, and it was identical to her own. The impact was so significant because Margaret knew they shared the same pattern. But until that moment Jo Ann had forgotten they ever discussed it.

When she regained her composure, Jo Ann begged me to sell it to her, or at least bequeath it to her. I said, "No, Jo Ann, the fact that she directed me to take it out and show it to you is enough for me — she obviously wants you to have it." After the viewing at Long's Funeral Home, I gave Jo Ann Margaret's best pearls that she wore during the viewing. I did it because I felt indebted to Jo Ann — because she had shown herself to be a true friend.

Yet another demonstration of Margaret's presence occurred around the same time, probably late in January. I had been attending church regularly after Margaret died. Just why, I wasn't sure; perhaps it gave me some measure of comfort to do so. One Sunday in particular, I was quite busy and I decided not to go — I didn't have to go every Sunday, did I? As it got closer to the time of worship, however, I felt a strong urgency to get to church. I fought against it; I really didn't plan to attend that Sunday. Guess what? I lost the battle, and the organ was playing when I arrived at the church.

Margaret's influence was powerful enough to take charge of me in a way that altered who I was, and this was before the transcendent experience I described in the opening chapter. You will hear more dramatic accounts of my remarkable experiences in the final chapter, but what I want to do here is to fill in a few blanks, things not mentioned elsewhere.

A Quest for Knowledge

I discussed some of my search with my friend, Helmut, describing my lack of understanding concerning the books of First and Second

Corinthians in the New Testament. (Margaret had specified readings from both for her funeral service.) His response was, "Well, perhaps you should read Corinthians again." But somehow there was much more — in fact, Margaret was leading me to a comprehensive study of the apostle Paul. I was already experiencing that "quest for knowledge" that governs my life to this day.

I discovered *Paul*, a little book by Edgar Goodspeed, on Margaret's Bible shelf. That book had been on her shelf as long as memory serves me; in fact, when we had been recently packing to move, I asked Margaret if we should dispose of it. "I wouldn't get rid of that," she replied without explanation. Now I was certainly glad we kept it. I began fervently reading the story of the apostle Paul, and when I finished it and leafed back through the book, I discovered that I had unconsciously underlined the text in many places. Suddenly, I "got it." Margaret wanted me to study Paul.

I discussed it with Pastor Mauthe, who suggested contacting Walter Wagner, a professor on the faculty of the Moravian Theological Seminary here in Bethlehem (they were close friends for many years). When I called Walter at home, he replied, "Meet me at Reeves Library at noon on Monday."

By then it was summer recess, but even so, for Walter to take time from his busy schedule to tutor me on Paul was incredible. But he did just that; we met every Monday, all summer long, so I could gain knowledge and understanding of Paul's letters. My gratitude to him for doing that is unbounded. Walter and I have spent many hours together in the classroom, and I anticipate spending many more.

Also that summer, Gordon Sommers replaced Carol Dague as Chaplain at Moravian Village. I stopped in to introduce myself and explain my circumstances, both that I had recently lost Margaret and that I was participating in classes at the Seminary. Gordon invited me to join the Wednesday afternoon Bible Study group at Moravian Village in their current study of the Book of Hebrews. He also invited me join the men's Bible Study group at Central Moravian Church that met Wednesday mornings at 6:45 a.m. It has been a very insightful experience being a member of this group, which Gordon leads each week.

I also participated in the adult Sunday School class at St. Matthew's. When Pastor Mauthe learned of my interest in Paul, he invited me to attend: "We're studying Romans at the present time," he said. Pastor Mauthe was an excellent teacher on Romans, and many other subjects.

I also did a lot of home study during that summer of 2011. I found "The Great Courses" DVDs to be of exceptional value, with lecturers like Luke Timothy Johnson, Bart Ehrman, and Amy-Jill Levine. I also read Barclay's complete series on the New Testament.

After Walter and I finished our study on Paul, I called the seminary to inquire about courses for the fall term. I was directed to Jill Peters, and surprisingly, she stopped by my apartment to discuss the program with me. I thought that was awfully nice of her, and didn't understand for quite some time why I was singled out for such special treatment, but I think Walter had a hand in it.

That visit led to my taking multiple courses over these past two years, many with Walter as my professor. A few that come to mind were New and Old Testament (taught by Walter Wagner), Theology (taught by Steve Simmons), Spiritual Formation (taught by Emily Wallace), Paul (taught by Tim Marquis) and, just recently, The Book of Hebrews (taught by Walter Wagner). It has been, and continues to be, quite a journey.

———

Pastor Mauthe announced his retirement, effective after Labor Day. That came as a shock to the congregation and especially to me, because he had been so supportive all through my ordeal. Our church now began the call process to seek a new pastor.

———

The holidays were difficult, and I won't deny it. I didn't decorate much, except for hanging the Moravian Star on my balcony. I mailed my cards early so people would know that Margaret was gone. A bright spot for me was the Christmas Eve candlelight service, and the inaugural use of the pew torches donated in Margaret's memory. She *was* a pillar of St. Matthew's Lutheran Church.

These are the pew torches, donated in Margaret's memory for the Christmas Eve candlelight service, that I discussed in the opening chapter. It is still difficult for me to attend that service.

Chapter 29

Moravian Village
2012-2014

During the winter of 2012 I attended additional Crossroads courses at the Seminary with Walter Wagner on the Old and New Testaments. (Crossroads is the lay leadership education program at the Moravian Theological Seminary.) My friend, John Norton, and I frequently had dinner together in the dining room at Moravian Village, and on occasion he discussed the bridge group that met on Tuesday evenings. At first I wasn't interested, largely because I had never played. But since I had a basic understanding of what constituted a deck of cards, John offered to teach me.

"Come down and sit in with me for a few sessions," he suggested. As I thought about it more, I realized it was an opportunity to try something new and to meet people. After watching for a few nights I became fascinated with the game, and was soon filling in and actually playing when a table was short one player. Jean Haney, our leader, has been most gracious in welcoming me to the group. It's been a process, and I do make mistakes, but everyone is tolerant and helpful. I always make sure to keep Tuesday nights open on my calendar.

Flying N 758HK to Bethlehem

During the summer of 2012, the "airplane bug" struck and I toyed with the idea of becoming a plane owner one last time. I had renewed my friendship with Ray Franke, who hangars a Cessna 195 at the Lehighton Airport, and I began spending more time there.

Considering my age, Ray suggested a Cessna 172, but not just an ordinary one; he suggested I look for an "XP" (extra performance) model from the late 1970s. Production was limited, so it was difficult to find a good one. The XP model came equipped with a 6-cylinder 210 horsepower Continental engine, versus the standard 150 horsepower Lycoming engine found on most planes of that type.

Many XPs were either high-time "run-outs" that had been used for training or repainted in color schemes of the owner's choice — however, I preferred finding one in its original configuration at a suitable price. "If it doesn't work out, just resell it," was Ray's suggestion.

In June, Ray found a promising candidate on the west coast. After a bus ride to Newark Airport, I boarded a nonstop B-737 flight to San Diego. I was surprised to find my old friend, "Albert," flying coast to coast — during the 1970s, the version I flew only traveled half that distance.

Everything went well at the ticket counter and I boarded the flight, which was packed to the gills with no more than one or two empty seats remaining. I warned Don Dixon (the owner's selling agent) to check with United before leaving home to pick me up at Lindberg airport. Arrival was after dark, and it was good of Don to pick me up; fending for myself at SAN would not have been fun, and I was exhausted after the long day. The Cessna was based at Ramona, a small town in the hills east of San Diego, and Don reserved a room at the town's only motel. It was dinner hour in California, but I was bushed. "Please, just take me to the motel," I said.

It doesn't rain in Ramona in June, so its climate is totally different than San Diego's, just 40 miles away. Jeff, the plane's owner, was at the airport when I arrived the next morning. The hangar was open and there, staring out at us, was N 758HK, the Cessna 172 XP. "HK" was a '79 model with some 3000 total hours, but the engine only had about 400 hours since major overhaul. I discounted any concern about the engine because of its low time and the excellent compression report from the last annual inspection. Jeff assured me it ran fine, and the mechanic from the shop was there to answer any questions I might have. We carefully reviewed the checklist for preflight, performed in an unhurried fashion. Jeff seemed to be quite competent.

"Let's go flying," he said, so we took off and flew around the airport. Everything seemed to work properly, so we only did a couple of landings and then taxied back to the hangar. Before I realized it, lunchtime had arrived, after which I asked about an instructor to check me out. "Sure, no problem — Tim Farmer will be out shortly to go up with you."

Flying the plane locally was no problem, but I soon realized I wouldn't be flying it home by myself, as I had planned. With no autopilot, it would be a lot more hands-on flying than I cared to do. During my checkout the temperature soared into the 90s, and I became severely dehydrated. By the time we got back to the hangar, I was exhausted.

I mentioned my concerns about the trip home to Tim, and he agreed that it would be unwise for me to fly home solo. In fact, he said he would be willing to accompany me in about a month, as he had relatives, and also some business to take care of, in New Jersey. While I was making arrangements for my trip home, Tim called me and said, "I talked it over with my wife, and for a flat fee and a ticket back home, I will be willing to fly to Pennsylvania with you, and we could leave first thing Sunday morning. Would that work for you?" Tim liked the XP, and that may have influenced his decision to accompany me. I was relieved to find a way to avoid making another trip to California. "Absolutely," I said. That plan would provide me a much-needed day to rest up.

Sunday, the 24th of June, began picture-perfect, with clear sky and a limp windsock. The folks at the airport had loaned me a car, so I made my own way to the airport. We had fueled the plane the day before, so it was ready to go. Being the first one there, I opened the hangar and began the preflight. Before long Tim arrived with his family, and I was able to meet his wife and their two small children. She didn't seem worried, but maybe a bit "concerned" that her husband was taking off on a cross-country journey with a stranger. I believe Tim filled her in a bit about my airline background so she wouldn't be anxious. "Do you have insurance on Tim?" she asked. "About a million dollars' worth," I replied. With that, I got a smile and a handshake, and we were off.

It was a gorgeous morning to fly, and fortunately the sun was not in our eyes. Before long, we were over some of the most hostile terrain I had ever seen, and I suggested to Tim that it might be advisable to follow I-15, dimly visible off to our left. Tim seemed to be unconcerned, and since he was flying I left it to his discretion, but I was a bit uncomfortable. "We're on a flight plan," he said. It was already quite warm when we landed for self-service fueling at Boulder City, Nev., where I spent over $200 in the blink of an eye. That's what was killing General Aviation: high fuel prices, in the range of $6 to $7 per 100-octane gallon. Some small planes ran on high-test lead-free auto fuel, but the XP could not. Soon we were off again for our next stop in Provo, Utah.

Before continuing our journey, let me briefly explain the rationale behind selecting the route we were taking. A glance at a U.S. map would show that we were clearly not taking the shortest route home. That would have been over the torrid desert of the Great Southwest: specifically, Arizona and New Mexico, and part of Texas. To consider that route at all would have required dawn departures, with all flying for the day completed by 11 a.m., for a yield of perhaps five hours per day.

It was the hostile terrain and high ambient temperatures that influenced me to select a more northerly route. However, we didn't escape rough terrain on our leg to Las Vegas, either, but it was soon to improve dramatically for the second leg and beyond. The other consideration was my fervent hope that maximum daytime temperatures along the high plains route would be more temperate. On that presumption, I was only partly correct. The temperature over the entire country was above normal that last week of June.

On the leg to Provo, we were quite comfortable at 11,500 feet, and enjoying a tailwind as well. In a light plane, that's as good as it gets. To avoid delay at Salt Lake City International we landed at Provo, a smaller airport, and while descending we hit a severe updraft that banged my head into the headliner. I directed Tim to alert Air Traffic Control that we had encountered "moderate turbulence," and being tracked on radar, the controller would know precisely where.

As we approached for our landing at Provo, the forbidding Wasatch Mountain range loomed immediately to the east. Recalling my stint on the B-720 out of Denver and flying into Salt Lake (descending into Farley's Canyon), I was now looking at the canyon critically and wanted no part of it in my Cessna 172.

After refueling, we began our third and final leg of the day to Rawlins, Wyoming. I recalled the Swift trip with PG Fellmeth in 1954 and how I passed out, requiring him to fly the plane for a time. That was over 60 years ago, and here I was flying a light plane over the same route again.

Unfortunately, we weren't there yet. We needed to climb, climb, and keep climbing, all the way up to 11,500 feet again so we could traverse Uintah pass at Ogden, Utah, where we would break out into the high plains. It was really the Rockies, but instead of high peaks all around us, it was flat tableland. Oh, I could see a few bumps far off to our south in Colorado, but they wouldn't bother us at all as we made our way to the east. Interstate 80 was our companion for the next thousand miles, much of the time paralleling our course to the east, usually within sight.

My goal from the start had been to escape the torturous desert heat and bask in these Wyoming highlands instead. Bask might be the wrong word, though, as Rawlins had just reported a temperature of 88 degrees. Provo to Rawlins was our longest leg of the day, lasting over three hours. We lost our tailwind, and were chugging along at not much over 100 mph. However, we had covered an impressive 1000 miles the first day. Finally, as our destination came into view, the first thing I noticed was the runway; it had been extended to 10,000 feet.

Rawlins had been a training base for bomber pilots during WWII. They wanted pilots to gain experience flying out of a high-altitude airport without the hazard of dodging mountain peaks. The old wooden hangar still stood, along with some modern ones. Rawlins Airport had changed markedly in the 58 years since my last visit.

The airport operator was most cordial, and offered to put our plane in the hangar for the night. "Looks like something might be brewing out there," he said. Hail damage was a real threat on the high plains. Downtown Rawlins was just a stone's throw away, and after we checked in at the motel it was a pleasant walk to a nice restaurant, and then time to call it a day.

Rawlins Airport, with its 7000-foot elevation, was where PG and I had sweated out our takeoff in the Swift so many years ago. We were unable to reach a safe altitude without circling the field a number of

483

times. This Skyhawk 172 XP was a lot different, and tomorrow we would see how that big engine up front would go to bat for us.

Tim was a little late the next morning. The weather was perfect, and I was anxious to get underway to enjoy the cool of the morning. East of us, in Nebraska, ceilings were down to 500 feet. Probably the weather would have improved by the time we arrived, but we couldn't depend on it. Much better weather prevailed not far to the south; Omaha was good, but out of range.

I decided to fly the first leg of the day to compare the XP's takeoff performance at Rawlins with that of the Swift I had flown so many years earlier. There was a noticeable difference, all right. Even though our ground run was long, once in the air, climb was quite satisfactory. However, it was necessary to lean the mixture.

In the cool morning air, we climbed steadily to our cruising altitude of 11,500 feet. Once in the air, the airplane didn't know we had just left a high-altitude field — it just climbed normally. When we arrived at North Platte, the ceiling was still quite low, and some deviation around clouds was necessary to get underneath. After refueling and eating lunch, we departed for Des Moines, Iowa, and encountered an unusual headwind that slowed us noticeably. Arriving at Des Moines, I exercised the Instrument Landing System (ILS) equipment on Runway 05, and all components worked fine.

Splitting Up

Taxiing in for service presented us with a clear view of the airline terminal, and sitting over there on the ramp was a United B-737. We were back in UAL territory again. I asked Tim if he would mind flying the rest of the way alone, so I could hop on that United flight to Chicago. I was reluctant to abandon him, but by that time, I was very tired. Tim replied, "No, I don't mind at all."

So, once we parked, I went to the terminal to check the schedule. The Chicago flight was leaving at 1 o'clock; that was perfect, and since they weren't busy, I asked the ticket agent to help me with a pass to Newark. Tim finished servicing the plane and brought my suitcase over. We shook hands and went our separate ways. At that point we were only a little over halfway home.

Checking the flight board at O'Hare, I noticed United Express had an evening flight directly to Allentown, a far better choice than the

Newark flight I was ticketed on. There was just enough time to make it, so I hurried to Gate F-4. At first they refused to let me board, but eventually they agreed to "fix" my ticket. Arriving in Allentown, I took a cab to Moravian Village. Thankful to be home, I called Tim Farmer to see how he had fared with the airplane. He was in Kankakee, Illinois, with less than 1000 miles to go, and expected to arrive at Lehighton the following day. The next morning, Tim called me from Mansfield, Ohio, during his last fuel stop, with an ETA of 1 p.m.

I left immediately to make it to Lehighton in time for his arrival. I had just opened the hangar and was talking to Ray Franke when Tim arrived. A cold front had passed through during the night, so a stiff breeze was blowing across the runway. Tim handled the crosswind professionally, and pulled up to my hangar. The plane was finally home; mission accomplished.

June 2012: 1979 Cessna Skyhawk Model 172XP. This photo was taken after a cross-country trip from San Diego, California.

As agreed, I paid Tim for his services and put him on the bus to Newark. I thanked him for flying back with me, and wished him well. The trip showed that I could still fly, and provided me with a pleasant memory.

So, what else did I do that summer? The answer was, not much. With no obligations, I could spend my time as I pleased. I went out to the airport frequently to have lunch with my friends. I did certain things on a regularly scheduled basis, such as the Wednesday morning gathering at Central Moravian Church and our own Wednesday afternoon Bible Study here at Moravian Village. Sometimes when Gordon was away, I would lead it.

Margaret's influencing spirit keeps surfacing. Just when I think she has left me to my own devices, something new takes place.

2014: Alverta M. Serfass

I would be remiss in concluding this narrative without relating my most recent experience of Margaret's healing influence.

Alverta Serfass and Margaret had been very close friends at St. Matthew's Lutheran Church since the 1970s. Because I didn't attend church very often, I didn't know her very well until recently, as a participant of St. Matthew's Adult Sunday School. Alverta was gifted, and could write a poem on most any subject extemporaneously.

Toward the end of 2013, I was aware of her absence and was told she was having surgery for stage 4 stomach cancer. As in many cases of late discovery, the operation met with only limited success. She languished in St. Luke's Hospital for several weeks before finally being released to the Moravian Village health center to receive therapy. (Since the hospital could do nothing more for her, the reality was that Alverta came to Moravian Village to die.) In spite of knowing about her general condition, I felt no compunction to visit her until I learned she was here at Moravian Village — from that point on, however, I felt an urgency to visit her that defies explanation.

On my very first visit she was lying in bed. She was weak, best described as "skin and bones" and, by her own admission, reduced 25 pounds from her normal weight. Her most objectionable encumbrance was a large bag connected to an abdominal drain tube that stayed with her at all times. I noticed a walker close at hand for assistance getting to the bathroom.

Alverta was quite lucid, and was resigned to spending her remaining days at Moravian Village, where hospice care had been arranged. I spent considerable time with her when she was not involved with family. Her son Jim had been summoned from Versailles, France.

Within a week, though, she displayed a remarkable turnaround, gaining strength (and weight) — the walker was gone and so was the onerous abdominal drain. We took walks together as I showed her the marvelous Moravian Village facility. Alverta didn't even need a cane and could climb stairs. We arranged to have dinner in the main dining room with another close friend from St. Matthew's who was also a resident.

In spite of the dreadful winter weather we were experiencing, the following Sunday Alverta dressed and I took her to St. Matthew's Sunday School, where she was warmly received. No one there ever expected to see her again. Shortly after that, she expressed a desire to leave Moravian Village and return home. All during her stay here she was visited by her friends, including members of the "Red Hat Society" that she treasured so much. Numerous awards usually bestowed after passing were graciously received while she was still very much alive. She even celebrated her birthday, and arriving home at the end of the week, she was welcomed by her neighbors on Livingston Avenue.

I took Alverta to Sunday School and church twice more before she was suddenly stricken with a blockage and taken to St. Luke's Hospice Center, where she died peacefully at the end of February.

What role did I play in her short, dramatic "remission"? I have no idea; I only know what I felt, and it was very powerful. Did I view it as a failed intervention? Not at all, because Alverta enjoyed a precious month, mostly pain-free, with her family and friends. I was very pleased to be a part of that. Her memorial service was wonderful, well-attended by family and friends as well as three pastors of St. Matthew's. She would have liked that.

So, what is the "gift of the Spirit" that I wrote about in the first chapter? Some refer to it as God's energy field. Look at me; I have been transformed by this gift. My life was changed dramatically in the blink of an eye by a transcendent born-again experience — invigorated with energy, and enjoying a level of good health I would not have believed possible for someone in his mid-eighties.

I am the recipient of spiritual gifts beyond imagination, the greatest of which is clarity: I'm quite certain about things I previously knew nothing about. Other gifts are significant as well, including healing and my quest for knowledge. My soul had been locked in materialism for decades, and was now suddenly released from bondage.

For the past two years, I have been taking courses at Moravian Theological Seminary. At the conclusion of the Old Testament course, before the holiday break, Walter Wagner asked a perplexing question: "What is truth?" Again and again he asked the question. No one responded, so I put my hand up and said, "Truth is clarity." Not liking that vague adjective, Walter's response was, "All right, what is 'clarity'?" In that context, Webster's dictionary says, "The quality or state of being clear: lucidity." That word, "lucidity," takes us a little closer to where I want to go, with: "1. Clearness of thought and a presumed capacity to perceive the truth directly and instantaneously."

For me, in the context of my spiritual gift, it translates to the quest for wisdom and knowledge. That sounds pious, so I don't like to go there. Likewise, "gnosis" is not my destination, either. Rather, I would describe my gift as having received insights about the path to salvation and eternal life as defined by the apostle Paul. I am quite sure now about many things that have puzzled me, if and when I thought about them at all, for so many years.

Margaret's spiritual return has demonstrated, beyond the shadow of any doubt, the ability of the spirit to alter any level of preconceptions with regard to the hereafter. I strongly resisted acceptance of such notions from the time of her death. Many had described it as a temporary phenomenon connected with the grieving process. But after four years, Margaret's influence is as strong as ever, and presents itself in so many different ways. The outward manifestations of my gifts of vitality, healing, a calm and serene disposition, a quest for knowledge and an ability to assimilate that knowledge — as well as the time-honored trilogy of faith, hope and love (and "the greatest of these is love") — indicate a measure of the scope of the "gifts of the Spirit." And, in accordance with Paul's teaching, we must not leave out "love." Therein lies the foundation of my theology as spelled out in the two Great Commandments: "Love the Lord thy God," and "Love Thy Neighbor as Thyself" (Deuteronomy 6:5, Mark 12:31).

I could never have imagined writing this account of my life, and I certainly could not have imagined doing so in a few short months, and with recall for detail that many have found to be astounding. Will this story serve any purpose? I have no idea. The writing was done as a response to higher power. Please let the concluding chapter serve to recount a few final dynamic elements of my experience.

Chapter 30

Not Flying Alone
2013

Oh, reader, you've been so patient. What about that letter to Mark Hanson? What is the meaning of it? Is it important? Accompany me on this journey and you decide. As I said long ago, I was awakened by Margaret at four in the morning with an urgent message to *"Write to Mark Hanson."*

But it really wasn't about Mark Hanson. Oh yes, I wrote to him about receiving my wonderful "gift of the Spirit," with a vague inquiry as to how it might be used. He was good enough to reply directly to me with a nice letter and a quote from Philippians ("the epistle of joy").

In order to write to him, I would need an address. Where would I find that? In *The Lutheran* Magazine, of course, so I referred to the October 2011 issue. Did I go directly to the magazine staff page at the front? No-o-o, I leafed through it page by page until I came to a commentary on retired Bishop Herb Chilstrom's autobiography, which had just been published. Why would I be interested in that?

I didn't know Bishop Chilstrom either, but I read the synopsis of his book, and I "decided" to order it. *A Journey of Grace* is 600 pages. Why would I order it? It looked like a daunting project just to read a book of that size.

Don't ask; it's Margaret's wish for some reason; who knows? It was a very interesting book, and I did enjoy it. With my exceptional acumen for assimilation, I read it in just a few days. I felt I must write to Herb Chilstrom and compliment him on his excellent book. Why? I don't know; for some reason Margaret wants me to.

Okay, drag out the typewriter again, and write to Bishop Chilstrom. As I'm writing to him, I suddenly get up and go to the Bible shelf in the bedroom. Why would I interrupt my train of thought to go there? Margaret wants me to.

As I pointed out much earlier, there were at least 10 Bibles on that shelf, and I take down this "one," and it's in a box. I open the box and right on top, there is a sheet of paper. What is it? It's faded, from 1966, describing a class on Hebrews that Margaret and I attended while members of Messiah Lutheran Church in Oakland, N.J. Oh-oh, look who conducted the class. It's none other than the same Herb Chilstrom to whom I am writing a letter out in the dining room.

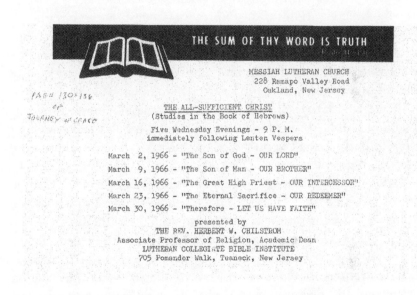

While writing to Bishop Chilstrom in the dining room, I suddenly felt an urgency to get up and go to Margaret's "Bible shelf" in the bedroom. The Bible I was directed to was in a box, and upon opening it, this is what I discovered. See text for the full implication.

Somehow, Margaret concocted this elaborate scheme. Why? Was it to be incontrovertible proof of her presence? At first, I thought so, but with Margaret's spirit at work, we must probe deeper. Oh yes, I was blown away when I realized what I was looking at. Such an elaborate scenario fabricated by the soul of one who was seriously demented in the final stages of her life — now fully restored, in heaven, able to return here in spirit to my apartment and work me over in this way. Pretty heavy stuff; do you believe it? I didn't at first, but I do now.

———

There's more, much more. I fell in November of that year and broke my foot (fifth metatarsal). An x-ray showed that it was a clean break. The orthopedic surgeon told me that I would need crutches and would have to wear a "boot" for quite some time, at least two to three months. He didn't want to prescribe a cast due to circulation problems inherent with the elderly. "Come back in three or four weeks and we'll take another look at it," he said.

I was in considerable pain and misery for a couple of weeks, and then, all of a sudden, the pain just started going away. By the time of my return visit to the hospital the pain was gone, the swelling was down and I walked into the office wearing a regular shoe, without even a limp. I passed the doctor at the nurse's station. "Where's the boot?" he inquired.

"I don't need it anymore," I replied. When he came in to examine my foot, he remarked, "It's not even swollen. Let's take another x-ray." Mounting the x-ray on the screen, he couldn't find the break, so he dug out the previous film. "Oh, now I can see it. It's healed. That's remarkable; I can't do anything more for you — you're released."

It *was* "remarkable." However, the possibility of divine intervention was beyond my perception at that time. I talked to some people with similar fractures, and it usually took months, in addition to physical therapy, to restore normal function. As I pondered over my orthopedic wonder, I realized that I hadn't been in to see my family physician since Margaret died. In fact, his office called me one day to see if I was all right. My health has been excellent, best in memory.

Before receiving my "gift of the Spirit" I had issues with anxiety, and even took medication for it. I no longer have any stress-related issues — my demeanor is one of calm and serenity. I seem to have received all of the "signs of the Holy Spirit" to some degree, except for speaking in tongues. I have written about my gift of clarity, which could possibly be interpreted as manifestations of wisdom and knowledge — I really don't know.

Returning to Margaret's marvelous "demonstration," I said earlier that there might be more, and I believe there is. In my lifetime, I have come to the Book of Hebrews four times. The first was in 1966, in Oakland, N.J. The second time was just a year ago when I met our chaplain, Gordon Sommers, who was conducting a class on the New Testament book of Hebrews here at Moravian Village. The third time was with the slip of paper in the Bible box, and the last was my recently completed course with Walter Wagner at the Moravian Theological Seminary.

These multiple encounters over such a long period of time seem like more than coincidence to me. According to my notes from class, this book of the Bible is seldom read in the church's lectionary used in Sunday worship. Why not? I think there is a mystical element to it, with Jesus being elevated to the highest priesthood at the right hand of God, as outlined in Psalm 110:4.

What does that mean? Hebrews teaches us that Melchizedek was the highest of high priests; he was a king, a shadowy figure who seemed to come from nowhere, and never died.

I believe this linkage to the Old Testament is significant because of the "covenant" (promise) that God made with Abraham and the Israelites. God does not lie. He was bringing Jesus (his risen son) to his side in the heavenly tabernacle as "High Priest in the order of Melchizedek" (forever). Hebrews establishes a new covenant (promise) of the highest order with Jesus at the right hand of God, and it was not just for the Israelites — all of God's people can attain salvation and eternal life through Jesus Christ.

The Book of Hebrews can be seen as an avenue to the entire Pauline corpus — into the beauty of Corinthians, the depth of Romans and the joy of Philippians. Is this what Margaret is trying to convey? I don't know, but what I do know is that I am being directed to Hebrews and Paul's letters for something, and I believe it has to do with salvation.

Recently I have been directed back to Paul's letters, especially I Corinthians 15. The eminent scholar William Barclay aptly titled that chapter, "Jesus' Resurrection and Ours." His thoughts on it were that it "is both one of the greatest and one of the most difficult chapters in the New Testament" — primarily because of the phrase we recite in the creed on Sunday, "the resurrection of the body." Although Paul's letter preceded the creed's formation at Nicaea, apparently bodily resurrection was preached on by Paul and others, creating a serious problem for the Corinthians in the early church by believing they were already saved in their earthly bodies, and they could therefore relax and enjoy life.

For me, Paul's explicit explanation in I Corinthians 15:35-49, in the analogy of the "seed," is quite adequate to dispel any notion that our rotted flesh will rise up out of the ground, as in "the rapture." Maybe this is Margaret's explanation as to why she can't appear to me in any substantive way, only spiritually.

I believe there is more excitement to come as I continue my journey. It's not over yet, and I plan to continue with my study at the Seminary. I do enjoy my limited teaching role here at Moravian Village. Regarding Margaret's persistent spirit, it has been a supreme comfort to me to know that I am "not flying alone" these last few remaining years of my life on earth.

Trust in God and praise the Lord, Amen.

Afterword

A Message From the Author

Not Flying Alone is an account, fundamentally, of the airline piloting profession — both struggling to gain entrance into this rather exclusive brotherhood of aviators and living the good life that membership in it provided. My partner throughout most of this journey was my deceased wife Margaret, about whom you have read a great deal as the story has unfolded.

Before Margaret's death in 2011, I had no motivation to write a book such as this. After her death, however, Margaret's spirit emerged quite suddenly and exerted tremendous influence on me in remarkable and amazing ways.

The "gift of the Holy Spirit" that I described receiving in the opening chapter of this book contained many elements that I have discussed in detail. Margaret realized that I would vehemently reject any notion of her spiritual return, so she took elaborate measures to convince me that her spirit truly was present, and that she was here to help me.

These miraculous encounters have produced, for me, a unique personal revelation. I use the word "unique" because I have not found another instance of anyone who has undergone a similar experience. The indisputable proof of Margaret's presence that I presented in the final chapter is truly amazing to me.

At the core of my experiences is the magnitude of the significant changes in me. As the previous chapters have related, for decades my life was completely immersed in achieving materialistic goals and just having fun. Religious pursuits were virtually absent.

My purpose in writing this book is to show that the Holy Spirit is alive and well in the twenty-first century, and that salvation is available to all who come to our Lord Jesus Christ — even to those of us in the twilight years of our lives.

Ray Lemmon

About the Author

Ray Lemmon was born in Erie, Pa., during the Great Depression and grew up during World War II and the postwar era. While working as a lab technician, Lemmon learned to fly and decided to be an airline pilot. After serving in an Army hospital in Japan during the Korean Conflict, his flying career was made possible by the G.I. Bill.

Lemmon met and married Margaret Taylor, a co-worker at the lab, who became his partner in his flying career and his off-duty adventures. After beginning his flying career with Capital Airlines, twelve years later he was promoted to Captain for United Airlines. His career spanned over thirty years during a time of major change and expansion for the airline industry.

Lemmon's hobbies have included restoring and flying vintage aircraft; owning antique and collectible automobiles; boating; and touring in trailers and motor homes. He lives in Bethlehem, Pa.

Printed in the United States
By Bookmasters